VOICES FROM THE GULAG

VOICES
FROM THE
GULAG

EDITED BY

ALEKSANDR
SOLZHENITSYN

TRANSLATED FROM THE RUSSIAN AND
WITH AN INTRODUCTION AND NOTES BY

KENNETH LANTZ

NORTHWESTERN UNIVERSITY PRESS

EVANSTON, ILLINOIS

Northwestern University Press
www.nupress.northwestern.edu

Published 2010 by Northwestern University Press. Originally published in Russian as *Pozhivshi v GULAGe,* copyright © 2001. This translation of *Pozhivshi v GULAGe* edited by A. I. Solzhenitsyn is published by arrangement with Русский Путь (Russian Path) Publishing House, Moscow, Russia.

Printed in the United States of America

10 9 8 7 6 5 4 3 2 1

Library of Congress Cataloging-in-Publication Data

Pozhivshi v Gulage. English
    Voices from the Gulag / edited by Aleksandr Solzhenitsyn ; translated from the Russian and with an introduction and notes by Kenneth Lantz.
        p. cm.
    "Published by arrangement with Russkii put (Russian Path) Publishing House, Moscow, Russia"—T.p. verso.
    Includes bibliographical references.
    ISBN 978-0-8101-2655-8 (pbk. : alk. paper)
    1. Political prisoners—Soviet Union—Biography. 2. Political persecution—Soviet Union—History. 3. Concentration camps—Soviet Union—History. I. Solzhenitsyn, Aleksandr Isaevich, 1918–2008. II. Lantz, K. A. III. Title.
HV9712.5.P6913 2010
365'.45092247—dc22

                                                                                2009032425

Contents

Translator's Introduction   *vii*

V. M. Lazarev
1937: An Eyewitness Account   *3*

N. N. Boldyrev
The Crooked Path of Fate   *71*

N. M. Ignatov
My Lot in Life   *139*

A. P. Butskovsky
The Fate of a Sailor   *171*

N. R. Kopylov
My Wanderings   *219*

V. V. Gorshkov
My Life as a Gift   *245*

A. E. Kropochkin
Memoirs of Former Prisoner SL-208   *357*

Translator's Notes   *401*

Translator's Introduction

The Polish writer Gustav Herling described the two years he spent inside Stalin's vast complex of forced labor camps known as the Gulag in a memoir he entitled *A World Apart*. Many other memoirists who passed through the Gulag also saw it as, if not another world, then at least another country whose inhabitants, the *zeks,* formed a distinct nation. Aleksandr Solzhenitsyn as well wrote of "the *zeks* as a nation." The Gulag had a country-sized population of several million during the peak years of its existence. It had its own territory, whose many "islands" dotting the map inspired Solzhenitsyn to call it an archipelago. It had its own government which, though not independent from Moscow, enjoyed more freedom of operation than any other institution within the rigidly centralized Soviet Union. The Gulag administration devised and enforced most of the laws that governed the daily lives of the hapless prisoners within it. New arrivals were quickly and brutally initiated into a way of life that was a cruel parody of the worst features of the world outside. Many memoirists who spent time in the earliest major camp of the Gulag, on the Solovetsky Islands, recall their greeting from the camp commander, Igor Kurilko, which made it clear that the newcomers were entering another world: "Here," he told them, "there is no Soviet power, only Solovetsky power."

Inhabitants of the Gulag spoke, if not a distinct language, at least a well-developed jargon—an amalgam of criminal slang, technical terms, and elaborate curses—that outsiders barely understood. (Several sizeable dictionaries of Gulag speech have been published.) They wore their own national costume, the quilted black cotton jackets and trousers. They had their own traditions and folklore: grimly sardonic sayings ("You can die today, but I'll live till tomorrow") and rigidly enforced customs (as one memoirist in this collection notes, the theft of personal belongings was rampant and almost accepted, but theft of the basic bread ration brought sudden and harsh punishment, often by death). Though the inhabitants may have had different ethnic origins (indeed, they reflected the multi-ethnic composition of the Soviet Union and also included citizens or former citizens of most of the nations of Europe as well as China, Japan, Korea, and North and South America), their common camp experience did create something approaching a "national character": camp veterans claimed that they could recognize one another years after they had been freed.

The Gulag had its own rigid social hierarchy. At the top of the pyramid were the privileged bosses who, particularly in isolated areas like Kolyma, could live on a scale as lavish as that of the wealthy Russian landowners a century earlier. Camp guards lived under conditions not much better than the prisoners, though they were adequately clothed and fed, well paid, and had immense power—even that of life and death—over their charges. The mass of the Gulag nation were the *zeks* (from z/k, an abbreviation of *zakliuchënnyi,* "prisoner"), but there was a hierarchy here too. The most privileged among them, ironically, were the most vicious criminals—murderers, thieves, rapists—who did little or no work and who terrorized the mass of "politicals," who had fallen into the Gulag under the notorious Article 58, whose eighteen subparagraphs covered a broadly defined range of "anti-Soviet activities." *Pridurki,* or "trusties"—prisoners who were not sent out on general labor and who had less demanding jobs in the camp administration—were relatively privileged. At the very bottom of the hierarchy were the "goners," prisoners who haunted the rubbish dumps seeking out potato peelings as they slowly wasted away from exhaustion and malnutrition.

The Gulag nation had its own economy. Its inhabitants dug canals, mined coal, uranium, gold, and copper, and built railways, highways, bridges, canals, airfields, and whole cities (Norilsk, Magnitogorsk, Vorkuta, Magadan, and others). Others toiled in manufacturing and agriculture. Timber cut by prisoners in the Gulag was exported to earn precious foreign currency, as was the gold they mined in Kolyma.

Like any nation, the Gulag had its unique history, one virtually as long as that of the Soviet Union. In fact, several weeks before Lenin toppled Russia's Provisional Government in October 1917 he wrote that those who would oppose his new regime would be "*forced to work*" in new state institutions.[1] Some eight months after the tsarist regime had been overthrown, Leon Trotsky was already writing of a "concentration camp" to house a group of unruly prisoners of war. Not long thereafter, he addressed the Soviet government in a memorandum calling for concentration camps to confine "parasitical elements" such as the bourgeoisie and former army officers who refused to join the Red Army; they would be forced to perform "particularly dirty work."[2] A number of such camps were formed, using abandoned facilities that had housed German prisoners during World War I. On August 9, 1918, Lenin telegraphed a police official in Penza, where there was an anti-Bolshevik uprising, with instructions to carry out "merciless mass terror against kulaks, priests, and White Guardists"; those suspected of opposition were to be taken to "concentration camps outside the city."[3] As Mikhail Geller writes, "The very first documents proclaiming the birth of the new punitive institution set forth its characteristic and unchanging features: the concentration camps were meant to inflict harsh punishment; potential enemies, not those who had already committed crimes, could be sent there; punishment by confinement in a concentration camp was essentially an extralegal measure."[4] Thus, even those who may not have overtly opposed the regime but who, because of their class origins, were likely to be hostile to it ("class enemies") must be made to conform, and forced labor was the means to achieve conformity.

At the same time, there were already professional criminals inside the prisons the Bolsheviks had inherited from the tsarist regime. The prevailing attitude toward them among the Bolsheviks was quite different from their feelings toward "class enemies." The Bolsheviks were heirs to a tradition that went back at least to the Romantic era and which, in Russia, was expressed in ideological terms by Russia's most famous radical thinker of the mid-nineteenth century, Nikolai Chernyshevsky (1828–1889). Crime, he wrote, was simply a rational response to an unjust society: the thief steals because he is hungry. Reform society, feed people, Chernyshevsky wrote in 1860, and "at least nine-tenths of all that is bad in human society would quickly disappear."[5] A few decades later, Maxim Gorky (1868–1936), who sympathized with the Bolsheviks, wrote popular stories and plays that romanticized tramps and outlaws as free beings who refused to be bound by the mores and restrictions of a corrupt bourgeois society. It was no great theoretical leap for the Bolsheviks, then, to come to regard professional criminals as incipient, though not yet politically conscious, revolutionaries. In other words, if the bourgeoisie were class enemies, the professional criminals were "class friends." Compelled to a few years of healthy, useful labor, in which they could devote their energies to the building of the new workers' state, these "fallen angels" could be restored to grace. Or, to use the more appropriate metaphor used by the regime itself, they would be "reforged" as components of the new state machine.

The number of camps grew rapidly as arrests mounted, and by the end of 1920 there were 107 of them, many in Russia's north, where their inmates were put to work cutting timber and building roads. The organization designated in July 1918 to run the camps had been founded only six weeks after the October Revolution: it was the All-Russian Extraordinary Commission for Combating Counter-Revolution and Sabotage, known by its Russian abbreviation, Ch-K, or Cheka.[6] Although the Gulag acronym (standing for the Main Administration of Camps) did not appear until 1930, the Gulag had already been born.

The history of the Gulag was long and complex, but a sense of its evolution can be had by looking at three milestones in its development: the first large-scale forced labor camps, on the Solovetsky Islands; the most famous construction project of the 1930s done with forced labor, the White Sea Canal; and the vast camp system of Kolyma.

The Cheka had been setting up camps in Arkhangel Oblast (i.e., province), in Russia's north, and in 1923 it took over the Solovetsky Islands, in the White Sea, some twenty miles off Russia's northern coast. The islands were the home of a fifteenth-century monastery that, in addition to its religious functions, had also served as a part of Russia's northern defenses. The area (often referred to as Solovki) would serve well. It was isolated: prisoners made the last part of their journey from Kem, the nearest port on the mainland, by a three-hour trip by boat, though in the six winter months navigation was impossible and there was no direct communication with the mainland. The monastery had stone buildings and churches that could be adapted to hold prisoners securely.

From an initial intake of a few hundred prisoners in 1923, the population of the camp grew to more than 6,000 by 1925. By 1930 there were some 50,000, with another 30,000 in the Kem Transit Camp.[7] "Solovetsky power" was wielded with a vengeance in the former monastery, where the earliest prisoners were confined in overcrowded cells. Conditions in the eight additional camps eventually set up elsewhere on the main island or on outlying islands were even worse. Both torture and arbitrary executions were much more common here than in the later camps of the Gulag. With meager rations, heavy work, overcrowded barracks, and appalling sanitation, it was not long before disease broke out. About 1,500 prisoners died in a typhus epidemic in the winter of 1925–26. Another typhus epidemic broke out on the mainland, in Kem Transit Camp, in 1928 and spread to the islands.

Reports on the abuses in the camps of Solovki eventually reached the highest levels of the Communist Party leadership, although it was not until 1930 that an OGPU commission was sent to investigate. (The OGPU, or All-Union State Political Directorate, succeeded the Cheka as the Soviet Union's security police agency; it, in turn, was incorporated into the NKVD, or People's Commissariat of Internal Affairs, in 1934.) More worrisome for the regime, however, was the problem that the camps, intended to support themselves from the labor of their inmates, actually needed substantial subsidies.

It was at this point in the history of the Gulag that the enigmatic figure of Naftaly Frenkel emerged. He had been sentenced by the OGPU to be shot in 1924, but over the course of his spectacular career he made the transition from prisoner to guard to OGPU officer and head of production of SLON (the Russian acronym for Northern Special Purpose Camps, the parent body for the Solovki camps) and eventually to the rank of lieutenant general.[8] Frenkel rose to power because he applied his organizational genius to the problems in Solovki that troubled the Kremlin leadership. He submitted to the OGPU in Moscow plan after plan for reorganizing and rationalizing prison labor so as to make the camps not only self-supporting but even profitable. One of the "incentives" he proposed to squeeze more work out of the prisoners was probably as old as slavery itself, but Frenkel seized upon it, refined it, and made it a Gulag institution. This was the notorious "work for food" system. Prisoners were classified according to the amount and type of work of which they were capable. Those who could meet the "norm" for a full day of heavy work would receive a full ration; those capable of less would receive a smaller one; invalids, able to do only light work, would receive a correspondingly light ration, about half what a healthy prisoner received. Failure to meet the norm meant a reduced ration. A full ration was originally set at eight hundred grams (almost two pounds) of bread and eighty grams of meat. In later years, the size and content of the ration would vary considerably from one camp to another and from one period to another, though the principle remained one of the cornerstones of the Gulag. It all but guaranteed the slow death by starvation of those already incapacitated; on the other hand, it did not necessarily ensure the survival of those in the first category. A Gulag proverb advises, "It's not the small ration that kills you, it's the big one." In other words, the effort needed to fulfill the often impossibly high work norm could quickly exhaust the prisoner, despite the larger ration.

Frenkel also expanded the scope of the camp's activities, gaining contracts to use forced labor to cut timber and build roads on the mainland. Frenkel's system did seem to achieve what the authorities in Moscow desired: by 1928 Solovki was showing a profit, at least on paper.[9] The OGPU's accounting system was a flexible one, however, and it allowed Frenkel to proclaim his new system an outstanding success, even though the camp was receiving a subsidy. Still, the production of lumber tripled from 1926 to 1929 (due in no small measure to the increased number of prisoners working in the forests).

The experience of Solovki provided a model for future camps. The regime saw the need for exploiting the vast timber and mining resources of the north. Frenkel's model showed that even unskilled labor could produce timber and build roads. And the Soviet Union had an enormous pool of unskilled labor . . .

Frenkel and his methods were tested on the next massive project, digging a canal to link the White Sea with Lake Onega and provide access to the Baltic Sea. The canal was a pet project of Stalin, and he insisted that it be built by prisoners supervised by the OGPU. The route was 140 miles long, much of it strewn with granite boulders, and the project was to be done urgently, within twenty months.[10] Nineteen locks had to be constructed. The actual building began in September 1931. No foreign currency was allotted for the project, which meant there were no tractors, cranes, or earthmoving equipment. Lacking iron, wood was substituted. There was not enough concrete for the walls, so frames of logs filled with packed earth and stone were used instead. The basic tools were sledgehammers, picks, shovels, and wheelbarrows. Most often, even these had to be crudely improvised on the site. Construction began with a prisoner workforce of some one hundred thousand; many more were added to replace those who perished during the project.

Those who managed the work clearly understood that Stalin's deadline for completion within twenty months was serious, and that failure to meet it might well mean that they themselves would be wielding pickaxes on the next construction site. A sense of urgency permeated the whole project. Driven mercilessly by the overseers, prisoners cut through granite with chisels and sledgehammers and moved the spoil in homemade wheelbarrows. Amazingly, the project was completed in June 1933, only a month past the deadline.

In the summer of 1933, not long before the canal opened, Maxim Gorky, the most prominent cultural figure in the Soviet Union and a writer who then enjoyed a world reputation, organized a group of 130 Soviet writers and journalists on a visit to the canal.[11] Thirty-six of them produced a collective work—a 600-page propaganda piece, in fact—to pass on their reactions to it. Gorky's introduction gives a good sense of the tone and content of the book as a whole. He writes:

> This is one of the most splendid victories of people's collectively organized energy over the elements of harsh northern nature. At the same time, it is a wonderfully successful experiment in the mass transformation of former enemies of the dictatorship of the proletariat and the Soviet community into qualified allies of the working class and even into ardent proponents of necessary labor for the state. The quick victory over a natural world hostile to humans, achieved by the friendly onslaught of thousands of heterogeneous individuals of different races, is astounding. But even more astounding is the victory won over themselves by people who, not long before, had been living lives of utter disorder under the bestial power of the autocratic bourgeoisie.[12]

Solzhenitsyn's comments on the book provide a sobering corrective to the giddy optimism of Gorky's group:

> The very grandeur of this construction project consisted in the fact that it was carried out without contemporary technology and equipment and without any supplies from the nation as a whole! "These are not the tempos of noxious European-American capitalism, these are socialist tempos!" the authors brag. . . . The whole book praises specifically the backwardness of the technology and the homemade workmanship. There were no *cranes*? So they will make their own—wooden "derricks." And the only metal parts the "derricks" had were in places where there was friction—and these parts they cast themselves. "Our own industry at the canal," our authors gloat. And they themselves cast *wheelbarrow wheels*

in their own *homemade cupola furnace*. The country required the canal so urgently and in such haste that it could not even find any wheelbarrow wheels for the project![13]

The authors of the book provided many snippets of interviews with workers on the project in which they claimed they had been inspired by it and transformed from hardened criminals into loyal, productive citizens. The book thus not only celebrated what truly was an amazing feat; at the same time, in stressing labor as a means of reforming criminals, it attempted to disarm the critics of the camp system and allay foreign concerns over the use of slave labor in the Soviet Union (accounts of conditions on Solovki, for example, had reached the West). Even more important was the book's goal of propaganda that would influence and inspire Soviet citizens generally. Its none-too-covert message was that despite the shortages, despite the difficulties, amazing things could be accomplished through hard work under the leadership of the party.

Perhaps the bitterest irony of all in this episode is that the canal was not widely used. Its planners realized that they could only hope to complete it within the deadline by keeping it narrow and reducing its depth to twelve feet, sufficient only for smaller vessels. It had to be substantially rebuilt, widened, and deepened in later years. Even with these improvements, ship traffic between the White Sea and the Baltic remained relatively small, and the canal is little used.

The building of the canal demonstrated, to the satisfaction of the party and OGPU leadership, that massive projects could be completed in inhospitable areas with a minimum of technology and masses of unskilled labor. Stalin's grandiose vision for rapid industrialization of the Soviet Union through a series of Five-Year Plans had been frustrated by a shortage of hard currency to purchase technology from the West on a grand scale, as it was by the reluctance of many Western countries to sell it. The Soviet Union did have masses of unskilled labor, and neither the party nor the police had scruples over sacrificing large numbers of them "for the building of socialism." Roy Medvedev comments:

> The widespread use of forced labor had dangerous consequences. In the first place, the harsh regime established in 1937 used up labor quickly, with a consequent need for rapid replacement. Secondly, because Stalin did not find a rational solution for the

problem of building in remote regions, he constantly increased the number of projects assigned to GULAG. Thirdly, the apparent "cheapness" and "mobility" of GULAG labor prompted many construction organizations and other economic units to employ such labor even in the central regions of the USSR. By the early fifties GULAG was working several mines in the Donbass and some sewing factories, ran virtually the entire lumber industry in Arkhangelsk oblast, and had built the Moscow University skyscraper as well as several other buildings in Moscow.[14]

Thus, the number of the Gulag's camps and the range of their activities steadily increased in the early 1930s; the mass arrests during the "Great Terror" of 1937 filled the camps and prisons to overflowing. Unlike the White Sea Canal, these camps and the projects they undertook were not widely publicized, and when they were mentioned, it was implied that the work was being done by free labor, not prisoners. Many projects built road and rail links to bring the largely untapped timber and mineral resources of northern Russia to the south. One of the largest and most prolonged was the Baikal–Amur Mainline (a 2,500-mile branch of the Trans-Siberian Railway System) undertaken by the BAMlag camp complex. Several of the memoirists in this volume spent time on this project.

The most notorious area containing these northern camps, however, was Kolyma. The historian Robert Conquest has written: "Just as Auschwitz has come to stand for the Nazi extermination camps as a whole, so Kolyma remains fixed in the imagination of the Soviet peoples as the great archetype of the sinister system under which Stalin ended, by hunger, cold and exhaustion, the lives of so many of his subjects."[15] The area itself, the most northeasterly part of Russia's Pacific coast, was also the most remote within the Soviet Union. Prisoners sent there from western Russia first faced a train journey across almost the whole of the Soviet Union, a journey that might last several months. Then, from the railroad's eastern terminus, Vladivostok, or nearby ports, they would await embarkation on overcrowded prison ships belonging to the NKVD's own fleet—aging merchant vessels whose holds had been crudely adapted to transport human cargo. The voyage, whose horrors have been described by a number of memoirists, including Lazarev and Kopylov in this volume, lasted about a week. Because shipping could take place only during the ice-free months between May and November, and because there were many prisoners to be transported, they were packed into the vessels in conditions whose like had not been seen since the notorious slave ships of the eighteenth century. From Nagayevo, the port of Kolyma's "capital," Magadan, the prisoners—those who had survived—would be marched several miles inland to holding camps. They entered a region of low mountains that became higher and more rugged farther inland. The climate is one of the world's harshest: winter temperatures regularly reach fifty degrees below zero Fahrenheit. (In fact, the settlement of Oymyakon, in western Kolyma, holds the record for the coldest temperature in the Northern Hemisphere—ninety degrees below zero Fahrenheit.) But the region had rich deposits of gold, one of the reasons the regime was so interested in it. Substantial finds of lead and tin came later, and uranium was discovered in the early 1950s. Free workers were reluctant to endure the isolation, hard labor, and extreme climate; forced labor provided a solution.

Kolyma was controlled by Dalstroy (the Far Northern Construction Trust), an NKVD agency set up in November 1931 and reporting directly to its ministry in Moscow. Its boundaries expanded over the years, and by 1941 they took in 860,000 square miles, a territory four times the size of France.

In the summer of 1932 teams of prisoners worked to build an infrastructure, including the major transportation axis, the Kolyma Highway running north from Magadan, the town's docks and, indeed, the city of Magadan itself. These early years, in which prisoners operated in chaotic conditions, took a heavy toll: in addition to the deaths from exhaustion, accidents, and illnesses, isolated camps were sometimes cut off by winter blizzards and every living creature in them perished. Yet roads were built, barracks erected, and organized gold mining began in 1935. By 1936 Magadan's population had reached 15,000; by the mid-1940s it had grown to 70,000. In fact, the years from 1935 to late 1937 have been described by the writer Varlam Shalamov, who spent eighteen years there, as Kolyma's "golden age."[16] The founder of the Kolyma camps, Eduard Berzin, believed that prisoners who were well clothed, well fed, and not utterly exhausted by work would be more productive. Berzin himself was arrested in 1937, however, and executed a year later. The camp regime generally became much harsher in 1937: rations were reduced, warm fur clothing was taken away and replaced by padded jackets, work norms were increased, and all prisoners convicted under Article 58 were sent to do hard physical labor. When gold production then began to decline, the NKVD authorities increased the working hours. The camps were becoming extermination

TRANSLATOR'S INTRODUCTION

camps. Executions of prisoners who had failed to fulfill the work norm (regarded as sabotage or counterrevolutionary activity) or simply random killings became common. Indeed, a special camp, the Serpantinnaya or Serpantinka, had been built some 375 miles west of Magadan as a place where mass executions were carried out.

Work in the Kolyma gold mines was a veritable death sentence. Shalamov wrote that a healthy prisoner would be reduced to a wreck after three weeks in the mines.[17] It is unlikely that anyone will ever know how many lives were claimed by the mines and camps of Kolyma. Adam Hochschild questioned four experienced researchers on the region about the number of deaths that occurred there: "One estimated it at 250,000, one at 300,000, one at 800,000 and one at 'more than 1,000,000.'"[18]

The camps themselves are depicted in vivid detail in the memoirs that follow, but a few general remarks can provide some context for the memoirists' accounts. First, the "camps" referred to by abbreviated titles—Siblag for the Siberian Corrective Labor Camp, Urallag for the Ural Corrective Labor Camp, and so on—were actually camp administrations, complexes of many smaller units, called *lagpunkty,* or camp sectors, each of which housed anywhere from a few hundred to several thousand prisoners. At the beginning of 1948, for example, Vyatlag, a camp engaged mainly in timber cutting, held 24,922 prisoners in fourteen camp sectors.[19] Camp sectors were often temporary: one involved in forestry or railway construction might be abandoned or used as the basis of a small settlement once the work in its immediate area had been completed.

Within their barracks the prisoners slept on closely arranged "bunks." Typically, these were *vagonki,* double-tiered frameworks with two platforms, each about two feet wide; two prisoners would sleep on each level.[20] Though they were formally prohibited, some barracks would be equipped with *sploshnye nary*—a long, undivided sleeping platform on which prisoners slept close together, side by side. Such arrangements were sometimes so crowded that, as Gorshkov recounts, one person could not turn over unless everyone else in the row did. Each long wall of the barracks was lined with bunks; the passageway between them might have a few tables, and it certainly would have a wood stove, made from one or two metal barrels; another passageway in the middle of the barracks, at right angles to the first, led to the entrance and divided the barracks into two sections. Crude washing facilities and the *parasha,* the latrine barrel, would be located here.

Depending on the type of bunks installed, the barracks could hold from 60 to 120 prisoners. Barracks were normally built by prison labor and were typically of wood. There were also barracks that were little more than excavations in the earth, roofed with logs and earth or semi-underground barracks (Gorshkov describes both in his memoir). In new or crowded camps, prisoners often had to live in tents, even in the Arctic.

Prisoners' rations varied not only because of the percentage of the work norm they fulfilled: general food shortages during the war were reflected in the Gulag as well, as they were during years of poor harvests and near famine. The heart of the ration was bread, and prisoners had an almost mystical attitude toward it. A daily bread ration of 800 grams would be considered quite good, but this would be given only after fulfilling 100 percent of the norm; 500 grams was more common, and only 400 for meeting less than 70 percent of the norm. For breakfast, in addition, there was a bowl of kasha—watery porridge that might be made from corn, oats, barley, wheat, millet, or almost any grain. Lunch was the remainder of the bread ration and a bowl of *balanda,* thin soup made from what was available: potatoes, cabbage leaves, beet tops, perhaps some fish or offal; dinner was often a bowl or two of thin gruel or soup with a spoonful of oatmeal. Official food norms also called for small amounts of fish or meat, oils and fats, and sugar, but these were often pilfered by the criminals. With an official working day of eleven hours (after 1940), at heavy labor and often at below-zero temperatures, prisoners existed in a perpetual state of hunger. Diseases brought on by malnutrition such as scurvy and pellagra were common.

The basic work unit in the camps was the "brigade," or work gang, comprising fifteen to thirty-five prisoners. The brigadier played a key role in negotiating work quotas that were as low as possible, since the brigade's rations depended on the degree to which the quotas were fulfilled. An experienced brigadier was also adept at *tufta* ("padding"), the many ingenious ways in which work output could be falsified.

A typical camp would have a medical unit (larger ones, a hospital), staffed by personnel who might range from highly trained specialists, who were themselves prisoners, to completely unqualified "medical assistants." Some memoirists comment bitterly on doctors who denied them any treatment at all, yet many others give instances of excellent, compassionate care by camp doctors, some of whom risked their own positions to save the lives of their patients. Medical personnel were themselves under pressure to turn away "malingerers" and report those who faked illnesses or mutilated themselves; they also had strict limits on the numbers of prisoners they could exempt from work.

Camp guards—both the warders (*nadzirateli*), who were responsible for the prisoners inside the camp, and the *konvoy,* those who escorted them to and from work—were on the whole poorly educated and heavily indoctrinated. Apart from a few who were genuinely sadistic, their harshness came from the idea instilled in them that they were guarding "enemies of the people"—spies, saboteurs, traitors, and "fascists"—who need not be treated gently. They were also part of a strictly disciplined structure that meted out harsh punishment for violations of orders. They were still human, however, and more than a few offered small kindnesses when they could. Gorshkov's memoir describes one guard who was genuinely loved by the prisoners.

The *blatnye* or *urki*—the professional criminals—were the most privileged among the camp inmates. The highest-ranking among them, the "thieves-in-the-law," subscribed to a code of behavior, and those who violated that code would face punishment at the hands of a primitive tribunal. The central points of the thieves' law were that all those who did not belong to their fraternity—the *frayery* ("pigeons" or "suckers")—were fair game, but fellow thieves were untouchable; and that the thieves themselves would neither work nor cooperate in any way with the authorities. This meant, among other things, that their rations came at the expense of the humble *zeks* who did work and whose rations were thereby reduced. The criminals spent their time playing cards, which they fashioned themselves (Ignatov's memoir describes the method in detail), and when one had lost whatever possessions he had, he would often select some item belonging to a hapless "pigeon," who would then have no choice but to pass it over to the winner of the game. There were criminals who had abandoned the thieves' law and did work—the "bitches" (*suki*), though they would be assigned the easiest jobs. Criminal jargon, "thieves' language," had developed over many years by criminal gangs, largely to enable them to discuss their activities in terms outsiders could not understand. In the confined conditions of a prison cell or a camp barracks, however, elements of the thieves' language infiltrated the speech of almost everyone.

The criminals' systematic terrorization of the hapless politicals was not only tolerated by the camp authorities but even encouraged as a means of keeping them in line. In the years immediately after the war, however, large numbers of battle-hardened soldiers entered the Gulag. They were disciplined, organized, and unintimidated by the tattooed criminals; many memoirists recount with considerable glee how the criminals in their barracks were at last subdued and, in some cases, driven out of the camp.[21]

Gulag memoirs were generally written by so-called political prisoners, though scarcely any of them had committed offenses that would be labeled political in any democratic country. The majority of them had been sentenced under one of the paragraphs of Article 58 of the Criminal Code of the Russian republic. Article 58.10, dealing with anti-Soviet propaganda, was one of the provisions most widely applied by prosecutors. The "offense" to which this article was applied might simply have been a passing remark that someone had interpreted as critical of the Soviet regime. Even listening to such a remark and not reporting it was covered by Article 58.12, "failure to report."

As Anne Applebaum has pointed out, the great majority of prisoners were peasants, caught up in the campaign to collectivize agriculture in 1929 or arrested for taking as little as a few heads of wheat to try to feed their families during the Ukrainian famine of 1932–33.[22] They left scarcely any memoirs, and their stories that have survived have done so because they were recorded in the testimony of others.[23] The peasants were, of course, much better equipped to survive the hard labor and scanty rations of the camps than were the intelligentsia. They knew how to wield an axe and a shovel and were accustomed to long days of outdoor labor.

The composition of the camp population changed as the twentieth century wore on. The Soviet occupation of Polish territory in 1939 brought many Poles to the Gulag; most were released in 1941 under the Polish-Soviet Treaty, and some seventy-five thousand of them joined the army of General Anders to fight the Germans. Much of the intelligentsia of Estonia, Latvia, and Lithuania was also shipped to the camps after the Soviet occupation of the Baltic states in 1940 under the Molotov-Ribbentrop Pact and a new Soviet occupation in 1944. German prisoners of war spent time in the Gulag, and many more came in the postwar period, as well as some six hundred thousand Japanese, though both groups were generally kept in camps separate from Soviet prisoners. Prisoners from Soviet Central Asia and the Caucasus, torn away from their sunny climates and forced to work in subzero temperatures, suffered greatly. Ukrainian nationalists who had fought for the liberation of their homeland during and after the war formed another large group. As Kropochkin's memoir shows, their relations with the Russian prisoners were often scarcely cordial.

There were fewer women in the camps than men (official statistics show that they made up 13 percent of the population of the Gulag in 1942, 30 percent in 1945, and 17 percent in 1952), but they lived under the same regime as men and were expected to fulfill the same work quotas.[24] As with the men, there was a contingent of professional women criminals and prostitutes who terrorized the "politicals." Some camps housed both men and women, in separate "zones." The prohibition of contact between men and women was strictly enforced in some areas, virtually ignored in others. Many women were sent to light regime camps where the labor was somewhat easier. As part of a plan to make Kolyma as self-sufficient as possible, farming was gradually developed in the more temperate areas. Such camps were largely staffed by women, as were several fish plants. Their work was onerous, though rations were often better and there were more opportunities to pilfer a bit of the food being produced. Eugenia Ginzburg, who for a time had a job tending chickens in Kolyma, was able to keep aside a few eggs and make porridge from chicken feed.[25]

Still, survival in the camps was perhaps even more of a challenge for women than for men. There was the constant threat of rape, either by guards, criminals, or male prisoners. Women were often forced into trading sex for extra rations or privileges or for simple survival. Many memoirists tell of a modest, frightened girl quickly transformed into brazen, well-fed mistress of a camp official. Women with families faced the added agony of worry over the fates of their children.

Other prisoners came to the Gulag as victims of religious persecution. Some were members of religious sects, others Orthodox, including nuns, and many of them stoutly maintained their religious vows, refusing to work on Sundays and holy days and suffering severe punishment for it.

Transport—from prison to a camp or from one camp to another—was a basic fact of life for the *zek,* and one that was much dreaded. A transport might take place when a particular project ended, but often it happened for no apparent reason. Gulag officials simply wanted to shake things up, since prisoners who had worked and lived together for a long time might develop a solidarity that was a potential threat to camp discipline. The typical traveling ration was several days' issue of bread (half-starved prisoners were often unable to resist consuming it all at once) and heavily salted fish which led to almost unbearable thirst; water was not always forthcoming. A transport might last only a few days or, if from one end of the Soviet

Union to another, several months, with stops at transit prisons along the way. (Kopylov's memoir describes his epic, yearlong transport.)

The news of Stalin's death, as several of the memoirists here describe, was greeted by prisoners in different ways. In some camps there was open rejoicing, in others only a stunned silence. Most hoped that amnesties or at least an easing of conditions would follow, but veteran prisoners generally did not dare believe that things would change. Things did change, though not immediately for the better. There were amnesties, but they applied to prisoners serving less than five-year sentences, and almost all of these were professional criminals. (In the postwar years, twenty-five-year sentences for political offenses had become more and more common.)

Stalin had shown great personal interest in the labor camps, but with his passing the regime was able to look at them more dispassionately. It was now clear that they had never been profitable. Rebellions and strikes by prisoners in Kengir, Vorkuta, Dzezhkazgan, and in other camps had made it difficult for the regime to ignore the inefficiencies of camp administration and the blatant abuses of the inmates. By 1954 the party's Central Committee was looking into the abuses of justice during the Stalin era and beginning a review of prisoners' cases. Khrushchev's attack on Stalin in his "Secret Speech" of 1956 came as a severe shock to the KGB and camp administrators. Camp discipline was eased, and the release and rehabilitation of prisoners proceeded at a much faster pace. In November 1962 the appearance of Solzhenitsyn's novel *One Day in the Life of Ivan Denisovich*, with its intimate look at a typical day in camp from the point of view of a typical prisoner, came as another bombshell. The broad public now had its own vivid picture of the inside of the Gulag.

By then many camps stood empty and decaying, though there were still camp complexes in Moldova and Perm to hold dissidents. Unlike the secrecy about the camps that prevailed during the Stalin years, however, information from political prisoners in the 1970s and 1980s leaked out to the Soviet Union and abroad. The camp regime, it seemed, had not eased from that of the Stalin years, apart from the brutal labor. Only in late 1986, under the new regime of Mikhail Gorbachev, was a general amnesty declared for political prisoners.

The numbers of prisoners confined in the camps, as shown by NKVD documents, ranged from a low of 179,000 in 1930 to a high of 2,561,351 in

1950. As has been pointed out by a number of scholars, these figures may represent the static population of the camps (as of January 1 in each year), but they do not reflect the very sizeable turnover in the camp population. The turnover came from deaths, releases, and amnesties for the old and the ill (it was not uncommon for "goners" to be released so that the camp in which they had been held would not have to record an abnormally high number of deaths). Neither do these figures include prisoners of war, "special exiles," and those in several other categories. Because of this, totals for the number of forced laborers during the existence of the Gulag derived by different scholars do differ. The figure accepted by Anne Applebaum, who has studied the most recent data carefully, is 28.7 million. The question of how many died in the camps is even more difficult to determine. The figure calculated by an American historian and cited "reluctantly" by Applebaum is 2,749,163.[26] She cites it reluctantly because it does not include deaths by execution, on transport, or during interrogation, of those released shortly before death, and many other categories. The full number of victims would also have to include those dependents who were left behind and perished without support, along with prisoners who died prematurely after release because their health had been ruined by years of malnutrition and overwork. Ultimately, statistics give little sense of the impact of the Gulag on human lives: it was, after all, Joseph Stalin who is said to have remarked, "One death is a tragedy; a million is a statistic." The devastation the Gulag wrought on its inmates cannot be conveyed by mere numbers. But the voices of those who survived remain as compelling evidence of its monstrous existence.

Notes

1. V. I. Lenin, *Polnoe sobranie sochinenii* (Moscow: Gos. Izd. Politicheskoi literatury, 1962), 34:311.

2. Mikhail Geller, *Kontsentratsionnyi mir i sovetskaia literatura* (London: Overseas Publications Interchange, 1974), 43.

3. Lenin, *Polnoe sobranie sochinenii,* 50:143–44.

4. Geller, *Kontsentratsionnyi,* 5.

5. Nikolai Chernyshevsky, "The Anthropological Principle in Philosophy," in *Selected Philosophical Essays* (Moscow: FLPH, 1953), 101.

6. The Cheka functioned as the "sword and shield" of the Bolshevik/Communist Party. It came to have immense powers of investigation, arrest, and punishment and to operate essentially outside the law at the behest of its Party masters. The responsibilities of it and its successors—the GPU (1922–23), the OGPU (1923–34), the

NKVD/NKGB (1934–46), the MVD/MGB (1946–53), and the KGB (1954–91)—shifted from time to time with reorganization, but these bodies had overall responsibility for the prison camp system during the Stalin era and beyond. Despite the name changes of their parent organization, its members often continued to be called "Chekists."

7. Aleksandr Solzhenitsyn, *The Gulag Archipelago Two* (New York: Harper and Row, 1975), 72.

8. Frenkel's rise can only be described as meteoric. In 1931 he worked as superintendent of the White Sea–Baltic Canal project, and the following year he received the Order of Lenin, the Soviet Union's most prestigious award, for his efforts. In 1933 he was appointed head of the OGPU's vast complex of camps called the BAM GULAG (the Baikal–Amur Mainline). Here he managed to siphon off huge sums of money, a good deal of which he used to bribe appropriate officials. Then in 1937 his past caught up with him, and he once again faced execution. Somehow, however, he managed to survive and in 1940 was released from prison by the direct order of the head of the NKVD, Lavrenty Beria. Two more Orders of Lenin followed. Frenkel's acute political instincts apparently alerted him that new purges were in store in the postwar era, and he made a timely retirement in 1947. Frenkel the pensioner was able to watch many of his former colleagues lose their positions and, not infrequently, their lives. He died in 1960 at the age of seventy-seven.

9. The camps as a whole were never profitable, however, and by the mid-1950s the regime itself became aware of the heavy subsidies needed to keep them functioning.

10. By way of comparison, the Panama Canal, 50 miles long, took ten years to build; the Suez Canal, 100 miles long, took eleven years.

11. Gorky had visited Solovki in 1929 and had produced a glowing account of how young prisoners were being rehabilitated there, even though he was, apparently, well informed of the horrors that were taking place every day on the islands.

12. Maxim Gorky, L. Averbakh, and S. Firin, eds., *Belomorsko-Baltiiskii kanal im. Stalina* (Moscow: OGIZ, 1934; rpt. Moscow, 1998), 12.

13. Solzhenitsyn, *The Gulag Archipelago Two*, 91.

14. Roy Medvedev, *Let History Judge* (New York: Columbia University Press, 1989), 660.

15. Robert Conquest, *Kolyma: The Arctic Death Camps* (London: Macmillan, 1978), 13.

16. Varlam Shalamov, "The Green Procurator," in *Kolyma Tales* (London: Penguin), 369.

17. Shalamov, "An Epitaph," in *Kolyma Tales,* 308.

18. Adam Hochschild, *The Unquiet Ghost: Russians Remember Stalin* (New York: Viking, 1994), 237.

19. Viktor Berdinskikh, *Istoriia odnogo lageria (Viatlag)* (Moscow: Agraf, 2001), 40–41.

20. Jacques Rossi, in his *Gulag Handbook* (New York: Paragon House, 1989), provides sketches of a typical barracks (p. 43) and bunks (p. 41).

21. See, for example, Izaak Filshtinsky, *My shagaem pod konvoem* (Moscow: Vozvrashchie, 1994).

22. Anne Applebaum, *GULAG: A History* (New York: Doubleday, 2003), 292.

23. Oleg Volkov's memoir, *Pogruzhenie vo t'mu: iz perezhitogo* (Moscow: Sovietskaia Rossiia, 1992), includes a number of perceptive and sympathetic accounts of peasants caught up in the "de-kulakization" campaign and imprisoned or exiled to the far north.

24. Applebaum, *GULAG: A History,* 311.

25. Eugenia Ginzburg, *Journey into the Whirlwind* (New York: Harcourt, Brace, Jovanovich, 1967); and Eugenia Ginzburg, *Within the Whirlwind* (New York: Harcourt, Brace, Jovanovich, 1981).

26. Applebaum, *GULAG: A History,* 583.

Notes by Aleksandr Solzhenitsyn or the original author are included as numbered footnotes. Translator's notes appear at the end of the book.

VOICES FROM THE GULAG

V. M. LAZAREV

1937: AN
EYEWITNESS
ACCOUNT

I am sixty years old now, as I write my memoirs. Ten of those sixty years I spent in Kolyma.

Back then, during the most arduous days and years in those icy concentration camps at the edge of the world, I often thought that I had to survive, if only to tell people the truth of what happened. I am convinced that once people learn this terrible truth, once they have a glimpse behind the facade of this "happy and joyous life," they will be horrified; they will realize that we cannot live this way any longer, that we need a cleansing storm to wash away this filth from Russia, to vindicate the innocent and sweep out the party bosses and their accomplices, the people's executioners.

CHAPTER ONE

Dismissal

We had moved into this apartment six months earlier, when I arrived here in Stupino and had taken a job in the chief mechanical engineer's section. We were building a huge aircraft factory—Kombinat No. 150.

In the autumn of 1936 I was unexpectedly summoned to the personnel department of the Kashira Hydroelectric Station where I was then working and asked to give up my job. The deputy director, Orlov, told me that I could be let go with the notation "at his own request" or "because of staff reduction," whichever I chose. I chose the latter, since I would then be eligible for severance pay. My wife and I had no savings and barely managed to survive from one payday to the next. I had married two years earlier, and Zhenya and I already had a plump and healthy little daughter, Lidochka, who was just beginning to take her first steps and say a few words. I worshipped both of them. I was then twenty-nine, full of energy, and easily bore the rigors of life at that time. I lived with the confidence that life would become easier in the future. Zhenya was two years younger than I. We met when she was working as a copyist and later as a secretary in the engineering and technical office of the trade union's factory committee. She was regarded as one of the loveliest girls in Kashira. She had many admirers, but the local ladies didn't have many positive comments to make about her behavior.

At the time I had absolutely no experience with women and shied away from them, the pretty ones in particular. But fate, apparently, brought us together. We saw each other at work every day and sometimes took the same way home.

My whole being rejoiced when she began to notice me, and I felt a little drunk from joy. Soon we married. The hand of fate, however, had already set us on different paths that were to diverge for many years.

Why did I go to the aircraft factory after the Kashira Hydroelectric Station? When I was let go they didn't tell me outright but led me to believe that I had fallen into the ranks of the "unreliables." Yet I wasn't aware of committing any specific offense and so, in order to check if I really had been placed on the blacklist, I decided to go to work in a military factory. It was, incidentally, twenty kilometers closer to Moscow.

They accepted me at once, with no questions. It's true that the head of the personnel department of the Kashira Station advised me to go off to some distant province; but at the time I didn't understand the full significance of his advice and, in any case, I had no money to spend on long trips looking for work. Overall, they had treated me well at the Kashira Station and everyone was sorry about my dismissal, but evidently there had been some pressure from outside. The director of the station, M. G. Pervukhin, loaned me a car to carry our things, and we moved to Stupino.

The factory that was being built was enormous, and its director, Vazirian, was the nephew of Sergo Ordzhonikidze.

Chapter Two

Arrest

It was a Saturday evening. We were going to have our tea and go to bed, since the next day we were planning to go to the forest to pick flowers. The table was set, and the new electric kettle was gleaming happily—in those days an electric kettle was almost a luxury item.

There was a knock at the door. Two strangers and a neighbor entered.

"Good evening. I need to check your documents."

I produced my passport.

"Last name? First name? Patronymic?"

"Take a look at this."

The taller man handed me a paper with the heading, in large letters, "Warrant for Search and Arrest." I couldn't make out the rest of the text.

The taller man headed for the bookshelf. I sat down at the table and rather inappropriately asked the others: "Would you like some tea? Why don't you sit down?"

They declined. The neighbor didn't know where to look and what to do with his hands. This role wasn't at all to his liking, and he had obviously been brought here against his will. The face of the second man expressed nothing: it wasn't the first time he had done this.

My wife, a dazed smile on her face, was standing near the table holding our child.

It was obvious that the search was only a formality. The tall man rummaged a bit among the books and took two with him, John Reed's *Ten Days That Shook the World* and A. O. Avdeenko's *I Love.*

"Get dressed."

I put on a light coat, gave Zhenya a hasty embrace, and kissed sleepy Lidochka.

"Will you be long?"

"I don't know, maybe three months."

We said our good-byes.

It was dark. I got into the box of an open truck and off we went. For a moment a thought flashed through my mind: "What if I just jump out along the way and make a run for it? But where can I run?"

The country at that time was being drawn more and more into the dark web of the NKVD. After hunting down the "ex-es"—the former privileged classes—they tackled the de-kulakization of the peasants, then the opposition and anyone who doubted the genius of the leader. Then came the engineers—the Shakhty Trial had taken place not long before, and the word "engineer" still had overtones of "wrecker."

Many engineers, particularly important ones, were being picked up even now; among them were some I had happened to meet and to work with.

The deputy director of capital construction in our factory was A. S. Golubtsov. He came from a working-class family, had graduated from the "Workers' Faculty," and become an engineer; now he was devoting all his energy to building hydroelectric stations.

Not long before, he had returned from Germany, where he had been sent to study problems of setting up our turbines. He had not been home for more than a year. His wife prepared a samovar for his return, but he couldn't wait for tea and rushed off in the evening to the cogeneration plant—he'd been missing Kashira. I was still in the machine room. He greeted me and asked how things were going, and in reply to my grumbling about a number of hitches, he clapped me on the shoulder and said: "Nothing to worry about! You're great fellows and you've done so much. More than I ever expected!"

They picked him up that same night. A few months later, though, he was released and sent to build the Berezinka Cogeneration Plant in the northern Urals. By the standards of those days, this station was considered to be a high-pressure one (sixty atmospheres), and there were great difficulties with its construction. He met his end there eventually.

There were cases when people were released two or three months after being arrested, and that's why, when my wife asked, the words "About three months" just came out.

What had happened to me did not worry me much at first. I even thought, "Well, to hell with them, let them check me out and investigate. Then I'll be cleared and beyond suspicion."

In my stupidity, I still believed that the NKVD was dealing with serious matters and state criminals, and I even felt a little awkward that they were being taken away from big things to waste their time on small fish like me.

Around midnight, they brought me to Kashira Prison and passed me over to the head guard. There was a search, then a corridor, a door sheathed in iron, more iron doors, and a horrid grating of keys in the locks.

Reason cannot reconcile itself with the idea that one person locks others like himself in iron cages—it's unnatural.

On the wall of the prison office hung a portrait of Stalin, "The Morning of Our Motherland." As in every institution, there was the state crest with the slogan, "Proletarians of the World, Unite!" Indeed . . .

Chapter Three

Prison Neighbors

There were six of us in the cell. In the narrow space between the beds two thieves—*urkagans* in the criminal jargon—were trotting back and forth like trapped wolves. They were in an animated discussion of why and how they had been "burned" and who it was that sold them out. They carried on their conversation in thieves' language, full of incomprehensible words: *faraony, shkery, kozha, smetana, frayer,* and so on.

Near the door on the right was the cot of a tall, red-haired lad. He was a blacksmith in some small shop in Kashira, and he happened to be living in a house that stood next door to the home of the head of the local NKVD.

The wives in the two houses were squabbling over the way they looked after their households: the chickens would sometimes get into the neighbor's garden, or the pigs would break through the fence and dig up the potatoes, or the washing would fall off the line. The two of them also couldn't agree on how to divide up the strip of orchard that lay between the two houses. The result was that Vasya found himself in prison charged with being a Trotskyite.

The next cot belonged to an elderly, gloomy-looking Pole, P—sky, with a puffy, sickly face. He ran the post office in our settlement, Kaganovich City, at the hydroelectric station. His parents were living in Poland, not far from Warsaw. He had been called up for service during World War I, and when Poland became an independent state after the war and revolution, he found himself in Russia—"abroad," in other words. He was homesick, and his entire crime was asking Moscow how he could make a trip home, even a brief one, to visit his dying mother. What resulted was not a trip to Poland but a trip to prison, with charges of having "links abroad" (Article 58, point 4, which promised nothing good).

The thieves had the best places, near the window. As the most recent arrival I had the worst place, near the door.

Next to me was a young and very nervous fellow.

His story was quite unusual. He had been a journalist in Golutvino or Ozery, had recently married, was young, ardent, energetic, and new ideas were always popping up in his head. He decided he was going to be a writer, and the hero of his novel was supposed to go to prison. To find out what life in our prisons was like (nothing was ever written about this, of course), he began trying to get permission from the authorities to visit a prison and talk to the inmates (Leo Tolstoy did the same when he was writing *Resurrection*). The authorities threw him out, of course, though they had already marked him as a suspicious character. Then he decided to get to prison "temporarily," on a legal basis. To do that, he went to Moscow and, in a teahouse near the Zatsep Market, began trumpeting his "underworld adventures" in hopes of meeting some real criminals. They knew at once whom they were dealing with, however, and he couldn't strike up any acquaintances. Then, toward evening, he began telling people that he had only just arrived from abroad and had nowhere to spend the night. There were various "vigilants" around, of course, and before long he did find himself in Kashira Prison:

having nowhere to spend the night, he took the night train to Kashira and there they picked him up. He found the first day interesting; on the second he was shocked by prison ways; and on the third he demanded to see the prosecutor, though in vain. His investigator told him, "We know, we know. We've been following you for a long time."

He had left a sealed letter at home which his wife was to present to the prosecutor in case he actually was arrested. In it, he explained his motives for wanting to learn about prison life. This did not help, however. An NKVD Troika gave him five years under the article "SOE," meaning "socially dangerous element." So now he could collect material—and of the most dramatic kind—to his heart's content. Did he ever write anything? Not likely . . .

And how his wife grieved and wept when he was packed off on a transport!

I learned all these stories later, of course. That same night I was summoned for my first interrogation.

The lock grated. Someone shook my shoulder: "Lazarev? Get dressed."

The guard led me down a long corridor and then upstairs.

CHAPTER FOUR

Interrogations

Interrogations, as a rule, took place at night. They would let a person fall asleep and then, after an hour or two, would wake him. Before he could even collect his wits, they would take him away for interrogation.

So what were the workers of the "glorious organs" trying to find out?

"Who were your acquaintances? When and where did you meet? What did you talk about?" As a rule they had in mind the people one dealt with at work.

"Did you know engineer such-and-such?"

"Yes, I knew him at work."

"What did he tell you about his counterrevolutionary activity?"

"I never noticed he was involved in any such activity!"

"So, in your opinion, the organs are arresting innocent people?"

"I don't know."

"Sign that you believe that the NKVD has wrongly accused citizen N. We want you to help the investigation. Confess your counterrevolutionary activity and things will be easier for you."

Once they called me out in the daytime and took me down the street to the building of the regional NKVD.

It was summer. There were flowers on the interrogator's desk. During the interrogation he kept picking up the telephone to talk to his wife or to his friends about going fishing, swimming, or to dances. He would order theater tickets, and so on. The whole point of this game was to make me "give up my accomplices," in other words, to write a denunciation or to slander innocent people. Various privileges were promised in exchange: the right to correspondence, meetings with relatives, receiving food parcels, and so on. His performance struck me as rather inept, however, and I quickly saw through it.

Many did take this bait, though, and helped the NKVD "fulfill the plan."

And there was a plan. There was competition as well. If one region picked up a hundred people in a week and another only fifty, the latter region was thought to be lagging and the head of the region's NKVD "lacking in vigilance"; that, in turn, threatened him with harsh punishment. In one of his "theoretical" articles the "Great, Wise Leader" noted that about seven percent of peasants were "kulaks' henchmen" or simply resisting the building of socialism. This seven percent had to be produced, lest the theory of the "Wisest Father" be cast into doubt and undermined. That could never be permitted, of course. There was no shortage of "game." Apart from people unhappy with the way things were going or who were suspected of dissent, they picked up relatives, friends, and coworkers of those arrested previously; they picked up people for quarreling with Jews—for "anti-Semitism"; they picked up Jews themselves, for "Trotskyism" and for "connections abroad." One of the subparagraphs of Article 58 proclaimed "Knew, but did not inform." Anyone they liked could be brought in under this point: the husband of a neighbor lady who had caught the investigator's eye or, to the contrary, who had quarreled with his wife—anyone on whom the investigator wanted to take revenge, any poor creature whose life he wanted to destroy, and so on.

The NKVD had its informants, its secret collaborators. If they failed to produce denunciations, then they must be hiding something or abetting, and so on; and then the collaborator became another victim. What occurred was a peculiar chain reaction: the longer it lasted, the more it expanded.

"The Wisest of the Wise," by the way, advanced a theory by which the greater the victories of socialism, the more furious the resistance of the dying world and the greater the number of internal and external enemies. Despite the blatant stupidity and illogic of such a theory, no one, of course, dared to doubt it. Every party organization had its official collaborators whose official party assignment was spying on and denouncing their comrades at work.

The methods of interrogation were varied. After a few sessions of "preliminary feeling out" that failed to produce the desired result with me, they went to a twenty-four-hour interrogation. This method was called "the conveyor," and its essence was not allowing the person to sleep. Interrogators took turns, of course. Over twenty-four hours they allowed me to doze off only twice, for half an hour; the rest of the time I sat at a table opposite the interrogator under the blinding light of a high-wattage bulb.

When my eyes began to close and my head fell on the table I would hear him shout: "Stand up! Do you think you came here to sleep?" And so on. On the interrogator's desk lay a rolled-up newspaper. If you weren't able to jump up immediately he would hit you over the head with this rolled-up newspaper or whatever was at hand. There was a piece of iron rolled inside the newspaper, and when he hit you with it, you either came to or collapsed senseless on the floor. By the end of the second twenty-four hours, I had completely lost my bearings; my head was whirling and all I wanted was to sleep. Once, after a regular half-hour break (they would take me to the washbasin and the toilet), they brought me back to the interrogator, and I simply took off my jacket, spread it on the floor, and collapsed on it. The astounded interrogator and a major—some official from the NKVD—howled:

"What do you think you're doing? Where's your respect for the organs? On your feet!"

Already falling asleep I could hear: "Well, that's it! We have to finish with him. Take him away!"

I don't remember them dragging me back to the cell. I collapsed into sleep immediately.

They didn't bother me or call me out for two days. The summons on the third night seemed rather different. An NKVD lackey appeared along with the guard. Looking at a piece of paper he checked: "Last name? First name? Patronymic? Year of birth?"

He led me into the corridor without letting me get dressed. "Straight ahead. No turning around!"

The usual procedure was to take me into the corridor where the investigators' rooms were, but now we went downstairs, into a semi-basement. I had heard talk in the cell that on the right were the punishment cells—stone closets without heat and light, while on the left was the place they took people to be shot.

The man leading the way turned . . . to the left! A few more steps and we stopped at a gray door sheathed in iron.

One of these lackeys stopped to the right of the door, the second behind me. The command came: "Straight ahead! Don't look around!"

The door swung open. Beyond it was a long, narrow room like a corridor. It was four paces wide and twenty long. It was bathed in blinding light. Four walls, a concrete floor, and a door at the opposite end. There were no windows. Two steps down. Blinded by the light after the semi-darkness of the corridor, I stopped. Behind me I heard the sharp cry, "Straight ahead, don't look around!"

My mind suddenly becomes exceptionally bright and clear. My body is tense, my step resolute and confident.

They'll probably shoot me when I get to the middle of the room. Well, to hell with them, I'm thinking; I've had enough of this! The corridor, though, seems endlessly long. The dozen paces to the middle seem like a long, long journey. The closer I get to the opposite door, the harder it is to keep going. Why are you dragging this out, you bastards? My legs begin to feel like they're going to fold under me. With my last ounce of strength, my heart beating madly, I reach the door. I climb the two steps . . .

The door swings open: "Move on!"

Once again, a semi-darkened corridor, a turn to the right, up a stairway—and there I am in the investigator's office. My knees are knocking, I'm out of breath, and my tongue won't move.

"What do you think you're doing, coming here looking like this? Why aren't you dressed? Take him away!"

They take me back to my cell; I put on my pants and jacket and present myself to the bright eyes of the representative of the "glorious organs."

The performance is over. Once again the same old words: "Give me more details about your connections with enemies of the people."

But I'm not in the mood for talking. This little show may have been directed by people without much talent, but it made a deep impression on me. I was only twenty-nine years old, after all, and had been married just two years.

CHAPTER FIVE

Prisoners' Conversations

They left me in peace for a time. The endless days dragged on, one just like the other.

Books, letters, and visits were all forbidden. It was the end of June. The cell was stifling. A bit of the stone wall of the prison could be seen through the window; but if, with the help of your comrades, you tried to climb up and look out they would shoot.

Even this little glimpse, though, was soon reckoned impermissible by Moscow, and prison windows all over Russia were hurriedly covered with "muzzles"—louvers made of roofing tin. Light managed to find its way through the louvers only from the top, through a narrow gap. I've heard that in the accursed days of tsarism, pigeons would fly through the prison windows, and the prisoners would feed them. Our authorities, of course, did their best to do away with such "survivals from the past." There was a shortage of roofing tin in the country, and everyone's roof leaked. In the schools of Kashira they had to hang sheets of plywood over the pupils' desks—otherwise their notebooks would have been soaked whenever it rained. Such problems were called "growing pains."

I can't recall what we talked about in the cells. In any case, there weren't any serious conversations. We told jokes and interpreted dreams in great detail. A dream of a church was supposed to mean you were going to be let out. Everyone tried to dream of a church, but for some reason no one managed to be that lucky.

The criminals—the *urkagany*—boasted about their successes and deals "on the outside." I was amazed when for the first time I heard the phrase "a good thief" used as a compliment. That's what they called those who didn't stoop to petty crime and kept out of jail, whether they were a pickpocket, a burglar, a break-and-enter artist, a specialist in stealing passengers' baggage, or a "Freemason"—one who palmed off counterfeit money. But they were contemptuous of "shoppers" (those who grabbed bags of groceries) and *sosochniki* (who robbed children).

Most of the stories were highly exaggerated and told with the aim of making an impression. Later, I learned that very few of the real, major criminals were talkative and almost never spoke about themselves. The prison authorities began to plant "broody hens" in the cell, especially for new prisoners. These were provocateurs, most of them prisoners themselves, but occasionally free people. They would try to turn conversations to political topics and sometimes brought greetings from acquaintances or unknown people; and they would suggest ways of passing notes to the outside, and so on. Somehow I was able to pick them out at first glance and would try to keep my distance; but when they became really insistent, I would turn the conversation to women and so make myself seem "not a serious person."

They took us out of the cell only to go to the interrogator (alone) or to the toilet (the whole group). In the toilet, you could sometimes learn a bit of news: you might come across a bit of newspaper, a scrap of paper, a few words written on the wall, or hear someone's name mentioned. Given the total lack of news from outside, such information seemed very significant and would give rise to a lot of speculation.

Chapter Six

Farewell, Moscow!

I was brought before the interrogator two more times. The first time he gave me a transcript of the interrogation to sign and told me that the investigation was completed (the process required a certain amount of time—no less than two or three months—and a certain number of sheets of paper of the "interrogation" to be written up, even though everything on them might be utterly trivial). This would be enough to show that the investigation was "up to scratch." By that time, my interrogator and I had come to know one another quite well and sometimes chatted about everyday matters: we'd had a hailstorm recently; some windows had been smashed in the factory; power lines had broken down . . . Sometimes I would tell him something about the history of technology, a subject he took an interest in. The prescribed two or three hours would go by in conversations like these, and the report would indicate that "the interrogation was begun at such-and-such a time and was concluded at such-and-such a time." Each of us left satisfied with the other.

The second time the interrogator sent for me was at the beginning of August. He took a narrow strip of paper out of his folder and placed it in front of me; it was a clipping from some long report. I read, "By decision of the Special Commission of the NKVD of the USSR for Moscow Oblast, Citizen Lazarev, Vl. Mikh., born 1907, is sentenced for counterrevolutionary propaganda to five years imprisonment, less the time spent in preliminary detention, in Corrective Labor Camps."

I couldn't make any sense out of it. There had been no trial, no speeches, no charges and—no acquittal.

There were just a few lines on a carbon copy of some typewritten words.

"Sign on the back."

"I refuse."

"Come on, you're only signing that you've been informed of the decision."

"It doesn't matter, I refuse."

We argued for a few minutes, then the slip of paper was put away into my file.

"You may go."

A few days later, those of us who had received our sentences were taken out with our belongings and lined up by fives in the prison yard. The roll was called, checked, and we were counted. The guard warned us: "No stopping, no talking. A step to the left or a step to the right will be considered an escape attempt! We'll open fire without warning. March!"

We marched. The few passers-by pressed themselves against the fences or slipped into doorways. "Keep moving, no stopping," the guards shouted.

A few women, not known to us, began to sob. Evidently their relatives had already been herded away earlier.

We reached the station, and our group was kept in a little square to the right of the building. Passengers from a train just arrived were passing by on the other side of a wooden fence. They were our people from the hydroelectric station, and they looked our way with puzzlement. I noticed a friend, Vasya, and raised my hand with five fingers spread out. He understood and nodded. He would pass the word.

A railway car rolled up, and we were taken on board according to the list. There were bars on the windows and guards on the platforms of the cars. The guard commander took a liking to my wallet, a leather one. He put it in his pocket: "Not allowed."

There was nothing in the wallet anyway. My entire capital—something around two rubles—I had shoved in my pockets.

The whistle blew, the train set off. At the Paveletsk Station a "Black Maria" was drawn up to the train. We were loaded inside and the doors closed. It was dark and stifling. The vehicle went careening through Moscow.

Maybe we could rock the vehicle until it turned over and run off every which way. In one of the little courtyards at the back of the Kazan Station we were loaded into a Stolypin carriage. This was interesting, though: here was the supposedly vicious reactionary Stolypin, and yet his invention had outlived both him and the tsar and found a happy place for itself in socialism. Incomprehensible are Thy ways, O Lord! The carriage was shunted about for some time and at last connected to a train. Through the narrow, barred window we could sometimes see passengers rushing by, people seeing them off, porters. The normal bustle.

The whistle blew. We set off. The last thing I saw through the window was the flaming red canna lilies in the flower bed in front of the station.

Farewell, Moscow!

It would be ten years before fate let me see it again—and what years they were!

Only then did I suddenly realize what had happened to me. Would Zhenya and Lidochka survive without me? Who would support them? Painfully aware that I was responsible for them and unable to help them, I buried my tearful face in the pillow.

CHAPTER SEVEN

Moscow–Vladivostok

The Stolypin car is not unlike a sleeping car. However, it has gratings on the compartments instead of doors; the windows, only on the level of the upper sleeping shelves, are tiny and also covered with gratings. Escort guards are stationed at both ends of the car. You're not allowed to leave the compartment.

I'm lying on one upper shelf, and on the other is a young lad in a striped sailor's vest. He's a hardened criminal who's already had a taste of camp life. Below sits a massive old fellow who strongly resembles Gogol's So-bakevich, though only in appearance. He's had a rather interesting life. He was a policeman in tsarist times, a neighborhood cop in Moscow's busi-ness area, near the Lubyanka. Given the nature of this area, he had scarcely any contact with ordinary people but dealt with offices, business firms, and transport. When he was young, he was given the task of going to Yasnaya Polyana to deliver some document to Leo Tolstoy. He couldn't explain just what sort of a document it was, but I think it was connected with Tolstoy's excommunication from the church. Tolstoy accepted the document and then took one of his books from the shelf and wrote in it: "Young man, I hope you will try to understand this story." He signed it and gave it to him, then showed him out.

The young policeman finished this book and then went on to read ev-erything that Tolstoy had written, and he still remembered it all. What was most remarkable was that he apparently read no other writers but Tolstoy—at least he never mentioned any.

Since he had never been involved in any cases dealing with revolution-aries, he went on serving peacefully in the Moscow city administration in Soviet times until at last in the 1930s someone remembered his past. A Troika labeled him a Socially Dangerous Element and threw him in jail.

In the middle of the night they brought a man of about thirty-five into the last compartment of our car. He was surrounded by a solid ring of guards with weapons at the ready. This was apparently somewhere near Kazan. A few stations farther on, though, they took him out. Who was he? Where were they taking him? To be executed? To be tortured? To a solitary cell in prison?

Three days later we were in Sverdlovsk. We were loaded into the back of an open truck and brought to a prison courtyard and told to sit on the ground. At the other end of the yard was a group of a hundred or more prisoners.

We sat waiting. The yard was U-shaped, walled in by the huge wings of the prison.

In one of the corners of the yard was a well-trodden circular path some 120 meters in diameter; on either side of the circle was a wooden sunshade under which stood soldiers with rifles. Around the circular path, hands clasped behind their backs and a meter apart, walked a group of women. It was exercise time. Suddenly, this orderly procession was disrupted. There were hoarse shouts, a woman's piercing scream, a child crying and a shot. What was happening? One of the woman prisoners had a boy about four years old; something among the stones on the ground had attracted his attention. "Ma, a bit of glass," he cried, and ran out of the ranks. A guard rushed toward him, rifle butt at the ready. The mother turned, cried out, and rushed toward the boy. The ranks of women got muddled, and the guard at the other end of the circle, whether out of panic or on orders, fired a shot into the air. Guards rushed out, twisted the woman's hands behind her back, and the whole group of women was driven back into the prison with kicks and rifle butts.

Many years later, when they began writing about the Hitlerites, we never heard that even they did things like that. But in 1937 this was all new to us, and it produced a painful impression.

Toward nightfall, they loaded us into cattle cars on a special prisoners' train.

The freight car had two-level wooden sleeping platforms on the right and the left. They loaded forty of us into each car, so that there were eight to ten men on each platform. You had to lie on your side and could turn over only when everyone else did, otherwise there was no room to move. The door on the side was barred shut, and the other door was blocked tight. There was a latrine barrel, a *parasha,* on the floor. No mattresses or straw, no water either.

For some reason I don't remember much about this long journey across Siberia. I can't recall who my neighbors were, how we prisoners were fed, or many other things.

What did we talk about?

All we learned about each other was the article under which we had been convicted, our sentences, our names, and the prisons we had come from.

Everyone, of course, was concerned with the big question: where were they taking us? But no one knew the answer to that. We stopped for a long while in Mariinsk (between Novosibirsk and Krasnoyarsk). There was a major camp distribution center here. At night, though, we went on. Someone said we were bound for Gornaya Shoriya, a land of mines, mountains, and camps and, apparently, a place where the law of the jungle reigned supreme. When we asked our guards where we were going, there was no answer. It was much easier, though, to find out how many of us were on board the train.

There were sharp curves as the train crept up into the mountains, and the fellow lying by the upper window could count the cars. There turned out to be no less than seventy. If even ten of them were for the guards, the kitchen, and so on, then every train like this was carrying no fewer than 2,500 prisoners.

Even though the little windows in the freight cars were covered with gratings, it was dangerous to look out of them or even get too close to them: the guards would shoot without warning. Nevertheless, this was our only link with the world outside, and the fellow lying by the window was supposed to tell the others where we were and what he could see. That person kept his right to this privileged place because of his descriptive talents and, often, the trust others had in him.

Stationed outside, on the braking platforms between the cars, were "archangels" or "devils"—cops, in other words. They were our soldier-escorts, armed with rifles and, of all things, wooden mauls. The farther east we traveled, the uglier and more terrible they looked: their coats were full of holes burned by some stray spark or a cigarette; their faces unshaven and covered with soot and grime; their hands blackened; all human notes in their speech had disappeared, and if they did open their mouths, only some inarticulate noise would come out. We didn't envy them and even felt pity: it was no easy task, especially at night, to be jostled about in all sorts of weather, under a penetrating wind and without shelter, hanging on to a rifle all the while . . . They were all half frozen, deathly tired and haggard. While we were sweetly dreaming, they were either on duty or having all sorts of inspections, training, and political education—studying the biography of Stalin, the history of the All-Russian Communist Party (Bolshevik), and so on.

To see what awaited a guard who made a mistake you needed only to look at the long line of cars. The cars not equipped with braking platforms had temporary timber decking and barbed-wire enclosures installed over the buffers. This was a blatant violation of railway regulations, and the soldiers who had to ride on such little platforms were not much different from condemned men. But such was the will of the NKVD. A person was only a little screw in the vast machine of the state. If the soldier perished, his mother would be informed: "He died carrying out his military duties." Let her believe that he was defending the Motherland. And what if his father or his brother was being shipped off in the same car he was guarding?

Whenever we stopped, the archangels would jump down and chase away any onlookers.

It was forbidden to throw any messages out of the cars, and if this did happen, it was only after the train had begun to move and when the archangels were running to hop back to their perches between the cars.

I recall once when a message, folded into a triangle, was picked up by a filthy, fair-haired lad of six or seven. He ran off with it some ten meters away from the railway line. The train suddenly jerked and came to a stop. One of the archangels jumped down and shouted to him: "Hey, boy, give me that note right now!" The lad, not a bit intimidated, thrust the note into his shirt and remained standing there. Meanwhile, the locomotive gave a whistle, the archangels rushed to their perches, and the young lad shouted in triumph: "Think I'd give you the letter? Like hell!" Then he unbuttoned his trousers and showed the soldiers what one might expect to be shown in such circumstances, to the sympathetic laughter of a few women who were standing by.

The train slowly picked up speed and many of us managed to get a look at the boy; then a bullet whistled past the window.

When the train made a stop, especially at night, there would be a savage search, a *shmon*.

The door would open with a clang, and we would hear the command: "Everyone move to the right!"

A pair of guards would burst into the car and begin pounding the floor and walls of the car with their wooden mallets. Then everyone would be chased over to the other side and counted while they pounded the other half of the car. All this took place to the light of torches held by guards outside, while German shepherds, trained specially for hunting people, snarled and strained at their leashes near the doors. If there weren't enough long stops, the guards would hammer on the walls and roofs of the cars during shorter stops at night.

As we learned later, this was done to deter anyone from escaping through partially sawn planks.

One day, at a large station somewhere near Mariinsk, the guards deliberately left the door of the car open after the soup had been given out so they could show us what awaited escapees. They led two young fellows—who had evidently run away from some camp—alongside the train. They were a terrible sight. The dogs, obviously, had torn their clothing to rags. One lad's whole face was no more than a bloody mask, and he kept spitting blood as he went. The second lad could barely drag himself along on his broken, bloody leg. Blood had dried on his head, and his hair was a dirty, bloody mass; there were bleeding wounds on his shoulder and back. The guards drove them past the car with their rifle butts; other guards on both sides led huge dogs on leashes . . . Despite all that, someone always escaped from every train on the way to Vladivostok.

Traveling around Lake Baikal was terrifying. The train never slowed, the cars rocked and shook, and at the bottom of the embankment below we could often see railway cars that had derailed earlier lying on the lake shore and in the water. These losses did not trouble the authorities, and they certainly didn't trouble the NKVD, who had caused them.

I became very friendly with one fellow in our car, Baturov, a tradesman from Kazan. He was about forty, very good looking, with well-defined features, a calm, confident person with innate decency and honesty. He was a communist, a veteran of the Civil War, in which he had been seriously wounded in the back. He had an operation in Kazan to implant silver disks in his back, but he was at risk of osteotuberculosis. On the advice of doctors, he went to work in a creamery, where he learned the trade and became a butter and cheese maker. This saved him from tuberculosis. He treated me rather protectively, like a youngster, trying to help me and sharing whatever he could. Later, in Kolyma, he worked as a carpenter.

We arrived in Vladivostok in October and were held in a large transit camp somewhere near the Pervaya River (I don't know Vladivostok). We could see the bay far in the distance; to the right, on the hill overlooking the shore, was the Japanese crematorium; behind us were mountains. There were a few areas inside the camp fenced off with barbed wire: one "zone" for the "contras," the "enemies of the people," another for women, and an area for those on extra punishment. Moving from one zone to another was forbidden, but within each zone people struck up acquaintances and made contacts. Taking advantage of the warm weather, people took off their shirts and killed lice while sitting in the sun. Amateur barbershops went into business. The criminals had their hidden razors and bits of soap and would take on customers for a small fee. Those who were penniless shaved with shards of bottle glass.

Our rations, of course, remained at the norm for transports: four hundred grams of bread and some watery soup with rotting vegetables. There was no sugar. We spent about ten days here, waiting for a ship, as it turned out. We had no idea of what awaited us, though, and all sorts of rumors sprang up. There was one, for instance, about the "Decree on Abolition of Transports." We were supposedly being held here "because of the coming vote on the new constitution."

This was the time when the new Stalin Constitution was being conceived and ratified (as it later turned out, the author of the constitution was the "enemy of the people," Bukharin). Many believed that after the election we'd all be turned loose to make our way back home.

It was the more philistine among the educated prisoners—bureaucrats, rank-and-file engineers, local political figures and lesser functionaries—who most eagerly grasped at and spread these rumors and "theories." It all reminded me of the conversations carried on by the "piqué vests," so wonderfully described in the Ilf and Petrov novel *The Golden Calf.* This marvelous book was and remains an unsurpassed chronicle of our society.

There were quite a few interesting people in the camp. Here I met D. A. Samoilov, a well-known engineer-specialist in power-generating and editor of the journal *Moscow Energy* (*Mosenergo*). I had to laugh when he asked anxiously if I had managed to send him the article I had promised (I had already published some articles in the journal). Here as well was Kostya Soloukhin, the senior dispatcher of the Kashira Hydroelectric Station, a very capable young engineer. Having time on their hands and, evidently influenced by accounts of the habits of political prisoners in tsarist times, a few scholars gave lectures in the barracks on academic topics.

Prince Sviatopolk-Mirsky, the famous Pushkinist and literary scholar, gave lectures on Pushkin and Byron, citing whole pages from their works from memory. This man was so well educated that he gave a course on English literature at England's finest university, Oxford. He came to the USSR by invitation of the Soviet government (Comrade Stalin) and a short while later was arrested. Not having any trade or practical skills, he was sent out on general labor in Kolyma, slowly starved, and, as a "goner" wound up doing road work in the settlement of Atka, where he perished of cold, hunger, and the harassment of the *pridurki* (this was the camp word for those prisoners, criminals as a rule, who had the soft jobs in camp administration and maintenance).

There was another old man, an astronomer from Pulkovo. I don't recall his name, but he was a specialist in small planets and told us many fascinating things about the solar system. His writings were well known in the rest of the world. And that was what did him in: in 1935 or 1936 a German admirer discovered an ordinary asteroid and named it in honor of his teacher. For such "foreign contacts" the astronomer was given five years.

One very important geologist (again, I don't recall his name) gave interesting talks on "the treasures of the earth," mines, mountains, and so on.

There were many doctors, including some important specialists. People from the regular army kept apart in their own individual groups.

The mass of the "contras" were mid-level intelligentsia and peasant "seven-percenters," arrested to fulfill the plan because of Stalin's claim that seven percent of the peasants were kulaks or their henchmen. Some of them had been picked up straight from their fields or from home after returning from work. They were wearing tattered straw hats and homemade rope shoes. Often, their only clothing was a pair of canvas trousers and a belted shirt.

At the time I still had no idea of the scope of destruction in the countryside and the annihilation of the hardest-working peasants. This madness had begun as early as 1930. Even in Moscow people experienced food shortages, and across Russia there was genuine famine. In Ukraine it reached the point of cannibalism. And even now, in our time, Russia still cannot feed itself!

CHAPTER EIGHT

To Kolyma in the Hold of a Ship

They put us on board the ship in darkness, and the loading, apparently, went on all night. First they herded us into the hold of some sort of iron barge that then moved up to the side of an oceangoing ship. We went up a gangplank to the deck and were then assigned to one of the ship's holds.

I found myself in the lower level of the forward hold; my place was on the lower range of bunks at the very bow of the ship. There were rough wooden bunks four and five levels high in the middle of the hold and along both bulkheads where the ship's hull broadened. The floor was wooden, and the hold was dimly lit by electric lights. One steep iron ladder led up to a hatchway through the deck of the upper hold. This hold was also fitted with bunks and was full of prisoners. Around the hatchway stood camp guards, chosen from the prisoners—criminals, as a rule. Their task was to keep anyone in the lower hold from going to the upper one. A bright spot could be seen from the upper hold: this was the hatch to the deck, which was reached by its own ladder. This exit was watched by guards armed with rifles.

Each hold was nearly the height of a two-story house. There were no deadlights, and air came in only through the hatch from the upper hold to the lower. We soon would discover what this meant.

They divided us into tens. The leader of each group of ten was responsible for collecting the rations and the water. Later, in Kolyma, we found out that four or five ships were used to transport prisoners; each one carried 3,000 to 5,000 prisoners per voyage, from May to November. A ship could make two voyages per month.

Our ship was the *Kulu,* carrying about 4,000 prisoners. (On some voyages the ship took more than 5,000.)

In the morning, we each got a piece of salted whale meat and a ration of bread. I came from Arkhangelsk and knew that you had to eat salt fish with caution, but hungry people, despite my advice, wolfed it down greedily. Soon everyone was gasping with thirst. The water ration was a half-liter, but by no means everyone managed to get his full share. The group leader would fetch water in a tin basin, but had to go up the ladder, pass through the upper hold and then through the hatch to the deck, where a guard would fill the basin from a hose. Then he had to go back down the steep ladder carrying the basin of water. This was difficult even in normal circumstances, and much more so when the ship was rolling. As he came down from the upper hold to the lower, the criminals in the bunks attached to the ladder would scoop up the precious water with cups, spilling so much that the group leader often had nothing left to give to his group. There were vicious brawls around the foot of the ladder when another basin of water appeared. The bestial essence of man was on full display.

By the end of the day, some prisoners were reduced to licking puddles of water that had spilled during the fights from the filthy floor. You could hear groans, cries, and shouts of abuse from all sides. Someone was weeping hysterically.

Toward evening the ship began to roll. We were already in the Sea of Japan. Most of the prisoners had never been in an oceangoing ship and they quickly became seasick. The first to suffer were those in the top bunks in the upper hold. They had no control over their vomiting, and the vomit flew downwards, often on the heads of those in the lower bunks. Toward the end of the day we were allowed another half-liter of water. Things went better this time, since most of the criminals were lying flat in their bunks and couldn't steal it.

We were taken to the toilet twice a day. The toilets were on the upper deck and were wooden lean-tos hanging along the side of the ship over the water. They rocked terribly, and when you looked down you could see the cold, white-capped waves.

The lack of ventilation began to take effect at night. There simply wasn't enough air in the hold, where people were so tightly packed together. The combination of rotting garbage, vomit, and the smell of dirty clothes and foot-wraps created an absolutely stifling atmosphere. To catch even a small breath of air you had to stand near the ladder; but there wasn't much room there, and as more people blocked the free entry of air, the hold became even more stifling.

Some lost consciousness. Those who had asthma or colds or heart disease suffered most. We spent most of the time in a half-sleep or semi-consciousness. When they gave us our regular portion of salt fish the next day, hardly anyone touched it. On the morning of the third day, there were a few corpses. We were not allowed to take them away, so their neighbors dragged them onto the floor, under the bunks. When the ship rolled, they would slide along the floor, from one side to the other, their stiff hands and feet knocking dumbly against the supports of the bunks.

It all reminded me of the scenes in *Uncle Tom's Cabin* and the descriptions of transporting Negroes in slave ships in the days of slavery.

The resemblance was not only superficial, in fact. For some time the NKVD had indeed been supplying slave-prisoners to the major projects of the first Five-Year Plans. These slaves built the White Sea–Baltic Canal, the factories of Kuznetsk and Magnitogorsk, the Moscow–Volga Canal.

The major slave-owning centers—Mariinlag, BAMlag, and others—supplied prisoners for mining coal and metals, timber cutting, railway construction, and other "projects to build socialism."

People were supplied to Kolyma by Dallag, and Dallag's owner was Dalstroy, a trust that answered to the NKVD and was part of its system.

I recalled that when I was a student at the Arkhangelsk Polytechnic I had an instructor who was an exile. When the English interventionists had withdrawn they left a Fraser lathe in our workshop; the Polytechnic traded it for him with the NKVD. This instructor used to say, "I never knew my real worth before, but now I know exactly what it is: I'm worth precisely the price of an English lathe."

That was accepted as normal even in 1928. But by the end of the thirties, such things were taking place on a massive scale.

Soon there were so many prisoners that new "projects of the century" were undertaken one after another, since there weren't enough places to employ this unpaid work force. And so we had the needless White Sea Canal, the Transpolar Railway from Salekhard, the famous BAM (Baikal–Amur Railway), and enormous harvests of timber in isolated areas where it couldn't be moved out, and so on.

CHAPTER NINE

Magadan

Our ship stood at anchor in a large bay surrounded by snow-covered, tree-less hills. It was already growing dark by the time our hold was unloaded. The sky was gray; the water in the bay was a dark leaden color; on shore a few scattered groups of lights showed at the foot of the hills. There was not a building in sight at the place where we landed. Dogs barked, rifle bolts clattered, the guards shouted as they assembled us into ranks of five on the icy road. This was a confusing process for those who had never served in the army or who were new to prison, and they were encouraged into place by kicks and rifle butts.

It was still warm when we had left Vladivostok, but winter was setting in here. The wind was cold, there was snow on the ground, and we were lightly dressed. I had a thin gray cotton coat and was shivering from the cold. It was even worse for the peasants from the south, who wore only shirts and straw hats. After days of sitting in the hold, our legs had swollen and we were unsteady.

Finally the long column had formed up.

"A step to the right or a step to the left will be considered an escape at-tempt! We'll open fire without warning! March!"

There was no lagging. You would be beaten without mercy, torn to pieces by the dogs, and shot "while attempting to escape."

The road rose steeply between the hills. It was growing quite dark and people often tripped and fell. In an hour or two we reached a huge camp surrounded by barbed wire, with guard towers at each corner and every fifty meters between. These towers always reminded me of the Martian tripods from H. G. Wells's *War of the Worlds*. They looked just as ridiculous and seemed to bear the same malice toward the human race as did the Martians.

At the gates, our transport was handed over to the camp guards. We passed through in groups of five.

"First group! Second! . . . Seventeenth!"

The human cargo was being accounted for. We were distributed among large barracks with three-tiered bunks. There was a passageway through the middle of the barracks, and at both ends stood stoves made from gasoline barrels lying on their sides. There were no fires in the stoves, of course. A few twisted stumps lay in the yard, but we had no way to saw or chop them into firewood. We flopped down on the bare planks. A few people tried to gather up some chips and rubbish to start a fire. But we were not the first transport to come here, and not much remained after the thousands of people who had already passed through.

A "census" began in the morning. Some long tables had been set up along the passageways in one of the barracks, just like the polling stations on election day. We were herded through the barracks and our names recorded alphabetically:

"Surname, first name, patronymic? Year of birth? Article? Sentence? Trade?" Local prisoners handled the process.

Since it was impossible to take all the names at once, a few groups were assembled and marched out in columns to work. I found myself in one of the columns—about two hundred strong—assigned to clear snow from the roads around Magadan. Compulsory, unpaid labor has no attraction for anyone, of course, and the guards themselves weren't particularly zealous. They had little interest in the work; their task was to ensure that no one escaped and no one was lost. On the other hand, they were interested in something else: a few soldiers began walking around the column, discussing something with the brigadiers. The news soon spread: anyone wanting to buy tobacco, cigarettes, matches, or anything else should just hand over the money and the guards would supply it.

People shook out their remaining change and ruble notes and passed them over to the guards. Of course, we never saw the money, the cigarettes, or the guards again, and three hours later we were herded back to the camp. This was how the warrior-Chekists of the "Glorious Organs" saw their task of protecting the Motherland and serving the people. I'm certain that this did not happen without the compliance of their officers. And yet the majority of them were probably members of the Komsomol or the party, "the conscience of the people." This conscience turned out to be badly stained . . .

The next morning, after we were fed and had our particulars recorded, we were herded off to the bathhouse for showers and disinfection. We entered one end of the building in our own clothes, stripped ourselves naked, washed under the shower, and exited clad entirely in camp clothes: a pair of underwear, a padded jacket and trousers, felt boots, footcloths, and a cap with earflaps. When one of the new arrivals tried to go into the bathhouse again to pick up some little thing he cherished from the pile of our "free" clothes, he would be stopped by angrily cursing *pridurki*.

They would rummage through the clothes, rifle the pockets, and pile the more valuable things in heaps, obviously to be sold off.

None of this could have happened without the knowledge and connivance of the camp authorities who, of course, got their share as well.

Chapter Ten

The Kolyma Highway

Over one of the camp barracks hung the slogan: "Kolyma needs bold, energetic people." This was a bit flattering to one's vanity: so, are we people like that?

I met a few people I knew from the hydroelectric station and asked Kostya Souloukhin, "So, where are they sending you?"

"I've signed up as a carpenter. I'm going off to a construction site."

I was signed up as an electrical engineer, even though there were plenty of engineers here without me, it seemed.

In the morning they loaded twenty or twenty-five of us onto trucks and we drove off along the road that went northeast from Magadan into the heart of the "continent." There were two guards in each truck: one sat in the cab and the other with us in the back; they changed places from time to time. Ninety kilometers down the road was the first settlement, Palatka.

It was much colder here than in Magadan, but there was scarcely any wind. Everything around was white from the deep snow. To the right and left were endless waves of rising hills. The road climbed higher and higher, sometimes twisting in a serpentine to overcome the steep rise through a pass. The road passed through uninhabited regions, though it carried a good deal of traffic. There were no railways here (now a narrow-gauge line has been built to Palatka), and the whole of this enormous area between the Sea of Okhotsk and the basins of the Kolyma and Indigirka rivers was supplied exclusively by vehicle. The farthest-flung gold mines were almost a thousand kilometers from Magadan.

From time to time we would come upon little camp settlements of three or four shacks almost buried in snow. These were for road workers and were called *komandirovki,* or remote camp sectors. The weather was clear and cold. Even though we were wearing padded trousers and jackets, felt boots with woolen footcloths, a second padded coat, and caps with earflaps, the wind from the moving truck could always find gaps to make its way inside our clothing.

The snow was blinding in its whiteness. The hills became ever higher, more formidable; the road often ran along the edge of a cliff, but the Kolyma drivers were used to this and scarcely reduced speed.

We arrived in Atka late in the evening. The settlement was high above sea level, with rocky hills all around. The right half of the sky was blocked by two enormous hills that resembled a double-humped camel.

Here we stopped for the night. We settled ourselves in a large barracks, which was a camp kitchen where the evening meal had just been served. We were each given a bowl of fish soup and a piece of bread. We lay down on the floor side by side to sleep. There were two truckloads of us here, about fifty men. We had traveled 206 kilometers from Magadan.

With morning came reveille, and on we went. Beyond the pass, the road began to descend; the hills became smaller and less sullen than in Atka, where they stood like gates into a magic kingdom of eternal ice and silence. Along the little river valleys we could see sparse growths of poplar, and in the gullies between the hills the bare trunks of larches.

By lunchtime we had arrived in the settlement of Myakit that stretched for about half a kilometer along the Kolyma highway. The little Myakit River (the name means "no fish") was on the right; on the left were low hills around which the road bent as it continued north. Poplars grew in the valleys, sickly larches and dwarf cedars on the hills. Myakit was half village and half bush. In the summer, the dwarf cedar was tall enough to hide a man, but in winter, under the weight of the snow, it hugged the earth beneath the snowdrifts, and so the hills seemed to be bare. Only the misshapen larches thrust up from the valleys and narrow ravines. Nevertheless, the dwarf cedar produced cones—small ones, a little larger than spruce cones—and the nuts were also smaller than usual.

There were no straight streets in the settlement. A one-storied building housing the Dalstroy Autotransport Administration stood on an elevation between the road and the hills, along with a few one-storied duplex apartments for the administrators. Farther along were a hospital and a post office.

To the right of the road, in a hollow closer to the river, stood a barracklike dormitory inhabited for the most part by "free workers" on contract— guards and ex-prisoners (three hundred of them); farther on there was a fire station, a mess hall, a generating station, and a jumble of private houses clinging to the riverbank.

Across the road from the Autotransport Administration was a garage, the dispatcher's office, and, in a hollow nearer the river, a camp where we were brought. There were watchtowers on each corner; within were a few whitewashed barracks and some canvas army tents. It was a small camp of about four hundred men. It was here I was to spend five years of my life.

CHAPTER ELEVEN

Myakit Settlement

Prisoners late for their dinner were continually arriving at the mess hall where we had eaten. We were struck by their happy, healthy appearance and their suntanned faces. They were well dressed in new clothing and they wore caps made of local rabbit fur, often with white flashes on the front, a feature considered particularly "chic." They talked loudly, joked and laughed. It was obvious that they were all well fed: they offered us bread and had also left a good many pieces on the tables. After the semi-starvation we had endured, we pounced on this bread, so much so that soon we could scarcely breathe. And so when I was summoned to the office for an interview, I could barely speak. The conversation here turned on where I had worked and at what profession. We had no documents to prove our education or work experience, and so our qualifications were determined by this interview.

I was taken on as an engineer in the planning office of the Autotransport Administration.

At that time, prisoners in Kolyma who had experience as specialists or workers were paid almost the same as free workers, with a deduction for food and lodging in the camp. I was assigned a wage of nine hundred rubles, almost 50 percent more than I had earned at my former job. The money left after deductions was not paid out but was credited to a personal account, so that when a person was released from camp he would have accumulated a nest egg sufficient to set himself up at something new. A portion of the money, by permission of the camp authorities, was paid out, and one could use it to buy whatever was not provided by the general norm: cigarettes, canned goods, candies, cologne, and so on. This system was sensible and humane, although it didn't last long when we were there. Truck drivers were particularly well rewarded. They were paid by the trip, and some were almost constantly on the road and so managed to earn 4,000 or 5,000 rubles a month or even more.

This reminds me of another story. In one of the tents I met a good-looking young fellow, Petya Vishnevsky. He was in prison on criminal charges and was a driver. I noticed that sometimes in the evening he would sit trying to write a letter but seemed utterly at a loss. When we came to know one another better, I asked him:

"So what are you working on there, Petya?"

"Here, have a look," and he passed me a crumpled piece of paper. It turned out to be a letter from his mother. First, there were the usual greetings and regards from his family and friends, and then: "Petya, thank you, son, for thinking of me, I've got the money you sent but you shouldn't have taken up your old ways, better try to set yourself on the right path we don't need anything just to see you soon." When he had become a driver and started to earn a good wage, he began sending money home; but his mother simply couldn't understand how he could earn so much in prison and so assumed that her son had taken up thieving again. He was desperately anxious to explain and vindicate himself to his mother, but Petya's meager education left him without the words to do so.

The task fell to me, and I was able to convince her; she, in turn, referred to me in her letters as "a good man who has set you . . . on the right path"!

Those who earned good money scarcely relied on camp food since they could buy groceries in the camp shop or through the free workers. The truck-driving fraternity was always on the road and ate in roadside cafés.

The daily routine was as follows: reveille was at 7:00, followed by breakfast in the mess hall; then we would form up in brigades at the gate, where the guards would escort us to work.

There were free workers as well as prisoners in the office. The only difference was that they wore civilian clothes.

Several good engineers worked in our planning office. There were the well-known heating engineer and metallurgist Grum-Grzhimailo; an automotive designer, Kolosov; a young engineer from Leningrad; and others. All of them were prisoners. There were two free-worker technicians whom I don't remember at all.

The projects we had to design in no way corresponded to our qualifications and resources, of course. They were for small boiler houses, bathhouses, heating stations, and other such rubbish. The guards would come to take us to eat at lunchtime, and then we would go back to work until seven o'clock. The working day was ten hours.

In the evening there was supper, a roll call between nine and ten, and then a stand-down when walking around the camp was forbidden.

For roll call we formed up by barracks; the senior prisoner of the barracks gave his report to the prison staff and the bookkeeper. Anyone who didn't show up for roll call or tried to avoid it was severely punished.

Specially assigned people—cooks, water carriers, kitchen helpers, barbers, barrack seniors, and orderlies—looked after the day-to-day running of the camp.

The orderlies were chosen from among the old men who were unable to work. Their duties included tending the fires in the stoves, keeping the barracks in order, tidying the bunks, and so on. Here we did not have the usual sleeping platforms but wooden trestle beds with mattresses filled with wood shavings. A few prisoners had the right to go out freely to the settlement; they worked as electricians in the generating station, looked after the projector in the club, served in the free workers' cafeteria, worked in the hospital and other places. A few were orderlies in the administrators' apartments. Here they would wash floors, keep the stoves heated, wash clothes, and sometimes prepare lunch for the family of some communist administrator. Such a family, as a rule, was only a man and wife, but the wife did not work and thought it quite normal to have her dirty clothes washed by some middle-aged man who was also a husband and father but who had been torn away from his wife and children and sold into slavery. It was like going back to serfdom.

If the orderly displeased the lady of the house in some way or showed any sign of dissatisfaction, he would be dismissed and usually sent to the gold mines. Few people returned from there. And so, even though the orderly's job was out of the cold (and in Kolyma this meant more than anything), provided him with decent food, and was not exhausting, scarcely anyone wanted to take it on. The job usually fell to peasants whose health was such that they could not be sent out to do heavy physical work.

On nonworking days we had to shovel snow in the camp or were taken out to cut firewood. We needed an incredible amount of wood, since there were no brick stoves. The barracks had old gasoline barrels stacked one atop the other. There was a fire in the lower one day and night; the moment the fire went out the barracks would get cold. Prisoners were housed in barracks or in tents. Barracks were much better, of course: double doors, walls plastered inside and out, and when everyone was inside for the night, the warmth of our bodies helped as well.

Twelve to fifteen men would be quartered in a tent. When I first arrived I was in a tent with some "Trotskyites" who had arrived earlier. They were soldiers in the regular army, serious, taciturn people. They immediately made their presence felt in such a way that the camp *pridurki* didn't venture to push them around or trouble them in any way. In the morning they would exercise, wash with water or snow, and then go off to work.

I only spent a few days with them and so didn't manage to make friends with anyone. On one side of me slept Lisba, the former leader of a divisional brass band; on the other an army doctor, a Jew named Glants.

They were all very decent, hard-working and honest people. I am sure that they were as much Trotskyites as I was the son of the Pope. Before long, they were soon all sent off to the gold mines, and I never heard anything of them again.

Prisoners were divided into two groups, which lived in different barracks according to the regime under which they were held: "regulars," meaning nonpoliticals of all stripes, and "contras." We contras were considered a socially dangerous element and we had a stricter regime. Thieves, rapists, and murderers were regarded as "socially friendly," temporarily isolated from the happy and irreproachable communist society. The entire administration inside the camp was in the hands of these socially friendly. They were the barracks seniors, the bookkeepers, the barbers, bathhouse attendants, cooks, storekeepers, and so on. The camp office had several sections: the Registration and Distribution Unit that kept track of personnel and work assignments; the Equipment and Service Unit, the Culture and Education Unit, etc. The Education Unit designated any swindler or big-time thief with a long term as an "educator." The work assigner was an important person for us: it was he who determined if we would be sent to work in the warmth or in the cold, at heavy work or light. There was also a bookkeeper—a timekeeper, more or less. If we were lucky, the infirmary would be run by a medical assistant with some qualifications. But wonderful stories were told about this job: since there were no documents, any newly arrived prisoner could declare himself a doctor and win a soft job. This job often fell to con artists—morphine or cocaine addicts—who had served time in other camps where they picked up a few medical terms and could "put on a front," pretending that they knew something about medicine.

The administration was content with them: they didn't ask for any special medicines or instruments; they made do with iodine, soda, alcohol, and, of course, soporifics like morphine, cocaine, etc. These "medics" (and they were called medics) would treat any dissatisfied patients with curses and threats to have them sent to the gold mines. The authorities didn't bother them much if a prisoner died, so long as there was no threat of an epidemic. In that case, these medics would find themselves in the gold mines. Thanks to Kolyma's healthy climate and sparse population, however, epidemics were very rare.

From the time of our arrival we prisoners were eligible for "credits." This meant that those who overfulfilled their work norm would have their prison terms shortened by a specified number of days per year—sometimes one day was counted as two. These credits were soon revoked, though, first for us and then for those sentenced under Article 56 (Banditism) and the Law of August 7, 1932 (Theft of State Property)—peasants, for the most part, who had made off with an ear of wheat or a carrot picked up from the fields. This was done in Jesuitical fashion, backdated so that all the time accumulated earlier was taken away. Those who had "pull" got their credits, often after doing scarcely any work. It all depended on the clerk or the work assigner who was "one of their own" and who would credit the work of a whole brigade—particularly if the brigade were not criminals—to one or two thieves. Complaining about it, of course, was pointless. There were also people called "colonists." The NKVD had made a peculiar agreement with them: their term was calculated without any credits, but in exchange they could live in some settlement, build a house, marry, and set up a household. They were not issued passports and could not travel any distance, but the authorities who regulated the lives of these prisoners saw them as potential settlers who would live out their lives as residents of Kolyma. Later on, they deceived them as well and, with very few exceptions, sent them to the camps.

Toward the end of 1937 the camp regime began to grow more severe. The first elections under the new Stalin Constitution were taking place in the country. More and more public figures were falling under the category of "enemies of the people."

The biographies of candidates for deputies would be torn from the walls and destroyed after only a few days. The journalist Radek, editor of *Izvestia,* Sosnovsky, the people's commissar of finances, Sokolnikov, Tukhachevsky, and many others who had once been acclaimed and famous were picked up and liquidated. The cover of *Krokodil* was graced with "Yezhov's Iron Fist," a hand clenched into a fist whose fingers were crushing "enemies of the people."

Since newspapers from the "mainland" arrived with a three- to five-month delay, they almost all turned out to be "counterrevolutionary," since they carried articles written by "enemies of the people" or were run by those very same "enemies." At first we had no radio, and we contras were strictly forbidden to read or have newspapers. Having a pencil or paper in the camp was also considered a crime. You could write a letter only in the Culture and Education Unit or somewhere in secret. Letters were turned in unsealed; there were no mailboxes in the settlement, and the free workers took their letters personally to the post office.

The camp administration's fear and hatred of any sort of printed material—books or newspapers—was quite astonishing, especially if such material was in the hands of the contras. They hated and feared culture and they confiscated and destroyed books and newspapers.

CHAPTER TWELVE

Camp Life

New instructions came from the NKVD after November 1937: all "enemies of the people," that is, those sentenced under Article 58 by Troikas as SOE (Socially Dangerous Elements); KRA (Counterrevolutionary Agitation); KRD (Counterrevolutionary Activity); KRTD (Counterrevolutionary Trotskyite Activity), etc., were to be used only for heavy physical labor. In our camp, such work was done either under escort—armed guard—or without escort. Work under escort usually meant moving earth.

Prisoners with picks and crowbars would hammer at the frozen earth or clay that would not yield to their blows. Nothing but tiny fragments would fly loose.

There was nowhere to warm yourself, and because of the cold you constantly had to keep moving. The guards also froze, though they were dressed much more warmly than we. Whether from malice or boredom, they would snap their rifle bolts, shout at us, or use their rifle butts to beat weak prisoners or those they disliked. It was especially bad if the guard was a Ukrainian, Mordvin, or Chuvash who worked by the book. They were trying to get ahead in their service, and anyone who shot a prisoner "attempting to escape" was given a reward.

Luckily, I never had to spend much time working under escort. Those of us who had worked in the Transport Administration were soon put together in a few teams and allowed to work without escort. We would be marched off to a site where we worked under the supervision of a prisoner-brigadier.

I worked in one such brigade grubbing out tree stumps and collecting sand in the flood-lands of the Myakit River, half a kilometer from the settlement. One of the members of this brigade was A. V. Makovsky, former secretary of the Ukrainian Academy of Sciences, a man of forty or forty-five. He was a very gentle, musical man, poetically in love with his Ukraine. He was broadly educated, and for this was persecuted by the authorities. He was in prison for having "connections with the Vatican."

These "connections" consisted in the fact that the Academy Library, like all major libraries, had an arranged book exchange with many other academies all over the world, including the famous Vatican Library. This was a tradition, yet because Makovsky was receiving foreign books for the academy he was imprisoned.

Another man in our brigade was Rabinovich, of French Jewish origins. He was a journalist and had worked as a guide and translator for Intourist; and he did resemble a Frenchman, being very jolly and sociable. He was serving time on account of the famous French writer André Gide. Gide had visited Africa and had published a book on the Congo in which he described the inhuman exploitation of the natives, colonialism, general lawlessness, the slave trade in the colony, and so on. Therefore our regime numbered him among the progressive writers, and in 1936 he was invited to Moscow. Rabinovich was assigned as his guide-translator. Gide was supposed to have a look round our country and learn how it had been transformed under Soviet power.

Gide rejected the proposed itinerary of visits to factories and construction sites, however, declaring that as a writer he was interested above all in people. Some time before the Revolution he had been in the Caucasus, and made known his wish to travel to Svanetia, the most isolated corner of the Caucasus, as he knew.

Rabinovich accompanied him on this trip. When they had made their way deep into the mountains and were on the road to an *aul* (a village) where they were to spend the night, a delegation of peasant-mountaineers suddenly appeared carrying on a red velvet cloth . . . some quotations from Gide's latest book, in his splendid French. Our authorities had clearly outdone themselves in arranging this little "incident," and the writer, painfully sensitive to anything false and prearranged, stopped the car, bade farewell to those who were greeting him, and announced: "I understand everything, there is nothing more to see here," and then turned back. He behaved quite differently on the way back, and all his attention was focused on watching how the words about our "happy, radiant life" failed to match that life itself.

It seems, though, that he wanted to get out of the USSR safely, and so he sent his thanks to the government and even burned a bit of incense for Comrade Stalin.

And as soon as he got back to France he published a book of impressions and observations in which he denounced and ridiculed the lies in our newspapers and, in general, dumped whole tubs of mud on us. He had some experience in this, since he had managed to escape safely from Africa in much the same way. He was able to get on good terms with the corrupt leaders and executioner-colonizers while he was there, but after he left he showed the whole world their true face and their cruelty.

Comrade Stalin could not forgive such treachery, of course. But André Gide was beyond the reach of the NKVD, and so Rabinovich was hauled in as a scapegoat.

The third man was Eduard Eduardovich Pukk-Pukkovsky, an Estonian and a navy veteran. He was a graduate of the Leshaft Institute and had been in charge of physical training on naval vessels. He was five or more years older than I, muscular, well-read, and a highly cultured person overall. His beloved young wife and little son had been left on the "mainland." She was expelled from Kronstadt after his arrest and ended somewhere in Kustanai. He was arrested because he had relatives in Estonia (which was an independent state at the time).

Another who worked with us in our first days in Myakit was the army doctor Mark Glants, a young, life-loving Jew, very witty and cheerful, although not nearly as well educated as the others. He had served in Mongolia and Russia's Far East and was arrested for expressing astonishment and doubts about the guilt of one very popular commander who had been arrested by the NKVD.

A man from Odessa, A. Vinglinsky—a Pole, perhaps, or a Jew, or a mixture of both—had been designated as brigadier and supernumerary for us and for one other brigade. He was a rather pitiful and villainous figure. Before his arrest he apparently had worked as some sort of minor official in the port, where he dealt with warehouses and lading, though he passed himself off as an engineer. He knew nothing about engineering, of course, and although he considered himself an intellectual, there was nothing in his head but bits and pieces he had picked up here and there—longshoreman's terms, a little medical terminology, and so on. He was dreadfully afraid of physical work, the cold, and, of course, fights. So he was hardly ever with us, and if he did pick up a shovel or a crowbar, it was only when the bosses were around or when it was absolutely necessary. At the first opportunity he would disappear into the office to "process the work assignments." They put up with him in the office because his "processing the work assignments" meant he would do various other office work for the free workers as well—making up time sheets, bulletins, lists, orders, and so on. He had worked as a tally man in the Autotransport Administration before the decree came sending us out on physical labor.

I had an innate revulsion toward servility and cringing, and so whenever I had the chance I would express my contempt to Vinglinsky for his degrading lack of personal dignity. We lived in the same barracks, and I couldn't restrain myself from tormenting him. One example I recall: Vinglinsky somehow found out that the free workers in the settlement needed shoe polish. It was nowhere to be had, and the bosses wanted polished boots and shoes. So Vinglinsky ran off to the administration and offered his services in making shoe polish. They turned him down for some reason, and so I got a piece of paper and made up a diploma for this "bootlicker and inventor of shoe polish." In the center of the diploma was a shiny boot set on a shoe brush, while Vinglinsky was depicted licking the sole of the boot. We tacked this diploma on the wall over his bunk.

I don't recall which great writer said: "The slave who is beaten deserves compassion, but the slave who kisses the hand that beats him is to be despised." Vinglinsky was a slave who kissed the hand that beat him.

Soon our "educated" brigade was disbanded, and I found myself cutting timber. Any real forest nearby was long gone; what remained were a few scattered trees, the remnants of earlier cutting.

The deep, loose snow made the work much more difficult. Because it never thawed in winter and there was no wind, Kolyma had a particular kind of snow: it was hardly packed at all but lay in a fluffy mass, like down. And so you couldn't walk across it even by breaking through the surface a little as on normal snow. You had to crawl or almost swim in snow up to your waist or even deeper. That was how you moved from tree to tree, and the trees were far apart.

There was no sense in cutting the smaller trees: it was a lot of work, and you couldn't get the required cubic meters from them. You had to wade through the deep snow to each tree, stamp down the snow around it, saw it through, divide it into two-meter logs, trim the branches, and then haul all these logs on your shoulders to a central point and stack them to be measured.

This was very heavy work, and by the end of the day I felt as if the bones in my pelvis were coming out of their sockets. It was good if we had any homegrown tobacco, *makhorka*. The ration for all this work was half a kilo of bread per day and some herring in the morning; for lunch there was thin fish soup with frozen potatoes and some porridge without any fats. We had more soup or herring in the evening.

We worked by the sun and didn't stop for a midday meal, and so in the evening we got what remained from lunch.

There was no possibility of fulfilling the work norm. But those who didn't fulfill it were punished: your ration was reduced to four hundred grams of bread, no tobacco, and you were sent to punitive work under escort.

Fortunately, this was where the criminals, the *urkas,* could help us.

"We'll have to do some *tufta* here," one of my mates advised.

"How's that?"

"Just watch." And we began our "laying on the *tufta*." In the middle of what was to be our stack of logs we would set down a few stumps or snags with many roots and then arrange two-meter logs on the sides and top to make it look like a solid stack; this would then be measured and accepted by its outside dimensions. That way we managed to pass off one cubic meter for two and sometimes three.

Huge amounts of wood were needed for the settlement. The generating station and the boiler houses ran on wood, and the iron stoves in the barracks burned day and night. Winter began here in October and lasted until May, and the winter temperature hovered between minus thirty and minus fifty-five.

The bosses generally weren't very severe in rooting out *tufta* unless we happened to have a particularly eager new careerist as tally man or brigadier. But we would soon get rid of those. Padding was profitable for everyone: the *zeks* fulfilled their norms, the camp bosses and settlement administration could show impressive production figures and be held up as an example to others as "those who managed to fulfill the norm." *Tufta,* eyewash, and "show," however, were among the most widespread methods of work in literally all areas of life—political, military, economic, cultural, etc.—and literally corroded the whole of society, though elsewhere they were not always called by their names as they were in the camps. Still, there was a shortage of wood. The needs of the free workers, the administration, and the hospital, mess hall, generating station, boiler rooms, and garages were met first. The camp would get the leftovers or whatever could be collected by people chased out to the hills after work.

As we came back to camp, each one of us would try to pick up some sort of stick, log, or bit of kindling for our barracks stove. At the camp gate, however, most of this wood would be seized by a band of camp *pridurki* and administrators—for the guardhouse, the mess hall, and the criminals. Often, there was nothing to keep the fire going in our stoves even for the evening, and by morning everything was frozen.

41

The clothes that we laid under our heads often froze to the wall and had to be torn loose in the morning. It was particularly grueling on days when the temperature fell lower than minus forty-five degrees.

The main area of timber-cutting was thirty kilometers away. Keeping the logging trucks working was a very hard job. The garages got cold, the trucks would not start, batteries and rubber tires would freeze, so the delivery of wood, already in short supply, would stop. We burned old tires, used oil, and anything that would burn.

At temperatures below forty-five degrees, synthetic rubber became so brittle that if one took an inflated inner tube outside and threw it, it would shatter into small pieces as if it were made of clay. Oil in the truck's differential would freeze, so that if the truck stopped there was no way it would move again; a fire would have to be built underneath.

There were times when all this created a truly terrible prospect—the whole settlement might freeze to death.

The drivers and mechanics, almost all of them prisoners, worked real miracles of heroism and resourcefulness in managing to keep the trucks moving—with difficulty, but moving.

In January and February, the time of the most extreme cold, another disaster was added to all this: water began to appear on the floors of some of the barracks and the buildings began to sink. By this time, the river had frozen to the bottom and, evidently, the groundwater as well. But underground springs found their way to the surface, forming ever-growing beds of ice crystals, particularly in low areas. The soil under the barracks was partially thawed, and the groundwater, finding no other exit, collected there.

We struggled with this disaster in various ways: the whole barracks was temporarily evacuated and allowed to freeze, but this was only a short-term remedy. Little runways were set up along the floor using wood blocks and planks from the bunks. The barracks were drained by ditches. The last method was the best, but it meant having to dig a ditch at least as deep as the height of a man, and that was beyond the strength of tired people worn down by months of heavy work. The soil was pebbles and clay.

Body counts and *shmony* were special torments. The count took place by signal at 10:00 P.M. Everyone was supposed to be in their places by this time, and a group of camp officials—the head of the guards, sometimes the camp commandant, the barracks seniors, and a tally man—inspected the barracks. The check lasted about an hour. Those not in their proper place or found in another barracks were punished. They would find fault with beds not properly made up, the general appearance of the barracks, and so on. Sometimes a few people would be called out to go to the punishment cells—the *kondei* or the *sobachnik*—for talking back to the bosses or for some other offense of which the man being punished wasn't even aware.

The *sobachnik* was an unheated cell inside the camp, and the *kondei* was something like a camp prison. It was in the settlement, and people were sent there for a term of three to ten days. It was a wooden shed, like a small barn or bathhouse, surrounded by barbed wire, with guard towers on each corner. A series of rails covered with earth served as a roof. The walls were not caulked, but a few of the chinks between the logs had been stuffed with moss. The building was divided into two unequal parts: the smaller one had a corridor and a tiny room where the "*kondei* commander," a criminal or some reprobate, lived. This room was heated by a stove; one side of the stove projected into the other half of the building, where there were bare bunks for about eight prisoners.

I don't recall what offense I committed—it might have been missing the nightly check or arguing with some camp boss—but one winter I had the pleasure of spending ten days in this *kondei*.

The ration was four hundred grams of bread, with cold prison soup once a day, and that not even every day. The stove, of course, gave off no warmth, though it smoked dreadfully. Since three-quarters of the stove was in the *kondei* commander's room, he was probably quite warm, the more so that he was able to seal up the chinks in his walls. The prisoners' quarters were hellishly cold, though, and it was impossible to sleep at night—you had to keep dancing around so as not to freeze. To make matters worse, your belt and scarf were confiscated (so you wouldn't hang yourself). Your pants wouldn't stay up, and cold air crept in everywhere.

The only reason I didn't reach the end of my rope here was that in the daytime, thanks to the insistence of the drivers, I was called out for work. There I could warm myself and get a bit more to eat. I served less than three days of my sentence: evidently they grew tired of having to escort me to and from work. My scarf, of course, was never returned to me.

Aside from this *kondei,* the prison authorities also had the RUR (Strict Regime Unit) and the ShIZO (Special-Purpose Punishment Isolator). The RUR was a separate camp where they sent prisoners from several camps in a given area. Work here was done under escort and, as a rule, was particularly hard—stone quarrying, mining, timber cutting, etc. Prisoners slept on bare bunks, the bread ration was four hundred grams, there was no boiling water, prison soup once a day, no tobacco. The guards were exceptionally vicious and were allowed to do whatever they pleased to the prisoners.

A favorite punishment in summer was "leaving them to the mosquitoes." A half-naked man was made to stand near a guard tower or tied to a tree in the forest. Mosquitoes would attack him. He wasn't allowed to wave his arms (that was "an attempted assault on the sentry").

It's hard to describe what the Kolyma mosquitoes were like: one had to experience them. Even animals could not stand their onslaught. Deer would take refuge in the water and stop eating. There were cases on the taiga where mosquitoes bit people to death. One could withstand such torment for only a few minutes; after that people would nearly go mad and would be ready to do anything. They were usually shot on the spot, either for "attempting to escape" or for "attacking the guards." In both cases the guard got a reward, the prisoner got death.

In the winter, at temperatures of minus forty or forty-five, prisoners were made to run barefoot from the guardroom to the barracks, and so on.

If a person in the RUR didn't "mend his ways" or if the NKVD thought he was especially dangerous, he would be sent to the ShIZO.

I never saw anyone who had come back from that place; it was rumored to be a real hell. People there were killed off by hunger, cold, and torture. I heard that in the winter, the guards would pour water over them until they froze. Aside from all that, in those camps, and to some extent in ours as well, there was the rampaging of the criminals, who would freely steal whatever they liked from the others, beat them, and bully them. The camp administration never interfered.

I remember one Ukrainian guard telling us flatly: "You enemies of the people have been brought here not to work but to be exterminated." Evidently, that was how his Stalinist leaders had trained him. In Myakit, one of the famous victims and martyrs of the *kondei* and the RUR—he hardly ever was out of them—was a young lad, a criminal, named Kolya Ladonin. He was tall, thin as a skeleton, and half insane. We would see him being herded past our group by a guard, on his way to another term in the *kondei*.

"Where are you off to, Kolya?"

"Hunting."

"Where's your rifle?"

"The goon behind me is carrying it."

"Good-bye, Kolya."

"Red Front, boys!"

He would stop for a moment, raise his clenched fist in greeting: "Red Front!"

I don't know how long his term was or what it was for. He was one of the *bezprizorniki* and was an amazing example of how much a human being can withstand. But he was mentally disturbed, even though he was always joking. He had a fierce hatred for the authorities.

For many years after I got out of prison I would have dreams about the compulsory body counts. About ten o'clock each evening I would always have a sense of heightened vigilance, an ominous expectation of something bad about to happen, of reprimands and bullying.

In the thieves' language, *shmon* means a search. Sometimes these would take place in a column of prisoners about to be let back into the camp. Here everything that the prisoner might have acquired outside—food, books, homemade knives, etc.—would be confiscated. The *shmon* in the barracks or tents took place later, after midnight when one is in the deepest sleep. The search was usually carried out by NKVD guards, sometimes with the help of our own bosses.

One by one we would be awakened with a shove and made to get up noiselessly. Barefoot and in our underwear, a few of us would stand near the stove while the guards rummaged around the head of our mattress, and if the prisoner had a bedside table or trunk these would be searched as well. They would seize any "free" food, books, newspapers, notes, "free" clothes, penknives, and sometimes even take away letters that had already passed through the censors.

"Why are you collecting these?"

To get caught with a newspaper was dangerous: as I said, newspapers quickly became counterrevolutionary. We kept them, though, not for their contents but as cigarette paper (we did get some *makhorka*).

Once they found a quarter-page of *Pravda* among my things, and for this they dragged me off several times to the punishment cells. Just what was in that scrap of paper (was there anything in it?) I don't know to this day. It was forbidden to leave the barracks during a *shmon*. The whole thing was a great torment: one's sleep was interrupted, it was cold, and there was the fear that they might find something. Once they found a "poem" about Vinglinsky, written on notebook paper, under my bed. There were people like him in other camps as well, so my "poem" was passed from hand to hand and copied out by others. When they had made a copy, they would leave the original under my pillow. I was afraid that they would seize upon this as grounds for punishment, but I found out later that the bosses just laughed and left the poem where it was; I wasn't touched.

We had a stricter regime than the nonpoliticals. They could read books, sometimes watch a film, and a few of them had little radios; all of these things were forbidden for us. In general, though, the criminals were not very literate and didn't read books.

Books confiscated from the educated prisoners sooner or later got into the hands of the criminals, who used them to make playing cards. Cards were made in a rather clever fashion, as follows: paper was cut to size and glued together with paste made from bread. Then a stencil was made for each of the suits, and with the aid of an indelible pencil and some bread paste, red and blue cards were printed using the stencil. Darwin, Shakespeare, Pushkin—all the best that the intelligentsia managed to bring along to Kolyma—went to make playing cards. From the end of 1937, however, no more books were brought—they were forbidden. Although the authorities tried to stamp out card playing, it was a favorite pastime of the hardened criminals, the "thieves-in-the-law." They gambled first for their own things, then others'. Any of your belongings might be gambled away without your knowledge. But these were minor problems.

In the more terrible camps, isolation cells, and transfer prisons, a person (any person) might become the stakes. The player who lost would have to kill that person or else be killed himself. There were even more senseless stakes: "to bet the office" or "to bet the barracks" meant that the loser had to burn down the barracks. There was no mercy here: the punishment for not acting on the bet was death.

In our barracks we played "goat" and sometimes chess, if the chessmen had not been confiscated. The Tadzhiks, Uzbeks, and Caucasians had their favorite, backgammon. This would happen usually after work—there was an hour or so of free time before the count. The criminals played cards if they could find a hiding place somewhere.

I once saw an unusual chess tournament. We were making road repairs; the work was not heavy since there was no norm. The guards took up their posts at the beginning and end of our stretch of road and usually took turns dozing in the sun. No one was watching us—there was nowhere to which we could escape, after all.

My attention was drawn to two men who had been standing motionless on the road, leaning on their spades for hours but not having a conversation. I walked up to them staring, thinking that they might have fallen sick.

"What do you want?"

"Nothing, I just . . ."

"Go away, don't bother us! We're having a tournament."

It turned out that they were playing a chess game in their heads, without a chessboard but for stakes. The winner would get the loser's portion of soup in the evening. One of them was a fifth-year student from a Vladivostok institute, Sergei Tretiak; the second I didn't know.

Beyond the tents in our camp was another zone surrounded by barbed wire in which stood a single tent; five women lived in it. Prisoners were strictly forbidden to enter this zone, of course. The gate was located near a guard tower. The women themselves were not allowed into the general camp without an escort.

They worked in the cafeteria and the settlement hospital. Most of them were criminals—thieves and prostitutes, no longer young. There was only one young girl, a Baptist, who had been imprisoned for her religious convictions.

It was amazing and incomprehensible, but she managed to lead a decent life in these circumstances, and all the filth around seemed never to rub off on her. The camp *pridurki* tried hard to win her favors by pestering or threatening her, but their efforts were in vain. Finally, one young lad fell deeply in love with her. He would defend her from the attempts of the other "fancy men" in the settlement and do his best to look after her.

I think he was an electrician at the generating station. She was let out a year before him. He helped her build a little house out of packing crates, and when he was released, they married, finished building their house, and set up a household. They had a child and, as far as I know, lived happily.

The other women were in the category of "tear one off, throw it away," as the saying went. An old Kuban Cossack, a former kulak, looked after them. He had once been the orderly in our tent and kept the stove going, carried water, and so on. This old fellow once let slip some bit of gossip about these women and they found out. In the evening when we came back from work, he was in the corner of our tent shaking with terror; from outside came the howls of one of the inhabitants of the women's tent:

"You old bugger! Show your face around here and we'll tear off your balls! You think you can spread stories about us? No whore on the outside would show you a piece of her ass from a ninth-story window. You lousy son of a bitch," and so on, and so on.

The old fellow never showed his face there after that and was transferred to other duties.

We could send letters, unsealed, only via the Culture and Education Unit. The coming of mail was a major event: the first ships arrived in Magadan at the end of May, the last in November. For half the year there was no mail at all. When the first ships arrived, there was a general call-up of personnel for sorting the mail at the post office: all the literate free workers were mobilized, along with members of the Komsomol and students. The camp mail was sorted, passed through the censor, and only then was delivered to the settlements and camps.

A letter took about six weeks to go from Moscow to Magadan, if there were no delays, and would reach us only after two months (in summer). And so to write a letter and get an answer to it would happen only once or twice a season.

Getting a letter was always an enormous event. By no means everyone wrote letters, though. The NKVD was terribly strict in persecuting people on the outside for any "connections with an enemy of the people," and so only the closest family members dared to write; those who had no close family got no mail. Criminals who had been *bezprizorniki* or orphans got no mail either.

Gradually, we learned to write in "Aesopian language." Our families understood us clearly, and the censor didn't notice. We'd write, for instance, "I heard that Sasha Smirnov has moved in with papa," meaning that he had died, since papa had died long ago; or "I haven't seen Filippov from Moscow since we parted and can't remember what he looks like," meaning "we haven't even seen white bread," since Filippov's was a Moscow bakery; or "We're as cozy, clean, and warm as in grandmother's bathhouse"—grandmother's bathhouse had long been neglected, had partly collapsed, and was always terribly cold.

On the whole, with a bit of ingenuity you could write whatever you pleased. People from the "mainland" would sometimes write us in the spirit: "Vitya Kamkin has already grown up; he had his tenth birthday on September 2 and got a lot of presents, especially from his godfather, M. Rozhdestvensky." This meant that on September 2 Vitya Kamkin was given ten years, was severely beaten, and had been denounced by M. Rozhdestvensky.

Prisoners began receiving letters about unfaithful wives and the breakup of their families. Early in the winter of 1938–39 I got a letter from my mother in which she wrote, "Your former wife..." I was expecting that and didn't blame Zhenya. There was no hope of my return, and she was not yet thirty. I knew that my family and my mother were looking after my daughter. I realized that Zhenya was being persecuted and humiliated as the wife of "an enemy of the people." I also recalled that after she had left Lidochka and me to celebrate New Year's in Kashira, I had told her that something would happen this year and we would no longer be together.

CHAPTER THIRTEEN

In a Remote Camp Sector

At the end of the winter I was part of a group of twenty who were sent to Kilometer 226 to cut wood for the settlement of Myakit. Such isolated camp sectors were called *komandirovki.*

This one had two little log huts roofed with turf-covered planks. The floors were bare earth; a rough table and a gasoline-barrel stove stood in the middle; there were crudely made bunks along the walls. In a separate hut was a storeroom and quarters for the head man or brigadier—I don't remember what title this "boss" had—who was, of course, one of the socially friendly, i.e., a criminal.

There were no guards, counts, or searches, nor was there any barbed wire or "zone." The hut was in the forest, away from the road, and apart from our drivers who came to haul out the wood, there was no one but us.

We worked from dawn till dusk, while there was light. Along with the head man lived a cook who made the soup and gave out the bread ration. The hut was lit by homemade lamps fashioned from a couple of tin cans inserted into one another. The lower can held some cotton soaked in gasoline; little holes had been pierced around the top edge of the upper can, like a gas heater. The joint between the cans was sealed with bread. These little lamps smoked, stank, and sometimes exploded, but they did give out a bit of light. On the whole, we got along with one another and everyone did his part. In fact, it could not have been any other way: if you didn't keep moving, you would freeze. Newcomers would at first try to light a bonfire at the work site so as to warm themselves, but soon we realized that this was pointless: the fire would warm only one side of you, and once you had got warm, you quickly began to freeze again, especially your face, hands, and feet.

Aside from that, it was dangerous to warm yourself by a fire. Once I had to go from the woodcutting site to the storeroom to get a saw; this was a three- or four-kilometer trip. It was minus forty degrees, and midway through the trip I spotted a fire and decided to try to get warm (I had a poor pair of mittens and my face was freezing). I stood there for a while and then went on, but I could smell something burning. I'd look around and not see anything, but as soon as I went on I could smell it again. Finally, I felt my shoulder burning. It turned out that a spark had fallen on my back, and while I was walking and swinging my arms, the padding in my jacket started to smoke and then catch fire. I tore off my jacket, stuffed snow into the hole that had burned in it, and then tried to get dressed again. But now my hands wouldn't work: my fingers had become wooden, and I couldn't fasten even one of my buttons. With enormous difficulty, almost weeping from the cold, I managed to get two buttons fastened and kept going.

Fifteen or twenty minutes later, I could smell the smoke again. I had to get undressed once more and stuff snow in the sleeve. I arrived at the camp with frozen fingers, and it was only inside the hut that I finally managed to put out the fire in the damned padding with water.

The trees grew sparsely: it was half taiga, half tundra. The commonest trees were misshapen larches; in lower areas, near the river, there were poplars. The trees had become so brittle from the cold that we didn't need an axe: we could knock off branches as thick as your arm with a club. Not everyone knew how to use a saw, let alone how to select, sharpen, and set one, so that the work went very badly if you had an unskilled partner. We had to produce, since on that depended the feeding of the whole *komandirovka,* and letting one another down just wasn't done.

Tolya Shitnikov and Sergei Leonov worked in my brigade. Shitnikov was a young lad, short and solid. He had formerly lived in Harbin, where he was a designer in the administration of the Chinese Eastern Railway. After the Japanese seized Manchuria and set up the puppet Manchukuo state, the work on the railway was broken off, and our government had to sell it to the Japanese. Russians who worked for the railway were offered the chance to leave for Russia or to stay and work for the Japanese-Manchurians.

Even though these people had been living there for decades, since well before the Revolution, most of them decided to return to Russia. Here, however, almost all of them were immediately imprisoned. The NKVD arrested them under the article "Suspicion of Espionage." And so it was that on the basis of unfounded suspicion, without any investigation or trial, people were sent to the camps for five, eight, or ten years. That was Tolya's fate. But he was young, did not lose heart, and worked honestly.

Leonov was altogether different, but an original in his own fashion. He was the son of an important Moscow professor, a surgeon; he had a wonderful education (he had graduated from both the university and a technical institute) and had worked in the L. Ya. Karpov Physics and Chemistry Research Institute. He had learned French as a child and had studied a little English in university. He had a wonderful knowledge of mathematics, physics, and physical chemistry. Leonov, though, was imprisoned not for political reasons but under Article 162(g), stealing state property. It was amazing how his innate inclination for deception and thievery went along with his sound knowledge of the exact sciences. He was proud of his "adventures" in petty crime and was happy to tell us about them. He had taken up stealing rare books and reference works from the Lenin Library after mastering the system of codes—the numbers and notations used to identify books. He made up some stamps and was easily able to take these books out and sell them. One fine day, however, the library changed the codes and he was almost caught. He had to sit and wait in the toilet until the library closed and then shimmy down a drainpipe to get out.

Tall, thin, his head tilted back and to one side and a bit swivel-eyed, Leonov was a man with a lot of cheek, but he never got his way through force or threats, only by good manners and slyness. That was how, he told us, he managed to get admitted to a banquet organized for the delegates to the International Conference on Atomic Physics in Moscow in 1935. Taking advantage of his knowledge of French, and after the official part of the conference had ended and the delegates were leaving, he got into an animated conversation with Langevin (a scientist with a worldwide reputation). Never leaving his side, Leonov managed to slip into the banquet hall where food and drink were aplenty. There was rationing in Moscow at the time, and people were going hungry.

Leonov got "burned" for stealing platinum crucibles. He would swipe these crucibles from his research institute and palm them off to Jewish dentists who were in private practice. Finally, one of the dentists was arrested and sold Leonov out. The dishonesty of his clients bothered Leonov more than anything.

They gave him ten years and sent him to the White Sea Canal, but he escaped from there and got on the Leningrad-Murmansk train. In the railway carriage he got a slide rule, surrounded himself with papers, filled them up with formulas, and got into a discussion with some engineer, thus managing to slip through the document inspection that took place in the train before Petrozavodsk.

Before long, though, they picked him up again in Leningrad, added two years to his sentence for escaping, and sent him off to Kolyma. He lived with the criminals, but since he was, after all, an educated man, he was always drawn to us, the more so that the big-time criminals didn't consider him one of their own, and he had nothing in common with the small-timers.

Also with us was a tall, very handsome but emaciated fellow, Galushko, a man of thirty or thirty-five. He was a Ukrainian, and after his family perished during the Civil War he decided to "try his luck." He tramped about the south, then crossed the Romanian border—family tradition had it that some relative of his, an uncle, perhaps, was living in Paris. He never made it to Paris, of course, but worked as a stevedore, a stableman, and a common laborer in Bulgaria and Romania. At last he made his way to Bucharest and there fell in with Russian émigrés. They helped him out and eventually managed to get him into the Slavic University that had been founded in Bucharest around 1921 for Russian refugees and their families.

The university was supported by funds from Czechoslovakia, Yugoslavia, Romania, and from our émigré organizations. Galushko got a scholarship, worked in the summers, and graduated in economics.

When he got his diploma, he found a post as a consultant to the Soviet trade delegation. Part of his job was to read the Balkan newspapers and compile economic summaries for the ambassador. The trade delegation was subjected to some cuts, however, and Galushko was reduced to half pay.

Then Galushko was offered a good job as an engineer-economist with a large firm. The work paid well, a good career lay before him; fate had something else in store, however.

Young, attractive, and educated, Galushko was successful with women. And so it happened that out of jealousy, one of his mistresses decided to poison him. The doctors managed to save him, but he was left with stomach problems. His firm gave him sick leave, and he went to a sanatorium for treatment. The treatment dragged on, however, and after three months Galushko lost his job.

At the time (1929–30), Europe was in the grip of an economic slump, and it was hard for him to find another job. The newspapers and radio were full of news about the major construction projects beginning in Russia.

Galushko went to our embassy and offered his services. He was greeted warmly, offered a contract, and sent off to Kharkov.

Two agents met him at the border—he was astonished at such consideration—and a car was already waiting near the station.

"Where are we going?"

"To the Krasnaya Hotel."

After circling around the city, they drove him up to some iron gates and Galushko found himself behind bars. In answer to his protests the investigator said: "What are you worried about? Back in Bucharest you were giving lectures about the White Sea–Baltic Canal. You know the place already, so that's where we'll send you!"

And so they did, and from there they sent Galushko to Kolyma. His wife, a Polish woman from Warsaw, refused to go with him to the Soviet Union, insisting, "You can't believe the Bolsheviks. They'll deceive you!" He wasn't able to change her mind, and she went back to her family in Warsaw. They agreed that if everything was as fine and good as Moscow propaganda insisted it was, he would write her to come and join him (he had a contract for three years).

The clever Polish woman turned out to be right, and Galushko himself climbed into the net spread out before him. He was receiving parcels from Warsaw right until the war began, and would weep and beat his head against the wall when they came. Correspondence with "abroad" was forbidden, of course.

There was also a Finn, Pustolainen. He wasn't friendly with anyone, knew only a few words of Russian and, indeed, was taciturn by nature; he also had an amazing tolerance for the cold. When the sun's warmth began to be felt in the daytime and the temperature rose to minus thirty, he could flop down and sleep right in a snowbank by the side of the road. At times he would sing some endless, mournful, and monotonous song through his teeth, a song without words in which you could hear the rustle of the pine trees and the lapping of the waves in the lakes of his homeland.

It was hard working in the forest in temperatures from minus forty to fifty. Icicles would form in your nose, and you had to get rid of them somehow; it was hard to breathe and your lungs burned. Bits of ice would gradually build up on your eyelashes, and it became difficult to open your eyes; you had to melt the icicles with your hands and brush them off your eyelashes.

Starting a bonfire in the deep, loose snow was not so simple either, but we soon learned how to do it. We usually found drinking water in some pool of ice crystals or spring that didn't freeze over. We would get down on our knees and take the water directly into our mouths since it was impossible to use a cup in such cold.

In winter, the only other living things that remained in the taiga were partridges and a kind of white sparrow. The partridges would peck at the buds on the trees and at night they would bury themselves in the snow, leaving only the ends of their tail feathers sticking out. We didn't have any rifles, of course, but once in a long while we managed to catch a partridge.

In winter, as a rule, the weather remained dry, windless, and clear. The stars at night seemed particularly huge and bright and often led us into discussions of life on other worlds. From that point of view, everything that was happening to us seemed petty, transitory, and insignificant.

Makovsky knew a lot about history, and if we managed to persuade him to talk about it, he would intrigue us for hours with tales of "bygone days" as we lay stretched out on the bunks after work, blissfully soaking up the heat from the red-hot stoves. Here we always had plenty of wood. No one confiscated it and, unlike Myakit, we could sleep in our underwear.

Galushko, using his knife, fashioned something resembling a fiddle out of tea boxes, and he and Makovsky would sometimes quietly sing Ukrainian songs.

I spent about two months at this *komandirovka*.

CHAPTER FOURTEEN

Encounters

Towards spring I found myself in Myakit again. We worked at various outdoor jobs, and then I got into a brigade that looked after heating and the boiler house for the garage. Here we chopped and sawed wood for the Shukhov boiler. The chief stoker was Vasily Bystrov, a broad-shouldered peasant of about fifty with an enormous red beard. He looked like a cross between a bear and Maliuta Skuratov. In the past he had been a locomotive engineer at the Putilov factory. He joined the party, served in the Civil War, and gradually rose through the ranks. Before his arrest, he was manager of a trust in charge of erecting cableways, trestles, and major steel assemblies.

He had been on work assignments abroad, in Italy, and on the whole was a prominent party man. He was imprisoned after being denounced because on the list of engineers he put forward to be awarded prizes was the name of . . . a Trotskyite.

In the camp, he saw himself as an Old Bolshevik who had wound up here by accident, and he managed to behave so that the camp administration looked on him favorably and allowed him a few perks—wearing a beard, for instance, something that no one else was allowed to do.

The criminals respected him because of his bearish physical strength and his violent temper—they were afraid of him. He worked furiously, like a peasant, never fell ill, and was in good standing with the camp bosses. He was the head man in his tent, insisted on cleanliness and order, and personally took pains to ensure that everything looked good. In front of the barracks he made a "flower bed" out of bits of bottle glass, bricks, and stones. The camp bosses liked this, but we thought it was just another useless job and quietly mocked him. Glants said, however, that making such designs was a clear sign of schizophrenia.

Bystrov's zeal sometimes led him to put his foot in it and place the bosses in a ridiculous position. Once in a while, the camp was visited by a review commission, and each camp head tried to ensure his camp would be held up as an example to others: everyone was working and fulfilling their norms, no one was ill, the prison regime was being strictly observed. The roads and pathways would be swept and sprinkled with sand, the barracks cleaned, and so on. I don't know what other "indicators of socialist competition" there were.

And so it was that during a regular period of "intensified regime" for the contras, a High Commission from Dalstroy in Magadan appeared in the camp. They immediately picked up on the curtains in the windows and the "flower bed" near Bystrov's tent.

"Who lives here?"

"Article 58ers."

"What are you thinking? You set up a resort for these enemies of the people, while your nonpoliticals are living in filth? Who permitted this? Is it opportunism?"

Soldatov, the poor camp commandant, was expecting praise, and suddenly he got this dressing down! His soul sank within him—he wasn't far from being slapped with that same article himself, after all!

"I'm sorry, we missed that, but we'll correct it!"

"Have those prisoners moved out immediately!"

When Bystrov returned from work in the evening, the criminals were in charge of his tent, and all his belongings and those of the others who lived in the tent had been hauled over to the filthy, ramshackle barracks where the criminals had formerly lived. The criminals, of course, never hesitated: when they ran out of firewood, planks from the bunks, floorboards, and tables went into the stove—everything, up to the roof. Needless to say, his comrades cursed Bystrov blue for his eternal striving to distinguish himself and be better than everyone else.

The regime eased after that, and Bystrov took up "aesthetics" once again. That was how it went—soaring to the heights, crashing to earth, and back up again.

Apropos of Bystrov's passion for fancying up his surroundings, Pukk-Pukkovsky recalled Dostoevsky's words about the convicts who at Easter would polish their shackles with a brick until they gleamed: "I'm entitled to celebrate the holiday too!"

Yes, it's hard to understand the psychology of a man! Bystrov treated the camp bosses with respect, but without a shade of that self-abasement and bootlicking that was characteristic of Vinglinsky. The prisoners addressed Bystrov as Vasily Vasilevich, the bosses as "Beard." His other passion, aside from his desire to win praise, was playing dominoes. He played marvelously, usually for stakes, and woe to a partner who didn't understand the game well enough and didn't support Bystrov's moves. Before your eyes he would change into a vicious bear, ready to beat up his unfortunate partner.

On Bystrov's initiative a shower room with shelves and a bench was built in the boiler house. Almost immediately, these showers became enormously popular with the free workers and prisoners alike. It was much more convenient for the free workers to come here than to the regular bathhouse, especially for the women, since the bathhouse operated by schedule—one for the *zeks,* others for the soldiers and for the civilian population—and so they could not get into it every day.

Everyone who came to the showers would bring something for Bystrov—sugar, butter, white bread, cigarettes. Soon there were so many wanting to get in that the settlement authorities once posted a list of "Pregnant Women in Myakit Settlement" who were admitted to the head of the line.

The prisoners, apart from those who worked in the boiler house, didn't use the showers and weren't particularly eager to bathe. They were interested in something else, though: there were knotholes in the plank walls of the shower room, and the young prisoners, desperately hungry for women, tried in every way possible to "have a little peep." Not everyone was allowed to do this because of the danger of possible complaints.

The women soon noticed these peepholes, however, and when they came for a shower they would carefully plug them or hang clothes over them before getting undressed.

Then one sharp fellow set a large iron lamp standard, supposedly for a light, in the ceiling of the shower room. There was no bulb in it, however, and instead of a socket there was a length of water pipe running through the ceiling. Through this "periscope," lovers of astronomy could spend some time "observing the stars."

It was practically impossible to catch such an "observer." If one of the bosses suddenly appeared, the observer could always stretch himself out on the roof and pretend to be sleeping. Unless someone knew he was there, however, there was no way to catch him: the roof was two and a half meters high, the roof of the boiler house was still higher, and it was always dark there.

The criminals called this peeping "taking in a show," and the whole establishment took on the name "The —— Movie Theater," with a resonant but indecent title. One of the duty stokers in the boiler house would even announce the program: "Today at 6:00 we are featuring an appearance by Nelly" (she was a pretty secretary from the administration).

Bystrov knew about this, of course, but did not take part in watching the "shows" and pretended that they did not concern him. In fact, it was beyond his powers to forbid the criminals this pleasure. The free workers, of course, suspected nothing.

I had a stroke of luck in the spring and got myself some good, steady work. The garage mechanic learned from the *zeks* that I was an electrician and found a place for me in the electrical shop. The shop was a long room, about three meters by ten, partitioned off along one wall of the garage, with windows looking out on the street. Our boss was Misha Kornev, a tall, good-looking young lad about twenty-four years old who was in prison under some nonpolitical article. Because of his good looks, the fine coloring of his face, and his propensity for blushing and suddenly flaring up, some people called him Masha, which made him very angry.

One person who was particularly taken with him was a driver, Belykh (nicknamed Beluga), who was in prison under Article 59 (3) (transport banditism). He was always teasing Misha, but at the same time looked after him in an almost fatherly fashion and catered to all his whims. If he brought something back from one of his trips, he would always give Misha a share. I suspect that Misha Kornev reminded Beluga of some love that he had left behind on the "mainland."

Misha didn't like heavy, dirty work and tried to avoid it, but he was very fond of dressing himself up and also of driving a truck with great style.

The second man was Vaska, nicknamed Rylo (Ugly Mug), a criminal and former *bezprizornik*. Somehow, he had managed to get back here from the gold mines, where he had also been an auto electrician. He was a stocky fellow with a very rough-looking face which at first glance gave no sign of intelligence, though he was very calm and resourceful when it came to technical work. He and I made many gadgets and devices for checking and repairing automotive electrical systems.

There was also Grisha Gorelov, another young fellow. He had already spent many years in various camps, was very industrious and diligent but rather stupid and never able to repair a relatively simple fault on his own.

Finally, there was one more handsome, kind, and trusting boy, Senechka Bela. I think he came from the Crimea, but he had no family and was in prison for vagrancy. He was always ready to help or to do a favor for his fellow workers. Sometimes this took a very unexpected form. For instance, one time a truck bound for the gold mines stopped by the garage. It was loaded with groceries, dried fruit in particular. Someone said, "Wouldn't it be great to cook up some stewed fruit." Ten minutes later, Senechka dragged in a bag of fruit. He had stolen it in full view of everyone, even though this was dangerous: for things like that—and the farther north you were, the stricter it was—they would "tack on another article" and add to your sentence. Nevertheless, our lads would get flour, cooking oil, and even sugar.

We didn't steal from our own trucks, of course, but our drivers often found ways to appropriate a portion of the groceries they delivered to the warehouse or the depot and share them with us. There were many ways to do this. For instance, they would try to take on a load of sugar during the day or toward evening, in dry weather. Before arriving at the designated place they would try to stop for the night near the river. The sugar would greedily suck up moisture, and they could manage to keep aside one sack and still meet their load weight.

It was very difficult to avoid theft from food trucks while they were parked in the garages for maintenance, despite the sentries and the ever-increasing security. And so food trucks very rarely came in for maintenance, only when it was urgently necessary. *Zek* drivers would do their best for their fellow prisoners, but if the driver happened to be a free worker and stranger, the mechanics would arrange for a prolonged test of the motor. The garage would grow dim from the exhaust gases, it would become impossible to breathe, and the driver and guard, dizzy and reeling, would rush outside. Meanwhile, the truck would be "cleaned out."

Eventually, particularly valuable loads—sugar, cooking oil, cigarettes, tinned goods—began to be shipped as follows: the sacks and boxes loaded on the truck would be covered with a tarpaulin lashed down with ropes. Atop this would sit a soldier with a rifle. The driver was also responsible for keeping his load intact, and he would not leave the vehicle for a moment either.

Nevertheless, even when a truck was guarded like that our fellows still managed to steal a few pails of sugar without either the driver or the guard suspecting anything. It was surprisingly easy to do: the truck was driven over the grease pit (a narrow trench a meter and a half deep that enabled the mechanic to work under a vehicle) for "preventive maintenance" and replacement of its springs. The guard would be sitting on the tarpaulin atop the load, the driver in the cab. In the pit, the mechanic would slit a hole in a sugar sack through a crack in the floor of the truck box, and sugar would sift down into a bucket. The whole operation, including the repairs, would last some forty minutes. It was not in vain that the hardened criminals were sent mostly to Kolyma—they knew what they were doing!

There were a lot of clever, capable fellows and some good technicians working in our garage and in the Autotransport Administration generally. There were no railways here, and supplies were transported to all the points along the highway, from Magadan right to the most isolated gold mines, only by truck. And to make the vehicles run in the conditions of Kolyma, with its long, snowy winter and cold of minus fifty degrees or more, one had to be selfless, a master of technology, resourceful, clever, and something of an inventor. And so the mechanics, drivers, and specialists were highly regarded here, and the bosses did their best to keep them out of the gold mines. On the other hand, we prisoners also appreciated our jobs: here we could pick up the odd "extra" on the side; they treated us like human beings at work and even had some respect for us; and we always knew what was going on, both in Kolyma and in the country as a whole, since we would speak to so many different people.

Aside from the electrical shop, the garage also had an engine shop, a chassis shop, a body shop, and a mechanics' workshop. Article 58ers worked in all of them.

The chief mechanic was A. A. Koreishchikov from Tver, a former prisoner and a gentle, rather timid fellow. The head of the garage was a free worker, Nikolai Kuzmich (I don't remember his last name). He was young and energetic and had been a driver or a mechanic. Both these men treated us very well and protected us as best they could from the camp administration.

Vehicle travel schedules were arranged by the dispatcher's office, which was staffed by criminals serving five- to ten-year sentences. I remember one of them, Esselevich, a short Jew or Belorussian (as he regarded himself) with a large black beard, a lively, agile fellow. He was imprisoned because he had posed as a cash collector and had made the rounds of stores just before closing time to pick up money from their cashiers. He had mastered all the ins and outs of this scheme and was caught only by chance. He was very keen to become an electrician and kept after me to take him on in the electrical shop. I taught him to repair truck batteries, and then he built himself his own "shop" out of old packing crates. From then on he was in clover, since batteries were always in short supply. He earned good money and ate and drank well.

It was here that I met one remarkable fellow who eventually became a close friend. This was Viktor Lvovich Grey. He was tall and thin, with a large nose and close-set black eyes. He was friendly and jovial but very quick-tempered. He came from Minsk and his father—a soldier, I believe—was killed when Grey was still young. His mother had some important job in the district, but he didn't go into details.

Grey began running afoul of the authorities even when he was in school, and it was apparently because of his lively, energetic nature and exceptional intellect. Finally they expelled him, declared him "handicapped," and sent him away to a special school for handicapped children.

At that time, children generally were educated in accordance with the ground rules of child behavior as defined by pedology, then considered to be a progressive science. The school curriculum was chaotic—Tolstoy, Esenin, Turgenev, Balmont, and all the Western classics were labeled "idealists." Instead of history, children were given a vulgar and semiliterate basic course of political indoctrination. Mindless "cud chewing" replaced genuine learning. There was a series of campaigns for this and that and the taking of measures against various other things. In classes of practical work, thirteen- to fifteen-year-old children were made to cut stars out of paper and engage in similar nonsense.

This suited the fools, but the capable children were dissatisfied and tried to find outlets for their energy in acts that were labeled "antisocial."

Grey usually spoke of his "normal" school with distaste, but his very best memories came from the school for the handicapped.

The windows of the school looked out on the market square where the flea market was held (O wise authorities!). Though he had often come late to his regular school and had to be forced to go, at the school for the handicapped he and the other students would lay siege to the building an hour before it opened. Here they were all equal, and no one divided them into normal and handicapped; educational specialists never showed their faces here; the pupils, as "incorrigibles," enjoyed relative freedom. There were a few genuine devotees of teaching among the staff—followers of Makarenko, who tried to instill a love of knowledge and books in the pupils and who treated them as friends. The overall conditions in the school, however, did not allow it to achieve very much. Makarenko's ideas were not accepted and understood by the pedagogy of the day; the post of school principal was usually given to some party man as a form of reprimand; the school was last in line for equipment and school supplies; teachers from "good" schools didn't take jobs here; and the city's Education Department regarded it as a necessary evil that would be best ignored. Circumstances such as these, a teaching staff collected from all over the city, the flea market next door, and the lack of consistent discipline led the children to seek adventures on the street and to make dubious acquaintances and connections with criminal gangs. Grey became involved in one such gang and was arrested during the attempted robbery of a store. He was sent to a reform school, escaped, was caught and sent to prison, and so was drawn into the unrelenting conveyor belt that was officially called "the system of reeducation."

His contact with criminals, the persecution and beatings of teachers, and the stigma of being a lawbreaker gave him no means to break out of this vicious circle.

Grey became embittered and quick to take offense. He picked up a thorough knowledge of the base and sordid sides of human nature. Nevertheless, those good things that had found a place in his soul survived and were not crushed by the filth around him. He learned to play the trumpet, worked on a lathe, and read a great deal. Painfully sensitive to any kind of injustice, with contempt for the high and mighty, the wealthy, and for authority of all kinds, he fell in love with the heroes of Schiller, Byron, Dumas, and Aleksandr Grin.

When there was a free moment, he and I would often talk about heroes, real-life and literary ones. What interested him most were those cases when some historical figure hid his true base and villainous essence behind a mask of ideology and nobility. We recalled the Jesuit fathers, Cagliostro, the conquistadors, Ivan the Terrible, some contemporaries, and, of course, Stalin and his henchmen. Pronouncing Stalin's name was too dangerous, of course, and we usually spoke about "wax," associating Stalin—moustache—moustache wax. Bit by bit, using such coded language, we learned to speak about whatever we pleased, arousing no one's suspicion and being regarded simply as eccentrics.

We contras were strictly forbidden to read books and newspapers and watch the films they showed ("They're smart enough without that," was the view of the camp bosses).

The nonpoliticals and criminals could use the small library in the Culture and Education Unit. There were very few books there, however, and they quickly vanished as the hardened criminals transformed them into playing cards.

At the beginning of the winter of 1937, they brought some new people to our camp. These were ex-prisoners, recently set free when their sentences ended, who had been working in nearby settlements. They had all been picked up on the same day. They were not informed of any charges against them and had not been interrogated; they were simply taken from their apartments, loaded onto a truck, and brought to the camp. Five of these "enemies of the people" were put into our tent. When they were asked "Article? Sentence?" at checks and roll calls, they would reply, "You tell us, we don't know."

The answer to this was curses and threats.

Things dragged on like that for a month or two until at last they were informed that they had again been sentenced to five years—and some to more—for "counterrevolutionary agitation." They refused to sign anything, of course. This was yet another action of the "Glorious Organs," headed by "The Great, Wise Leader" of the most humane and just party that was building socialism in our progressive country. The only crime these people had committed was that they had already been imprisoned—though not for any crime, of course.

Among them was a Leningrad automotive engineer who, after his release from camp, had been the chief engineer of the truck station in the settlement of Strelka, about seventy kilometers north of us. His name was Aleksandr Kolosov. His wife had come to join him not long before, and they were expecting a child. He was desperately worried about her, but there was nothing he could do to help.

Another of these men, Artavazd Tevosovich Aivazian, I came to know much better after the following thing happened. One evening after work, one of the "rotten intellectuals"—some know-it-all like Vinglinsky—began to talk a lot of nonsense in the barracks about the atom, the structure of matter, and so on. His brazen ignorance bothered me, and from my bunk I shouted something like, "Don't babble on about things you know nothing about, just shut your mouth or someone will shut it for you!" The fellow snarled a bit, but he did stop talking, and then I saw a short, bearded Armenian come up to my bunk and sit alongside it. He offered me a smoke and said, "Still, it would be a good thing to know just how matter is structured."

So we began to chat. He looked a lot like Pushkin—sideburns, a large nose on a thin face, and astonished eyes that always looked expectantly, curiously, and with great interest at the person he was speaking to. We soon became friends. He came from a poor Armenian family living not far from the place where the Turkish, Soviet, and Persian (Iranian) borders meet on the Aras River.

Following the practice of many generations of Armenians, he decided, when barely in his teens, to go and seek his fortune abroad. He had no money or official documents, however, and he decided to go on foot, seeing as the border was nearby. This was in the middle of the 1920s during the time of the NEP. To cross straight over the Aras meant one would be in Turkey, which at that time would send back refugees; besides that, the memory of the last massacre of Armenians by the Turks in 1919–20 was still fresh. It was possible to get to Iran, but for that you had to cross to the Turkish side somewhat lower downstream and then cross a tributary that formed the Turkish-Iranian border.

In summer, both the Aras and its tributaries are very shallow and almost dry up. And so, following his plan, Aivazian crossed the Aras at night, walked for several kilometers through the underbrush and again crossed a small river, assuming that he had reached Iran. At dawn, when he traveled a bit farther from the river, he was met by . . . our border guards. It turned out that he had got lost in the darkness and crossed the Aras twice, to Turkey and back again.

Given his youth at the time, the matter was let pass. Then Aivazian got into a theater school and was studying to be a film director. His childhood passions for travel and adventure were forgotten, and he seemed to see a clear, straight road ahead of him.

As it turned out, though, the NKVD had not forgotten, and in 1933 Aivazian was given three years for "suspicion of espionage."

He was a man of rare goodness and understanding, a man with the same sense of good and evil and justice that one finds only in children, and not even in all of them. If he saw someone in trouble he would rush off to help them without thinking. When he managed to get an extra bit of something to eat, he would always try to share it with his neighbors.

He knew many bits of verse by memory and even whole poems by Lermontov, Pushkin, Byron, Tumanian, and other poets. All these qualities often led to his being unjustly wronged or punished by the camp bosses.

As we became closer friends, I called him Arto and he called me Volodya. I can't recall exactly, but I think he finished his sentence and was let out of the camp before a year had passed. After he was released, he found a job as a bookkeeper in the Autotransport Administration and often helped me out by bringing food or sending money home for me; sometimes he would come just to have a chat. I wonder if he is still alive. I wish I knew . . .

I heard that during the war he was tossed into the camps again, and I think he may have perished there. I'd like to believe that's not so.

CHAPTER FIFTEEN

The Daily Grind in Camp

I didn't keep any diaries, of course, and so I can't describe our life day by day or even year by year. What I remember are only isolated events—perhaps not even the most significant ones, but ones that somehow left a trace in my memory.

I recall one early morning at the beginning of winter as we were leaving for work in our garage. It was foggy, with a temperature of minus forty-five. In the parking area in front of the garage was a group of fifty people or so—evidently newly arrived from the last ships of the season—surrounded by guards and dogs. Almost all of them were frostbitten, and a few of them, their strength gone, had collapsed on the ground. The two trucks that had been carrying them had broken down and were waiting for repairs; no arrangements had been made to keep these people warm or fed. The guard commander was shouting at the drivers, but no one could make repairs in that kind of cold, and there was still no room in the garage—our own trucks and buses were getting ready to move out.

"These people are bound for Maldyak!"

Maldyak was one of the gold mines that had become notorious as a death camp. I found out later that of 4,000 prisoners brought there in the fall, no more than 500 were alive in the spring.

People from our camp were sometimes mobilized to clear snow from the highway. I once found myself in such a group. We were taken off work earlier than usual, loaded onto a truck, and taken in the direction of Atka. Late in the dark of evening, we reached the pass called Granddad's Bald Spot. There were a few huts scattered in a little gully between the bare hills; this was a *komandirovka* station for road workers. Our trucks turned around immediately and set off for home in the hope of getting back before the blizzard blocked the road completely. The blizzard had moved in from the direction of Magadan, but it hadn't yet picked up strength here. We made our way into one of the huts where a brigade of road workers were living.

In the middle of the hut stood an enormous iron stove made from an old gasoline barrel; hanging from the ceiling was an oil lamp made from a food tin that cast a dim light; road workers who had finished their shift were sleeping in the bunks that stood around the walls of this, the only room. We managed to find places on the floor, though there was not enough room to lie down, and we dozed off. Two hours later, around midnight, we were roused and herded outside. The weather had grown much worse while we slept: the blizzard was raging at full force, seeming to blow from every direction and driving masses of sharp, stinging ice crystals into our faces.

The local brigadier or head man issued us shovels, and we moved out onto the highway. As soon as we had made our way up from the ravine to the road, the wind attacked us in a fury. If it could find even the tiniest hole or gap in our clothes it would penetrate right to the bone. We needed to protect our faces somehow. The road gang that worked here regularly usually wore homemade masks fashioned out of old padded jackets. The mask had three holes, for the eyes and mouth, and looked very much like the hoods worn by the Ku Klux Klan, but even uglier. A cap with earflaps would be worn over the hood.

We had no such masks and tried to walk sideways, sheltering ourselves from the wind with our shovels. It was pure hell in the pass: in places the road had been swept clear almost to its surface, in other places it was completely blocked by deep snowdrifts. Shovels were useless in such conditions: the wind immediately blew the snow away and tried to tear the shovel out of your hands. Aside from that, we had to work almost blind since you could see nothing. On one side of the road was a steep cliff with masses of hanging snow that threatened to fall on us, on the other an abyss.

It was senseless work, and we didn't manage to clear any snow; but we had to keep moving so as not to freeze. The wind in our faces gradually drove us back to the *komandirovka*. They wouldn't let us into the huts, though, and chased us back to the road again.

Several times we made the same retreat and return. Many of us had frostbitten hands and faces. It was nearly dawn before they finally left us in peace. I made my way back into the sloggers' hut and curled up on the floor, half lying down. At 7:00, the road gang began rousing themselves and getting ready for work. A thickset fellow got up from the bunk next to where I was sitting and put a teakettle on the stove. When the kettle boiled he beckoned to me, set down a mug covered with a chunk of bread and said, "Please, have some tea."

I was surprised at his English accent and his politeness and asked him, "Where are you from?"

"I'm from Canada!"

Soon he and the others went off to work, but he pointed to his bunk and said, "Why don't you lie down and get some sleep." He had been one of the secretaries of the Central Committee of the Communist Party of Canada, Comrade Fedak. He was indicted for his communist and antigovernment activities and was facing a year in prison and a fine. He was released on his own recognizance, signed on as a sailor on a Japanese ship, and eventually made his way to Vladivostok, where he came ashore to our "promised land."

At first he was welcomed, given some money, and sent to Moscow. In Moscow, though, the NKVD took an interest in him. It was 1937, after all . . . Fedak was accused of illegal entry with the intent of espionage, and a Troika gave him five years of hard labor under the article "Suspicion of Espionage."

And so he found himself in Kolyma, where he was now able to study communism not just in theory but in practice. Fedak wasn't a very talkative fellow and still didn't know Russian well, but he was delighted when I managed to say a few words to him in English. I learned his story mainly from his neighbors, since he himself was reluctant to talk.

The blizzard began to blow itself out during the day. We cleared the road and the next day went back to Myakit.

Meanwhile, Grey had met with misfortune. Because of some insolence or other, he was transferred to a work team under escort, grubbing up frozen stumps and mining sand near the Myakit River, beyond the settlement. Here he hurt his foot (later it was found to be broken) and could neither walk nor stand. The guards, Ukrainians, thought he was faking an injury and began beating him with their rifle butts. When the column was being escorted back to camp he was able to walk at first, dragging his leg and leaning on his neighbor. Finally he could go no further and he sat himself down in the snow. This was considered an offense.

The column halted, the guards began beating him again, and he lost consciousness. The German shepherds, responding to the guards' command, would tear at his clothes as long as he could fight back and move around; but now they withdrew and lay down in the snow, growling angrily. To assure himself that the *zek* had breathed his last, a guard came up to him and jabbed a bayonet into his back twice. Then the column was herded back to the camp, and Grey was left lying in the cold as a corpse. Some camp slogger hauling brushwood with a horse noticed him, loaded him on the sleigh, covered him with branches, and brought him to the settlement hospital. Meanwhile, the guards had submitted their report about an "escape attempt," and a team of "angels" was sent out to recover the body.

These angels were harnessed to the sled they used to haul bodies to the camp morgue. There was no body to be found, though.

The alarm was raised, troops were called out, and soon the guards appeared in the hospital, demanding that Grey be handed over immediately. But here they met with the determined refusal of the chief surgeon. This courageous woman, a free worker, threw them out of the hospital, declaring that she would not allow wounded and ill patients to be further tormented and that she would complain to Moscow.

Her husband was some high ranker in the army, and they didn't dare touch her. Thanks to her concern and attention, Grey stayed on in the "free" hospital and was back on his feet in a couple of months.

Among the denizens of our camp was one reprobate everyone feared and hated. His name was Stefanovich, and he was serving time for suspicion of espionage. He had formerly been the editor of a newspaper in the Belorussian Military District. A despicable and repulsive dwarf, Stefanovich was an informer who made regular denunciations for which he received favors from the camp administration. Just the same, he met his end when he was drowned by prisoners in the river where he had been sent to cut timber.

In the summer I barely escaped being sent to the gold mines. Some camp *pridurki* who had it in for me put my name down on a list of those to be transferred, and we were sent off. My mates found out and informed the bosses. Kuzmich, the head of the garage, was furious that he hadn't been asked about it and quickly set off after us in a bus. He caught up with us at the Strelka settlement. Somehow, he managed to take me away, feed me in the local mess hall, and by evening had brought me back to Myakit. And so I was saved by a miracle, and they didn't dare touch me after that.

CHAPTER SIXTEEN

The War

One night there was a special reveille and search. It was done with unusual strictness and haste. Then we found out: war had been declared. Our regime immediately became more severe. We found out from the nonpoliticals working in the Registration and Assignment Unit that lists were being drawn up dividing the prisoners into two groups: those on one list would be sent to the front; those on the other would be held under a strict regime and would work only under escort.

In the fall of 1941, we began to get prisoners who had served on the front. One of them was nicknamed Lieutenant Blackbeard. He organized a gang that would flag down and rob trucks on the highway, leaving a note saying, "Cargo received in full, Lt. Blackbeard."

In the late autumn of 1941, I saw in a passing truck a prisoner who turned out to be a former colonel of the General Staff who had been released from camp and summoned to Moscow.

It was the spring of 1942. My sentence was to end on May 12, though I had little hope of being released. Usually, before our sentences were over we contras would be called into the special unit where our files were held and presented with a decision from the Troika specifying a new sentence but without any charges.

And so, in this limbo, almost without hope, the months of May, June, and most of July passed by. And then, finally, on July 28, 1942, I was set free; it was my birthday, as it happened. Friends joyously welcomed me to their room, and I was given a bed. I sent off a telegram home: now I was a free man.

Soon I received an appointment from Magadan as an engineer on the construction of the Electric Generating Station in Arkagala, two hundred kilometers to the north. Here I was to spend more than four years.

But that's another story.

N. N. BOLDYREV

THE CROOKED PATH
OF FATE

CHAPTER ONE

My Forebears

My father, Nikolai Nikolaevich Boldyrev, was born on July 9, 1884, in the village of Ukriantsevo, Insarov District, in Penza Province, on the estate of his grandmother, Olga Vasilevna Litvinova, née Ustinova.

My father's father, also Nikolai Nikolaevich, educated as a jurist, was a third-generation nobleman. He could not boast of any illustrious ancestry since his forebears had been simple Don Cossacks. According to my parents' recollections, they were adventurers who had served bravely on many a campaign.

It was my father's great-grandfather, the dashing Don Cossack Vasily Yakovlev Boldyrev, who was the founder of the noble "dynasty" of Boldyrevs. For his brave deeds during Suvorov's crossing of the Swiss Alps, Emperor Paul I granted him noble status and lands in Poltava Province, the villages of Krutets and Vasilevskoe. He had three children: Maria, Olga, and Nikolai.

Nikolai Vasilevich Boldyrev, my father's grandfather, was born in 1814. He graduated with great distinction from the School of Military Engineering in St. Petersburg and then completed officer training. The school, later transformed into the Nicholas Academy of Military Engineering of the General Staff, kept him on. Here, in 1838, he taught mathematics, land surveying, and later fortifications. He supervised the construction of fortresses along Russia's western border.

At the end of 1860, on instructions of Emperor Alexander II, he was invited to the Imperial Palace to give lectures on fortification to the heir to the throne, Nicholas. With the death of the heir in 1865, Nikolai Boldyrev again gave lectures now to the second son of Alexander II, the future emperor Alexander III.

He retired in 1879 with the rank of lieutenant general of engineers, as a professor emeritus and member of the board of the Nicholas Academy of Military Engineering. He had been given almost all the honors the Russian Empire had to offer, including its highest orders, the White Eagle and the Alexander Nevsky. He died in 1882.

He had four sons and a daughter. The eldest son, Vasily, graduated in 1867 from the Faculty of Law of St. Petersburg University. He loved carousing and would astonish the prudish Petersburgers with his reveling and eccentric escapades. In summer, for instance, he would arrange to have the Nevsky Prospekt covered with salt and take some music hall actresses for a drive in a sled driven by a cabby; or he would organize "Egyptian Evenings" in restaurants along with his friends, the sons of wealthy merchants. He got away with everything, and even the police left him alone. Once, while driving along the Nevsky in a cab, he was stopped by two young nuns who were collecting contributions for building a church. He dropped a hundred-ruble bill in the collection cup and then hoisted the nuns into the cab, sat them down beside him, and rushed off with the young women, who were half dead with fright. The story reached the metropolitan, and the procurator of the Holy Synod, Lukyanov, ordered him to leave Petersburg within twenty-four hours. He was banished to the town of Blagoveshchensk, where he died in 1928.

The second son, Pyotr, a cavalry officer, was killed by a maddened horse while training it to accept a saddle.

The third son, Sergei, lived in the country on his estate in Penza Province; he was married to a peasant girl, one of his own former serfs.

The fourth son, Nikolai, graduated from the Imperial College of Jurisprudence at St. Petersburg University. In 1884 he returned to Krutets, his estate in Penza, and served in the zemstvo. He married a graduate of the Smolny Institute, Vera Dmitrievna Litvinova, my future grandmother. She came from an old noble family. My grandfather died rather early, leaving his wife and four children almost without support.

My father completed the Second Penza Classical Gymnasium in 1902 and then entered the Physics and Mathematics Faculty of Moscow University. The students were caught up in the revolutionary movement of 1905, and my father was part of a team of them that tended to the wounded during battles on the barricades in Krasnaya Presna. For this he was expelled from university with a "wolf's ticket," a passport that marked him as politically unreliable and meant that he did not have the right to continue his studies and had to earn money by giving private lessons. For almost six years, he lived by his wits to earn enough to support himself. He continued to attend university lectures surreptitiously. The ban was lifted at the beginning of 1911, and he was permitted to take the exams for his whole university course without having formally attended lectures. When he had passed his exams, he was given his diploma and a post as an instructor in chemistry and technology at the Kovno Agricultural College. That same year he married a cousin, Nadezhda Nikolaevna Kropotova, who had graduated from the Saratov Institute for Noblewomen.

My mother came from an old noble family listed in the "Velvet Book" of the nobility along with others who traced their ancestors back to Rurik.

My great-grandfather, my mother's grandfather, Sergei Mikhailovich Kropotov, served in the Grodno Hussar Life-Guard Regiment as a cornet. In 1840 Lieutenant Mikhail Lermontov, a distant relative of his, was transferred to his regiment from the Caucasus. Contemporaries say that great-grandfather and Lermontov became fast friends (see the book *Lermontov Remembered by His Contemporaries,* published not long ago).[1]

In 1849 S. M. Kropotov was among those under investigation in the Petrashevsky Affair and was discharged from the army. Given the absence of any direct evidence against him, he was merely required to settle in Saratov, where he lived on his prosperous estate. That same year he freed all his serfs, dividing the land among them without any redemption fees.

He was a friend of Nikolai Chernyshevsky, and when Chernyshevsky was imprisoned in the St. Peter and Paul Fortress my great-grandfather assumed responsibility for supporting his wife, Olga Sokratovna, and his two sons (he enabled them to complete their higher education).

Sergei Kropotov was married to Maria Vasilevna Ustinova, the sister of my great-grandmother, Olga Vasilevna Litvinova. His son, Nikolai Kropotov, graduated from Moscow University and later served in the Samogit Grenadier Regiment, participating in the Russian-Turkish War and in the taking of Plevna. When he retired from the army he married Aleksandra Dmitrievna Litvinova, the sister of my father's mother.

CHAPTER TWO

Our Life in Omsk

My parents lived in Kovno until 1915. In the summer of that year, the Germans broke through the front, and in a rapid advance they cut the railways

---

1. S. M. Kropotov is mentioned twice in *Lermontov Remembered by His Contemporaries* (*Lermontov v vospominaniiakh sovremennikov;* Moscow, 1989, pp. 264, 266). This source does not confirm any familial or friendly links between Lermontov and Kropotov, however. *Editor's note.*

linking the city with central Russia. The members of the Kovno Agricultural College, along with other refugees, made their way on foot to Panevezhis, and from there by train to Moscow. My mother and elder sister went directly to their family in Penza, while my father, who had taken a post in the Omsk Agricultural College, went to his new place of employment.

I was born on November 28, 1915, in the village of Ukraintsevo, Penza Province. In 1916 my mother, now with two children, joined my father in Omsk.

That year my father and the students were laying out a park and nursery farm on the experimental fields of the college; they were also fitting out a hydrological modeling station on the Irtysh River and conducting soil studies.

The Revolution was in progress in Russia: the monarchy was being toppled and power was shifting to the Soviets; in Siberia power was held by the Siberian Provincial Duma, controlled by the Socialist Revolutionary Party. There were new upheavals and new coups. In September 1918 the Siberian Duma was replaced by a Directory, established in Omsk on the initiative of the Samara, Ekaterinburg, and Siberian governments. As a result of this coup, Admiral Kolchak was elected as the supreme leader of Russia on November 18, 1918.

In the fall of 1919 the entire teaching staff and student body of the Agricultural College were mobilized to provide internal security. Two months later the Kolchak government fell, and father voluntarily enlisted in the Red Army. In December 1919, near Chik Station, he was seriously wounded in both legs and was admitted to the Novonikolaevsky Field Hospital for treatment.

While father was away we had to move out of our apartment and settle on Syezdovsky Street, near the approach to the bridge over the river Om. Mother found a job in the Provincial Food Commission (headed by Smolin), where she could earn a salary and support the family.

In the summer of 1920, father came back from hospital with a leg amputated. He was not able to go to work since his wounds had not yet healed. Famine in the city was imminent, and father decided to accept a proposal from two enterprising Germans, Kindsfarther and Liebrich, who had invited him, as a chemist, to work in a soap-making cooperative.

Our family agreed, and we all moved to the German village of Pobochnoe in the Odessa Region of Omsk Province. Here father began to manufacture soap, while the partners supplied the raw materials. The business flourished, but in 1921 famine came to the village. There was no bread to be had. Mother and father somehow managed to "harvest" switchgrass and other weeds in the fall, and from the switchgrass seeds they ground flour and baked green-colored bread. Many beggars wandered from village to village looking for something to eat, and one episode I particularly recall: my embarrassed mother gave a poor man begging for food a piece of our bread-surrogate, apologizing that all she had in the house was bread made from weeds. The beggar replied, "My dear, we have eaten not only weeds but human corpses to save ourselves from starvation."

It was a red-letter day in our family when oil cakes or meat from dead animals we had found appeared on our table. From time to time the peasants shared their meager food with us, such as flatcakes made from potato peelings or bread made from chaff they had swept up.

The cooperative was running smoothly. They manufactured various kinds of soap—marbled, regular washing soap, toilet soap—that the partners sold in the villages and in the city.

In the spring of 1922 father was offered a teaching position in the Omsk Polytechnic College and in the Communist University. When the Omsk Polytechnic was closed and the Communist University moved to Sverdlovsk (about 1925), father got a position as a chemistry instructor in a school, while working at the same time in a technical school for industry.

In 1930 he was appointed professor in a veterinary institute, and we moved into a house belonging to the Omsk Veterinary Institute, 47 Tobolsk Street.

These were the years of radical change—the collectivization, the campaign against the kulaks—and every day we could see from the windows of our apartment endless columns of prisoners being led off to the prison at 72 Tobolsk Street or to the station for transport.

At that time the city was inundated by hungry bands of Kazakh nomads, sitting in the city squares; these ranged from wizened elders to infants. They would stretch out their tin cups to passers-by hoping for a handout and imploring, "Oh, pap-mam, the belly's empty!"

When my father saw all this happening, he and the medical personnel from the clinic and pharmacy of the Omsk Medical Institute set up a free kitchen for the starving. This "feeding station" did not last long. The organizers were summoned to the NKVD where they were told in no uncertain terms to cease this spontaneous initiative, thereby offering the Kazakhs the opportunity to starve to death. At the time a malicious little verse circulated:

When I at one time was Kirghiz
I ate my meat and drank koumiss.
But now that I've become Kazakh
The front of my belly meets my back.

Times were very hard, and we had to get up at 3:00 A.M. to get a place in line for bread. Food had disappeared from the bazaars and starvation was on the doorstep.

CHAPTER THREE

The Fateful "Running Off to America"

In 1930, on an accelerated program, I was finishing the seventh and eighth classes in the local school, named "In Memory of the Paris Commune." They were closing down the school and, by decree of the Peoples' Commissariat of Education, were setting up an economic and financial technical school in its place. The profession of a financial manager did not suit me, and I enrolled in a factory school attached to the electrical shops of the Omsk railway. My school friend, Oleg Spiridonov, was not intending to go on with his education; he had read a lot of adventure novels and had decided to run off to America, to the Klondike. He and his friend, Stanislav Zaikovsky, the son of a professor at the Agricultural Institute, proposed that I take part in the escape they were planning. I flatly refused since I did not want to leave home, enjoyed school, and was not prepared to abandon my native land.

One fine day I heard a rumor that both my acquaintances had run away from home to parts unknown. Zaikovsky, as part of the plan, had robbed his parents and pillaged his father's laboratory, carrying off anything made of gold. The fugitives' parents informed the police about the flight of their sons and asked their help in locating them. For a few days the Omsk newspaper, *The Worker's Path* (*Rabochii put'*), published an announcement in large type: "Stanislav, Come Back!" A month later I learned that Oleg Spiridonov had returned; Stanislav Zaikovsky *came back somewhat later.*

I never dreamed that this ridiculous little event would have such terrible consequences in my life.

CHAPTER FOUR

"Wrecking" the Grain Harvest

I carried on with my studies and graduated from the factory school; then I enrolled in the third year of the Workers' Faculty of the Siberian Transport Institute. I graduated from it, and in 1933 I was accepted into the Auto Mechanics Faculty of that same institute. That same year we students were sent off to help with the harvest on the Sosnovka State Grain Farm. All the boys from our faculty were assigned as combine harvester operators, while I, as an electrician, worked at repairing the electrical systems of tractors and combines. That fall was very rainy; day and night, in two shifts, the boys harvested grain with combines under heavy downpours. And so it happened that during one night shift two of our combine operators were involved in an accident: a wrench fell out of a toolbox on the combine platform, dropped into the header, and was pulled into the drum. The combine was put temporarily out of commission.

At the same time, the Sosnovka State Grain Farm was graced by a visit from Vyacheslav Molotov, who arrived on one of the airplanes of the "Pravda" Propaganda Squadron and immediately began dispensing "justice" and savage punishments. On his order, the student combine operators were arrested as wreckers; also arrested was the foreman of the seventh section of the farm. Thereafter came the arrests of the men in charge of the drying floors. They had not been able to load the threshed grain into the overflowing granaries and had left it on the drying floors covered by tarpaulins to keep it from the rain.

When the students had returned to town from harvesting, the NKVD began harassing everyone who had been on the farm, demanding confirmation of the police's version of what had happened: that the arrested students were supposedly agents of some fascist secret service. No one, including me, would corroborate the accusation that our comrades had been

79

involved in sabotage. The enraged investigator, pounding the table with his fist, shouted:

"You're all in it together! You're obstructing my investigation. I'll smash your gang, I'll expose the lot of you!"

And he threw me out of his office. Our lads were sent to trial nevertheless, but only for negligence.

CHAPTER FIVE

Arrest, Investigation, Trial

In December 1934 Sergei Mironovich Kirov was assassinated. An epidemic of arrests began in town, picking up those who had survived the arrests of 1930–31. In those years they had arrested former officers of the tsarist and Kolchak armies, members of the clergy, and former entrepreneurs from the NEP era. Now, however, they were picking up former Socialist Revolutionaries and anarchists and had begun arresting students and people who had relatives abroad.

On the night of June 5, 1935, I was awakened by a harsh shout: "On your feet!"

Before me stood a man in a Chekist raincoat of steel-gray color holding out a piece of paper. Only half-awake, I could not understand what was going on. I rubbed my eyes: was this a dream?

"It's a search warrant. Get up and get dressed!"

I got up and asked, "What are you looking for? Please, go ahead and search."

A thorough search was done. I had a collection of rifle cartridges from firearms of various countries, including a Russian 30-caliber. I was very keen on military things and was getting prepared for service in the Red Army and studying military history. I used to buy books on military science from the used-book dealers in the central bazaar. The people making the search collected all these things as evidence. When they had gone through my room and had found their evidence, I was told to go into the dining room. I went in and saw that the door to father's study was open and heaps of paper were scattered about. Father was sitting down, mother was beside herself, and a group of people were rummaging through father's desk.

The search was finished by six o'clock. Two cars drove up, and the compromising evidence seized during the search was loaded into one, my father and I into the other. We didn't have far to drive—the NKVD headquarters was located in two brick buildings of the former bishop's palace. We were taken separately to the preliminary holding cells, first father, and then me. The building had once served as the bishop's stables, but now it had been adapted to hold prisoners. After a humiliating body search, during which my buttons were ripped off, my shoelaces pulled out, and my belt taken, I found myself alone.

The cell was a meter and a half wide, about four meters long with a two-meter ceiling; it contained two narrow trestle beds, a little table, a stool, and in the corner a spittoon that served as a toilet. High up was a small barred window. The building contained nine single cells and five larger ones for five or six people.

I was stunned by what had happened. For two weeks no one summoned me from my cell, and I was left alone with my own thoughts. It was especially difficult in the evenings and at night when the scent of blooming lilac and the sound of a brass band came from the nearby Aquarium Park.

During those two weeks, a few suspicious characters were planted in my cell. They were curious about what crime I thought I had committed. The days passed monotonously. Three times a day the door would open with a clatter of the bolt: in the mornings, for the toilet; afternoons, for exercise; evenings, for roll call. At last I was called out for interrogation.

The investigator's office swam with the heady scent of "Red Moscow" cologne. At a desk sat a man in his early thirties who introduced himself as the senior investigator for major cases in the Chief Directorate of State Security of the NKVD, Captain Tarasov.

The conversation began with trivialities. He inquired about the state of my health, both physical and emotional. With a Jesuitical smile, he apologized for being forced to disturb me; then he took the interrogation record from a drawer and began recording the usual factual information. I was asked to list all my relatives and acquaintances. I willingly began to enumerate all my living relatives and everyone I knew. This procedure, the interrogator's "getting acquainted" with the "detainee," took up the first day. He pressed the button on a buzzer, and a guard wordlessly escorted me back to my cell.

There was another interrogation the next day, and again the interrogator Tarasov began with riddles.

"What am I accused of?" I asked.

"You should think carefully about it and tell us. You see, I've put you down in the proceedings not as 'accused' but as 'detained'—until we can clear up a few things. Once we've cleared them up we'll let you go. When you go back to your cell you'll have a lot of free time, you can search your memory and tell me everything." Then he began discussing unrelated issues.

This struck me as a cat-and-mouse game.

And so the days dragged by.

At one of the interrogations I was asked whether I had ever made an attempt to flee the Soviet Union, whether I had relatives abroad, and whether I knew Zaikovsky. I felt as if I had been scalded when I heard that name.

I laughed and told him about how some schoolboys of fourteen or fifteen with overactive imaginations had decided to run away from home. He recorded this whole epic in the proceedings, though Tarasov would not agree with the year I had indicated—1929—and tried to convince me that it had all happened in 1934–35. I refused to sign the proceedings, since the interrogator had falsified the dating of this childish adventure.

When I returned to my cell, stunned by the conversation with the interrogator, I tried carefully to collect my thoughts. The question about relatives abroad had deeply disturbed me. I had some, of course. My parents' second cousin, Count Mstislav Nikolaevich Tolstoy, was an émigré and owner of a large farm near Paris; my grandmother on my father's side had corresponded with him in French, but my parents had no connection with him. Grandmother had died in 1929, and my parents had burned all the letters she had kept.

Mstislav Tolstoy's brother was the writer Aleksei Nikolaevich Tolstoy, who, when he returned from emigration, had become a favorite of Stalin and wrote works that reinforced and exaggerated the cult of the "Great Leader" by turning history inside out (in his novels *The Defense of Tsaritsyn* and *Bread,* for example).

In 1931 my mother's sister, Maria Mozzhukina, had come from Penza with her three children and moved in with us. Her husband, Aleksei Mozzukhin, was a former officer in the tsarist army and a veteran of World War I. He had settled on the estate of his father, Ilya Mozzhukin, who once managed the estate of the Obolensky princes in the village of Kondol,

Penza Province; there he took up farming. His two brothers—Ivan Ilich, a movie actor, and Aleksandr Ilich, a singer in the Paris Opera—lived abroad, although they were not émigrés. They had left the Soviet Union on tour at the beginning of the 1920s and had not returned, but they maintained their Soviet citizenship and Soviet passports for the rest of their lives.

At the end of 1930 Uncle Aleksei was arrested as a self-employed farmer and a tsarist officer. The shock of this killed his father, Ilya, and my aunt and her children sought refuge with us. In 1934 Uncle Aleksei was freed, came to Omsk, collected his family, and moved to the town of Kalachinsk in Omsk Oblast.

It was these family relationships that frightened me. Did the interrogator know about them? If he knew, then things looked bad for both my father and me.

The question of the time of the proposed escape abroad was raised at another interrogation. I tried with all my might to prove that the events took place in 1929 when we were only schoolboys of fourteen or fifteen (I was the youngest), while Tarasov stubbornly maintained it was in 1934 or 1935. Finally Tarasov proposed to put down 1930 in the proceedings and I gave up and signed off on this date.

A new guest appeared in my cell—Ivan Shutov, the secretary of the Kirov Regional Party Committee of the city of Omsk. He was amazed by what had happened to him and, at the same time, angry at the treachery of the head of the NKVD, who had invited him in for a friendly chat and then hidden him away in an interrogation cell.

I was again called out for interrogation and presented with the charge of involvement in a counterrevolutionary conspiracy headed by a supposed rabid enemy, a former colonel of the tsarist police—my father. When I heard these charges I felt my hair begin to stand on end.

"Soviet power has put the squeeze on you. You don't like the existing regime and so you spend your time dreaming about toppling this system you hate and that's taken away your privileges," muttered the interrogator. "And there is no way you can prove your loyalty to us."

What could I reply to that?

Thereafter there were nightly interrogations; I would come back to my cell only at reveille. Sleeping in the daytime was not allowed. After a few sleepless days I could barely understand what they wanted from me.

"We have extensive factual information about your criminal activity. Here is your testimony at your first interrogations and your sincere confession."

The interrogator handed me the proceedings in which the year 1930 had now been changed to 1932! "Here is the testimony of Zaikovsky, where he sincerely confesses that you were planning a terrorist act against Comrade Voroshilov, that you were planning an armed insurrection and printing counterrevolutionary leaflets."

I demanded a face-to-face confrontation with Zaikovsky. They brought him into the office and, not blinking an eye, he told a complete cock-and-bull story that confirmed his testimony.

Tarasov, furious at my stubborn refusal to accept the accusation of a crime, pounded the table and shouted:

"If you're going to be this stubborn I'll have to arrest your mother, brother, and sister!"

I was horrified by this threat.

The grounds for the accusation of an armed insurrection were my collection of rifle cartridges and, possibly, my undue frankness. When asked if we had any weapons I answered that we did. Oleg Spiridonov had a broken Belgian Browning that would not shoot and Zaikovsky had a small-caliber six-shooter revolver loaded with "Bosquet" cartridges.

I had no visits from my mother. I was plagued by thoughts of what was happening on the outside and whether my mother was at home. After the confrontation with Zaikovsky I decided to use cunning. So as to get a little time at home and check to see if my mother was all right I took the risk, to my own detriment, of making a "confession" at the next interrogation and giving the following testimony: "Feeling threatened by Soviet power, I make a sincere confession (this was the interrogator's preamble, *N.B.*). We in fact did distribute anti-Soviet leaflets (no such thing had ever existed, *N.B.*), printed with a hectograph made by the accused Zaikovsky and brought to me. The hectograph gel is contained in a box of Chlorodont tooth powder and is in my room."

The interrogator's face stretched into a sugary smile.

"You should have done that long ago," and he offered me some cigarettes. "Now where is that box? I'll send a man to bring it here at once!"

"You'll never find it without my help. Your agent can come with me, and I'll hand over the box to him."

I went home with an escort. My amazed and overjoyed mother greeted me at the door, exclaiming, "At long last!" and embracing me.

"Mama, you have to understand that I'm not alone and I have to go back. I just have to hand over one little thing to this man. Don't worry, everything will soon be cleared up and I'll come back home. I don't know anything about papa."

At home I was fed dinner, supplied with food, and, after handing over an empty box of tooth powder to my escort, I returned to the preliminary detention cells with a lighter heart.

Now I had to wait for the trial. The Soviet court is a just court; it clears the wheat from the chaff and will establish my innocence.

The Russian-Chinese-Japanese phrase book published by the General Staff at the time of the 1905 Japanese War and seized during the search of my room served as evidence that I was a Japanese spy. Personnel in the highest echelons of the Main Administration of State Security of the NKVD took an interest in me. One of my interrogations was attended by the head of the section on counterespionage, Kostandolgo, a tall, thin man with a long beard whose appearance somehow reminded me of the famous polar explorer Otto Schmidt. After sitting through about an hour of my interrogation he gave up and departed.

I was summoned before the "clear eyes" of the head of the investigation section of the NKVD State Security Administration, Makovsky, who told me:

"We believe you when you say you are not a counterrevolutionary, but you will be one in the future. You are an alien element and so we must isolate you from society."

Between interrogations I chatted with my neighbor in the cell. He was told he was being charged with forging his party card and being an impostor.

If I am not mistaken, the exchange of party cards connected with the change in name from the Russian Communist Party (Bolshevik) to the All-Russian Communist Party (Bolshevik) began in 1935. Arrests of some party members came with the verification of their party documents. This was how Professor Fridolin of the Agricultural Institute was arrested—as a former member of the Central Rada of Hetman Skoropadsky. The director of the Rosa Luxemburg Factory in Omsk, Gavrilov, was arrested in the same way. He was a member of the Regional Party Committee, a deputy of the Supreme Soviet, but his real name, it turned out, was Dubrovin, and he had been a colonel in Kolchak's army and commander of the "Death Train." The trial of Dubrovin-Gavrilov was widely publicized in the Siberian press.

They were trying to shove Shutov into this same group. His party card, along with all his other documents, had been lost in the Amur River when he was thrown off the bridge of a gunboat by a shellburst during the storming of the town of Lakhassusu during the conflict along the Chinese Eastern Railway. His sidearm and his clothing were pulling Shutov down to the bottom. He unbuckled his weapons, cast off his pea jacket, his trousers, and the tunic that held his documents and, in his undershorts and vest, was picked up by a lifeboat.

The testimony of eyewitnesses to the event helped him get his documents restored, and he was issued a duplicate of his party card; some time later he was transferred from the Far East to Omsk. And then came the finale. Shutov's membership in the party was confirmed, but in the prison where he was awaiting the end of the process of verification of his version of the loss of his party card he had told someone a joke, and got six years in the camps under Article 58 (10).

The investigation of my case was coming to an end.

For the first time in the course of the investigation I at last met my father, by the Black Maria that was sending us off "to visit Auntie" (that was the name people gave to the Omsk Prison at 72 Tobolsk Street).

High brick walls formed a rectangle around an ancient building with small towers on each corner, built in the shape of the letter "E." Prison oldtimers explained the building's configuration as an attempt to immortalize the name of the one who had instituted it, Catherine (Ekaterina) II. It was three stories high, with a basement and stout wooden gates and internal security guards. The first small courtyard, called "the well," served as the reception area where they searched those brought in to the prison from freedom. Then the gates would open into the prison yard itself, from which the corridor warders, jingling their rings of keys, would march the prisoners off to their cells.

We were taken up to the third story of the right-hand investigative wing and placed in a cell where the accounting clerk and the corridor cleaners lived. The clerk, who was awaiting the decision from the Special Board, was a teacher in the Omsk Pedagogical Institute, Vasily Zuev. While taking up the works of Demyan Bedny he incautiously informed the students that Bedny had graduated from university and had received a scholarship through the resources of the governor-general of Moscow, Grand Duke Sergei Aleksandrovich, uncle of Tsar Nicholas II. This cost him five years. The two other cellmates kept the corridors clean and delivered the prison rations of bread and thin soup. One was an elderly peasant, Falchenko, sentenced for counterrevolutionary activities and sabotage, as evidenced by his reluctance to become a member of a collective farm; the other, Abram Shengaruz, was a Polish Jew and defector who had been sentenced to ten years imprisonment by a Revolutionary Tribunal.

This was the first time I saw a "real" spy. I was interested in his case and questioned him about why he had crossed the border. Jumbling Russian and Polish words, he told me that he had crossed the border to visit his brother who was living inside Soviet territory. He was detained by border guards and turned over to the NKVD where, being questioned and barely understanding Russian, he replied to the interrogator's question about his place of employment in Poland by saying that he served in the Polish *Defensywa* (security section). This was sufficient for the tribunal to give him ten years. And what did his service consist of? He was a tailor by trade and made "ufinorms" (i.e., uniforms) for the Polish police.

The cell had a special status and was locked only at night. There was a little shop in the prison yard where one could buy food during exercise time.

One could quite often find graffiti made in pencil on the walls of the prison toilet: "Abandon hope, all ye who enter," and in another place someone had scratched with a nail, "Those who come here, do not grieve; those who leave here, do not rejoice. He who has not been here will be; he who has will forget this shit." Some cheery optimist had written, "They can't chase you any farther than the sun, they can't drive your cock into the ground." This author's optimism proved to be unjustified: they could. And how they could. How many of them remained of those driven into the ground in nameless graves? How many never came home again?

The head of the prison, Kokin, made his rounds of the cells once a week, collecting petitions and hearing the complaints of the prisoners. He was short, lively, and took care to keep the regular criminals separated from the politicals and those charged with civil crimes.

One of the criminals called him "little boss-man," to which Kokin replied, "I may not be tall, but I'm the boss here."

Books from the prison library would be brought round to the cells, including some that had been removed from libraries long ago to be destroyed as "harmful," such as Savinkov's *The Scales of Life* and *Pale Horse,* the works of Plekhanov, and a number of others.

Within a week I received the final list of charges against me, and they included a full range of subparagraphs of Article 58 of the Criminal Code of the RFSFR: 2, 6, 8, and 11.

My father and I, two of my friends from the institute (arrested by Tarasov in hopes of making a case for a well-established organization), and one more young fellow I did not know were surrounded by seven guards with rifles and taken away to court.

I was astonished to learn that this unknown boy brought to court with us was one of my "co-conspirators." Zaikovsky, who had been "assisting the investigation" by denouncing "enemies of the people," was brought from the preliminary detention prison with another group.

Court proceedings took place behind closed doors. Apart from the judges and the accused, who were surrounded by a reinforced group of guards, there was no one in the room. Even the defense attorney who had volunteered his services was not admitted to witness the judicial procedure. During the session it became clear that the materials for the prosecution had been put together hurriedly and that the accused did not know one another, as was the case, for example, with this boy named Pavlin (his last name was Melnikov), whom I saw for the first time in my life on the day of the trial. According to Zaikovsky's testimony, he was something in the order of a treasurer who had collected seven rubles to carry out the escape. Investigator Tarasov's forgeries were revealed in court, as were the illegal methods he had used, and the judges choked with laughter as they listened to the accused. The court dismissed subparas 6 and 8 (espionage and terror).

The sentence was read out: "In the name of the Russian Soviet Federated Socialist Republic . . . under Article 58, subparagraphs 2 to 11 of the Criminal Code of the RSFSR . . . the sentences are: Zaikovsky, Stanislav Yanovich, five years in corrective labor camp; Boldyrev, Nikolai Nikolaevich (son), five years in corrective labor camp; Melnikov, Pavlin, two years in corrective labor camp.

"With respect to Boldyrev, Nikolai Nikolaevich (father), professor at the Omsk Veterinary Institute and the students of the Autotransport Institute, Pustovarov, A. I., and Mikhailov, V. I., brought to trial under Article 58, subparagraph 12 (failure to inform), because of the absence of *corpus delicti* the case is to be dropped and they are to be released from custody."

Now it was just one guard who escorted Pavlin and me back to the prison. They took Zaikovsky back to the NKVD preliminary detention prison again. Evidently, Investigator Tarasov could not get along without him.

CHAPTER SIX

In Prison, Waiting for Transport

Back in the prison I asked Pavlin what had become of Oleg Spiridonov. It turned out that Oleg had spent a long time hanging about after quitting school, then signed on with a fishing cooperative on the Pacific coast where, according to rumor, he managed to get married.

In the prison (which in those years bore the name "House of Correction") the cells in the wing for those awaiting transport stood open and prisoners were allowed to mingle freely. There were nonpoliticals, politicals, and a small contingent of criminals in this wing; the mass of criminals were held in the half-basement. The administration would punish violators of the prison regime by sending them "to India"—to the criminals in the basement where there was "nonstop singing and dancing."

The professional criminals would greet a new arrival to their cell by throwing a towel at his feet. An experienced criminal would wipe his boots (*prokhorya* in criminal jargon) on the towel and casually toss it to the latrine barrel.

"One of us!" would be the relieved sigh that went around the cell and, depending on his "service record," he would get a place on the sleeping platforms amidst the criminal elite. Lower-caste criminals, called *syavki*—petty crooks who had no connections with well-known criminals on the outside who could vouch for them as thieves—spent their days under the *yurtsy* (bunks) and were servants of the senior criminals, the *pakhany*.

But when a noncriminal "pigeon" (*frayer*) or some poor devil of a collective farmer happened to find himself in the cell he would pick up the towel from the floor, shake it out, and lay it down on the edge of the sleeping platform. Then a competition for the belongings of the new arrival would begin.

"Why don't we have a bite to eat, chum? Now then, let's take a look at your bundle." And his bag of food would instantly disappear before his very eyes. "Wanna have a little game of cards? *Bura* or *stos*? Don't be shy, chum, sit up closer."

Within a few minutes the stunned newcomer's own sound clothes and shoes would be gone, replaced by some tattered rags. More "jokes" at the expense of the newcomer followed. An exhausted man sleeps soundly. A strip of cotton wool would be carefully placed between his toes and lit. Awakened by a terrible pain and, still half asleep and unable to comprehend what was happening, the man would wildly kick his legs until he realized he had to splash some water from the teakettle on his burned feet.

"Well done, chum," the criminal would say approvingly, to the laughter of the cell. "I s'pose it's been a while since you've been on a bicycle."

I also had to spend three days in the basement. I slipped up and came running out for roll call when all the others were already formed up in the corridor. They shoved me into a cell at the same moment all its inhabitants were breathlessly listening to one of the criminals "stringing out a historical now-vel." The story as told blended the Middle Ages with the twentieth century and its technical advances: the king of France sat in his luxurious office and chatted on the telephone with Cardinal Richelieu, and the musketeers crossed the English Channel on a high-speed cruiser to get the queen's "jewweled" necklace. The performance stopped . . . The eyes of the cell's denizens all turned to this new arrival. They asked me who I was and if I had any grub.

I laid out all my supplies on the table and said: "Let me tell you a historical novel," and began to tell the story of Princess Tarakanova from Gleb Uspensky. My story delighted the criminals, and I spent three days there like one of their own. After I introduced these dregs of society to the poetry of Pushkin and to other Russian literature, they nicknamed me "The Student."

Three days later I was settled back in my own cell. The people in the basement had now come to know me, and when I went out for exercise they would greet me, shouting out the window, "Hey, Student, come visit us, we'll keep you in *vantazh* (show you respect)."

In those years the prison regime had not yet become very harsh. Visits and parcels were permitted without limit. Those who wanted to spend some time in the fresh air were taken out on work projects. I was twice taken out to sort brick rubble from the Omsk cathedral that had been blown up. The cathedral was a remarkably beautiful building, and a number of famous artists—Surikov, Vrubel and others—had helped paint its frescoes. The brick from the cathedral went into the construction of a new NKVD building and a new internal prison.

The prison contingent changed daily. Some left on transport, others arrived at the prison to wait out the judicial process.

CHAPTER SEVEN

Siblag

At the beginning of November 1935, I was put into a special transport along with Zaikovsky, even though my case was under appeal.

The *zek* car was crammed to the bursting point. There were fourteen people in each section and no room to move. You could only lie on your side with your head toward the grating that divided the section from the corridor. The journey was long and exhausting. The first stop was Novosibirsk Prison, where I spent several days waiting for the next train. It was another *zek* car, called a Stolypin carriage, and once again we were on the move.

At Yurga Station, where we were supposed to change trains, the train guards for some reason never appeared and a special guard took us on to Anzhersk Prison by raft. We spent the night in the prison and the next morning were back at the station, only to set off in the direction from which we had come.

After a long series of ordeals, with stops at the Kemerovo and Stalinsk (Novokuznetsk) prisons, we finally reached Akhpun Station. Here, in the town of Temirtau, was an ore enrichment plant where the 9th Akhpun Penal Section of the Siblag NKVD worked. Those sent here had for the most part been convicted of banditry or under one of the "heavyweight" sections of Article 58.

The reception area was in the first commandant's camp sector. The area was surrounded by two rows of barbed wire; along the wire inside the zone was another strip of fenced-off territory called the buffer zone. Guard towers jutted up everywhere, and German shepherds on sliding leashes ran along the buffer zone.

The long rows of barracks within the zone were army tarpaulin tents stretched over frameworks of wooden rails. Inside the barracks were two-tiered bunks made of unpeeled rails; at either end was a stove made from metal drums. By morning your hair would be frozen to the wall. You would sleep in your clothes—otherwise they would be stolen. Noise, squabbles, fights breaking out continually, card games in progress, scores being settled—and all this in a barracks where bandits and KRs—counterrevolutionaries—were neighbors.

The first time I entered the tent I stood bewildered. A crowd of people had gathered around the stoves. Some were drying their clothes, others were toasting bread or cooking food in tin cans. There were about four hundred people in the tent, and conversations in several languages blended with traditional Russian obscenities. I sat down on the edge of someone's bunk and thought: Where on earth have I come to? What more is in store for me?

"So, just got here?" said a voice from the upper bunks. "What article? What term? Crawl up here. There's two of us, but where there's two, there's room for a third. We'll be a bit cramped, but it's fine—warmer for sleeping."

He did not have to repeat the invitation. I crawled up to the "attic" where I got acquainted with my neighbors. There was a fine-looking old fellow with a long beard and wearing a cassock who introduced himself as Arbuzov, a priest. The second man was a Leningrad archpriest, Aleksandr Remizov. He initiated me into the secrets of camp life.

Reveille for the camp inmates is announced at 5:00 A.M. by a sharp series of blows on a length of railway track hanging by the guardhouse. Duty bread distributors from each brigade, carrying basins and surrounded by a dozen or more lads from the brigade to guard them, rush off to the bread-cutting room. The others hurry to the washstands. Given the conditions in the camp, the bread distributors absolutely must be protected because of regular attacks and theft of the bread rations. Once the bread is distributed, breakfast is brought into the barracks: thin prison soup and hot water in huge metal boilers.

Then the metal rail is struck again. The work assigners burst into the barracks and use their clubs to chase the brigades to the guardhouse, where they form up and march to work. Those who still linger are thrown off their bunks, beaten with clubs, and driven out of the barracks with shouts, "Out of here right now, and nobody better be last."

The brigades form up. Various camp bosses, all of them prisoners—brigadiers, section leaders, the superintendent, people from the Registration and Distribution Section—stand under the lantern by the guardhouse carrying little squares of plywood on which they keep the tally of the men. Outside the gate is a crowd of guards with dogs. The brigades form up in columns of five men per row.

The gates open with the command, "First five, move out! Second five…"

Within the zone the work assigners count the fives, outside the zone the senior guard does the same. After their tallies are confirmed, the guards accept handover of the brigade.

Every morning there are the usual parting words:

"Attention, party! Do not spread out along the way; no talking. A step to the right, a step to the left will be considered an escape attempt! The guards will open fire. Without warning! Understood?"

"Understood," a chorus of voices responds.

"Move out!" shouts the senior guard, and the column of prisoners sets off.

I was assigned to timber cutting. The work did not worry me since at home we had been used to physical labor from childhood. One of my jobs was cutting and splitting firewood.

We had to break a trail to the forest through the deep snow. Up to our waists in snow, linking hands by fives, we pushed our way through with our chests, tramping down a trench leading to the work site.

Part of the brigade would flounder about the tract of forest; the criminals would build a bonfire and warm themselves until the workday ended. Our tools were "Stakhanovka" bow-saws and dull axes. My partner was the archpriest Remizov, who had built up a lot of experience in camp work (he had been in prison since the early 1920s and had been in a number of camps, including Solovki). He taught me how and in what direction to fell trees. We worked without a moment's rest. After the branches were cut from the fallen tree, the log would be cut in lengths for different uses—pulpwood, railway ties, mine props—and stacked. When the work was done, the section leader and brigadier would measure the stacks and put their stamp on them.

But we couldn't keep this up for long. Almost everything we produced was credited to the criminals warming themselves by the fires, and after three months' work in the forest we were on our last legs—"goners," as the prisoners said.

On four hundred grams of bread and watery soup (for those who did not fulfill the norm) we very quickly became as thin as candlewicks. There was no way to overcome the injustice of the system. The saying in the camps was, "You die today, I'll live till tomorrow."

I was saved from emaciation and certain death by a stroke of luck. A medical commission that arrived in the camp in February 1936 certified me and both clergymen and sent us to a Sanitary and Nourishment Section. A hundred camp goners were gathered up and placed in Rest Column No. 13 under medical supervision. For about three days I had a real rest. No one chased us out to work; the food was the same as for hospital patients; you could sleep if you felt like it or stroll about the zone.

One day the work assigner came running in and announced that a reply had come to my appeal: I was summoned to Omsk for reinvestigation. It was a simple matter to gather up what remained of my belongings in a pillowcase. Once more, in an empty *zek* car, I was on my way home.

CHAPTER EIGHT

Reinvestigation: Second Sentence

The trip to Omsk took about a day. When I arrived at the prison, the head physician of the medical section of the Prisons Section, Dr. Krikoriants, put me in the prison hospital. Two weeks of treatment and proper food (I immediately began receiving food parcels from home) set me back on my feet again, and I appeared before Investigator Tarasov.

There was no new interrogation. With a mocking grin on his face he examined my haggard face and emaciated body and asked:

"Well, how were things at the 'rest home'?" And pounding the table he shouted, "If you refute the material of the investigation again I'll have you packed off even farther, to the backside of the moon."

With that our last meeting ended.

I was put on trial once more. A new person appeared in court, Oleg Spiridonov, who had luckily avoided arrest and trial the first time but who had come home on leave for some reason and had been arrested.

The new court with new members did not delve very deeply into the essence of the case and the forgeries of the investigator. The stereotypical answer to everything was, "The court is well aware of this!"

The new court brought in a new sentence: Zaikovsky, Spiridonov, and I each got ten years of prison. Pavlin got seven years; my father and my two classmates, Mikhailov and Pustovarov, who had been acquitted earlier, were sentenced to two years each but were released on a signed undertaking until confirmation of the sentences.

After sentencing I was transferred to No. 5 Manufacturing Settlement of the Prisons Section. The head of the settlement was named Lesnikov. I worked as a technician-designer in the mechanical shop. The head of the shop was Povetkin, an elderly, stout free worker, the soul of kindness. There was a foundry, with a small cupola furnace; a modeling shop; a forming shop; an electrolysis shop; a tinning shop; and an electric welding shop. There was even a shoemaking shop run by the craftsman Mashebo. The mechanical shop produced beds with Warsaw and English mesh; it made nails, filled individual orders for window bars, metal gates, and so on. There were between 100 and 150 people in the settlement.

The head of production was the prisoner Aleksandr Kiselev, former director of the Kiselev Coal Mine, named after him (a town in Kemerovo Oblast was also named after him). He had once supported the opposition, but he was sentenced under Article 109 of the Criminal Code (malfeasance in office) to five years in prison.

The most interesting personality in Settlement 5 was the engineer-economist Goloushkin, former head of the Economic Section of the Omsk Aircraft Factory. He had spent 1924 and 1925 in America pretending to be an immigrant. The Soviet government had given him the task of getting into the Ford factories using any means possible to study the production line system ("industrial espionage"). After many ordeals he managed to do this and returned to the USSR at the end of the 1920s. His motherland showed its appreciation of his work by shipping him off to Omsk and sentencing him to ten years in the camps for malfeasance.

At the end of May, my father's sentence came into effect.

My father, not awaiting his armed escort, came on his own to the head of the settlement, Lesnikov, with an extract from the decision of the Supreme Court and asked permission to serve his sentence together with his son. My father's request was granted.

In June father was summoned to the yard, where he found students of the Veterinary Institute who had received permission to take their oral exams from Professor Boldyrev. He gave them their exams, but this brief transformation of a prison yard into a college lecture hall reflected badly on Lesnikov, and he was dismissed from his post. His deputy, Goldyrev, another decent person who harmed no one, became head of the settlement.

Father kept looking for work that was within his powers; idleness weighed heavily on him, though he would say, "Finally I'm getting a proper rest. I haven't had a real rest for a long time." The head of the Culture and Education Section, Kobrin, offered him a job in the settlement's Cultural Section, setting up the wall newspaper *Reforging* (*Perekovka*). Pointed verses and caricatures would be created on the basis of reports from correspondents (father was a master at drawing and writing little humorous poems), and this won the newspaper great popularity, not only among the *zeks* but among the free workers as well.

In August the prisoners were examined by a medical commission. The doctors pronounced father incapable of working and, under Article 458 of the Code of Criminal Procedure, he was released. Dr. Krikoriants and the head of the Prisons Section, Sege, helped father to make his way out of this "educational institution."

I made out estimates for repairs to the settlement buildings and the prison, and submitted a proposal to find a substitute for the metal tubes that were used in headboards for beds. These were in very short supply. The proposal was accepted, and I set to work designing a tube-stretching machine. I had to potter about for a long time with calculations and drawing of parts. The model builders prepared wooden replicas of the cogwheels that were then cast in the foundry. The whole machine was put together locally. I was given some substantial bonuses—credits toward time served—and was already dreaming that within four years I would be let out. But on April 30, 1937, on orders of the NKVD, I was sent back to prison.

CHAPTER NINE

Omsk Prison Again

There was now a strict regime in prison. Cells were kept locked. Baffles covered the windows. The prison was crammed full of people. Exercise in the yard was cut back to fifteen minutes. Family members now had a hard time arranging visits or sending parcels. Trips to the toilet were limited to morning and evening. There was a latrine barrel in the cell a meter high and a meter in diameter. It had a plank on top on which you could perch like an eagle. The cell was stifling and it stank.

My cell had a motley group of inhabitants—people of every kind! There was a group of criminals, some nonpoliticals, KRs (counterrevolutionaries), some who had already been sentenced, others still under investigation. Among my cellmates were people like the professor from the Department of Surgery of the Omsk Medical Institute, Bek-Dombrovsky, a German and former member of Germany's revolutionary government (the minister of health). After the putsch headed by General Kapp he had been put into Moabite Prison, from which, through an exchange organized by the Soviet government, he was released along with Karl Radek and two other German communists whose names, unfortunately, have escaped my memory. He had been a member of the Comintern and had worked as the deputy to the commissar of health, Semashko, but because of some sort of "deviations" he had been exiled to Omsk. He was arrested in 1937 as part of the Radek affair, and after some futile interrogations by the Omsk NKVD was transferred to Moscow.

Also in the cell was the former mayor of the city, Ostapenko. In 1900 he acquired the drawbridge that had been on display in the French Pavilion at the Paris World's Fair and donated it to the city. The bridge was placed across the Om River and linked Republic Street with Lenin Street.

The son of the shipbuilder Plotnikov was here; the son of the former supervisor of the Imperial Palace, General Potapov, was here; there were three peasants accused of participation in the Ishimsk-Petropavlovsk uprising of 1922 against the food surplus-appropriation system; there were three former ensigns from Kolchak's army, Sergeev, Kazymov, and Lopatin.

There was the former chairman of the Ishimsk City Soviet, Daniil Sharonov, a man who maintained his military bearing. It's worth mentioning him in more detail. A communist, he had helped Uglanov defend Petrograd against Yudenich in the years of revolution. He headed the Tosno group that captured an armored train from the Whites.

There was also a frail eighty-year-old "terrorist," Lukyanov, who had once (in the 1800s) been procurator of the Holy Synod, a very wealthy Kiev landowner (even the prison built on his land was called the Lukyanov Prison). He had spent time in Solovki, then was exiled to the Ishimsk District. He was arrested again and sentenced by tribunal to ten years in the camps "for planning a terrorist act against Stalin." After the trial he thanked the judge for extending his life by ten years.

The old Germans Wirth and Göse and the soldiers Schell and Bossart were also here because they had each accepted twenty-five marks "in aid of starving Germans in the USSR" from the German government.

Here too was Starovoitov, a tailor from deep in the provinces, the former head of a tailors' cooperative that the NKVD had declared a counter-revolutionary organization. When he came back from his interrogation, he asked his cellmates fearfully, "What's a 'kroksyist'? The interrogator put me down as one in his report and made me sign it."

A twelve-year-old romantic, Kolya Ginter, was there along with his father. He and some of his classmates had set out to run away to Africa, but instead of Africa he ended in prison.

There was a sizeable group of students from various city colleges, a small group of criminals, and a group of provocateur-informers headed by the former trade union activist from Vagai Station, Isai Grishin. He was an elderly man with legal training who introduced himself as a Trotskyite. Many people in the Omsk Prison fell victim to these provocateurs, who would put together spurious "cases" from the cell that brought new terms to previously convicted prisoners or sent them to the firing squad. Among those who practiced the trade of informer-"witness" were the insane Trans-Baikal Cossack Semenov, brother of Hetman Semenov, and the collective farm chairman Vasily Stepanenko. Fourteen-year-old Stepan Kudriavkin, who drove a handcar for a section chief on the Omsk railway, was also drawn into this group. This young lad was in prison because once when he was chasing away sparrows from the Omsk depot by shooting at them with a slingshot, he accidentally hit a portrait of Kaganovich that was hanging there. Well, that was enough to get him eight years as a "terrorist."

Soldiers accused of membership in a military-fascist conspiracy in the Siberian Military District began arriving. They shoved Major Shalin and Lieutenant Trashakhov into our cell. The prison simply couldn't hold any more people. The cellars of clubs in the city were transformed into prisons.

They hung powerful loudspeakers on the guard towers that deafened the prisoners in the cells with the shouts of people at rallies: "We must tear out all the rotten roots of the Trotskyite-Zinoviev bands! The death penalty for enemies of the people!"

The whole prison, oppressed by gloomy forebodings of events to come, grew silent. Even the little gang of criminals who had been trying to impose their dictatorship in the cell calmed down and fell into a kind of stupor. Rumors floated about the prison, each more ominous than the last. A wave of arrests began among the upper echelons of the city administration.

The secretary of the Oblast Committee of the party, Bulatov, was arrested, as were the chairman of the City Council, Kondratiev, the head of the railway administration, Fufriansky, who not long before had replaced Kavtaradze, who had been recalled to Moscow and had himself been arrested somewhere along the way. When Fufriansky had arrived in Omsk, the newspapers had published pictures of him along with testimonials that he was Stalin's faithful comrade-in-arms.

The procurator of the railway, Mazur, was arrested, as were the head of the local NKVD, Salyn, and the head of the Special Section of the Chief Administration of State Security of the NKVD, Makovsky. Sege, head of the Prisons Section, was accused of being a Polish spy. There was more than one occasion when an arrested NKVD investigator would meet his former investigatee, already convicted, in a cell.

The director of my own institute, Garshtein, a Latvian, was arrested along with several institute professors.

CHAPTER TEN

Deeper into the Swamp: The Sentence of the Troika

On the slightest pretext the cell was put on punishment regime: three hundred grams of bread, hot food—thin prison soup—every other day, and no trips to the toilet. We were no longer taken out for exercise because the prison was so overcrowded.

Visits and food parcels were canceled. For some reason I alone among my cellmates was in the good graces of the prison authorities, and once a week I was brought a parcel of food that I shared with all my cellmates.

The nerves of the people in the cell were strained to the limit. Quarrels often flared up, and the provocateur Grishin took advantage of them. Isai Grishin left the cell almost every day, explaining his absences by saying he was writing appeals for those already sentenced. In fact it was the *kum,* the "godfather" (security officer), who summoned him. During one of his absences he sold out Sharonov to the *kum.* Sharonov would often try to put down Grishin, who was always starting conversations in the cell on the slippery subject of the situation in the country. Grishin's entourage chimed in to support the slander against Sharonov, and Sharonov—along with Lopatin, Kazymov, and Sergeev, who all slept near him—was packed off to the cellar.

In the course of those terrible days of August 1937 the prison administration informed me that my "case" had been reexamined by the Supreme Court of the USSR, the new sentence quashed, and the former sentence of the Special Judicial Collegium—five years—left in force. A few days later, however, I was called out to the prison *kum*. The Prisons Section investigator Trianov demanded that I sign an interrogation report confirming that D. V. Sharonov was carrying on counterrevolutionary agitation and supposedly was the head of an insurgent group organized in the cell. I tried to show how absurd this accusation was by saying, "Everything Sharonov is accused of was concocted by the informer Grishin. The whole cell knows that he's an out-and-out provocateur and his cellmates are afraid even to discuss what they said at the interrogation in front of him."

A little while later I was called out again.

"You've been sharing your food parcels with the accused. That means you must sympathize with those criminals. They've all admitted that you've been recruited into their gang."

I was amazed at what Trianov had said and told him, "How can I be part of their gang when they've made no attempt to recruit me? As for sharing my parcels, well yes, I did share. Not only with the people you're accusing but with my other cellmates as well. If I sympathize with hungry and exhausted people, that's my own business. I don't categorize people by the articles of the Criminal Code."

So now I was tangled up in a new affair. I hoped that the new trial the investigator was promising would be able to clear away all the nonsense that had been concocted in the prison.

So I signed the indictment accusing me of sympathy for a counterrevolutionary group, expressed by sharing with them my food parcels from home.

I was told that I was to appear before an NKVD Troika.

Back in the cell I tried to learn something about this judicial organ from those with more experience of the prison system. Those criminals who had been sentenced in 1935–36 and had appeared before a Troika explained:

"They call you up, ask a few questions, and decide on the spot what to give you: a year, two years, or five—that's the full ticket. They don't have the right to give you more than that. The whole thing lasts no more than fifteen or twenty minutes; it's just like making pancakes."

The prison regime grew even harsher. Searches became more frequent. They would beat you up if they found you had the stub of a pencil or a needle. The head of our prison wing, Borodin, was particularly vicious. He was tall and thin, with malice written in his small eyes. He would burst into the cell at night, accompanied by ten or fifteen warders. In a frenzy he would kick at those sleeping on the floor. Shouting "Everyone to the side of the cell!" they would throw off the people sleeping in the bunks and start the *shmon*.

People huddled in one half of the cell, watching as their meager prison possessions, thrown from the bunks on to the floor, were ravaged.

After they had tossed their things about in this way they would herd the prisoners to the other side of the cell, and the same procedure would begin again. When they found no forbidden articles, the party of searchers would move off, their footsteps receding down the corridor, leaving the prisoners to spend the rest of the night crawling around the floor searching for their things under the dim light.

In December all the inhabitants of the cell were transferred from the third story to the basement. The cell was twenty-five square meters in the left inverted "L" of the prison. They pushed about thirty people into the cell. The floor was now concrete, not wooden. We could only sit by tucking our knees up to our chests. The people had come from various cells. Some of them were still dressed in summer clothes: they had been brought here after being arrested in southern resorts while on holiday; others had been taken directly from work. It was winter outside, but the ventilation window was never closed: it was the only place fresh air could get into our "Turkish bath."

More than once I regretted that I had not been taken on the 1935 transport to Kolyma along with the others involved in my case. But then at the end of March the bolt on the door clattered and the prison work assigner began calling out names from a list. Mine was one of them.

"Grab your belongings and get yourselves out to the corridor, right now!"

We were taken out of the basement and up to the first floor of the left wing, to the transport cell (it had formerly been the prison chapel). The cell was already full. People were taken to the bathhouse in groups and carefully searched. A medical commission was here as well, determining the fitness of people to be transported to camps.

The senior prisoner in the cell was Shuisky, a former prince, a strapping dark-haired fellow who looked like a Gypsy. He managed to keep order in the cell without any fuss.

"They're bringing the swill!" came a happy shout from one of the prisoners. "We'll fill our faces, boys!"

"Quiet, comrades!" came Shuisky's voice. "We must maintain order. Act like civilized people with a sense of our own dignity. There's no need to keep using expressions that don't exist in the Russian language—'fill our faces,' 'swill.' They are bringing us soup, I repeat, soup, and I ask you to get into line and approach the canister with no pushing. You'll be served a bowl of soup."

Shuisky stood out sharply from the mass of people who had picked up the manners of criminals. In the nightmare of prison he was able to maintain the self-control, nobility, and dignity of a cultured person. He had been an emigrant. As a cadet in the Kiev Military Academy, he and the other students and staff had been evacuated to the Crimea during the days of revolution. When the Crimea was taken by the Reds he set off along his thorny path of wandering across Europe. In 1927, under the amnesty declared by M. I. Kalinin for émigrés whose hands had not been stained with blood, he returned to the Soviet Union along with many others. In 1937, as a planner in a factory in Omsk, he was picked up by the "iron hand" of Yezhov.

Our articles and sentences were announced. I learned of the resolution of the Troika from the words written on a narrow strip of cheap paper. On the left were my last name, first name, and patronymic and my year of birth. On the right, "The NKVD Troika for Omsk Oblast resolves: For counter-revolutionary activity, to be sentenced to ten years incarceration, sentence to begin March 18, 1938."

That was all. Clear and concise.

CHAPTER ELEVEN

A Familiar Route: Gorshorlag

A column of more than a thousand men, surrounded by guards, stretched out along the road to the station. Passers-by froze as they stared at the prisoners being transported: some stared out of curiosity, others in hope of spotting a familiar face. The bolder among them would call out a name, begging for a response from anyone who had run across him.

Awaiting us at the station was a long line of cattle cars surrounded by searchlights and a tangle of barbed wire; there was also a crowd of friends and relatives whom kind people had informed of the transport. Among those seeing us off was my mother.

The loading began. Forty people were herded into each car. At last the loading was finished. Amazingly enough, the people outside had managed to persuade the guard commander some to accept hastily assembled food parcels for the prisoners, and there was a parcel for me as well. On the third day the prison train arrived at our destination, Mundybash Station in Kemerovo Oblast. Once again I was in the Akhputin Ninth Punishment Section of the NKVD Siblag, but now it had been renamed NKVD Gorshorlag and it had a new camp administration.

The head of the camp, Makarov, and his deputy, A. Mosevich, met the contingent at the transport camp. Passing through the ranks of fresh reinforcements he gave a brief, unusual speech to the new arrivals:

"Comrades! You have arrived at the construction site of a railway line to the iron ore deposits at the taiga settlement of Tashtagol. Working conditions are very harsh, but I trust that you will be able to overcome these difficulties and, once you've built the line, to earn early release. Now you'll be assigned to construction columns and taken to your future places of work."

Later on, I learned that a number of the camp bosses of Gorshorlag—former members of the Leningrad NKVD, including Makarov and Mosevich—had served time in the camps of Kolyma in connection with Kirov's murder. Their former ranks were restored when they were released, along with the right to work only within the Gulag and the GULZhDS (Main Administration of Railway Construction Camps).

They assigned me to Column 5 at Kilometer 25 (run by Ignatchenko). When we arrived there I was summoned to the Registration and Distribution Office, where its head and the planner Malinovsky (both *zeks*) were making up the brigades.

"Were you in the Komsomol?" they asked.

"I was at one time."

"Can I put you down as foreman?"

I tried to make excuses, saying that I knew nothing about the work.

"Doesn't matter, we'll teach you. Tomorrow morning go out with the brigade when it forms up at the camp gate. After a bit of instruction on the details of the job you'll have your mandate: don't let the brigade down; keep your mates fed."

I went back to the barracks to meet the brigade. Overall, they were an able-bodied lot. Two of them were frail. I decided to assign one to keep count of the wheelbarrow loads, and the other to repair the wheelbarrow ramps. But the brawny fellows—in particular, two Kazakh brothers, Bupe and Sadvokas Tulegenov—formed the backbone of the brigade.

The barracks were reasonably sound, not like the tents of Siblag. There were two rows of two-tiered bunks with a broad passageway and a long table between them. Unfortunately, there were no railway workers among the new arrivals. They had all been separated from us nonprofessionals back at the transit camp and had been assigned to the track-laying column.

Not one of the fellows in my brigade knew anything about building a roadbed. Well, what would be, would be . . .

I met a few people I had known in Siblag and asked them what had happened to the prisoners who had been here before. All those capable of work were transported to Kolyma, while the weak—the sick and elderly invalids along with those on a list sent by Moscow—were taken to a little gully at Kilometer 15 of the railway and shot. (And thus, I was lucky enough to survive thanks to the summons to Omsk when my "case" was reexamined.)

The next morning, escorted by rifleman Dasov, I went off to our assigned site with the brigade. The scenery was magnificent. We were surrounded by the Altai hills covered with evergreens. In the valley below roared the little alpine Mundybash River. Walking along mountain paths, we reached our construction site, a fill on a rocky hillside. The rate-setter, Roman Dolinsky, a former member of the Political Directorate of the Belorussian Military District, came up and showed us the direction to fill along the hillside, and work began in earnest.

I have to say that there was exemplary order in this camp. Makarov kept a very tight grip on the warders and guards and would tolerate no abuse of prisoners. All the criminals were held under special security in Column 15, and the key positions in the columns were held by Article 58ers, which eliminated thievery in the supply sheds and the kitchen.

When we formed up to march to work the work superintendents did not have to endure being cursed by the camp bosses, and the work assignment clerks did not thrash the "goners" with sticks. The assembly took place peacefully, without any fuss.

The foreman, Misha Pogonaichenko, a nonpolitical, provided the rocky construction site with a portable furnace and anvil so that we could put the dull crowbars and spades into shape on site and not have to drag them back to the camp blacksmith. Work went on in full swing. When we finished one section our brigade moved off to the next.

One fine day I was called in to see the head of the column, who told me that we were getting a hundred criminals from the Strict Discipline Barracks. These were people who had always refused to work, and he was transferring this brigade to me, with a promise that he would expand the work area and place a cordon of guards around it.

The new men were all very emaciated. They had been living on punishment rations for six months, but they firmly maintained their camp precepts: "If you eat, you'll sweat; if you work, you'll freeze"; "What you can do today, put off until tomorrow"; "Work's not a wolf, it won't run off to the forest." Their basic precept was "Horses croak from working."

So that was the sort of crowd I had on the construction site.

For the first three days they all just lay about as if they were at the beach, soaking up the sun. The planner and the rate-setter had agreed that I could put them in for Stakhanovite rations. Five days later I asked their brigadier, Sasha Stroganov:

"Your people are going to have get busy, even if they only do a little. Don't put me in a spot with the bosses. Get them at least to move small loads in the wheelbarrows. I can't go on forever padding rations to feed you!"

I don't know what Stroganov said to them back in the barracks, but the next day there was a line of wheelbarrows, not full ones to be sure, and the embankment was being filled.

How they covered me with abuse! I'd never heard cursing like that in my life.

"Listen, boss!" they would shout. "You'd better watch yourself. One day a crowbar might fall on you."

Dolinsky, who heard this, gave me some advice: "Why are you pussy-footing around with them? 'Would you mind,' 'Please.' They don't understand those words. This isn't a school for young ladies. You have to throw the same abuse right back at them, like a real camp veteran!"

Manners were set aside, and Stroganov's men gradually began to be drawn into the general tempo of the work and even became one of the better brigades. At a gathering of shock workers, the brigade was awarded wheelbarrows with ball bearings.

We spent a few months at Column 12, and once the basic work of building the roadbed was finished, in August 1938, some of the personnel and the administrative and technical staff were transferred to Tashtagol, the final section. This was Kilometer 95 of the future railway, in Column 14. The head of the column was Bublik, a prisoner; the work superintendent was another prisoner, Vasily Kuznetsov.

At the same time, an order went around the camp that the detached camp sectors (that was what the columns were now called) would shift to self-provisioning. All of the Gulag salted beef that came to feed the *zeks* would now be turned over to the sausage factory in Temirtau, and the money earned from its sale would be used to buy food for the prisoners from the local population, the Shortsy. This was yak meat, which cost one-seventh as much as the Gulag salted beef.

Little shops opened in the detached camp sectors and small cafeterias were set up. (In Detached Camp 14 there was a cafeteria whose cook could, for a fee, prepare any dish you ordered. Vasily Shteingart, a former chef from the Metropole Restaurant in Moscow, ran it.) Engineering and technical workers received a supplementary "administrative-command" ration that Berman had introduced when he ran BAMlag.

People coming from other camps marveled at our camp sector, saying, "You've got a proper summer resort here."

Bublik ordered the cook, the accounts clerk, and the supply unit to provide soup that a spoon would stand up in.

Everyone was dreaming that they would soon be freed. Instructions about presenting candidates for early release appeared on the door of the Registration and Distribution Office. It seemed that some sort of review of cases was in progress, and a few people were released. We all thought that the wave of repressions was subsiding. Yezhov was dismissed, but it turned out that the mechanism of oppression kept running.

In the spring of 1939 a new transport from Belorussia arrived. The inhabitants of the town of Orsha had, to a man, been accused of spying for Poland and planning to sabotage the bridge on the Dnieper.

Only one man from the newly arrived contingent, the former chairman of the oblast trade unions, Anis, turned out to be a "Latvian spy," and he testified during his investigation that he had already blown up the bridge on the Dnieper. The next day Anis was viciously beaten by the interrogator for giving false testimony, but he continued to insist on his version. Just the same, he was sentenced by a Troika to ten years in the camps.

The camp bosses were hurrying to finish the railway lines by the deadline. The brigades worked within a cordon of guards. Every worker had a meter of frontage. Explosions resounded along the rocky sections of the line—there was no scrimping on the ammonal. People worked like lions. Everyone wanted to earn an early release.

I was transferred to the Topographic Section, where I worked in the office. This is how it happened. Working with the brigade one time, I was restoring the axis of the line on our site; it was difficult to maintain the axis in the excavations while moving earth only with wheelbarrows and rakes. I made up a rope twenty meters long using the laces from old bast shoes (our footwear), and with the help of stakes marked in decimeters I laid out the curve.

I didn't notice a group of bosses that had come up and were standing behind me.

"Are you a surveyor?" a voice said.

I turned around and saw the head of construction and his assistants, the head of the Topographic Section, V. A. Shevchenko, and the head of the Civil Installations, D. I. Chechelnitsky.

"I'm just the foreman. I'm laying out the curve so as not to overfill the cutting."

"And what's the surveyor doing?"

"He's working at another site."

They asked my name again and then left.

That evening I was summoned to the head of the Registration and Distribution Office.

"I have an order to put you in the Topographic Section. You'll go to work there tomorrow."

The topographic group stayed inside the camp zone, in a spacious room where they both worked and slept.

The senior surveyor was Pavel Pobezhimov, a former cadet in a military academy who had a five-year sentence for agitation: he had asked a political instructor at a meeting, "Is it true that Trotsky was a good public speaker?"

The transit man, Mikhail Smolkin, had been a senior lieutenant in the NKVD guard troops. He had happened to tell a political instructor of his doubts about the degree of guilt of the people he escorted on transports. The price of his doubts was Article 58 with a five-year term.

And so I settled into this little cabin and set about working at calculations and drawings.

Among the "pleiade" of topographers in Detached Camp 15 was one Kostya Muzykin, convicted under Article 59, subpara 3 (Banditism). A most unassuming fellow, he did nothing to warrant the charge under which he had been imprisoned, even though he was living in a camp that had gathered in the whole criminal elite, along with some Chinese from the army of General Ma who had been pressed across our border by the Japanese. A student from Kharkov, he and two classmates had been completing their practical training by making a topographical survey in the Pamir Range close to our border. Their whole group was kidnapped by the Basmachi—Moslem anti-Bolshevik guerrillas—and carried off to Afghanistan. The Basmachi, expecting a substantial ransom, kept them imprisoned in a pit for a time until a chance event came to their rescue. One of his guards had a broken rifle, and Kostya managed to fix it. News of this technical expert reached the *Kurbashi,* the local commander. People in the East have great respect for such technicians, and the *Kurbashi* decided to hand over his captives to the ruler of Afghanistan, Amanulla-khan, as a gift.

Amanulla-khan and his wife Sarie had just come back from a long trip to Europe, and they had also spent some time in the Soviet Union. He was determined to introduce some reforms in Afghanistan and give his country a form of government closer to European models. He reorganized the army and ordered women to abandon the chador, something that particularly upset orthodox Moslems.

The khan had enlisted a bodyguard of Europeans, and Muzykin and his companions in misfortune were added to their numbers. A coup organized by Kurdish tribes led by Bachai Sakao forced Amanulla-khan to flee. All those in his closest circle managed to go into hiding, while Kostya Muzykin and his comrades set off for the Soviet Union. They were detained when crossing the border and later convicted as Basmachi.

Some time later, the head of the Topographic Section (I have forgotten his name), a senior lieutenant, paid a visit to the camp where Kostya was being held. He found Kostya cleaning a theodolite. Looking at the scattered array of parts of the instrument, he angrily demanded to know how Kostya dared delve into high-precision optics without permission.

"There was a bit of trouble," Kostya replied. "The fellow carrying the instrument tripped and fell, dropped the theodolite, and bent the optical axis of the tube. But I've straightened it out by using a birch log and tapping it gently with a hammer."

"Why hasn't there been a report on this? Why wasn't it brought to my attention?" the topographic chief continued to storm.

He sent a report to the head of construction, Makarov, about the disgraceful way the surveyor had cared for his instrument.

As soon as Makarov read the report he shipped that same senior lieutenant to the Personnel Department of the Gulag Railway Construction Administration, and replaced him with an ex-prisoner, Vladimir Shevchenko, who had served out his five-year sentence and stayed in the camp system as a free worker.

The nearness of the freedom promised by the camp bosses led the workers to redouble their efforts. Brigades refused to leave the construction site, and the exhausted guards on the site had to be replaced by fresh "screws."

And so in 1940, for Red Army Day, a telegram flew off to Moscow to announce the completion of the railway line, although the bridge over the Kondoma River to the ore deposits was far from finished. Newspaper correspondents from the capital arrived for the opening ceremony, along with movie cameramen and a whole collection of people from the upper echelon of the Gulag, GULZhDS, and the People's Commissariats of Transportation and Ferrous Metallurgy.

During the night, three gondola cars had been loaded with ore carried across the Kondoma by horse-drawn wagons. In the morning, to the accompaniment of whirring movie cameras, the camp administration finished loading the gondolas with a few pieces of ore that had been specially left for them. A locomotive drew up, and to the thunder of a salute organized by the head of the blasting crew, Karpov, the trainload of ore (three cars full) moved off to the enrichment plant in Temirtau. The newspapers loudly celebrated the completion of the railway line as "a great feat of construction by the Komsomol."

The basic earthmoving had been done. What remained was finishing the bridge, some shoring up, and the ballasting of the line. The camp did not get much financial return for this work. We had to come up with a way to show more work was being done. The head of construction told the topographers who had gathered for a meeting with the camp administration:

"Come on, you fakeographers, figure out something so we can feed our people. We've already moved all the earth we need."

We topographers did, and for nearly a year the camp was supported by selling cubic meters of nothing, approved and properly signed off by inspectors from the Transport and Ferrous Metallurgy Commissariats.

Most accommodating was the inspector from the Ferrous Metallurgy Commissariat, Fyodor Liutov, who willingly signed what sometimes were completely faked reports on invisible work. When signing certifications for probing collapsed embankments, he would sigh and say, "What's to be done? We can't leave the camp without funds, and we can't leave the workers without the bread they've earned."

"Godfathers" began prowling around our camp regularly. A frequent visitor was the security officer, "Uncle Vasya" Shiriaev, who was sounding out the mood of the inmates. His every appearance in our camp set everyone atremble, from the humblest *zek* to the head of the detached camp, Senior Lieutenant Chuprin, the replacement for Bublik, who had been released.

"Somewhere in our camp there's a real son of a bitch," Chuprin complained as he dropped by our cabin. "Someone's squealed on me. They think I'm using *zeks* to repair my apartment, doing the plastering and whitewashing. And I'm supposed to have used camp horses to go to Spassk on personal business! Any idea who might have passed that on to the Security Department?"

We were puzzled ourselves. Not long before they had called in the transit man Smolkin, wanting to know what we were talking about among ourselves. And now they were shaking down the barracks of the admin and technical personnel.

The camp began to resemble a turned-up anthill. Each one suspected the other of "rapping"—being the stool pigeon. In the barracks one day Mitya Pavlovsky, the monitoring foreman, said, "Well, now I know who's doing all the rapping around here . . ."

"Who?" asked the men in the barracks, suddenly freezing.

"It's the riveters on the Kondoma bridge, lads, they've been rapping out there for a long time!"

But the real squealer was caught red-handed (I will not mention his name because his children are still alive). A package addressed to the head of the Security Section was found by chance in his desk, and it contained slanderous fabrications about a number of admin and technical personnel and free workers.

The whole camp learned about the slander, and Senior Lieutenant Chuprin ordered the informer to be put on general labor and sent to the punishment cell; his things were thrown out of the barracks.

A few days later the informer was sent back to the headquarters staff column.

Chapter Twelve
Building the Konosha–Kotlas Railway

Rumors circulated that NKVD Gorshorlag was to be closed down and its inhabitants handed over to NKVD Siblag to do finishing work. Makarov would be transferred to a new construction project. He would be allowed to take with him fifty prisoners from the administrative team and a few construction brigades.

In the spring of 1941, our topographic group was transferred to the headquarters staff column, and we were loaded onto a waiting train. We went north, accompanied by our guards. We stopped in Omsk to go to the bathhouse. Some of the prisoners were taken off in Konosha, the rest of us went on to Velsk, where we finally disembarked.

We heard the command: "Put all your hand luggage on the sleds; it's not far, and we'll go on foot."

The trip turned out to be some seventy kilometers, all on foot. There was no road, and we went through the forest following the tracks of the train of sleds that had left before us with all our belongings. It was late at night when, barely able to drag our feet, we managed to limp up to three tents pitched near a pine tree; there was a blaze on the tree marked "Column 5." Two tents were for the prisoners, one for the guards. There was taiga all around, and food was cooked in a huge kettle over a bonfire. The bread, dumped off earlier, had frozen, and a single two-kilogram loaf was shared between two men.

The first task was to build the camp zone, with guard towers and barracks for the guards; inside the zone was a kitchen, dining hall, bathhouse, and an infirmary.

The admin and technical personnel set about building a plank road. On March 18, as I can recall, we grew so warm at our work that we were able to take off our padded jackets. Sweaty and overheated, we stopped for a smoke. I was a bit slow putting my jacket back on, and the next day my temperature soared. I was sent to the infirmary at the future Shangaly Station with pneumonia.

The hospital was in tents. There were no individual bunks, just sleeping platforms made of rails, and all the patients, infectious and noninfectious, lay mixed together. There were no medicines apart from pills for vitamin deficiency. The doctors were from the Kremlin Hospital; they had been convicted as part of the case of Pletnev, the chief surgeon of the hospital who had gone through the trial of the Trotskyite-Zinoviev opposition. The chief surgeon here was an army medical officer, Captain Logachev. Among the nurses was the writer Galina Serebriakova.

There were very many patients here with dysentery; they had come from the timber-cutting camp, Kulailag, which had become part of Sevdvinlag.

Every day several men departed this world. There was even a case of a completely healthy criminal who somehow had managed to persuade a medical assistant to give him an admission slip to the infirmary to take a rest; he died five days later, having come down with dysentery.

My youth won out, though: the carotene pills helped, and gradually I began to recover. I had some codeine pills back at the column for my cough, and I began asking to be discharged.

I couldn't recognize the column when I returned. The zone was already fenced off, barracks were built, there were guard towers at the corners, and it was full of people. They had shifted two camps from the Soroka–Obozersky railway branch line (NKVD Soroklag) and some camps from Medvezhegorsk to our site. The plank road linking us with the world outside was already finished. I. I. Kolomeitsev, a prisoner from Soroklag, had been appointed commander of Column 5. No one knew what his job had been before prison, but evidently he had been a big boss. Even the commander of the guard platoon would not enter his office without knocking. He lived outside the zone, took his meals at the free workers' dining room and, it seems, wasn't a bad fellow.

I didn't spend long at Column 5. Through May and the beginning of June I managed to rebuild the route over a six-kilometer sector and laid the profiles of arcs on sections where there were embankments. When I ran across old-timers from Velsk at work I would try to find out the latest news. But in this godforsaken wilderness it was impossible to find out anything. We didn't get newspapers, there was no telephone or radio, yet the old-timers all stubbornly said the same thing:

"Just watch, lad, there's bound to be a war. Look at all the crows that have come; and the women have started in whoring . . . That's a sure and certain sign; it was just the same before the German war."

The plank road really was dotted with crows picking out grubs of the bark beetle.

CHAPTER THIRTEEN

The War Years

June 22 came. Germany attacked the Soviet Union. I was ready to go to work but they didn't let me. They took away my pass and told me to collect my belongings quickly and, along with the transit man Peterson, an Estonian from Niandom Station, I was sent under guard to Column 7, where a "fragrant bouquet of enemies of the people" had already been gathered in from all the nearby columns. There was Faina Bliumkin-Braun, sister of the Chekist Bliumkin who had assassinated the German ambassador, Count Mirbach; two representatives of the Hungarian section of the Comintern, the section secretary Matyas and another young man whose name I can't recall; General Todorsky; a Belgian citizen, de Klerk; Astakhova, wife of a former staff member in the Soviet embassy in Germany; Mironenko, married to the daughter of the Czech premier Masaryk, something that gave cause for him to be charged with espionage; Baroness Takke-Doloresco, a Romanian; a mechanical engineer named Kopf, a twenty-five-year-old American who had been assembling the American machinery at one of our factories; Poles, Estonians, Lithuanians, Latvians, German nationals—people from every corner of Europe!

We were all on "guaranteed rations," i.e., not dependent on work quotas. In fact, we were not taken out to work. Everyone was in an agony of expectation of the unknown. Could they have gathered us here to shoot us all without leaving any obituaries?

Two months passed in this way.

During this time the construction site of the Konosha–Kotlas Railway had been included within the zone of the front and was under military jurisdiction. Work on the line slowed, and the camp prepared for possible evacuation. But Moscow decided otherwise, and work resumed.

I went back to Column 5 to watch over the construction of a section of roadbed. But it had become more complicated to go to work outside the zone. Now I was taken out by a guard with a rifle.

On one of these excursions I met Makarov and his staff on the railway line. When he recognized me, he came up, greeted me, and told the others, "Here's another one of our crew from Gorshorlag."

"How's the job going?" he asked. Then he noticed the guard and asked, surprised, "And who's this fellow?"

"He's my personal bodyguard, and he's going to defend me in case there's a landing by airborne troops," I replied.

Makarov called the head of the camp guards and asked, "What salary is that rifleman getting?"

"Seven hundred rubles," was the reply.

"Listen, I'll transfer that much to you. Now order the immediate issue of a pass for Boldyrev."

Thereafter I was able to go to work without a guard.

The camp sections were filling up with fresh arrivals. There were the "singletons," people with one-year sentences under the new regulations on being late for work; there were people from construction battalions, prisoners of war, and interned Poles, "special migrants" like the Volga Germans—every sort of wretched folk came to these parts!

With the coming of the first frosts we got busy in areas where no ground work had been done, uprooting stumps and laying down branch lines with the rails right on the earth. Where we had to cross a stream we laid down stacks of railway ties to make temporary bridges. Toward the end of 1941 the first trains carrying wounded soldiers began passing through.

The food situation in the camp grew worse with every day. The bread in the ration became lighter and the food norms were lowered. Bread was baked with additives like oil cake, vegetable peelings, and chaff, all the so-called sweepings. The "guaranteed norm" of bread dropped to four hundred grams. The prisoner-bookkeeper, in the hope of saving meat, fats, and cereals, gave instructions to replace them all with flour. In place of soup and porridge they cooked a swill from two ingredients, water and flour; it was something like paste. People gradually began to be transformed into "goners," and cases of scurvy appeared.

The first to die were the *ukazniki,* those sentenced under special ukases; they had served only a small part of their time. They worked at only half-strength. They would root through the rubbish pits, picking out potato peelings and gradually being transformed into walking skeletons until they died from emaciation. Their corpses would be carted into the zone after work and piled in a storeroom attached to the barracks so that the next morning, after we had gone to work, they could be taken out to the cemetery. Each corpse had a small plywood label with the requisite information tied to the foot.

At the guardhouse the duty sentry would thrust a sharpened metal rod through each corpse to ensure that no living person was being taken out.

The long-termers from Gorshorlag turned out to be the hardiest. They would not surrender their presence of mind, lose heart and courage. The iron law for every long-termer was to survive at any price and live to see the day of liberation.

It was certainly easier for me. I could go about my work without a guard following me. The *zek* without a guard is an imitation free man, a bogus citizen of his country, something like a hobbled horse without a herder. He can go off to the free settlement, visit the shop and the club. So long as he doesn't run into a security officer.

When I left the zone I always had the opportunity to pick some mushrooms and berries. People from my former crew, who had been allowed to work without guards on the basis of my guarantee and who then transferred from the Topographic Section to the bakery, were able to keep me supplied with a bit of bread despite all the strict rules about bread consumption.

In the winter, at the end of 1941, instructions came to send me to Kotlas to lay out the axis for a bridge across the Northern Dvina River. It was a very harsh winter. The temperature would often sink to minus fifty degrees. As was the practice in transports between construction sites, I set off on the long journey on foot, my pass for working without a guard in my pocket and a guard closely following me.

We walked along the roadbed, past the toiling brigades, and stopping only to warm ourselves at large bonfires. Along the way my feet became frozen and I was sent back to Column 5.

"Third-degree frostbite," was the verdict of the medical assistant.

The head of the medical office of Section 3 of Sevdvinlag, the doctor Major Ter-Masevosian, arrived at the column. When he saw my blackened feet he gave instructions to have me sent to Shangal Field Hospital, where they planned to amputate my gangrenous feet; I flatly refused.

"Well, you'll have to cure yourself then," he said as he left.

I spent a month in bed in my little cabin. The column's medical assistant and two young nurses who had come here for their practical training and had been trapped by the war looked after me.

Makarov's arrival brought some improvement in the prisoners' food. The bookkeeper who had been cutting back on food supplies (who was also an informer for the security officer Sushko) was removed from his post and sent out on general labor; later he was tried and got a "second helping"—ten more years. The food improved, and a barrel of salted *khamsa,* a small White Sea fish, was placed by the mess hall. We could take as much of it as we wanted.

The medical assistant managed to come up with some anti-scurvy medicine (dried peas and fish oil), and the column was declared a Sanitary and Nutrition Point—a facility for badly weakened prisoners.

In February 1942 a very senior official visited our road project—the head of the Gulag himself, the builder of the White Sea Canal, Frenkel. He ordered that the workers on the railway line each be given a hundred grams of alcohol along with little pies, pirogi, that the prisoners, since the time of the Baikal–Amur Railway project, had named "Berman slippers."

Frenkel issued an order: "Give me a list of the best workers for early release."

There were some star workers in our column: the digger Zavgorodny, a powerful, broad-shouldered peasant who could fulfill four or five norms in a day. He was presented to Frenkel and on the same day was freed, despite his ten-year sentence for counterrevolutionary activity.

Former military people began leaving the camp. They went straight to the front as soon as they were let out. Recruiting officers came from the front with offers to nonpoliticals to volunteer for service. And people did leave most willingly.

My petitions to the Procuracy of the USSR and to Voroshilov and Kalinin to volunteer for service in the front line remained unanswered.

Polish prisoners—interned residents of Polish towns to whom we had extended our "brotherly hand" in 1939—began leaving to join the Polish army of General Anders that was being formed. Elderly bearded fellows from Arkhangelsk now staffed the guard towers of the camp, replacing the young soldiers who had been called up to defend the Motherland. More than once I witnessed scenes like this: some poor camp "candlewick" would crawl under the barbed wire of the inner zone to pick up a cigarette butt under the guard tower. Instead of the shout, "Stop or I'll shoot!" you would hear the commonplace words, "Listen, lad, don't go crawling under the wire. The boss will be after you if he sees."

The troops guarding the brigades were not the same as they once were. They spent most of their time outside their towers. Often a soldier would sit down in the middle of the brigade, announce a smoke break, and even treat the workers to some homegrown tobacco from his pouch.

"They're going to let you out soon, they need people on the front. Maybe we'll even have to serve under you," they would often say.

The prison regime changed visibly. Yet there still were those who tried to preserve the traditions of the tough regime that had prevailed inside the camps. These were the security officer and his helpers, the "screws"—the warders who were responsible for camp informers.

Barchuk, Bardakov, and Tretiak were particularly noted for their zeal. The latter, while I and the brigade escort were watching, whipped off prisoner Boboshin's cap and tossed it into the bushes, ordering him to pick it up. The dimwitted Boboshin went after his cap and was killed by a shot in the back of the neck for attempting to escape. Tretiak earned ten days' leave for this exploit.

Camp "cases" were put together, charging people with defeatist attitudes. The "cases" were concocted by informers, and the outcome was never in doubt: one person would be shot, another would get an additional sentence.

Pobezhimov, a surveyor from the Kotlas camp section, was sentenced to be shot in this way (the sentence was later changed to a longer term in prison). I met him in the Shangal infirmary; he had suffered a great deal of emotional damage. In 1943 a medical commission had him released under Article 458 of the Criminal Procedural Code. He worked in the camp for a time and then was sent to the front. There another medical commission pronounced him unfit for service and he was released.

New transports were filling the camp. One new arrival on a prison train was the former head of the NKVD of the Stalin Region of Moscow, Ivan Stukov (the son of an Old Bolshevik who had also worked for the NKVD). There was Mitrofan Ivanov, superintendent of maintenance of the Kremlin apartments; Malbakhov, a prosecutor responsible for surveillance; and the Moscow prosecutor Tsvirko-Golytsky, sentenced to a five-year term by a Special Board of Moscow's MVD troops for dereliction of duty.

Stukov was immediately appointed head of the column at Podiuga Station; Ivanov became work superintendent in the staff column; the prosecutors Tsvirko-Golytsky and Malbakhov were sent to Column 9 at Ileza Station.

Prosecutor Malbakhov was very unhappy about the arbitrary way the column was being run and launched a war against the security guards responsible for this lawlessness. He was sent to the punishment cell and when he was released he refused to work, demanding to see a prosecutor. The head of the Security Section, Sushko, had him brought before a tribunal. After getting a "second helping" of ten years, Malbakhov found a way to send a petition to Moscow through the free workers. It was 1943, and the political climate was changing, as was the prison regime. A commission arrived from Moscow, questioned the prisoners, and went back to Moscow, taking Malbakhov with them. Sushko was transferred to Vorkuta, but on the way there he was arrested, tried, and, according to rumor, was shot.

In the second half of 1943 Stukov was released. He told me that he was expecting to be dropped into a detachment of partisans operating deep in the German rear. His worried look clearly conveyed his state of mind: it was a case of out of the frying pan and into the fire.

The attitude of the security guards to the prisoners moderated as well. The prison regime began to relax noticeably, and one day the guards invited the *zeks* to a general meeting.

The chief of the security guard political section gave a report on the international situation and told us what was happening on our front lines; then he asked us to donate money to a defense fund. Both the free workers and the *zeks* responded enthusiastically to this patriotic call. Almost every *zek* had some money in the so-called Release Fund, and this money was donated to the country.

All the young prisoners who were released, no matter what they had been charged with, were sent to punishment battalions at the front—to Rokossovsky's army. Rokossovsky himself had been serving his sentence in these same northern areas until 1940 and, as I heard, ran the bathhouse at Izhma Station on the Kotlas–Vorkuta Railway.

A new draft of Poles was sent to the Second Polish Army of Colonel Berling. All those who remained after the last draft were sent, and they even accepted Russians with Polish last names.

Prince Sviatopolk-Mirsky, now a ragged camp "candlewick," was brought in from somewhere along the Vorkuta line. They hastily made him a decent suit out of dark blue officers' material, and when he had assumed a normal appearance he was handed over to members of the Polish consulate in Kotlas.

The surveyor from Podiuga Station (the Konosha-Velsk camp section) also went to the front. So as not to leave the camp section stripped bare and without technical supervision, the head of the camp assigned me to replace him and monitor the work on the project. Thus the responsibilities resting on my shoulders had grown to some 160 kilometers of the line, and I became a "nomad."

At Ust-Shonosha Station, where the *zek* Lunev was head of the column and work superintendent, I inspected the lines around the station that had been built on an arc with a 600-meter radius. They seemed to be squeezed together and had been laid down crooked. I checked the centers of the switches on the western mouth and found that eighteen of them had not been laid down according to the plan. I reported this to Lunev and gave him my conclusion: all the switches on the western mouth had to be installed as per the plan. Their centers had to be shifted from one to one-and-a-half meters westward. Lunev protested at once: "It was the surveyor who laid these out!"

How can you prove anything different? The surveyor is at the front, Lunev is here, and he'll answer for it. The security officer is always looking for some pretext to justify his job. Someone will inform . . . so Lunev covered himself.

"Get the brigade moving the switches and put it down as ballasting. I can always find a way to cover up the extra cubic meters."

The work on moving the switches was done. The switching tracks and the radial lines at the station now looked smooth. And then trouble came along. The head of the PRO (the Production Section), Engineer Major Vologdin, paid a surprise visit. He noted the line workers who were installing the last switch according to plan and asked Lunev to inform the Control and Planning Section by intercom that they credit three hundred thousand rubles for the eighteen switches that had been installed.

Lunev confessed that he had already submitted that sum earlier, and now he was only moving the switches to their proper places on instructions of the engineer.

"What? Is some *zek* running things here?" Vologdin flew into a rage. "Get on the intercom and find out where he is immediately. I want him in my office tomorrow!"

People in the administration called Vologdin's office "the steam bath." Those summoned to his office would quickly adjust their tunics, knock politely on his door with the knuckle of their index finger, and in an obsequious voice ask permission to enter. Often, after a routine dressing-down, people would fly out of his office like a shot, wild-eyed and distraught.

And so it was my turn to face the "dreaded eyes" of the big boss. I opened the door, announced myself, and explained why the switches had to be moved on lines that had already been laid; but Vologdin, his voice breaking into a falsetto, hurled a torrent of threats at me:

"I'll have you tried on charges! You're a wrecker! You'll be in front of a tribunal!"

These threats seemed absurd to me. I had grown so accustomed to the life of a *zek* that I could no longer imagine people living and working in freedom without warders or guards.

"Fine," I told him. "I'll go to prison, but you'll be sitting in the prisoner's box next to me."

It seemed to me that even the shoulder boards on Major Vologdin's tunic stood on end with rage. Fists raised, he jumped from behind his desk, seized the telephone, and hurled it to the floor.

"Get out!" he shouted, stamping his foot. "Get out of my office! You're on general labor! Off to the shithouse (the punishment cells, *N.B.*) with you!"

What was I to do? Fate had turned its back on me. I stayed in the headquarters column waiting for my bitter lot to be determined. Days passed, and I was not sent to the punishment cells as one under investigation, nor was I assigned to the general labor brigade; and my pass for traveling without a guard was not taken away. A week later I was called in to see the deputy head of the Production Section, Yuvenitsky.

"You're going to work on a bridge we're building across the Yerga River. It will eliminate the Yerga bypass. Whatever you do, make sure you use the existing piers for the bridge, no matter what changes you have to make to the axis of the line. The axis of the bridge has to use the piers that are already there."

The prehistory of this project is as follows: soldiers from a construction battalion had worked on the bridge and its approaches. They lived even worse than the prisoners. Hungry, in ragged uniforms that should have been written off long ago and threadbare overcoats with charred skirts, these unfortunates labored at their task. Their only crime was that they had been collected from among the "special settlers"—people of German nationality or Baptists exiled for their religious convictions. They had managed to raise a pier on the riverbank and lay the foundations for the other pier and for two intermediate ones. The approaches to the bridge had been fully laid.

The surveyor who had been working on the bridge went off to the front, and one of the free workers (whom I won't name) arrived; by some incomprehensible method he determined that the bridge was being built thirty-four centimeters off the planned axis.

The camp bosses went into shock. There was a war on, and now an emergency like this! There would be an investigation, a trial, and under the laws of wartime military justice, the firing squad was a certainty!

Construction of the bridge was temporarily halted and the construction battalion transferred to the Kotlas bridging factory. The project remained under suspension for about a year, but the date for handing over the line to the Railway Commissariat was drawing near. They had to find some way out of the situation, and I was sent to scout out the site.

I reestablished the route of the railway line, carefully marked out the curve, since the bridge was located on an arc with a 2,000-meter radius, and established that the bridge piers were in their proper places. I passed on the news to the bosses via the intercom, and a few hours later a train arrived with two bridge bays and a bridging machine, workers, and equipment.

We unloaded the concrete mixer, a trough, a portable generator, electric motors, and some hoists. The next day the work was in full swing. In three months we had finished building the piers and had pushed out a spanning structure made by the Kotlas bridging factory from steel alloy taken from the framework of the disassembled House of Soviets. (That building had been begun but had been stopped on account of the war. The framework was disassembled and used for military purposes and for bridging on the Konosha–Kotlas railway line that was being built.)

By November 7, 1944, the bridge was handed over, ahead of schedule, to the Railway Commissariat. The camp administration recommended everyone who had helped build it for early release.

Arkhangel Oblast. A land of marshes and forests with scarcely any roads. To get into the remoter areas one had to go either on foot or by a horse-drawn travois. By vehicle one could go only from Velsk to Kotlas on the plank road along the railway line that was under construction.

In the taiga there were scattered settlements of descendants of Novgorod Old Believers who had fled from the oppression of Tsar Peter I. The bearded old men who lived in such remote villages were very unhappy about the building of the railway.

"They want to colonize us with their iron road," they would say of the construction workers. "They built a railway that will bring in some bosses to squeeze taxes out of us. Till now, lad, we used to go to Konosha on foot and buy our peace and quiet with money, but now the tax inspectors come along, and it's 'Give us a chicken. Give us some eggs.' Before that the bosses left us alone."

It was hardly a land of milk and honey. There was little land suitable for cultivation. There was a local saying, "There's no misfortune mixing pigweed in the bread; without misfortune there'd be neither bread nor pigweed." They planted peas and potatoes—goodness knows what else they lived on. They raised a few cattle. In this taiga wilderness they sometimes managed to get potatoes by trading for clothing.

The mother of N. D. Kuznetsov, the commander in chief of the navy, was a humble schoolteacher who lived on her own in the settlement of Sum-Posad.

CHAPTER FOURTEEN

The Early Postwar Years

At last the long awaited Victory Day arrived! They tested the radio links in the camp barracks and hung up loudspeakers.

Levitan's powerful voice solemnly announced the end of the war and Germany's complete capitulation. I can't describe how happy the prisoners were. The rejoicing was beyond measure. Joy in the victory and hopes of the possibility of imminent release seized everyone. Even the *urki,* who had once insisted that "It's all the same for us who's in power, Stalin or Hitler, we'll go on thieving just the same"—even they rejoiced.

"Our boys have done it, mates!"

I didn't manage to get past the guardhouse before falling in with a band of railway workers celebrating Victory Day, and when I got back to the guardhouse I was crawling on all fours. That day the guards did not drag drunken *zeks* coming back from work off to the cooler but simply suggested they go and sleep it off and keep out of the way of the warders.

Food rations improved. They began supplying us with food from Arkhangelsk that had come from America under Lend-Lease. There was tinned pork in food warehouses; our bread, baked from Lend-Lease flour, now had no additives; we were given fats—margarine, hydrogenated oil, lard—that had been in such short supply during the war. Transports of soldiers sentenced by military tribunals for various crimes, mainly looting, now began arriving in the camp. Things that had been overlooked in wartime on German territory were no longer overlooked after the victory. For example, the dashing Major Vasya Orlov, who had spent a good deal of time in punishment battalions, arrived in our camp. He had commanded a reconnaissance company relocated from Germany to Lithuania, where his men had shot a pig belonging to a Lithuanian.

"They wouldn't have bothered us about that in Germany," he complained bitterly, "But now in that lousy Lithuania I was hauled up in front of the tribunal."

Interned "civilian" Germans from the city of Schwiebus arrived; right behind them was a trainload of German prisoners and some Slovaks who had served in the German army. Vlasovites and *Polizei* with twenty-five-year terms came through, bound for Vorkuta. In short, the great resettlement of nations for the "grand construction" of the Stalin epoch was in progress.

The interned civilians and German prisoners of war were housed in vacant buildings and assigned to general camp labor. Prisoner of war brigades were headed by a *Zugführer* or brigadier who could speak Russian. Most of them had lived in German settlements near Odessa or were *Ostdeutsche* called up for service in the German army.

When the Germans wanted to ask some question of a Russian, be he a free worker or a prisoner, they had to address him as "Mister Rifleman," or "Mister Engineer"; they would stand at attention before the most wretched "goner." Prisoners were addressed as *Krieggefangenen.*

There was a paradoxical difference between the way war prisoners and the soldiers guarding them were fed. The war prisoners received rations in accordance with the accepted norm in Hitler's army: 1.2 kilos of white bread, sugar every day, butter, and some decent cooked food. The half-starved soldiers who guarded them received six hundred grams of bread-surrogate and the ration of soldiers serving in rear areas.

A year or two after the end of the war (1946–47) some of the Germans were sent to the GDR (East Germany). Those who remained were shifted to the reconstruction of cities destroyed during the war.

A state commission accepted the Konosha–Kotlas Railway for use. There remained the work of building railway barracks and depots, living accommodations, and other civil construction.

Sevdvinlag seemed about to be abolished. Makarov, the head of construction, was transferred to another construction site.

These were the years in which America and other Western powers entered the Cold War with the USSR. The BBC and the Voice of America filled the airwaves with accounts of slave labor in the Soviet Union. The United Nations was preparing to send a commission to inspect the living conditions of prisoners in northern camps.

In expectation of this commission the camp regime changed. The tiered wooden bunks in the barracks were taken away. Metal cots were installed, sets of bedding were issued, prisoners were given wages, with deductions for guard security, food, and equipment (some 90 percent of the wages), but the remainder was paid out. Food improved, and little shops where one could buy basic food items and tobacco appeared in the camp sectors. Medical services improved. The upper echelon of the camp hierarchy was removed: the camp was headed by Colonel Barabanov and his deputy, Bodridze (in Azhaev's novel *Far from Moscow* they appear under the names Baranov and Beridze), who replaced Colonel Kliuchkin.

Captain Andrei Mosevich put together a transport of construction workers who had been exempted from work under escort to go to Kemerovo. I was among them.

In the spring of 1946, on our arrival in Kemerovo, work was in full swing on building cottages for miners at the Severnaia mine.

I lived outside the zone in a barracks full of "special settlers" (that was what they called the contingent of former prisoners of war who had been sent to Kemerovo for special settlement for a term of six years). These were our own soldiers who had been captured by the Germans in 1941. They had been through all the camps of Germany, had escaped more than once, and had at last been sent to a death camp in Norway to build an underground factory for producing heavy water for the atom bomb. Their stories of the first months of the war were full of drama. German tank columns separated our forces into segments, but our lads kept on fighting while surrounded until they ran out of ammunition and grenades. When our troops were unarmed, hungry, and wounded, the Germans easily took them prisoner. When the Anglo-American forces landed in Norway the prisoners, working with Norwegian partisans, seized the camp and handed over all its staff to the Allies.

The Allies equipped the surviving prisoners in accordance with their rank, paid them an allowance for the whole time of their captivity, and tried to persuade them not to return to their Motherland, letting them know that they could expect nothing good to happen to them there.

Our own "patriot" agitators wasted no time in getting there as well, with posters saying "The Motherland awaits you." Officers painted rosy pictures for the prisoners, claiming that at home they would be greeted with flowers and honors. The Allies provided the departing Russians with a ship. Keeping in mind the voyage across the high latitudes to Arkhangelsk, the Allied command gave each soldier two camel-hair blankets. They were sent off with flowers and a band.

They arrived in Arkhangelsk on a rainy day. The wharf was deserted. A military detachment was drawn up not far away. An NKVD officer approached the passengers coming down the gangway and commanded:

"All of you put your belongings in one pile and form ranks."

They were immediately surrounded by machine gunners with dogs. A command rang out: "Remove the stars from your caps and shoulder straps! You're turncoats, traitors to the Motherland!" And with a cordon of guards they were marched from the wharf straight to prison.

They were moved from prison to prison for about a year. Interrogation followed interrogation. First by SMERSH, then by the NKVD: "Why did you surrender? Why didn't you shoot yourself?" After a year, they were informed of the decision of the Special Board of the NKVD: each was given a six-year term of special settlement, some in Kemerovo Oblast, others in the Krasnoyarsk Region.

The soldiers here had been placed at the disposal of the Kemerovo Housing Authority of the NKVD as a labor force. Every day someone among them was pulled out to face a tribunal and given twenty-five years in the camps "for betraying the Motherland." They were sent to Kolyma and to the Transpolar Region to build the Vorkuta–Labytnangi Railway (Project 501).

A wave of camp uprisings swept over the north in 1948. Soldiers with twenty-five-year sentences who had endured the terrible German concentration camps could not endure the horrors of Stalin's camps. In Labytnangi they managed to overpower their guards and, now armed, advanced through the marshlands toward Vorkuta under the command of an ex-prisoner, Colonel Voronin, in hopes of seizing the radio station and telling the whole world about the lawless acts taking place in the USSR. On their way, they disarmed the guards at the camp sectors they passed and freed the prisoners.

The camp garrisons, accustomed to shepherding unarmed people, could not put up any resistance. Regular troops were called out, with artillery, tanks, and airplanes. Vorkuta was already preparing for evacuation, but the reinforcements arrived in time and stopped the insurgents outside the city. They were strafed by aircraft, and those who survived were shipped to the mines.

This happened later, but now I'm talking about 1946. We were building "the government's gift to the miners"—well-appointed cottages costing twenty thousand rubles; this was to be paid off in installments over twenty years. This "gift" was presented to the miners for their selfless labor during the war.

The work was organized like a production line. A housing plant provided prefabricated sections of the houses, and they were assembled on prepared stone foundations, after which the water, heating, and electricity were connected.

I could barely manage to mark the outlines of the buildings and outdoor structures as per the plans before the excavators arrived, followed by stonemasons to lay the foundations and then the assemblers.

Japanese prisoners of war from the Kwantung Army transported the wood to the housing plant. The Japanese didn't consider themselves captives and would explain, "Mikado—ours, Stalin—yours," and clasping their hands in a handshake: "We help you."

There was a tense situation in the town. People said that a large gang called "the Black Cat" was running riot. Local stores were on the verge of collapse, having suffered one robbery after another. Soldiers with machine guns patrolled the streets, and the town was truly under siege. Our warder Bardakov fell victim: in broad daylight he was cracked over the head, stunned, and robbed of his pistol. They stole a dump truck from the quarry where we got the stone for the foundations.

In February 1947 I had to go to the Severnaia Mine to work out a number of problems with the mine administration and the Mining Inspectorate. It wasn't far—about ten kilometers—but the temperature was minus forty degrees. The head of the column had his horse harnessed to a sleigh and, with one of the special settlers as a driver, we set off.

We arrived at the mine administration and I left the horse and driver, asking him to stay put. I went to settle the various issues that had come up on the job. I hadn't been gone for more than an hour, but when I came out and looked for the horse and driver I could see no one. Well, I thought, he's obviously got cold and made a run back to the camp. I'd have to hitch a ride with someone going in my direction.

There was a teahouse next to the mine administration building. I'll step in and treat myself to a cup of tea, I thought; and then I saw the driver coming out of the teahouse to meet me.

"Where's the horse?" I asked.

"I just stepped in for a minute to warm up; the horse was tied to the hitching post . . ."

They had managed to steal the horse and the sleigh.

When I returned, I wrote up a report explaining what had happened and assumed the matter would end there. The security officer seized on the opportunity to start a new "case"—the theft of a sleigh—under the Law of August 7, 1932, by which a worker found with a dozen nails in his pocket, or someone who had picked up a few ears of wheat in the fields after the harvest, was given ten years in the camps, the same sentence as for major thefts.

At the very same time a decision had come from Moscow on the reduction of my sentence, and I was due to be released any day now. I am so grateful to Andrei Mosevich, the head of the Kemerovo Housing Authority, who put an end to this new case that had been whipped up and who had the horse and sleigh written off as production losses!

CHAPTER FIFTEEN

A Little Time in Freedom

I was released on June 18, 1947. They strongly urged me to remain in the camp as a free worker and hinted that with a six-month passport under Article 39 of the Passport Instructions it would be very difficult for me to make a living. I categorically refused. I wanted only to go home, to my parents.

The leading specialists in the camp, the professors and doctors of science Shchukin and Levanovsky, who already knew me from Gorshorlag, wrote excellent references for me. (Shchukin and Levanovsky had earlier been tried as part of the Industrial Party affair. They had served their time on the White Sea Canal and had been released early and awarded Orders of the Workers' Red Banner.) With my certificate of early release and my references I left for Omsk.

I was living in Omsk illegally. Through friends I made attempts to get a job on the railway. The head of transportation services looked at my certificate and my references and offered me two positions: as head of the Kulomzinsk ballast quarry or as head of the Railway Section in the town of Kalachinsk, adding that he truly needed people like me. The NKVD railway service could solve the problem of a residence permit. He collected my documents and promised to let me know the results of his efforts on my behalf.

A month passed in expectation. I was recovering at home from all the battering I had endured. One day, however, an instructor from the Omsk Pedagogical Institute, Grachev, dropped by to see my father. His many questions about camp life marked him at once as a suspicious person. I tried shifting the conversation to trivial topics.

Grachev turned out to be an informer, a *stukach,* and two or three days after his visit a black car pulled up and I was taken to the NKVD.

After some lengthy explanations they let me go, giving me four days to get a certificate releasing me from work in the railway system and to leave Omsk; otherwise I was threatened with arrest and prison.

So without waiting for the decision of the Moscow railway service of the NKVD, and having had an invitation from Severozheldorstroy (the Northern Railway Construction Administration), I went off to see the camp administration of Kniazh-Pogost, in the settlement of Zheleznodorozhny. At Velsk Station I went out to the platform and encountered the head of the Technical Production Unit, Apparovich. When he found out where I was going and why, he made me an offer: "Collect your things from the car, you needn't go any farther. You can work for us in the Velsk Section. I'll sort out your change of address."

And so I went back to my old post, but in a new capacity—as a free worker with a six-month passport.

I found an apartment in Velsk, 64 October Street, in the house of an old woman named Kessler.

Even though the wartime conditions were over, the work habit of sitting at your desk until late at night was still much in fashion.

My landlady marveled that I could spend so much time at work—fourteen hours or more.

"My father," she would say, "was called 'Your Excellency.' He was an Actual State Councilor. He managed the Department of Crown Property. The civil servants in his department began work at ten o'clock and finished at five."

Once some Grand Duke from the imperial family came to review the department. The department head told his staff: "I want you to stay at work a bit longer these days to show His Highness your dedication and diligence. Perhaps he will take note and give you a bonus."

The Grand Duke, of course, noticed this and asked the department head: "Why is your staff still here after working hours?"

"They are very dedicated, Your Highness."

"Do you mean to say that they can't get their work done in the course of a day? Why don't you fire them?"

That was the view of the Grand Duke. The comparison was, of course, not favorable to our forced rush to increase production.

It was 1948. In May a telegram arrived sending me to Kniazh-Pogost, to the settlement of Zheleznodorozhny to lay out the foundations and the axis for a bridge across the Rakpas, a tributary of the Vym River.

The people in the hotel where I stayed treated me with great respect: evidently they took me for some important personage. I had a separate room, the dishes in the hotel dining room were prepared especially for me, and they would not accept any payment for my stay, assuring me that I was a rare and respected guest. Something akin to Gogol's *Inspector-General* was going on. Or perhaps the Komi Republic had already achieved the high ideals of communism. I tried checking with my own office but they just laughed: "Never mind," they told me, "If they won't take your money, then just enjoy yourself."

I quickly finished work on the future bridge and submitted a report with my layouts and was getting ready to go back to my home base. On the day of my departure someone knocked on my door. A man I had never seen before entered and introduced himself as the regional secretary of the party. He asked if I was satisfied with everything and whether I had any instructions and guidelines to pass on; then he asked me to present a report to the constituents.

"Whom do you take me for?" I asked.

"What do you mean, 'whom'? You're our deputy, you're the great engine driver on the Severo–Pechorsk Railway, Boldyrev!"

I had to disillusion my visitor and, after paying for my stay, bid farewell to my excessively hospitable hosts.

Lying on the bunk in the railway car, I recalled the former technician and transit man Miasnikov, who was let out of prison and went to the front in 1943. He was a swindler of the highest order, one who could forge any signature at a moment's notice. People would bring him a tray with money tied up in a blue ribbon, as they would to Ostap Bender.

When the war was over he came back and spent some time with me, boasting of the decorations he had received, his party card, and telling me about his adventures at the front. Over a bottle of vodka I asked him: "So, are you going to get a job in the camp system?"

"Of course not. Why waste my talents on small stuff? I'm going to take up my old line of work. There are still lots of trusting fools here in the Soviet Union, people you can just wrap around your little finger."

As a front-line veteran, he was offered a job managing a restaurant in Kotlas by the town's authorities. After a month of work, Misha Miasnikov escaped to parts unknown, carrying off not only the cash receipts but all the tablecloths and curtains. He did leave the dishes and the furniture.

In 1948 I was issued a five-year passport, stamped with Article 39.

The camp administration began to petition for removal of my previous conviction so as to consolidate my position in the Main Railway Construction Administration. But at the same time (as I learned later), a secret order had been sent out to the whole of the NKVD to isolate all those who in 1947 had served out their sentences under Article 58, with the exception of subpara 10 (Agitation). The order was signed by Beria. Once again they began pulling in those who had been released earlier. People began disappearing, just as I had in 1937.

CHAPTER SIXTEEN

Sentenced to Eternal Exile

In the summer of 1949 I was unexpectedly summoned for a medical examination. The waiting room was crowded with people waiting to be examined. I reached the head of the line and entered. The doctors sitting there were wearing NKVD uniforms; there was a short examination that ended with: "Healthy." The procedure was finished.

I carried on working but noticed that one by one they had begun picking up everyone who had been summoned for the examination. I waited for my turn.

On November 12, 1949, I was arrested again and taken away to Arkhangelsk.

A new investigation, and more interrogations. They tried, without success, to tack on some new "crimes" of shaking the foundations of Soviet power.

The investigation was completed. I signed the transcripts that stated that the investigators possessed no new incriminating material, i.e., that there was absolutely no evidence for a charge.

"So now can I start living in freedom?" I asked the investigator.

"No, we're sending you to another area where you can live freely and find suitable work, but this is a prohibited area and you, as an ex-prisoner, can't stay here."

I was transferred to Petrovsky Prison. There was a spacious cell holding about forty "guests," mainly Jewish doctors from Arkhangelsk, as well as a correspondent from the newspaper *Northern Pravda* (*Pravda Severa*), some engineers, geologists, and only two or three people with no definite profession.

All the Jews were in prison because of Golda Meir, the prime minister of Israel. They were all accused of "Zionism." Golda Meir's arrival in the Soviet Union gave rise to a wave of anti-Semitism in the government— toward Jewish citizens of the USSR.

At the end of March a transport was put together and we were shipped off to Vologda Transit Prison. Here I shared a cell with people from all the prisons of the country. My attention was fixed on a taciturn fellow suffering from dropsy; he reminded me of someone, but I couldn't recall whom. His last name, Radomyslsky, didn't tell me anything; all I could find out was that he and his whole family were being exiled to Kustanai.

Several cells were let out for exercise at the same time, and we were able to exchange information about who was where and where others had already been sent. Here I found out that Radomyslsky was Zinoviev's brother. His resemblance to his brother was striking.

The transport was formed up. We were loaded into cattle cars surrounded by barbed wire. Guards from the famous Vologda detachment, notorious among prisoners for their atrocities, provided the escort.

At every stop they hammered away on the wall panels and floor of the car, using wooden mallets on long handles in hopes of discovering secretly sawn-away openings that could be used for escapes.

Omsk Station. We were off-loaded car by car and taken under reinforced escort to the bathhouse. A crowd of people gathered by the train. We could hear voices: "Have you seen so-and-so? Have you heard of him? Is —— on this train?"

The guards would shout: "No more talking! Move away, you motherfuckers!"

Bathing was done "sprinter style"—a little tub of water and five minutes for washing.

Then the command, "Get out!"

Whether you managed to splash yourself with a bit of water or not, you had to rush like a shot into the changing room in order to dig out your clothes from the delouser, get yourself dressed, and not try the patience of the guards.

They herded us back into the railway cars like sheep: "Get a move on there, you motherfuckers," the sergeant shouted, waving his mallet and striking a straggling old man in the back. "Stir your stumps, you old fart."

The blow knocked the old fellow off his feet. We carried him into the car and demanded to see the head of the guard detachment.

We absolutely refused the breakfast and the bread that had been brought. We lodged a protest with the head of the guard detachment and demanded to see a prosecutor. Our car refused to accept any food until the prosecutor came.

Some young fellow arrived and introduced himself as a prosecutor. He listened to our complaint and then solemnly announced that he was not empowered to take any measures against the sergeant and recommended that we write a complaint to the NKVD when we got to our destination.

That was the end of the conversation. The door of the car rumbled as it closed and the bolts clattered shut.

Driven to impotent rage, we began simultaneously to sing:

> My native land is broad and fair,
> With forests, fields and streams.
> No other such land do I know
> Where a man can breathe so free!

The whole train took up this song. The guards rushed up, shouting: "Stop the singing! We'll open fire!"

In answer came shouts: "Go ahead and fire at us 'free people.'"

A locomotive was coupled to the train and it was moved away to a dead-end siding at Moskovska Station. The people who had crowded around the train waved their kerchiefs. Women were crying.

In the night, like a thief, the train left Omsk.

We were unloaded at Novosibirsk Station. We were herded into Black Marias and taken to a transit point at a new prison in the Dzerzhinsky Region. After a few days in the transit prison a transport was formed up.

The head of the transit prison announced to the group: "You are free people and you will travel to your new place of residence in a passenger car with escort. I ask you to maintain order and discipline. You'll be taken to the train in trucks."

At the Novosibirsk Central Station we passed two gray-bearded porters on the platform and took our seats in the car indicated by our escort. No one told us where we were bound.

Chany Station. We disembarked and immediately walked into a circle of troops with machine guns and dogs. And yet we had come here with only one escort. And even he was unarmed!

They took us to the village of Vengerovo. We were herded into a wooden barn that was called a club. There was a sentry at the door. Various peasants began coming into the club: "Any bookkeepers here? Any stove-menders? Machine operators? Construction workers?"

Questions . . . questions . . . One person would have his name written down in a notebook, another would be called out to "freedom."

I sat deep in thought. This whole scene in the club reminded me of the slave auction in Beecher Stowe's novel *Uncle Tom's Cabin*.

A balding peasant approached me and introduced himself as the chairman of a kolkhoz.

"Are you a bookkeeper?"

"No, I'm a railway builder."

"Oh, we need engineers." And he persuaded me to go to his kolkhoz. At that point I was absolutely indifferent to where I went.

"I'm going to run off to the NKVD chief, Sudarev, and ask him to change my application for a bookkeeper to one for an engineer. I'll take you to our kolkhoz."

My name was called. I went out. An escort had come to take me to the Vengerovo NKVD.

At a table in the room where I was taken sat the NKVD chief, Major Sudarev; the first secretary of the Regional Committee of the party, Yevstratov; the deputy head of the Regional Executive Committee, Surmilo; and two NKVD officers from Novosibirsk. They let me read the resolution of the Special Board of the NKVD stating that I had been sentenced to eternal exile for counterrevolutionary activity and would face a twenty-five-year term in the labor camps if I attempted to escape.

"Sign to show that you've read it," said one of the officers.

There was little choice but to sign it, even though the text of the resolution was in contradiction with Marxist dialectics that maintained there was nothing eternal in nature.

"And once again you want to have it your own way," Sudarev said. "You still refuse to 'lay down your arms'? Why go to a kolkhoz when you can stay in town?"

"No one offered me a job in town. And you can't find anything that matches my work background. Going to a kolkhoz is my own personal decision."

"So you want to work for ticks (that was what workday units were called)?" Strumilov joined in. "A tick mark gives you two hundred grams of grain, and all the while you're up to your knees in manure."

I replied indignantly, "So are you comparing the socialist system of agriculture, where the finest people in the country work, with a manure pile? Write it down: only to a kolkhoz!"

The conversation over, I left. I was met by the chairman of the Lenin Collective Farm, Vasily Girgoriev.

"I heard your whole conversation," he said. "Here's a hundred rubles; there's five more people coming with you, carpenters and a machine operator. Go round to the teahouse and get something to eat and drink, get a room in the hotel for the night, and someone will pick you up in the morning." He shook my hand and left.

In the morning a cart drawn by a team of horses came for us. We loaded our belongings, and after a twenty-five-kilometer trip we arrived at the village of Orlovo, a part of the kolkhoz. They had arranged a welcome for us. Tables laden with all sorts of food had been set up in the middle of the street. We ate, drank, and then went to our rooms. In the evening I was summoned to the kolkhoz office.

"We've decided to make you the brigadier of a cattle-raising brigade, with a construction brigade under you. The former cattle brigadier, Agania Kudrik, is going to be secretary of the village council."

I didn't have to work long on the kolkhoz. I had only managed to get the offices sorted out and had begun repairing the cattle sheds and clearing the manure from the cattle yards when out of the blue appeared the superintendent of exiles.

"Report to Major Sudarev in Vengerovo tomorrow."

"If the major needs to see me I'll wait for him here. I've a signed document that forbids me from crossing the boundaries of the village, and I don't intend to violate it." But inside my heart was pounding: were they going to tack on a new sentence because of what I'd said to the NKVD?

I met the kolkhoz chairman, who asked: "Why do you want to move to town? The superintendent told me that you were transferring to Vengerovo. Are things really that bad here?"

I told him about my conversation with the superintendent.

"Fine, I'll call Sudarev and sort it all out."

Three days later the superintendent came again on a motorcycle with a sidecar. He had instructions from Sudarev to bring me to the town with all my belongings.

In Vengerovo I spoke to Sudarev's deputy, a captain (unfortunately, I don't remember his name).

"We have instructions to place you in a job here in town. Now you have to report to the chairman of the Executive Committee."

The chairman's deputy, Surmilo, was in the chairman's office.

"Well, how's work on the kolkhoz? The Soviet state has spent money on your training, yet you don't want to repay your debt to the government. Report at once to the head of the Village and Kolkhoz Construction Section, Comrade Popkov. You'll be working for him."

I went to see Popkov, secretly pleased that everything was working out for the best. He wrote out an order enrolling me in the section as a senior engineer with a salary of eighty rubles a month (that was an enviable salary at the time), and I went to work in my new role.

I got to know Vengerovo and its inhabitants. The local people were a fine, hospitable group. More than half of them were exiles.

The caretaker in the hotel was ex-general Koniukhov from the Political Directorate of the Belorussian Military District. The bookkeeper of the Regional Communal Housing Office was the ex-chairman of the Executive Committee of the Nagorno-Karabakh Autonomous Region, Suren Mirzoian (who told me a lot about Beria, things that only now the newspapers write freely about). Grigory Budagov, the son of the man who had built the bridge over the Ob River at Novonikolaevsk, worked in the Department of Land Use. Other workers had been engineers in the Moscow Likhachev Auto Plant. There was a performer from the Odessa Opera Theater, Larisa Shvarts; the Belorussian writer, Bialik; the major Ukrainian engineer and land reclamation expert, Poddubny. Chief engineer of the Vengerovo Communal Housing Office was Mstislav Pokrovsky. A Polish ex-corporal, Leva Ketslakhes, who had never taken Soviet citizenship, worked for the Housing Office as a plasterer. In 1955 he left for Poland, taking his wife, who was a local girl, and the troop of little children he had acquired in his years of exile. Jan Kagian, an engineer, worked as a technician in the Department of Rural and Kolkhoz Construction. I can't list them all.

Working on the periphery and visiting kolkhozes to check on the state of cattle pens, I would run into many fascinating people. Among them was Aleksandrovich, a dedicated and principled anarchist. For nearly thirty years he had migrated through various prisons and exiles, along with a wife and a troop of children, but he never abandoned his convictions. Another one was Nikolai Medvedev, an ex-cavalry captain of the Alexander Hussar Regiment ("the Black Hussars"), who had fought on the Romanian front in World War I. After a number of battles, their regiment was quartered in Kishinev for remounting. Rumors of a revolution in Russia reached the regiment. Medvedev assembled his squadron, announced the toppling of the autocracy to his hussars, and declared: "The war's over for us. Anyone who wishes can go back to Russia."

He himself stayed in Bessarabia. In 1939 our troops invaded Bessarabia. By that time Medvedev had become the director of the Kishinev Museum. He was arrested on charges of betraying his Motherland (!) and got ten years in the camps followed by exile. In the kolkhoz he was a watchman for the threshing floors.

My work involved regular official travel in the area. I checked on the condition of buildings on the cattle farms that formed part of the kolkhozes and sovkhozes. I would make recommendations for setting up brick-making, using reed fiber for making woven fences and tiles and cedar shingles for roofing.

When I got permission to buy a shotgun I would go hunting in my spare time.

By now it was 1953. From home came the sad news that my father had been arrested. The minotaur was still lying in wait for his victims. I can't find words to describe my state of mind.

Stalin's death brought a little emotional relief, although the "meat grinder" continued its work simply by inertia. We exiles rejoiced at Beria's arrest and execution: now we expected a change for the better.

Rumors circulated about cases being reexamined, and there were changes in the upper echelons of the regional authorities. The chief of the Vengerovo NKVD, Major Sudarev, was dismissed from the "organs," and

Yevstratov was removed as well. Investigators from Moscow arrived to review individual cases and to investigate complaints.

In August came an answer to my complaint to the Supreme Court that inspired hope: I was told that my case would be reexamined in the near future and that I could expect a positive outcome. In October I was summoned to the NKVD. I was informed that I had been freed in accordance with a list (I think there were nineteen or twenty names on the list) received from Moscow, and I was issued a five-year passport.

CHAPTER SEVENTEEN

But Even Now, Is It Freedom? . . .

I arrived in Omsk at the beginning of March 1955 bearing my new passport. I got a permanent residence permit, registered with the Military Registration Office, and by March 5 I had a job with a field party in the Omsk Road and Transport Planning Office.

Soon my father returned. He had been sentenced by an NKVD Military Tribunal to twenty-five years of hard labor for telling a "terrorist joke." He had been completely rehabilitated.

The long, arduous journey home was over.

N. M. IGNATOV

MY LOT IN LIFE

CHAPTER ONE

Tashkent Prison

On the night of March 14, 1935, when I was a cadet at the NKVD's No.1 Central Asian School of Radiotelegraphy in the city of Tashkent, I was arrested and held in a solitary cell. Everyone who gets picked up by the NKVD thinks at first that there's been a mistake, that it will soon be sorted out and you'll be released. Thousands of *zeks* who were in the camps under Article 58 told me that. I thought the same.

On my very first day in the cell I made up a daily routine that involved a lot of time devoted to gymnastics. In 1933 I had graduated from the Technical School of Circus Arts with a routine called "Flying from the Trampoline." During exercise periods in the inner courtyard of the prison I would do back handsprings with round-offs and end with a somersault. I'd repeat this several times. The NKVD employees used to watch my jumps from the windows.

On the sixth day they took me for interrogation. The interrogator told me that I was accused of betraying the Motherland. I was going to be shot and all my relatives would get ten years in the camps.

After that they would take me out for questioning almost every night. One time the interrogator's office window was open. I got the idea of throwing myself out of it head first (we were on the fourth or fifth story). But if I'd done that I would have been found guilty and my relatives would have gone to the camps for ten years.

So every night they would take me out for questioning, while in my cell during the day I could hear music from the movie theater where the picture *Jolly Fellows* was playing. Utesov would be singing "Darling, how wonderful to live in the world."

Some time before this I had come to Tashkent in a heated freight car and wound up in the radio school. There I immediately got into an amateur entertainment group doing some simple balancing acts and playing the drums in the orchestra. They provided us with officers' boots and a good uniform for performances. Everything was going fine: we studied the Morse code, practiced on the telegraph key, and I was in good standing.

Once we were doing a forced march of fifteen kilometers with full kit. This was a test of our endurance. We had covered two kilometers when they asked me to carry another rifle along with my own because another cadet couldn't carry his any farther. And so I made it to the finish carrying two rifles, while the cadet whose rifle I was carrying had to be supported to reach the end.

A day after our forced march there was a meeting, and the fellow whose rifle I'd carried gave a little speech. He said that we had met the test well. I stood up and asked who allowed him to say that, when someone else had to carry his rifle and he himself had to be held up for the last two kilometers.

The cadet who had spoken turned out to be the secretary of the Komsomol group, the son of the secretary of the City or Regional Committee of the party. People's attitude toward me changed immediately after I had spoken up at the meeting. The elite among the cadets decided to teach me a lesson. One of the cadets was a Category 2 boxer, and I was all but forced to fight a match with him.

I had a lot of experience fist fighting. For four winters I had taken part in the bare-knuckle fights in Babiy Gorodok. These were organized every Sunday and holiday about 150 or 200 meters from the point where the Moskva River separates from the canal. There were slopes a few meters wide down to the water there, and in summer a ferryman would haul various cargos to Khamovniki and back. The fights began about ten or eleven in the morning. They would start with kids of twelve to fifteen, then fellows a bit older, and toward evening the coachmen, draymen, and cabbies would come. Fellows from Khamovniki and Zamoskvorechye would form lines and the fight would begin. There were very strict rules: you weren't allowed to have anything in your fist. You could fight with the fellow standing in front of you or on your left and right. If someone had hit you very hard or you got tired, you could turn your back to the fighting line and drop out; someone else would take your place. Once in a while mounted policemen would arrive to break up the fight. But the coachmen would stop the horses and pull the policemen off them. Then fire engines would come and spray the whole group with a hose. And so the fights gradually ended.

I learned fighting skills in these contests. When I'd come home black and blue with swollen lips and my mother asked what had happened, I'd tell her that I'd fallen while sledding down the hills.

My bout with the Category 2 boxer lasted only one round. Over that time I knocked him down twice, and he threw in the towel. Not long after I was arrested.

The interrogator kept insisting that I had deliberately wormed my way into the radiotelegraphy school. My reply was that I had been sent to Tashkent along with some others by the Moscow Military Registration Office. This went on for several sessions. Once they took me to the interrogator in the daytime. He had a cadet from the radio school with him. The cadet began telling the interrogator a story that I had supposedly told: during a reception for the French ambassador and his wife, Mikhail Kalinin had unraveled the yarn from the skirt of the ambassador's wife until she was bare from the hips down. I'd never heard this story before (and it wasn't funny in any case).

After that I was taken from the interrogator's office to a common cell that already held ten or twelve people. Among them were a mullah, a teacher, and a bookkeeper. It was there I saw how the *zeks* made playing cards. First they would take a soft piece of bread and chew it carefully; then they would force this paste through a rag using the back of a tablespoon and then collect the smooth mass from the back of the rag. This very sticky paste was used to glue together two pieces of newspaper or regular paper. When the paper dried out it was very strong, and they would cut playing cards from it. They would make their own black ink by burning a bit of rubber over a bowl, collecting the soot, and mixing it with the glue. Blood served as red ink. Then they would use a stencil to put the color on the cards. The edges of the cards would be rubbed with garlic to make them more durable.

Our cell was long, with a high ceiling. The card games always took place on the bunks nearest the door. The cell door had two locks. I rehearsed a routine with one *zek,* a muscular fellow: while the guards were opening the cell door, I would get up on his shoulders and hide the cards inside the shade of the electric light over the door. When they took us to the showers, the guards would make a careful search—a *shmon*—of the cell. They would also search our underwear in the change room of the showers. Then we'd go back to our cell, collect the cards from the lampshade, and sit in the middle of the cell to have a game. The whole thing would be repeated soon after, and we got a good deal of fun out of it. The guards wanted us to turn in the cards and we did, in exchange for some checkers.

A few days later, I was taken back to the radio school where I had a show trial before a military tribunal. The prosecutor called me a cosmopolitan and a parasite. I was given four years in the camps under Article 66, part 1, of the Uzbek Criminal Code (equivalent to Article 58.10 of the Criminal Code of the Russian Federation). When I made my final statement, I called it a farce, not a trial. Two cadets and the commandant escorted me through the whole city to the prison. The prison guards took me to a cell.

In the cell one of the *zeks* came up to me and said that he liked my boots, to which I replied that I liked them too. Then he hit me in the face. In response I hit him so hard that he flew two meters backwards. He got up, grabbed a plank from the bunk, and began threatening me with it. But I pushed it away with my left hand and flattened him with my right. Then he ran to the door and began kicking it. He produced a bit of razor blade from somewhere and slashed his shirt and his chin; then he pinched the skin on his stomach and used the razor to make a cut some ten centimeters long so that there was a lot of blood. The guard opened the door and took him away, and they gave me his bunk. That's how I spent my first day in prison.

A couple of days later, food parcels arrived. Everyone in our cell who had got something put it down on my bunk without looking at it. I told them to take back their parcels and pass them on to anyone they chose.

A few parcels contained *anasha* (the *zeks* also called it *plan*). I tried smoking some then, but never tried it again.

One day they took me to the prison office and asked me to write a statement renouncing my final remarks at the trial.

CHAPTER TWO

Central Asia Camp (Sazlag)

About five days later we were called out for a transport and taken to the transit camp in Kuliuk. They marched us right across the city, and on the way about five prisoners escaped. In Kuliuk they took us to a large field surrounded by a double row of barbed wire with guard towers. A couple of hours later I was called in to the commandant, who asked me what kinds of things I could perform (there was a small stage with a tiny dressing room in the middle of the field). I told him that I needed some props. Then they took me to the carpenter, and I told him what he should make and drew him some sketches. By evening the props were ready.

I began performing three times a week. One of my other responsibilities was to call out the names of *zeks* listed for transport. They fed me well, but I didn't work for long because I came down with malaria. My temperature went up sharply, and they took me to hospital. There I was given quinine shots and acrichine. But that didn't help: I still had ringing in my ears, and during the day my temperature would go up to forty-one degrees; at night I would have chills and my teeth would chatter. I was moved from one ward to another until I arrived in the last one; the next move would be to the morgue. By then my weight had dropped by fifteen kilos. The doctors on their morning rounds no longer paid any attention to me. There was a pharmacist with them, and one day when the other doctors had gone he came and asked me when my attacks usually began. I replied that it was at 3:30 in the afternoon. He told me that an orderly would bring me some medicine, and at 3:00 I was supposed to go and bathe in a little pond that had been dug along an irrigation ditch. I jumped into the water at 3:00, but I was too weak to climb out on my own. Some ambulatory patients helped me, and when they found out which ward I was from they were quite amazed and took me there. Back in the ward I took the medicine. The malaria didn't torment me that night, but I sweated a lot. Just a few days later they moved me to another ward. I felt better but couldn't eat. Then they gave me thirty injections of arsenic (fifteen in each arm) that made my right bicep swell. After that my appetite grew so much that I sold my boots so I could buy bread and grapes each day after breakfast and lunch. I got back on my feet very quickly, and to get in shape for gymnastics I made myself a skipping rope and did 1,500 jumps before each breakfast and lunch. Within a week I could do a running somersault, back handsprings, and comfortably do handstands.

The hospital sent me back to Kuliuk. The commandant told me to move into the dressing room on the stage and, just as before my illness, I took up the same job (my props were still there). And everything went on as before.

Two weeks later the commandant called me in. He said a directive had come ordering that everyone convicted by a military tribunal under Article

58 (with a notation in their files) be used only on work with a pick, saw, spade, or wheelbarrow. Any commander who failed to comply would be punished. He added that tomorrow morning, after the next group of *zeks* was called for transport, I would go to the brick factory; but he'd have a word with the factory boss to fix up a place for me.

At the factory they made me a foreman. One of my duties was to receive, along with the factory inspector, the adobe bricks the *zeks* had made. I soon found a way to submit the same brick twice, and that allowed the *zeks* to "fulfill the norm." This meant they would get eight hundred grams of bread and the right to receive food parcels. The majority of the prisoners were Uzbeks.[1]

Thievery was flourishing in the camps at that time, and it didn't happen without some help from the camp authorities. When a new transport arrived, the nonpoliticals and 58ers would be stripped of their belongings. There was another practice as well: one of the "thieves-in-the-law" would announce: "You lot don't need to worry about who's boss, I'm gonna be your brigadier."

I soon got used to living in conditions like that and even went back to rehearsing.

CHAPTER THREE

Through BAMlag in an "Agitbrigade"

Early one morning, after we'd had a medical examination, some trucks arrived and all the Russians were transferred to another camp. Before we left the Uzbeks presented me with a *chapan* (a camel-hair robe), a pillow, and a bag of oat flour.

A day later we were all loaded on trucks in alphabetical order. We sat in the back, the two guards in the cab. The guards warned us that they

1. Most of the Uzbek prisoners had been convicted of corruption of minors. The Uzbek tradition that had existed for centuries was for men to marry girls between ten and thirteen. But in 1934 a law was passed making this punishable by ten years in prison; anyone who tried to conceal such a thing would get three years. (The same law applied to homosexuals. When the law was passed I was working in a Moscow music hall. One day when I came to rehearsal I found that all the male dancers had been arrested.) *Author's note.*

would open fire without warning on anyone who stood up. They took us to the Tashkent Freight Station where they handed us over, along with our documents, to a new group of guards. They loaded in alphabetical order into dual-axle freight cars, forty men per car. I was first on the list from our truck. I got into the freight car, climbed up to the upper sleeping platform, and got a spot near the narrow barred window. There were two ranges of bunks in the car, to the left and right of the door. The door opposite the entrance was blocked tight and a toilet (*parasha*) had been fitted into it. As soon as I came into the freight car I decided to quit smoking. Every morning when we stopped I would do some back handsprings, somersaults, and back walkovers on the spot. I had a length of rope and used it for skipping; I would stand on my head, do some handstands, and then have something to eat. I did that every day. We were going to somewhere in the north. After ten days they issued us with a week's ration of tobacco, half a package of *makhorka* per man. I had quit smoking and traded my *makhorka* for sugar. They gave us two pieces of lump sugar per day. The *zeks* would play cards for sugar and tobacco. I played just once. I lost my tobacco and won a week's worth of sugar.

I remembered playing a game called *rasshibalochka* at Easter time in 1923. The game was played as follows: two lines were drawn five or six meters apart; each player would bet a coin and set it on one of the lines; from the other line the player would toss his "bit"—these were the large five-kopeck coins from tsarist days. Whoever could toss his bit closest to the line was the winner. I was able to beat all of the kids from our courtyard and from the neighboring ones as well. Toward evening some older kids came by and began playing cards in a loft by candlelight. They were playing *bura,* and they went on playing until they had nothing left to bet. My elder brother was standing behind me, and by the rules of our world he wasn't allowed to play for me. I won a lot of money and various other things. I gave everything to my elder brother. He gave me some money. I had two friends. We bought a bottle of vodka. I drank a glass of vodka for the first time in my life and it made me very sick. After that I drank three cups of milk, and ever since I haven't been able to drink vodka or wine. Whenever I saw people drinking vodka my head would spin and my legs would give out, even though I was now an adult and an acrobat.

The *zeks* tried to persuade me to perform again but I refused. We traveled for forty-five days. We arrived at Pasheny Station in the Trans-Baikal

Region. Right away they herded us *zeks* out of the car to the disinfection chamber. I was the only one in our car who didn't have his head shaved (at the time they allowed us politicals under Article 58 to keep our hair). Those *zeks* who weren't able to walk under their own power were helped out to the disinfection chamber by the guards. We had a shower and our clothes were put through a steam chamber. Then we were marched off to a newly built locomotive shed with concrete floors; it was minus fifteen degrees. I spread out my camel-hair robe, laid my head on the pillow the Uzbek in Sazlag had given me, and tried to get some sleep. Soon two *zeks* woke me and asked who I was. When they found out that I was a circus performer and acrobat, they offered me a place in an entertainment troupe—an "agitbrigade" (they needed a partner). This was a routine thing in the camps: when a new transport arrived, the camp boss would send some of his representatives (*pridurki*) to find any specialists he could use. I replied that they'd told me in Sazlag that I had a note in my file saying that I was to work only at general labor, with pick and shovel, saw and wheelbarrow. But they talked me into joining them, so I collected my things and went back to the disinfection chamber. I took another shower there and was given new underwear, a suit, a newly altered jacket, and boots; and off we went. A passenger car and two freight cars were waiting on a siding at the station. One of the freight cars had four axles, the other two. The *zek* performers lived in the passenger car, two persons per compartment. The four-axle car had a kitchen and dining compartment, and this was where we rehearsed while on the road. We would move the tables and benches off to one side. In the two-axle car lived a tailor and a shoemaker—wonderful craftsmen. That's also where the props were kept, and where the two *zek* conductors for the passenger car lived. I met my future partner, Grisha Voldgendlir; he called himself Grigoras. He took me to the passenger car and introduced me to the brigadier of the troupe, Stepan Matusevich.

The performers and musicians lived two per compartment, and they showed me my bunk. The next day we began rehearsing a simple clown number. Grisha told me that they'd taken me out of the transport because he needed a partner. Five days later we demonstrated our clown number and were included in the program. We were very well received, and a month later we put together a power acrobatic number.

On the Baikal–Amur Line they called camp sectors "phalanges." When we made stops we would rehearse in local clubs or cultural centers; on the road we would use the four-axle car. Our troupe served the Baikal–Amur

Line from Chita to Khabarovsk. A second, parallel line was under construction, and we performed at the phalanges (camp sectors) building the line. There was a Ukrainian poet, Yuri Zahul, in the brigade. He would write odes for ceremonial occasions, and these would be read by the brigadier, Stepan Matusevich. We also had two sisters who were singers, the singer Georgi Vinogradov, two actors (a husband and wife)—they performed sketches—and some musicians.

Our base was Urulga Station, where we put together our programs and got our supplies. This was in Sector 2 of the Baikal–Amur Line. Bolshakov was in charge here. When we had our program ready we would travel along the line and return to Urulga. We were very well fed. In the corner of the dining compartment stood a table that always had bread, butter, and red caviar. Between lunch and dinner you could stop by and have a sandwich. When we arrived for a concert in the evening our cook, Uncle Fedia, would come into our car and ask each person what he'd like for breakfast. We were also well dressed: our own tailor and shoemaker made everything. Our cars sometimes stayed at big stations, and then we could go into the other restaurant cars for cigarettes, fruit, and sweets. We could have escaped any time.

I wouldn't write home to my family for fear that they might be arrested. Once I was performing at a phalange. A janitor who had lived in our building in Moscow came up to me and called me by name. I gave no sign of recognizing him and told him that he was mistaken; still, he wrote his wife that he had seen me. His wife went to my mother and told her that her husband had seen me in the camp and that I was a performer in an entertainment troupe.

We had a very good program and often gave paid shows in cities and towns. Once we arrived to do a show in Urulga. I went to the stadium where the local football team trained. I asked permission to kick the ball around, and they let me. After my workout, the chairman of the sports society came up and offered me a chance to play for his team; they were to play the Lokomotiv team from Chita. I agreed. The match was the next day, and we won 3–0; I got all three goals. The commander of Sector 3 of the Baikal–Amur Line (the head of the NKVD's BAMlag) was at the match. Our brigadier Matusevich called me in and told me that I was to go to the town of Svobodny the next day to play football.

I thought back to the time when I started playing football. It was in 1922. I was living in Second Babyegorod Lane. It ran parallel to the Moskva River, and at that time there was only wasteland between our lane and the river—people would pasture goats and cows there. But in 1922 they built the stadium for the Zamoskvorechye Sports Club. The footballer Fedor Selin played there. We kids would go to the stadium, root for our team, help clean up the field, and carry lime for marking the lines. Selin was in charge of marking. They would give us old footballs for helping them, and we'd take these to a shoemaker. He'd repair them and patch up the bladders. Selin taught us various ways to kick the ball, and so I learned the ABCs of the game. At that time, a player from each team would be chosen to run the hundred meters before each match. Nikolai Sokolov, the goalie, always ran for Zamoskvorechye and he was always first.

I traveled in one of the BAMlag *zek* cars. Along the way, ten pregnant women who were having difficulty giving birth were put on board. They were being taken to a prison hospital in the town of Svobodny. Before we got there, our car derailed and ran along the railway ties for about two hundred meters. As it was bumping over the ties, almost all the women gave birth without any help at all.

I arrived in Svobodny. Some people were there to meet me and take me to the stadium. There I got documents in my name saying that I was working in an exploration party for BAMlag (a *zek* didn't have the right to play football). I didn't get the documents, though; they were kept by the captain of the team. And right away they hooked me up to two guards in civilian clothes. We lived at the stadium, and next to my cot there was always another cot for the guard.

We were playing for the championship of the Far Eastern Region. We played two matches and won both. Our third match was in the city of Blagoveshchensk. We arrived there two days before the match. The next day we had practice. After the practice I met a girl and walked her home. She lived near the Amur River. A huge dog met us in her yard and immediately started growling at me. The girl calmed him down, and we went into the garden. There was an arbor there. While we were sitting, the dog kept growling and barking. I left her about 12:00. I got to the stadium, where a big panic was in progress. My guards thought that I had escaped and were about to send word to the head of Sector 3. The guard who had followed the girl and me had tried to climb over the fence, but the dog ripped his trousers and bit him in the leg. But everything was sorted out.

We played our match the next day. On one side of the stadium was a covered stand with a box for government officials. In the middle of the first half, something whistled over our heads. It turned out that a sniper had fired a shot across the soccer pitch at some local bigwig. In the first minutes of the second half, I was close to the opposing goal when I was hit very hard in the right leg, so badly that I had to be helped off the field. And I was sent back to Urulga.

I went back to Matusevich's troupe. The doctor prescribed massage, and ten days later I went back to work. I worked out a dance routine with acrobatics that I called "The Little Apple." I had a costume made. The dance was a great success, and I was also signed up as a drummer in the jazz orchestra. I had a lot of things to do in the program.

One day we came back from work early. One of our musicians told me that I was to go and see the brigadier. He said that the head of the phalange wanted to see me. This man introduced me to his daughter and said that the two of us could go for a walk outside the zone. We left and the guard let us pass. We strolled around outside the zone for about two hours. She told me that she had seen our show ten times at various phalanges and would go with her father to the places where we performed.

Once we were performing at a phalange where they produced crushed stone for the railway bed. A *zek* came up to me and said that he was a musician and had been part of the trio "Crain, Pinky, and Short." In the early 1930s they were performing abroad, and when they came back to the USSR they were arrested and given five years under Article 58. He showed me his calloused hands. Tears were flowing down his face as he told me he'd never again be able to work as a musician.

It was now the fall of the year. In Urulga our cars were hitched to a locomotive and we went off somewhere without making any stops. They took us to Khabarovsk. It turned out that the party conference of the Far Eastern Region was going on, and they didn't have any entertainment to offer for it, so our troupe of prisoners was urgently summoned from Urulga. After our performance, Bliukher himself mounted the stage and shook everyone's hand. The next day we were taken to the Zeia River. A military detachment there was building a second bridge across the river. A ceremony was being held in honor of this event, and we gave a concert in the mess hall. We used the storeroom and the kitchen for our changing room. I met the supply clerk of the detachment there. He was from Moscow, and we'd lived not far from one another. He was able to give me a lot of oranges, lemons, mandarins, and candies from the banquet. I took off one side of the bass drum, and he filled up the whole thing. After the performance they gave us a vehicle to go back to the station.

When we arrived in Urulga we got busy preparing a program for the new year, 1937. But on the night on December 13 two NKVDers arrived and took me to a holding cell. December 15 was my birthday. All the performers from our brigade came to visit. We arranged for the visit to take place in the cell, and they brought me fruit and sweets. The next day I was sent to Svobodny. When we arrived there I was taken to Skolpa (a prison in the mountains). The next day I asked for some paper and wrote to the commander of Sector 3, asking to see him. I don't know whether it was because of my statement or whether he had some business in the prison, but a day later I was taken to the prison office to see him. I told him that I hadn't broken any laws. He asked me to be patient for a bit longer.

CHAPTER FOUR

Kotlas–Chibiu

A day later I was taken to the station and put into a Stolypin car (a car in which the sleeping platforms are joined together at night so that they hold three people) in a passing train. In those days every train had a car for *zeks*. We were going westwards. As we went through some station or other I heard a radio broadcasting the chiming of the Kremlin bells and Stalin's greetings for the coming new year of 1937. That day my heart was giving me a lot of problems. They took us to the city of Kotlas. Kotlas had a huge transit prison in which there were many barracks with three-tiered bunks. We were assigned to barracks, and a day later they herded us off for a medical.

The whole thing went on for three days. They kept a very close eye on our physical health—so as not to send sick people to Vorkuta. One evening they took us by truck to the Kotlas freight station. They shoved us into freight cars with no bunks and we set off at once. We arrived at Murashi Station. There we were off-loaded and handed over, along with our files, to another detachment of guards. And we set off down the road on foot.

After fifty kilometers of walking we came to a small transit camp. The guards that had escorted us from Murashi handed us over, along with our files, to the guards standing at the camp entrance. Our footwear was worn and torn. When we got settled, we dried out our foot-wraps and our boots, put them on again, had some hot water to drink, and lay down on the bunks to sleep. Detached transit camps like these were looked after by criminals with short terms. They carried water and stoked the stove—made from an iron barrel and standing in the middle of the barracks.

Each day we were given 600 grams of very poor bread mixed with some other substance and 150 grams of salt cod. The bread and fish were given out in the morning, and almost all the *zeks* would eat it up at once; in the evening they would drink hot water. I always went first. I had a little bundle containing my bell-bottom trousers, a sailor's striped vest, a pair of low shoes, and a "doughnut" used for headstands. One day after a transport we came into a barracks. I drank a mug of hot water, dried out my boots and footcloths, put them on again so they wouldn't be stolen, and went to sleep with my bundle beneath my head. I soon woke up when I felt someone pulling my bundle from under my head. I saw the *zek* who looked after the barracks. He had an axe in his hand. I did a tuck and leapt off the upper bunk at his head, just they way they jump in the circus; in the process I kicked aside the loose planks on the bunk. I grabbed the axe and made a move to the second *zek,* who was standing about four meters away holding a knife and a sack full of stolen things. He ran toward the barracks door where he threw down the knife and the sack and then headed for the guard tower. I grabbed the sack and tossed it to the *zeks,* telling them to sort out their belongings. The thieves had taken one *zek*'s gold crown along with his tooth. Ten minutes later, the head of the guards came in with two more guards armed with rifles; he demanded the axe and the knife.

I lay down and tried to sleep. Someone woke me up and told me to go to the doctor (he lived in a little room behind a partition in the corner of the barracks). The doctor gave me a tablespoon of cod liver oil, and each morning and evening afterwards he would do the same.

After the attempted robbery our transport became much more united, and in the barracks in the evening we would sing the Cossack song "Chub-chik."

The doctor and his medicines on our transport would travel by sled. There was another sled for the guards, and they would take turns resting on it. I can't remember how many days our transport walked from

Murashi Station to Chibiu. When we got to Chibiu we went on another fifty kilometers or so; we stopped in the forest, sawed down a few pines, and made a fire with them; when they had burned we raked aside the coals and lay down on the warmed earth (the temperature was minus forty-five degrees).

CHAPTER FIVE

They Take Me into the Theater

As we were passing through Chibiu I had noticed a theater poster (the play was *Lev Gurych Sinichkin*). The next morning I asked the doctor to give me a referral to the local clinic because of a swelling on my right biceps; using that referral I was able to get a pass for all the checkpoints on the way to Chibiu. I got to Chibiu and headed straight for the theater. I found the director and told him that I was an acrobat; he told me he didn't need any acrobats. Then I told him that I had a dance number. I was told to come back the next week, at 2:00 on Thursday. I was very upset about this. I went to the clinic, had my pass signed, and went back to the camp. A tarpaulin tent and two stoves had already been set up (when I left there was nothing at all there). Going to Chibiu and back I'd been stopped six times to have my pass checked. I was very upset when I got back to camp. The doctor asked me how things were. I told him that I had to go to the theater at 2:00 on Thursday. He told me not to worry. The rest of the camp had already gone out cutting timber. The doctor gave me an exemption from work.

I worked hard preparing my dance number, "The Little Apple." Thursday morning I got my certificate and set off for the theater. There I met with the director, who introduced me to the pianist. I explained the dance rhythm to him. I went behind the wings and changed (I still had the costume from BAMlag). I waited a long time. The pianist was so nervous he was chewing a piece of canvas from the scenery.

The audition took place during a break in rehearsal. The dance was built around various acrobatic feats. At the end of every musical phrase there was a somersault or a back handspring. Through one whole musical phrase I danced on my hands and ended with Arab Wheels on the spot in very quick tempo. The actors and director were very keen on my dance number. The director called in one of the theater staff. He took me through some offices where I was taken on in the theater and put down for allowances. Then they took me to the barracks where I'd be living. A corridor ran through the middle of the barracks, and on both sides there were rooms with four cots, two by each wall. There was a stove in the middle of each room. The theater staff lived in the barracks. The *zek* who brought me there showed me my room and bed. I began getting acquainted with my roommates. To the left of the door lived Georgi Dutchenko, a Ukrainian—an opera singer, a baritone. He had been a member of the Kiev Opera before he was arrested. The second was Alyosha Popov, a choirmaster who had worked until his arrest with Olga Vysotsky, an announcer in the Central Radio. On the right side was Mikhail Nazvanov, an actor from the Moscow Art Theater. He was arrested after a trip abroad and given five years under Article 58. The next day I was introduced to the ballerina Valentina Ratushenko. We began rehearsing together and immediately worked out a dance number. Ratushenko was originally from Ukraine, but she had lived in the USA. She went to China, to Harbin. When the USSR turned over the Chinese Eastern Railway to China, they offered to accept anyone who wanted to come back to the Motherland. Ratushenko was one of those who took up the offer. But instead of going to Ukraine she found herself serving five years under Article 58 in the Ust-Vym camp. She had been a ballerina in the theater and a ballet mistress in operettas. She made me her male partner. Aside from dancing, I joined up as a drummer in the jazz orchestra.

The theater organized a variety troupe that traveled around putting on concerts in various camp sections. Once we performed at a camp where the prisoners were relatives of Zinoviev and other important political people. They were working with radioactive water. At first those who began working in this camp would put on weight and feel well, but then their flesh began falling away from their bones.

We had our own theater dining hall and a barracks just for the theater staff. Ratushenko and I put together several new dance numbers. Ratushenko was on friendly terms with Mikhail Nazvanov.

And so I became a useful member of the theater staff. The barracks had brick stoves that wouldn't hold any heat at all. When we came back to the barracks in the evening we would stoke up the stove for the night, and in the morning, if the temperature outside was minus thirty or forty, it would be only about ten degrees warmer in our room, and that's if there was no wind. My roommates would grab their underclothes and get dressed under the blankets, while I would get up and go for a run along the street and then get dressed as soon as I came back to the barracks.

CHAPTER SIX

In a Special Camp Sector: I Declare a Hunger Strike

And so I went on working in the theater until December 1937. At the beginning of December, two guards came and took me to a preliminary detention cell. The next day I was transferred to a camp, a special camp sector. This was not a camp for timber cutting or for building a railway to Vorkuta; it was for exterminating prisoners convicted by a military tribunal under Article 58. We were fed on three hundred grams of bread, half of which was sawdust, and a half-liter of *zatirukha,* flour mixed with water. There was no sense in working, since that kind of ration couldn't keep anyone alive anyway. I spent two months in that camp. The guards were serving punishment terms themselves, and they were fed four hundred grams of bread along with cooked food three times a day. They brought in *zeks* from other camps. There I saw the guards shoot two *zeks* (one had a nice pair of boots, the other a jacket). These murders were categorized as "attempted escapes." The *zeks* there soon turned into "goners" and were sent to die in hospital.

In the camp I became friendly with a *zek* who slept next to me (I never learned his name). Once we were behind the barracks and the goners were there near the kitchen picking up potato peelings from the garbage heap. My friend recognized one of the goners as his former boss and told me about it. That evening we lay there for a long time and weren't able to get to sleep. We just couldn't get the thought out of our heads that we too would soon be brought to such a state. The next day he talked me into going to work cutting timber. We sawed down two trees, trimmed off the branches, built a bonfire, and sat down next to it. A little while later he got up and went to a tree stump, put his left hand on it, and cut it off with an axe. The guards took us back to camp immediately, and they took him away. This upset me a lot. I couldn't sleep all night. I wouldn't be able to cut off my hand. I was an acrobat and truly loved my profession. My work brought me joy. I made a pact with myself that I wouldn't let them reduce me to the state in which I saw my friend's former boss. I decided to die of hunger and declared a hunger strike. After that, the camp authorities began doing "experiments" on me. Every day they would bring me potatoes fried in pork fat. I held out for four days, and on the fifth they stopped bringing me potatoes.

Usually, after five days without food a person loses the strong craving for it. I lay there for twenty days without food. The camp doctor would come each morning and take my temperature. I lay in my bunk and my whole life passed before my eyes, from the time when I had my first memories.

In 1914 our father was taken away to fight on the front. My mother and five children stayed in Moscow. Until the war, my father had worked as a sales clerk in the store of the manufacturer Prokhorov, and the Prokhorovs helped us out right until the Revolution. They would give us children summer and winter clothes at Christmas and Easter.

When my father first went to the front, he sent a letter asking my mother to have her picture taken with all the children and send it to him. Mama did that. I remember how in November 1914 she got a cab and took us all to be photographed. Mama and my two sisters sat in the droshky, my younger brother and I sat at their feet, and our eldest brother sat alongside the cabby.

After that, I was sick from November until May. I was in the Morozov Hospital. When they took me home I couldn't walk, and my brothers and sisters would take me around in a baby carriage that they had found somewhere. I had had measles, scarlet fever, and diphtheria.

When I was four I was beaten up by another boy. I came home to complain to my mother, who was washing clothes at the time. She left her washing and said, in a compassionate voice, "You poor boy." And then she took a strap from the wall and began whipping me across my backside, saying, "Don't ever come complaining!" I realized that it was up to me to overcome my problems ("We may have bloody noses, but we'll win!"). That was the way Mama taught me to build my character, and by that fall I was already winning fights with kids my age.

After the Revolution, Mama would make trips to the village of Liabinka, where our relatives would give her some food. We celebrated the new year of 1918 without a Christmas tree. Instead we decorated a fig plant and danced around it in a ring.

After our New Year's celebration, Mama and my elder sister Katya came down with the Spanish flu, and there was no one to go to the village for food. We soon ran out of groceries, and the family began to starve. We would get tiny pieces of bread measured in a matchbox. To feed ourselves we—my younger brother, my older brother Vasya, and I—would go around to stores and bakeries. One time, at a bakery where they were loading bread on to a horse-drawn cart, we managed to break off a few crusts without anyone noticing. The carters finished loading and drove off. We saw a tram come out of the bakery gate loaded with bread (there were rails going into the bakery), and then the iron gates closed behind it. At the bottom of the left side of the gate was a plank with a cutout for draining water, and there happened to be a watchman sitting right beside it. Vasya told my younger brother and me to take off our coats (we were wearing coats that had be-longed to our older sisters, and the sleeves, too long for us, had been tied up with string at the ends so we wouldn't freeze our hands) and crawl through this cutout. We took off our coats and managed to squeeze under the gate. On the other side, to the right, was a platform where there was a little trol-ley loaded with loaves of bread. We climbed up on the platform, took a loaf of bread each, again squeezed under the gate, dressed, and went home.

At home we found a doctor who had come to see my mother and sister, who were now running high temperatures. My older brother cut a small piece of bread from the loaf and gave it to the doctor. The doctor wrote out some prescriptions, and my younger brother and I went right off to Ferein's pharmacy on Serpukhovskoy Square. We bought the medicine and went home, had something to eat, and went around the shops, breaking off bits of wood from the fences along the way so that we would have something to burn in the stove. And so, over the course of two weeks, we went to the bakery every day and brought back two loaves of bread each.

One day we came home and our elder sister told us she had heard from her friend that the building manager was going round the apartments and making space for other people to live in them, so we should lock the door and not let anyone in. That's what we did. Soon we heard someone knock-ing at the door and the voice of the building manager demanding that we open it. When we didn't open it, a few people began breaking it down. Then we decided to take up arms: my elder brother grabbed an oven fork, I took a poker, and my younger brother an oven tongs (we had a Russian stove in the kitchen). Meanwhile, the intruders had already torn one side of the double doors from its hinges. But then a neighbor, a crippled man, happened to be passing, and when he saw what was going on he put them to shame and they had to leave. A few minutes later, the housebreakers returned and broke down the rest of the door. In the entryway my elder brother hit one of them with his oven fork and opened a cut on the side of his head. Blood gushed out of it, and the whole band had to retreat. My elder brother put the hinges back and hung the doors, but the housebreakers never came back again.

One morning my younger brother and I set off for the bakery. When we had crept up to the trolley we found that there was bread only on the top shelves, and so I had to climb up after it. Meanwhile, two women came out of the bakery. They caught us, took us inside, fed us some bread and butter (they used the butter to coat the bread pans), and asked us where we lived and where our parents were. We told them about our father on the front and about our sick mother and sister. Before we left, my younger brother asked if we could come into the bakery the next day. They agreed, and gave us some bread crusts as well. And so we began making regular trips to the bakery.

Mama soon got back on her feet again, and we managed to get a job for her in the bakery. But that turned out to be a very bad move for us: Mama had to send my younger brother and me to a children's shelter. This was a distribution center on Shabalovka Street, a two-story building behind a carburetor factory. Formerly it had been a soap factory.

Mama brought us there and left. We both had black hair, and the other kids began taunting us that we were Jews. When the teachers left, they wanted to fight with us. I said that my brother wasn't going to fight. I fought with each of them in turn and beat up thirteen boys. After that, I said that I wouldn't fight any more that day. And on the next day no one wanted to fight with me.

And so began our life in a children's shelter. Before long my brother and I were sent to the shelter at Podosinki Station (now Ukhtomsky), where we lived in the former dacha of Peltzer. This was a beautiful area. While we lived there we often had cocoa and bread rolls (they came from American aid).

Once some of the older kids climbed up into the attic of the dacha. Behind the chimney they found a leather bag full of greenish bills. The watchman had asked them to find something he could use for rolling cigarettes, so they gave him a few. The director quickly spotted the watchman rolling a smoke with one of those papers and asked where he had gotten it. The watchman said the children had given it to him. The director called in the children, and they showed him where the bag was hidden. The director took the bag and no one in the shelter ever saw him again. A new director, a woman named Averbakh, was sent from Moscow to replace him. She came with three children.

We slept in the dacha itself. The kitchen and dining hall were about two hundred meters away. There was also a large stable there, and some Red Army soldiers were living next to it. Sometimes they would let us ride their horses, and we'd all go to wash them in the pond near the dacha.

On the other side of the pond, nearer the railway, were two aircraft hangars. Once Trotsky flew in from Moscow to visit the airmen. He came on the airplane *Ilya Muromets*. A stage was set up in one of the hangars from which Trotsky made a speech, and various performers gave a show. The people from the children's shelter took us to see it all.

The airplanes at the time were tiny. Sometimes when they were landing they would catch the treetops and crash. In the winter we'd run off to the places where planes had crashed, and we'd strip off the rubber straps that held back the tips of the airplane's skis. Naturally, we found many uses for these straps.

In the summer we would often go with our teachers to the fields that were being irrigated (irrigation was then only beginning to be developed, and the first systems were being tested on these fields); they were closer to Liubertsy. They were called "Williams Fields." We liked going there because the workers always gave us carrots, radishes, and turnips.

In the children's shelter there was a butterfly collection in a case. We would steal in and use the pins that fastened down the butterflies to make fishhooks and then catch carp in the pond. While we were watching our fishing rods, a lot of cats and kittens would collect behind us and pull off the fish we had just caught as we hauled them out of the water.

Once when we had been formed up in pairs to go off swimming in Kosino we were taken to a table; lying there was the broken case of butterflies. One of our teachers asked each of us who had done this while looking him steadily in the eye. No one admitted to it. Then we were all taken swimming. As we were going through the village of Podosinki, my brother and I climbed over a fence and went to fish for carp. A couple of hours later, a boy came running up and told us that while everyone was coming back from swimming, two kids had found a bomb and had dropped it. The bomb exploded and many children were injured: those who were standing near it had leg injuries, those farther away were struck in the chest. Only one boy had bomb fragments in his head, and he died. It was just by a stroke of chance that my brother and I remained unharmed—because we had gone fishing.

One day a teacher came to me leading a boy. She took my hand and led us both to the end of the garden. As we were walking, the boy told her that I was the one who had pulled the pins out of the butterfly case. I kicked him in the face with my right foot so hard that he even fell down. And then I tore my hand away from the teacher's (probably she herself had let go) and ran off. I came back in the evening, near supper time, thinking that I'd be punished immediately. But no one even mentioned what I had done. No one in the shelters had much use for squealers, while in the camps informers were simply killed. I always hated people like that. It's probably something I was born with.

And so my brother and I lived in the shelter until winter. That winter Mama came and took us back home; she told us that Father had come back from the front. After he came home Father began teaching us to read and spell properly. Mama also made trips to the village for food.

Papa fell ill in the summer of 1919, and Mama took him to the village to recuperate. We were left at home alone, and Mama was away for a long time. Before she left, Mama had been feeding pigeons at the window, and they had grown used to it. When there was nothing left to eat we would catch them, roast them, and eat them.

Mama came back, and once again put my brother and me in a shelter because Papa had died in the village.

When a child is sent to a shelter or an orphanage, it's much worse for him than prison is for an adult. But we had been in shelters already and so we knew how these places worked. My brother and I were in the shelter right until 1920, when he was taken back home and I stayed on alone. The children's home was in a building somewhere between Mayakovsky Square and Tsvetnoy Boulevard.

In the summer of 1920 we went off to a dacha in Serebryany Bor. There, on Khodynka, there were weapons depots; people had set fire to them in 1917 and the fires and explosions had gone on for a long time.

One day after breakfast, when all the kids in the children's home had gone their separate ways, I decided to go to Khodynka. There I found a grenade (at the time I still didn't know what it was). I unscrewed a little tube from it that looked like a cartridge, with something black inside. I traded this tube to a boy for a broken penknife. He decided to dig out this black stuff so he could make a cap for a pencil from it. He put a nail into the tube and struck it against a rock. The tube exploded and he lost his left hand.

Soon we moved from the dacha back to Moscow and our director returned from his holiday. One day he called me into his office. He paced around the room for a long while and kept asking me why I had taken the detonator out of the grenade. Then he came up to me and gave me a good slap across the face. I grabbed his inkstand and threw it in his face. Then I jumped out of the open window from the second story and hurt my right leg a bit. I ran out on the street, got onto the bumper of the "B" streetcar, and went home, across the Krymsky Bridge. I didn't go into the house right away but waited until it got dark, then crept into our entrance and crawled into one of the boxes between the second and third storys where people kept groceries in the winter. There I went to sleep.

In the morning I got up and went to the market to swipe a few things to eat. After six days of living like that they caught me. Mama wanted to send me back to the children's home, but I said that if she did I'd run away again and never come back. And so I stayed at home.

Mama was still working in the bakery. The other kids and I would often go down to the wharf where they had recently begun renting out boats. We'd help wash the boats, and the boatman would let us use a two-person boat on Sundays. We'd use it to take picnickers across the river to the Sparrow Hills. People would take their families out for a bit of relaxation. As a rule, they would take food and samovars with them.

In his free time, the man who ran the boat station during the day taught us how to swim the breaststroke and how to save drowning people. First you had to turn the person onto his back and calm him down; if he started grabbing onto you in a panic you had to take a deep breath and let yourself sink toward the bottom. Then he'd let you go. All these lessons were very useful to me in later life.

In 1932 I broke my right foot, but before that, in 1931, while in my first year at the School of Circus Arts, Anatoly Gavrilov and I had put together an original number for our practical training. It included "Icarus stunts," tossing one another by our feet, and other acrobatic feats using a table and a little barrel. After my injury I couldn't take part in the number any more and a student named Kurepov offered me a part in a parody of the movie actors Pat and Patachon. The bones in my foot hadn't knit properly, and the doctor gave me an orthopedic shoe with an arch support and lacing that began right from my toes. I wore the shoe all day and didn't take it off even at night.

One day we were rehearsing in the hall of the school. My partner beckoned to Voinov, a student in our same year. He was sitting in the front row, while some jockeys were rehearsing in the riding hall. When Kurepov approached him, Voinov knocked him right toward a galloping horse. But my partner managed to turn, push himself away from the horse, and fall behind it. I went up to Voinov and told him that he could have crippled his classmate and that maybe we should go outside and clear up our differences. As he got up he butted me in the face. At the last moment I managed to ward off the blow with my left arm, and with my right I hit him so hard he flew back into the second row.

Early in the morning of the next day, when we arrived for rehearsal, Voinov came out of the side passage carrying a knife. He jumped across the barrier and waved it at me. I grabbed his hand, twisted it, and punched him so hard that he struck his head against the barrier. After that the administrator, Smuliansky, came and told us that he was going to be taking us out on performances. We showed him our number and went to work in Tula Oblast, in an area where they mined brown coal. We used to sleep in local cultural clubs.

One morning we went for a swim in the river. While we were swimming, a herd of cattle was being driven nearby. We were wearing red shorts, and when we came out of the water and made our way through the herd, a bull caught sight of the red color and chased after us. To get away from him we had to jump back in the water. The bull wouldn't go into the water but kept walking along the bank pawing the earth. We were freezing sitting there in the water and so we took off our shorts, hid them under our arms, came out, and walked through the herd where women were milking the cows.

Another time in Tula Oblast my partner and I had gone to swim in a pond, and since we were late for work we decided to swim across it (the pond was about a hundred meters wide, but going around it meant a walk of three kilometers). We bundled up our things, tied them to our heads, and began to swim. I made it to the other bank, but my partner had swum no more than twenty meters when he started shouting that he was drowning. When I swam up to him he immediately grabbed my hand. Just as the man who ran the boating station had taught me, I began sinking toward the bottom, and he let me go. I swam a little distance away and told him that if he was going to grab me, I would leave him. Once he understood that I pulled him out.

In 1923 there was a rubbish dump opposite the Zamoskvorechye Sports Club Stadium that ran all the way to Neskuchny Park. The dump was buried, the stadium closed, and they began building something over the whole area. They built a wooden bridge across the road at Krimsky Val and later set up some pavilions there: this was the first agricultural exhibition. It was opened at the beginning of 1923. The tickets were made of thick paper and cost 50 kopecks. I kept a close eye on the ticket takers. In the morning, after the exhibition opened, they would tear the tickets, but later they got tired of this and just threw them into the litter bin whole. When the ticket takers happened to be looking the other way, my friend and I changed some full bins for empty ones, gathered up the tickets, and then sold them near the wicket where there were long lineups. We did this for three days until the people who ran the exhibition caught us shaking out the bins. Our "wages" from this enterprise then came to a stop. But the money I "earned" over those three days was enough to buy shoes and blouses for my sisters.

In the fall, Mama again sent me to the children's home distribution center on Polyanka Square. I didn't spend long there. At the very beginning of my stay I climbed up to the attic by the fire escape. Hanging there I found several rings of horsemeat sausage; they had been left by the Tatar janitor (at that time in Moscow all the janitors were Tatars). I took two rings, hung them round my neck, buttoned up my shirt, and climbed back down. The other kids and I ate up all the sausage and found it very tasty. The next day I didn't find any more sausage there: the janitor had discovered some of it had gone missing and took the rest away.

That was the winter Lenin died, and our teachers took us in pairs to pay our respects to the leader. It was very cold, and my nose and ears got frostbitten.

Mama soon took me home again. By that time our eldest sister already had a job. My brother also was working at the Prokhorov Textile Mill ("Trekhgorka").

We spent most of the summer on the Moskva River. On the other side of the river they had built the Dynamo Water Sports Center. You couldn't get in unless you had a member's ticket, though children could get in for twenty-five kopecks. We would put twenty kopecks in our mouths and swim across the river. There were tennis courts and a gymnastics court on the other side (we were already doing some quite advanced acrobatic jumps). Only the staff of the Lubyanka and party workers could be members of Dynamo. And to play tennis you had to be quite well off, since a racket cost three months wages for a regular person, and then you had to buy tennis shoes and an outfit.

In 1925 the kids from our building went off to the District Committee, where we were sent off to workshops. These workshops were in a building that had once been the Rukavishnikov Children's Shelter. It was next to the Ministry of Foreign Affairs at 30 Smolensk Boulevard. We were assigned to the chemical workshop, since there were no vacancies in the other ones.

Netting made from bast fiber was being dyed in vats in a green camouflage color for use by the military. There was a dining hall attached to the workshops where we would play ping-pong on the tables after the noon meal. A man from the District Committee named Mezdrekov was attached to the workshops. He was a fellow with a round face badly scarred by smallpox. He stopped us playing and would always be checking the dining hall. But we would jump out of the windows and he couldn't catch us. Once he brought three fellows with him: evidently they were also party workers, since the party District Committee was next to the workshops. They took up positions by the windows, and Mezdrekov took away the ping-pong paddles and net. They tore up the net and smashed the paddles, calling ping-pong a bourgeois game that we must not play. They always reminded us of that later.

In the workshop we prepared aniline dyes and did various analyses. In 1928 I passed the exam for a machine operator in the chemical industry. The exam was held in the Department of Nonferrous Metals and Gold. I had to do a test to determine the percentage of silver in the tsarist twenty-kopeck coins. I did an analysis and found that the coin was made of 60 percent silver and 40 percent copper. I was given a certificate with a good grade and went to work in the Central Scientific Experimental Laboratory, where they made equipment for factories. I worked there for a year and a half until 1930, when I enrolled in the School of Circus Arts. I graduated after three years, presenting a routine called "Flying from the Trampoline" in which two others took part. They were Boris Gusev, who was the "catcher," and Ivan Mukhin, who did jumps on the trampoline. I was the vaulter from the trapeze.

We didn't perform that number together for long. In 1934 we were supposed to go to the city of Yuzovka (later renamed Stalino, and now Donetsk).

Before I left Moscow, my brother came from Yuzovka and told me that it was so cold there that your hands would freeze to the trapeze cables. I decided not to go. So I was eligible to be called up for army service.

After that I got a job in the Moscow Music Hall. At that time, they were presenting the shows "Variety Artists," "The 14th Division Goes to Paradise" (in that show we played devils while wearing rubber harnesses as we leapt from gridirons), and "The Seducer of Seville." In that show the director gave me a small part in the episode of St. Bartholomew's Night. Dressed and made up like a rabbi, I ran out onto the stage fleeing from my pursuers and ran toward the side passage at the other end. In the middle of the stage I did a somersault onto my stomach; the police agents caught up and cut off my head with a poleaxe. One of them held up my head (the props man passed the policeman a copy of the head through a trapdoor in the stage floor), displayed it to the audience, and threw it toward the footlights. I picked up my head, they cut it off again, and with that the scene ended.

One day the head of the Bureau of Literary and Publishing Affairs arrived and said that it wasn't possible that the police couldn't cut off the head of an old Jew at one go, so the scene had to be dropped from the show. And it was dropped.

CHAPTER SEVEN

The Hospital—The Camp Sector for Convalescents— Timber Cutting

The camp doctor began listening to my heart and checking my pulse twice a day. Lying constantly in my bunk helped me to feel better, and during the day I would leave the barracks and take walks nearby. One morning the doctor came to check my temperature. About twenty minutes after he left they put me on a sled and took me to the camp hospital. On the way there some unfamiliar but beautiful music kept ringing in my ears.

I knew the head surgeon in the hospital. In 1937 we had walked together on the transport from Murashi Station to Chibiu and he had fed me cod liver oil during the whole trip.

I had scurvy. The head surgeon brought me a kilo and a half of sugar and told me to eat nothing else until I had finished it. Every day he would bring me young shoots of pine and spruce; I was to chew these and then swallow. Thanks to the efforts of my friend, I quickly began to recover and was soon on my feet again.

After my recuperation they put me back in the camp sector where they kept goners and convalescents who, like me, had been sent here from hospitals. We were well fed: six hundred grams of bread and cooked food three times a day. Despite that, many patients died.

In place of regular work, the camp gave me the job of walking each morning to the camp sector near the Vorkuta railway line to bring back the mail. This was a wonderful job. I'd walk through the forest and often see a lovely wood grouse atop a spruce tree or an elk peering through the underbrush. But soon they took me off this job and made me a sawyer, cutting planks for coffins.

By that time I had recovered enough that I could begin acrobatic jumping and weightlifting to strengthen my arms.

The doctors at the camp sector gave us regular examinations. After one of these exams they sent me off to cut timber. One day there was a meeting of technical personnel in the camp and I was called in. They asked me if I had been a circus performer and I told them I had. They offered me a job breaking up logjams on the river where the timber was rafted away, and I took it. I remembered how, as boys, we would run across the ice floes on the Moskva River during spring breakup. We'd use a crampon tied to a piece of rope to fish anything that would serve as firewood out of the water and drag it back to shore. We managed to keep ourselves supplied with firewood that way and sometimes even had some left over to sell.

The camp head had me signed on with the crew breaking up logjams. They made me a pair of boots and gave me a horse that I shared with the log-rafting engineer.

Logjams happened only twice in the whole area of timber rafting, and both times at the same bend in the river. You had to run out on the logs to the middle of the river, knock out one or two logs and then, as the whole raft began to move, run back to shore. In 1937, lots of logs were left on the bank after a logjam.

Even before my hunger strike I had stopped shaving, and while I was on strike I grew a curly black beard and moustache. Because of that the *zeks* nicknamed me *Pakhan*—the boss or "godfather." One day I asked the camp head for permission to use the bathhouse, and he agreed. While I was washing, three *zeks* came up and tried to push me away from the tub of hot water. I pushed them back, and one of the *zeks* hit me. I punched him back. Then all three of them jumped me. I was a good soccer player and fought them off mostly with kicks. These *zeks* were carpenters and were making furniture for the head of the camp. They complained to him, and he told the barber to shave off my beard and moustache. After that one *zek* said about me: "He was the *pakhan,* but now he's just a *patsan*" (a teenager or young thief).

On the whole, the timber rafting went well, and the rafting engineer praised my work in front of everyone.

After that, the head of the camp sector gave me a job running the food warehouse. I was to take delivery of food supplies from the supply manager and send them to the kitchen; in the mornings I would distribute the bread to the *zeks.* There were quite a few goners among the young kids serving their time, and I was able to slip them some extra food. Many of them recovered and were able to fulfill their work norms so that they began getting eight hundred grams of bread and Category 1 cooked food.

Two months after I began that job there was an inspection of the food warehouse that turned up a deficit of three hundred rubles. Because of it, I was to be tried for "sabotage on the food supply front" (at the time, starving kolkhoz farmers who picked up a few ears of wheat from grain fields that had already been harvested were given five to ten years in the camps under Article 58). But since I was already serving my time under Article 58 and since I was running the food warehouse and was to be punished by the head of the camp, my deficit was written off as loss by shrinkage and spillage. That finished my chances for a job in the food warehouse, of course, and so they sent me to a brigade of firefighters who put out the bonfires left by timber cutters.

By that time I was physically well and had started performing tightrope walking for the prisoners. But after my hunger strike I was dead inside; nothing interested me and I didn't feel like doing anything.

CHAPTER EIGHT

I Get My Life Back

One day I was fishing in the river (they let me leave the zone) and caught a two-kilogram ide fish. After that apparently insignificant event, something inside me seemed to turn around. I felt that I was alive again; I went back to my "Little Apple" dance performance with acrobatic moves and put together a number with a female prisoner. We even went out to perform in nearby villages.

One day the food ran out in the camp and no supplies were coming in for another day. The camp commandant called me and two other prisoners in and told us that one of the local Komi people was going to take us out to catch some fish. Our Komi guide told us what we'd have to do. I was to stand in the prow of the boat and harpoon pike; the second *zek* would sit in the middle of the boat and kill the fish I caught so they wouldn't thrash around. The Komi would steer the boat. Twenty centimeters above the prow of the boat was a "goat"—a little wire grating where we burned pine roots (they gave off a lot of light).

We got into the boat and moved upstream. After three hours of rowing we made a stop, lit a fire, and had some tea. Then we burned some pine resin on the "goat" and quietly drifted downstream. In the darkness you could clearly see the dorsal fins of the pike near the riverbanks. I speared one with my harpoon, lifted it out of the water, and passed it to the fellow sitting in the middle. He killed the fish on the harpoon and quietly laid it in the boat so as not to frighten the other fish. In the morning we came back to camp with a boatload of pike. The camp commandant was delighted; he hadn't expected a catch like that.

At that time I was performing in three numbers: the tightrope, "The Little Apple," and lifting my female partner. We often toured the nearby villages and camp sectors and gave shows along with other performers. Besides us the program included a singer, a storyteller, and an accordionist.

When you were going to a village with the wind in your face, you could always catch the distant aroma of *shanga*—pies made from slightly fermented fish.

So that's how I lived until 1939. Early in the morning of March 14, the camp chief issued me a certificate stating that I had served my term, and I set off for Syktykvar to pick up my documents. It was about twenty kilometers to the main road, and when I reached it I sat down on a stump by the roadside; I was surprised to find tears rolling down my face. Trucks were passing by, but the tears kept flowing and flowing, though I didn't know why. When the tears finally stopped I got up, washed myself with some snow, stopped a truck going to Syktykvar, and showed the driver my certificate. And off we went . . .

A. P. BUTSKOVSKY

THE FATE OF
A SAILOR

CHAPTER ONE

My Life Before My Arrest

I was born into a peasant family in the village of Peschano-Ozerka, Amur Oblast, on September 30, 1926.

The first thing I can remember is collectivization. We had a hard life and a large family, nine of us in all. My parents didn't go into the collective farm, and we moved to Blagoveshchensk in Amur Oblast.

At the beginning of the 1930s there was a terrible famine in Russia. We lived in the city in poverty and hunger. One day I went to the market with my father and saw hungry, abandoned children there. They were lying under the market stalls and on the sidewalk. Alive but no longer able to move, they were being eaten up by flies and worms. This was such a terrible sight that even though more than half a century has passed, I can still see it as if it were today. There were many, many abandoned children.

In order to save us from starving to death, my parents took us to the island of Sakhalin.

In 1937 we came back from Sakhalin to Blagoveshchensk. My father couldn't get a residence permit, the reason being that he had left his village without joining the collective farm. That same year father was exiled to the village of Mazanovo in Amur Oblast. I didn't hesitate a moment to share my father's exile so as to try to ease his lot. The train went as far as Belonogovo Station, and from there we had to make a long trip on foot. It was October or November, the beginning of winter, and there was already a lot of snow. We walked, pulling a little sleigh with our belongings, and kept on for two hundred kilometers or more. I was eleven at the time.

I spent the winter of 1937–38 with my father, or rather my father worked in the taiga the whole winter, some sixty kilometers from our village, and came back home once a month. One day, while walking home from the taiga and crossing the Selemdzha River, he fell through the ice and nearly drowned. I was anxiously waiting for father that evening, but instead of his usual time of ten o'clock he didn't arrive until nearly two, quite frozen. He

173

survived, thanks to his strong constitution, and the next day he went back
to the taiga to cut timber.

Timber was cut by hand, and one man's norm was fifteen cubic meters.
The pay was far too low: 150 to 180 rubles a month (in prewar money).

I was in the fourth grade of the little village school. It was cold in the
classrooms, though the stoves were stoked up twice a day. The pupils were
children of exiles, just like my father and me. There wasn't much to eat, and
I didn't always have enough bread and always felt hungry. And to make
matters worse, we were plagued by lice that were very hard to get rid of.
Everyone, adults and children alike, slept on the floor since there were no
beds.

Toward the end of April 1938 my father was allowed to go and see his
family, and once again he and I made the 200-kilometer trip on foot. There
was still snow on the ground; we had fastened skids to a plywood box to
hold our belongings, and we had to drag it across the snow. The trip took
almost ten days. By the time we arrived at Belonogovo Station again the
snow had melted. Then we had a train trip with three changes before we
came to the settlement of Kivdo-Kopi in Amur Oblast. Here I met my
sisters, Anna and Polina, my brothers, Afanasy and Viktor, and the person
dearest to me, my mother.

The year 1938 was drawing to a close. One October night, NKVD
agents burst into the room where our family of seven was living. I woke up
from the loud hammering at the door, and when I opened my eyes I saw
people dressed in black. There were three of them: one stood in the open
doorway, two by our bed (we all slept on the floor). One of these people
kicked my father and demanded that my mother show him all our documents. Mama was trembling and crying, but the agents swore at her for
taking so long to find the documents, though she hadn't been looking for
more than a few minutes.

They kicked me as well and ordered me to close my eyes. I was terrified that they would take my father away, but this time nothing happened.
The agents left, slamming the door behind them. My sisters hadn't seen or
heard any of this—they slept through it. My mother and father couldn't
get to sleep until morning. No matter where I went in the years that followed, I could never forget that day.

We had to work very hard in those prewar years: cutting and stacking the
hay, digging the garden and, in the fall, gathering in the harvest and bringing it six or eight kilometers to where we lived. The whole family helped

bring in the harvest. In the winter there was school. We didn't have enough clothes, and two of us had to share a pair of very large-size shoes.

It got even harder in 1941 when the war began. A year later, when I turned sixteen, I volunteered for the army after adding two years to my age; but they soon released me as underage. I went to work operating an engine in a mine. Times were hard: there was food rationing, basically for bread, and there weren't any other kinds of food. If you overfulfilled the plan you would get two little pies when you left the mine.

In 1943 I was called up for army service. When I left to fight in the Great Patriotic War, I never imagined that when it was over I would have to spend long years rotting away behind prison walls, in the camps of Sakhalin, on Cape Lazarev, in Kolyma and frigid Yakutia, and that when I did get back to freedom I would run afoul of the tyranny of the authorities more than once. But that was all in the future. In the army I served in the 12th Independent Rifle Brigade as a machine gunner, as number two on a Maxim heavy machine gun team. I weighed 48 kilograms; the equipment I had to carry weighed 43 kilograms.

I saw a lot of injustices and harsh treatment of soldiers in the army. After basic training our battalion went on exercises in the forest. For a whole week we were ordered to strip down to our underwear at nights and sleep on branches laid on the snow. We had summer tents that weren't heated. Many people got sick. Twice I objected to such treatment and was punished.

Eventually I was transferred to the navy. I thanked fate that I was there. Things were easier, and at least they fed us better. We often had American tinned meat, tinned sausage, and cheese in our rations.

The war ended triumphantly, and along with other sailors I spent some time in Alaska at the American naval base in Cold Bay, where we were taking delivery of some warships for the Soviet Union. It was in one of these, frigate number 25, that I returned to the USSR.

I served in the war with Japan and took part in the liberation of the ports in North Korea. In 1946 I had a stroke of luck—another trip to the USA. I saw the cities of Portland, Chicago, New Orleans, San Francisco, Seattle, and the Panama Canal. We were again buying ships for Russia. When I came back to the USSR I went on serving in various ports—Vladivostok, Sovetskaya Gavan, Kamchatka, Port Arthur—never suspecting that, having once mentioned in my documentation that my father had been exiled in 1937, I myself would become a victim.

There was a good deal of talk around the fleet about people being arrested: Lidia Ruslanova, People's Artist of the USSR; Kuznetsova, the wife of the secretary of the Leningrad Regional Committee of the party. Some sort of "Leningrad Affair" had been discovered that involved the arrests of hundreds of people. A rumor went round that some of the sailors who had been in the USA had been arrested. Like an echo, these rumors were heard by every sailor.

And so the ominous date in my life arrived: March 4, 1950. I, a sailor on the torpedo boat *Vedushchy*, was arrested by agents of the MGB Military Section 25084. I was accused of praising life in the USA. The interrogations went on at night, and my testimony was wrung out of me by force.

The court sentenced me to ten years in prison and five years disenfranchisement with a ban on living in major centers: this meant, in effect, "voluntary" exile to Siberia after I had served out my time. And that's what I want to talk about in the chapters that follow.

CHAPTER TWO

Arrest and Prison

The coming of the new year of 1950 brought no sign of the bad things that were to come on my job. At the end of 1949 we had returned from the city of Komsomolsk-na-Amure in the new torpedo boat *Vedushchy*. By that time the weapons systems on the ship were as advanced as those anywhere.

I began thinking about civilian life and demobilization. Although I was already serving my seventh year in the navy, there were still sailors born in 1921 and 1922 serving on the ship, and so no one knew when the demobilization of those born in 1926 would begin. These were anxious times. Rumors of repressions spread like lightning around the fleet. I was soon convinced that the rumors were absolutely true. My friends in the merchant navy, the Kovalenko brothers, told me about arrests taking place there. Everything they had told me was confirmed when I, too, found myself in prison.

I think that they had had me in their sights for some time. It must have been a month or two before my arrest that I noticed they weren't putting me on duty details and that they held back my leave. By that time I was married. Married sailors would be given an overnight pass on Saturday or Sunday, but I was allowed to leave the ship only from 7:00 to 11:00 P.M. All this put me on my guard. One day I noticed a man in civilian clothes on board, in the cabin of the political supervisor. It was probably that same night I dreamed that someone had torn off the little finger of my left hand and it was very painful. Two days later, on March 4, 1950, I left the ship at 2:00 P.M. to go home. On the way I stopped by my wife's workplace to pick up a pair of shoes and take them in for repairs. When I came home I decided to change into civilian clothes. I put on a raincoat, put the shoes in a bag, and went outside. I hadn't managed to go more than twenty or twenty-five meters from my door when two unknown men ran up to me, grabbed my hands, struck me in the neck, and dragged me into a car. I didn't lose consciousness, and in the car I realized that these were MGB agents: this was their handwriting, the handwriting of the year 1937.

There was another man in the car besides the driver and the two who had grabbed me. Now I knew for sure that I was saying good-bye to my freedom for a long time. They took me to the MGB on Kitaisky Street. Everyone in Vladivostok knew this sinister building. I had walked past it a number of times when I was on leave. This was where they held prisoners, and this was where they interrogated and tortured them, though their cries and groans were muffled by the trams clattering along their rails. They shoved me into one of the three cells in the basement. I spent three days there; they never took me out and didn't feed me. I slept sitting on the concrete floor. Then they took me to an office where a colonel was waiting. They put me in a chair that was bolted to the floor. When I was seated, the colonel said with an ironical smile, "So, my friend, we've caught you as well. No one ever leaves here, and you'll not leave here alive either." Then two more people came in and forced me to sign some sort of document, an arrest warrant, I think. And that same day (it was March 7) I was sent to prison.

Sitting in my solitary cell in Vladivostok Prison and realizing the injustice of it all, I came to the conclusion that it would be best to kill myself. But how? The solitary cell had nothing in it that I could use for that purpose. The cell was on the second floor, two by four meters; the walls were more than a meter thick; the ceiling was vaulted; the window was barred by louvers and the door was of strong metal. There was an electric light in the ceiling, about two meters above. The first thing that came into my head was to grab both of the electrical wires, but I hesitated: I didn't know the voltage of the electrical system. A couple of days later I managed to find out from a guard that the voltage was only 127, but I still decided to try touching the wires. For a few days I practiced jumping up as high as I could and easily reached the bulb and the socket, though they were secured inside a metal cage. I could use the cage as a handhold.

I was alone in the cell. Well, I thought, it's time to make up my mind and do this. Suddenly out of the corner of my eye I caught a flash of something behind my back. I turned around involuntarily and saw a small folded piece of paper on the floor, a page from a book. I unfolded it and began to read: it was about Bolsheviks who had been sentenced to be shot. Sitting in their solitary cells and knowing that on the very next day they would be executed, they would do physical exercises. This gave me some strength, and I gave up my suicide attempt. I knew, after all, that I was not facing execution but ten years in prison: that was the sentence given to all those who were "uncooperative," those who wanted to know the truth and who saw injustice.

The interrogations began, and they took place by night in the building on Kitaisky Street. The interrogators used physical force. As a rule, two of them would do the beatings, using rubber boots to hit me in the kidneys. This went on for about ten days. After the exhausting interrogations and beatings were over, they transferred me to another cell that held two criminals. So there I was, a political, along with them. From that time onwards they relied less on beatings during the interrogations; besides, I had decided to resist. At one regular interrogation Guryanov grabbed his pistol and came up to hit me with it; he waved it around a few times, but I told him that if he ever hit me again I would strangle him. At the time I still had enough strength left to do it, regardless of the consequences. Then the MGB held me all night, gave me nothing to drink, and didn't take me to the toilet even though I urgently had to go. Twelve hours later they sent me back to the prison.

In April 1950 I was transferred to the third floor into what now was my third cell. In the cell were Anatoly Boev and two Japanese: one of them, Sawamura, was a simple worker; the other, Imai, was a genuine samurai. A little while later they brought in Tolya Yemshanov, a soldier.

And so now there were five of us in the cell. My interrogator was still the same Guryanov, but he no longer tried using force on me. He realized that he was physically weaker and wouldn't risk tangling with me one on one.

But using various lies and deceit, he began to concoct a transcript of the interrogation. He made me sign blank sheets of paper and then would write in whatever he needed to make a charge, and he did that more than once.

Prison was hard on my morale: we didn't get newspapers, food parcels were forbidden, and I couldn't exchange letters with my wife.

On one of those days I put the issue to the interrogator: if they wouldn't allow food parcels, I would lay hands on myself or on the interrogator. After that I was allowed to get food parcels from my wife.

Over this whole time, of course, my wife had no idea where I was, even though she did everything she could to find me. She also went to the ship. The captain, Captain Third Class Zherebin, knew where I was but told her that my whereabouts were unknown. Only later, when my wife and I had managed to establish an illicit correspondence, did I learn how she had been treated by the "organs." The direct intermediaries in our communication were the prison guards, though they didn't realize it. There are various ways of secret correspondence. The means I used had been worked out in prison by a sea captain, Pozdnyakov. He had lived in Vladivostok some time before, on Dalzavodsky Street, No. 2, and was sentenced to ten years in a trumped-up case. Our communication system began operating, but I'll say something about that a little later. First, a few words about our cell.

As I mentioned, there were five people in the cell where they brought me this last time. The concrete walls around us were a meter thick, the ceiling above was shaped like a cupola. An iron door with massive locks was set in the front wall; it had a small, covered window through which the food was passed. Above the window was a round hole four or five centimeters wide, the "Judas hole" through which the guards outside could watch those sleeping in the cell. On the ceiling there was an electric light inside a metal dome. The bulb lit up only half the cell, and reading by its light in the evening was virtually impossible; but they never gave us anything to read in any case.

The wall opposite the door had a window with a metal grille; outside there was a louver that shut out the light of day. The building itself, in any case, was situated so that the rays of the sun never made their way into the cell, and so even in daytime we lived in darkness. Within this cell of eight square meters there were five cots embedded into the concrete floor and a little table made of two planks. In the corner stood a foul-smelling barrel, the *parasha,* that was carried out to the toilet and emptied every morning at 5:00. For bedding we had a mattress stuffed with cotton, a flannelette blanket, a cotton pillow, and a single sheet of indeterminate color. The sheet was changed every ten days. They would take us to the bathhouse inside the prison at the same time.

All five of us were under investigation, and we were all being accused of holding views that were in some way harmful. At night they would take us away in an enclosed vehicle for interrogation, and they would bring us back to the prison in the morning. We weren't allowed to sleep during the day. There were usually two interrogators doing the questioning, and when they attacked people physically, one interrogator would leave the room so that there were no witnesses. As I've already said, the interrogator who was fabricating my case was Guryanov from the 25084 Military Detachment of the MGB. The interrogations and the humiliations went on for two months.

It was difficult to stand up to the coercion inside the prison walls, and in order to save my life I decided to sign everything that the interrogator wrote down. The lack of any links with the world outside and the loneliness inside the prison walls played their parts, and I began to feel that I was a genuine victim of the MGB. We in the cell would share advice on how to behave during the interrogations and, later, in court. We studied Japanese. We began to take an interest in how the prison administration worked. We would calculate how many people came into the prison and how many left on transports. Each month they sent over three thousand people to the camps. There was only one consolation—getting food parcels from my wife. The day a parcel arrived was like a holiday. We all—the Japanese as well—would share the contents: everyone was equal in the cell. The Japs were grateful for our help and thanked us for everything. How I wish I could meet these two Japanese again, my cellmates from 1950; but they were convicted and given twenty-five years in prison.

And so the days of our gray lives passed by, each day like the others. Two months inside these walls and never a single meeting with my wife. What were the state security organs doing with her? It was only her parcels that kept me believing that she was alive.

So they cobbled together a case, and I was waiting to go to trial, not just to a court but to a military tribunal, a Troika. And so it happened—Soviet justice. There was no one in court, a secret trial. There was one frightened witness (as I found out later, they wanted to use my wife as a witness). And that was all. The whole thing took half an hour, and the path to freedom was cut off for ten years (not counting the serious aftereffects), which was what I had anticipated.

Prison again, but now a different cell, one for people who had been sentenced. Anatoly Boev was already there; he was given ten years, and there were a few more who also got ten years each. Tolik Yemshanov was tried the next day—ten years. It was in this cell that I met the man who managed to set up a secret link with the outside, Captain Pozdnyakov; he had also been given ten years.

All those convicted were allowed one visit with relatives. The visit took place near the main gate of the prison in a special room cut in half by the prison's main walls. There was a window in the wall without any glass but with metal gratings on each side. These gratings were very fine and were set a half-meter apart so that you could barely make out the features of the face of the person opposite you, though you could hear very clearly. A prison warder stood in the half of the room where the prisoner had come for the meeting, though the warder would leave from time to time; I think this is how he showed a bit of compassion. When the warder was away you could talk about anything you wished. About two or three days after I had been sentenced, I managed to pass on the news to my wife. By that time I had already become acquainted with Pozdnyakov. He had been given permission for a visit, and I wrote a note for my wife explaining how she could write to me using an ordinary newspaper and giving her an example of how to do it. I gave it to Pozdnyakov, and he managed to pass the note over to his wife, who then gave it to mine. There was no doubt that the code had become known on the outside, since two days later I received a parcel and a brief note. This gave me strength, and I firmly made up my mind that there was a way out of any tough situation and you just had to look for it. I had to use that same code more than once, but then another way to communicate opened up. The difference lay only in that Pozdnyakov's code worked in both directions, while other channels of communication only ran into the prison.

A great deal of time has passed since then, and yet if people reading my memoirs understand how the code works, they may be able to use it some time and be grateful for it. First you compose the text you want to send on a piece of paper, keeping it as brief as possible. Then you take an ordinary newspaper and, starting from page one, pick out the information you need as you read it page by page. When you find the letter of the alphabet with which your text begins you make a pinprick beneath it, and go on doing that until you've picked out your whole text. When everything is ready, you wrap some item from your food parcel in the newspaper and take it along with your parcel to the prison. In prison everything would be brought to your cell. Without anyone batting an eye, you had to take the food and then, using another newspaper with a text you had already prepared, you would wrap up the dishes and give them to the duty warder; he would return them to the person who had brought the parcel. Back home, the person would hold the newspaper up to the light and find out everything you wanted to pass on. And so a secret means of communication was established. There were times when they wouldn't allow newspapers in the cell, but people on the outside found out about it immediately and communicated by other means. One time, after a regular secret message had been passed, something so unexpected happened that it was hard to believe it.

In prison everything has a meaning: the banging of the doors in the corridor; the number of pairs of feet that walked past and the weight of their step; how long the corridor door remained open; and how many times the key turned in the lock—you had to pick up all those things by ear. The sound of the key in the lock told you which warder had come on duty, the sound of footsteps told you the time of day. Overall, each one of these observations added something to our understanding of the workings of the prison administration.

The prison warders performed their duties zealously and didn't allow us any slack. The food was terrible. In the morning a spoon of sugar, or rather a measure of ten grams, and the sugar was damp; a soupy gruel (*balanda*) for lunch, with some kersey porridge, and more gruel for supper. The senior warder usually gave out the sugar, and we learned that he was the one who carried out the death sentences. We went on strike and demanded that he be replaced. Eventually the duty warder on the floor began passing out the sugar.

The warders were dedicated to their profession and to their duties. Still, among them was an elderly fellow who attracted our attention. He seemed somehow different from the others. When he was on duty on our floor we managed to find out a few things: how many prisoners there were in the prison, the daily counts of new arrivals and of those leaving on transport, both politicals and criminals. The figures he gave us confirmed our guesswork and calculations almost exactly. From brief conversations with him we managed to find out that he was not well, that he had a large family and they lived in great poverty. We decided to give him something from our food parcels, and he began accepting our gifts. After a few shifts with this warder we got quite friendly and even found out from him how things were in the city. He told us that arrests were being made, that there was some disarray in the ranks of the MVD, that the prison was overflowing with prisoners, the camps were overcrowded, and yet the arrests went on. He told us how to behave in interrogations and in court, though that was of little use to us now.

Usually when the warder brought a food parcel he would come up to the window in the cell door and ask who was expecting a parcel. He would give the first letter of the name of the man whose parcel it was, and that person would add the remaining letters of his last name; if everything tallied, the parcel was given to the person to whom it was addressed. But now, when our old fellow was on duty, he would give out the parcels by an unwritten law. The person who had a parcel would be called out to the corridor and receive it there; in return we would share some of our food with the warder.

And then came the incident I wanted to mention. It happened on a day in May. My wife had brought me a parcel. Our friend was on duty, and he called me into the corridor and began handing over the food. It was a substantial parcel that contained, among other things, two large smoked Atlantic herrings. I offered him quite a number of things, but he said that he would like something salted. I gave him one herring, and he led me back to the cell with the rest of my food. I told Boev about this. He was older and more experienced and said that I should be more careful doing things like that. And then we sat down to devour what was in the parcel. About ten minutes later, the window in the cell door opened and the guard called my name. "Outside," he said. Everyone was puzzled and trying to guess what had happened. I was puzzled as well. But everything was explained when I came up to the duty warder's little table. He was alone, and his modest lunch was on the table; there too lay the sliced herring that I had given him. But sticking up from inside the herring was something made of paper and about the size of a thin pencil. It was a note. The warder said, "Take it and read it." The note was from my wife, and she wrote that the people from MGB Military Detachment 25084 were trying to frighten her. They would question her and tell her that I was an enemy of the people and many other things as well. Then the warder lit a match and we burned the note. I went back to the cell and told my cellmates everything. From that day on our links with the warder became very close, and when my wife found out what had happened she would bring parcels on the days when our man was on duty.

So the note in the belly of the herring and our friendship with the warder strengthened my wish to live and not give in. They sustained my dreams that a time would come when all this would be explained, that truth would still triumph in our society.

CHAPTER THREE

The Death Cell

In the misty, distant childhood that I never had, when I was in exile with my father in 1937, I heard tales from exiles about prisons and death cells, those cells holding people sentenced to death without a trial or an investigation.

Many distinguished Soviet military leaders, scholars, doctors, and ordinary people passed through these death cells. And now, in prison in Vladivostok, I personally became convinced of the existence of death cells. This is how it happened.

While waiting for the confirmation of my sentence, tormented by interrogations and beatings, I decided to tell everything to my wife, not in code but in open text on paper. There was little chance that my message would ever reach her, but if the warders intercepted it they would at least know what was going on within the walls of their prison and within the investigatory organs. I knew very well that if the prison warders read my letter I would certainly be punished, but I was ready for anything.

It didn't take long to figure out how to throw my message over the prison wall, but as I later learned, the distance between the place where I threw out the little bundle and the street where people bringing food parcels might pick it up was more than 150 meters. Throwing a little wad of paper that distance, even from a height, was almost impossible, and the whole undertaking was doomed to failure from the outset. But, as they say, risk is a noble thing. I'll explain how it happened. Our cell was on the fourth floor, in the corner, close to the prison wall. In front of our cell, which was covered by a metal door, was a platform made of metal grating with another locked metal door. The door of the platform went out into a common corridor in which there was a huge window covered with a grating made of widely spaced bars. Through this window you could see the prison wall, the guardroom, and people coming with parcels. We passed fairly close to this window each day when they took us to the toilet. How could I throw out my letter when the warder was right there? But my plan had been worked out for a long time, and I had to take the risk.

When they took us to the toilet, the cell door stayed open and they closed only the door to the platform. On the day I decided to throw out my letter one of the more lenient warders was on duty. At 4:00 he opened our cell door and said we were to go to the toilet. As we left we closed the cell door and the automatic lock clicked shut; when everyone had come into the corridor, the guard closed the door to the platform. After spending the usual ten minutes or so in the toilet we went back to the cell; I was the last in line. The warder opened the door of the platform and told us to go into the cell. The first man in line shouted that the cell door was locked. The warder went to the door and all the prisoners clustered around him, blocking his path and thereby winning some time. Then I took two or three large paces to get near the corridor window and with all my might I threw my letter through the grating in hopes that it would land on the street. Then I hurried back to the platform where everyone was crowded together. The warder had already opened the door and we went in. Anatoly Boev asked whether I had seen my letter fly over the wall. I couldn't say that I had, because as soon as I had thrown it I went away from the window. We were quiet for a few minutes, mentally measuring the distance from the window to the street, and we came to the conclusion that my attempt had failed: the distance was too great. My message had fallen near the wall facing the prison building, in the forbidden zone. A warder picked it up and passed it to the head of the prison. The rest of the day was full of tension, and that night I dreamed that a little mouse had got into the pocket of my naval overcoat.

About 2:00 the next day I was called out to see the head of the prison. Everyone in the cell knew at once that our enterprise had failed; I realized that as well. I was brought to his office. The head of the prison sat at his desk, smug and radiant; his eyes shone and he had a triumphant air. The distance from the door where I stood to his desk was four or five meters, and among the papers lying on his desk I could see the gray pages of my letter.

The prison head picked them up and showed me and then asked if they were mine. I replied that they were.

I took pride in the fact that we hadn't yet been completely broken and that we could still put up a struggle in prison conditions. When he heard my answer, the head of the prison called in an officer and said, "Send this sailor *there* for five days." Just where "there" was I didn't know, but I realized that it was somewhere far away. We went down the stairs to the lower floors; iron doors would open and close in front of us; and then we began going down farther and I guessed that this was "there." It was the underground section of the prison. There was a narrow corridor lit by dim electric lights and cells along one side. A door was opened and I was shoved inside. I realized that this was a death cell. At first I was seized by horror. What first caught my eye were the walls on which were scratched the names of many people who had been condemned to death. In one place I read, "My last day. Tomorrow I'll be shot," and a signature. I no longer doubted that this was one of the death cells where they carried out the sentences and where they sometimes put rebellious prisoners to pacify them. Two or three times a month they would whitewash these cells and paint over the inscriptions on the walls, but despite their careful painting you could still make out the words. The cell was about five square meters; it had a concrete floor, and along one wall was a concrete shelf about ten centimeters high: this was the bed. Here as well was a huge iron ring cemented into the floor to which they shackled prisoners. There were marks from the chains. Everything suggested that something had happened in this cell not long before I arrived. When I looked carefully at the walls I found blood. The concrete floor was saturated in human blood. The smell in the cell was familiar from wartime; it was the smell that hung over dead bodies.

I had none of my belongings with me. There was no bedding. There was a barrel in the cell (a *parasha*). The daily ration was two hundred grams of bread plus a cup of water, also two hundred grams. I spent two days under these conditions and decided to declare a hunger strike. They wouldn't give me any paper to make a written statement of my hunger strike, and they wouldn't give me my allotted two hundred grams of bread either. The third day was drawing to a close. I had firmly resolved to eat nothing until the end and was ready to die in this cell. The warders usually changed shifts in the prison at 6:00 P.M.; it was about that time that the "Judas hole" in the door of my cell opened and I saw a warder I recognized. There was another warder with him. Then the Judas hole closed and I tried to imagine what this might mean. Before long the Judas hole opened again and the warder I knew told me that there was no point in my going hungry, that I wouldn't achieve anything by it and would only damage my health. He brought me some bread and porridge and I couldn't help agreeing that, truly, a hunger strike would undermine my moral and physical health. The next day he again added a bit to my ration, and now I had only a little more than a day to stay in the death cell. That time passed, and precisely at the end of five days I was taken back to the common cell.

There the fellows fed me and told me that they had known where I was. And so I had paid a visit to the death cell. Even now, as I write these lines, I tremble with the fear I experienced at the time. But after that the usual prison days went on, as I waited for my sentence to be confirmed.

And so the sentence was confirmed, and they soon sent us all on a transport to the transit camp at Vtoraya Rechka. My wife knew the day on which we were being sent away and she came to the prison. Here I was able to see her for the first time since my arrest. They didn't let us speak to one another, though: all prisoners had to squat down and stay that way for a long time. Free people weren't allowed to come near; they had to keep about fifty meters away. I shouted to my wife that we were being taken to Vtoraya Rechka but had no idea of where we would be sent from there.

Vtoraya Rechka was the transit prison that supplied the work force for the MVD Dalstroy. I spent about a month there, and then we were shipped off on another journey.

CHAPTER FOUR

Cape Lazarev

On one of the last days of August 1950 we were taken under reinforced guard with dogs to the freight station in Vtoraya Rechka, where they loaded us into stinking freight cars. There were no beds, just two levels of sleeping platforms made of planks; there was also a toilet in the car, or rather a chute in the slightly opened door. It was still very hot, but they gave us nothing to drink. They didn't feed us on the first day either. And so the train took us away to parts unknown, and only toward the end of the third day did we begin to get a vague notion of where we were going. But it was clear enough that we could expect impenetrable taiga. The freight car took us to the town of Sofiisk in Lower Amur Oblast. There they loaded us onto trucks, and on we went. On the way we learned that we were being taken to work on a tunnel under the Tatar Strait. Each truck carried thirty men, and we drove for more than a day. And at last we came to our appointed destination, Cape Lazarev. This is the most easterly point in our country. The distance between the cape and the island of Sakhalin across the Tatar Strait is eight kilometers. Even before the Revolution political prisoners had escaped through these places, and it was here that the song, "The tramp fled from Sakhalin along a narrow bears' path" originated. We didn't see any tunnel. The tunnel project was classified and was referred to simply as "Project 500."

And so it was Cape Lazarev and Project 500. The camp had only just been finished. The barracks were built of unpeeled logs, with two-tiered sleeping platforms made of rails. On the second day we were taken out to work, clearing the way for a road through the impenetrable taiga. But this was more like the roadbed for a railway than a route for vehicles. Our tools were handsaws, spades, and crowbars. We not only had to saw down the trees but grub up the stumps, remove the topsoil, and build embankments and drainage ditches. About eight hundred men were set to work on this sector. There was a long trip to the work site, almost seven kilometers one way, and we went there and back on foot.

Each day we built eight hundred meters of railway bed. Our machinery was the traditional prisoner's wheelbarrow. The days passed; there was nowhere to wash, and winter was on its way. The lice bred furiously. I wore my sailor's striped vest instead of an undershirt, and there were so many lice in it that it's terrible even to recall. The lice wouldn't let you get a decent night's sleep, and in the morning you had to go to work. A rumor went round that the road we were building led to the tunnel, but no one knew how many meters we had to build. They were pushing us hard to get the work done.

One Sunday we were resting in the camp. There was a bonfire inside the camp zone and I decided to get rid of my lice, so I took off my vest and burned it. But that hardly reduced the number of lice—they just crawled about my outer clothing. I don't know if it was because of the lice, but an epidemic broke out in the camp. Many people fell ill. Those who were seriously ill weren't forced to work but could stay back in the zone. Those who stayed in the zone would burn their lice over a bonfire, shaking their underclothes over the flames. In the camp there were Estonians, Latvians, Tatars, Russians, Uzbeks, Georgians, and prisoners of other nationalities as well. Everyone was weak and emaciated, though the Russians turned out to have more endurance. It's scarcely worth mentioning the food: there wasn't much of it, as the camp saying explained: "Project 500—500 grams of prison soup, 500 of bread." People asked where they might find "Project Two Kilos." And it's true that everyone did get 500 grams, and that it was called Project 500.

We spent months working day after day, deprived not only of our freedom but of all human rights. I came down with scurvy, lost the use of my right leg, and blood trickled from my mouth. My condition became critical, but I had always kept something aside for truly hard times. I had a hundred rubles hidden away inside a book. I gave this to the doctor, and over the course of ten days he gave me five or six injections of ascorbic acid. Slowly I began to pull myself out of my miserable condition.

And who was there to tell my sorrows to? You would just lie there, sick, not needed by anyone, and no one could help you.

Even worse, you knew that your family was being persecuted on your account. Once you began thinking that way, your life seemed senseless. Many people were overcome by a terrible state like this. A number of people hanged themselves.

After I got on my feet again I was given a job in the wood shop, since with my bad leg I wasn't able to work on road construction. In the shop I would carry planks and haul sawdust in a wheelbarrow. The shop did carpentry work for the camp and for projects of the Ministry of Transport.

At first we got no mail and, in all likelihood, the camp administration burned our letters; but then they began allowing us two letters per month. Then I remembered the code and decided to write my wife to tell her where I was and how she could get to Cape Lazarev. Our letters were checked, and the censor was the camp security chief, Nadeikin; but our code wasn't broken and didn't even arouse the suspicion of the camp administration. After a couple of months had passed I became convinced that my wife knew all about my situation. We prisoners would say in our letters that we were getting along fine, wonderfully fed and well treated. What else could we do? If we wrote the truth we would lose our right of correspondence. I had already received several money orders from my wife. I used the money to buy food: bread, sugar, tinned fish. I managed to buy some underwear. On my new job I gradually got rid of my lice.

It was the summer of 1951. We found out that a huge amount of work lay ahead in building a causeway and railway across the Tatar Strait. But how this was going to be accomplished no one knew. We hadn't spent all that much time on Cape Lazarev, and yet how many things had happened: cases of people hanging themselves, criminals who killed an economist prisoner with an axe, two people stabbed to death and several others attacked with knives; and then one day some criminals managed to escape.

I had heard a good deal about escapes from prisons and camps by revolutionaries and prisoners at hard labor during tsarist times, but here, it seemed, there was nowhere anyone could escape to: everything was closed off, water and security checkpoints lay all around, yet suddenly there was an escape. To tell you the truth, I felt relieved: there were some strong people left after all, people capable of finding daring solutions to any problems.

Here are a few words about them.

CHAPTER FIVE

The Escape

Even as a child I had heard of prisoners escaping from prisons and camps. There were coal mines operating in our little village of Kivdo-Kopi in Amur Oblast even before the war. Prisoners worked in one mine. Our neighbors in the barracks where we lived were the Petrenko family. They had many daughters, and the eldest was friends with a guard from the camp. His name was Fedor Goncharov, and it was he who told us how three people had escaped from the camp. You could tell from his story that he wasn't particularly eager to go searching for them. I heard about escapes when I was in prison in Vladivostok as well. There were escapes, or escape attempts from many places. As far as I know, the political prisoners rarely took the risk, though they would do their best to help those who did. In practical terms escaping was impossible. The whole taiga was dotted with camps and security posts. And how far could you go without any food?

Even in 1950 I heard about escapes from other camps in Project 500, but the result was always the same—back to the camp again. The Okha (Sakhalin) to Sofiisk oil pipeline crossed Cape Lazarev; this was the area described in Azhaev's novel *Far from Moscow*. In the village of Lazarev, famous as the site of the country's first oil pipeline (built by prisoners even before the war) lived a man named Yegor. He didn't have any job but lived on what he got from the MVD for catching escapees. For one *zek* he would get a "decent" payment, as he expressed it: five thousand rubles in cash, alcohol, white flour, meat, and tea. And Yegor would justify the rewards he was given and put his heart into his work. Whenever there was an escape the MVD agents would go to Yegor and give him his assignment: "Find him!"

Yegor would take his rifle, a good supply of ammunition, and some dry rations and go off after the escapees. Sometimes it would take him a whole month to catch up to his victim. He wouldn't take the escapee back to the camp but would kill him on the spot and bring back one of the hands he had cut off the victim. The camp administration would take fingerprints from the hand and check them with the ones they had on record; if everything matched Yegor would get his reward. People said that he'd even been given the Order of the Motherland for his dirty deeds. The people of the village hated him, but there was nothing they could do since he had a secret bodyguard.

One day we were being taken back from work. One guard told us: "That's Yegor over there, and he always gets his man."

It was already late fall, and from the camp zone you could see ice beginning to form along the shore. The fishermen were getting ready for winter, preparing their craft for winter storage, but there were still many boats in the water. The camp woke up that day as usual. By 7:00 A.M. everyone had already been chased out to the guardhouse ready to be escorted to work. Almost everyone in the brigade I worked in was a political. About twenty minutes after we arrived at the project, a guard came from the camp, formed us up again, counted us several times, and then escorted us back to camp. Here we found out that three people had escaped. The escapes had left no traces at all. No one knew when they had fled, whether in the evening or late at night. On top of it all, that morning we woke up to find fresh snow. There weren't any footprints, and even the well-trained dogs couldn't find a thing. The escape was so clever and so bold that we didn't find out how it had happened until the escapees had been captured.

It happened this way. Over the long period when they were working at the construction site, the criminals had hidden civilian clothes in various nooks and crannies. Once they had put together the essential supplies they fled. Regularly each week a truck (the "shit wagon") would come to the camp to empty the cesspools. The driver was a prisoner, but his term was almost over, and he worked without an escort. This shit wagon would come into the zone some time after 11:00 P.M. on the appointed day. That day it arrived at the proper time, but it didn't pump out all the contents of the toilets. There was quite a lot of space left in the tank, and it was here, into this liquid human waste, that the three men climbed: they were standing up to their chests in shit.

The shit wagon was stopped at the control post, the guard opened the hatch, looked in and saw the liquid contents, and let the truck out of the camp. Slowly and without any problems the truck made it to the work site where the escapees' clothes were stored. The fugitives climbed out, washed in the icy water, changed their clothes, got into a boat, and rowed across the Tatar Strait to Sakhalin. Meanwhile, the search for them was taking place here, on the cape and in the areas nearby. Five days passed, and the whole time we stayed in the camp; they didn't take us out to work. When the fugitives got to Sakhalin they hid in the forest until their food supply ran out. Hunger forced them to go into one of the villages. Notices had been posted everywhere about the escape, and people on Sakhalin knew about it as well. The fugitives went into a little shack and asked for something to eat. The man who lived there was suspicious of the strangers and quietly sent his son to a settlement where there was a village council to inform the MVD that these might be the men they were looking for. The owner of the house fed his guests and gave them a place to sleep, promising to help them make their way to Aleksandrovsk. Early the next morning, at 5:00, he woke them up; they went outside and saw that the shack was surrounded by local Chukchis and Nanais. They had nowhere to run. One of the fugitives tried to get away, but they shot him in the legs. Then they were all tied up and taken to a larger village that had direct contact with the MVD. And the MVD arrived as soon as they got the news of the capture.

We saw them when they came back to the camp. A guard was riding one horse, the wounded fugitive was tied to another, and the two remaining men, hands tied behind their backs, were tied to the tail of the second horse. Two more guards rode behind them. And that was how this escape ended.

From that moment on, the regime in the camp became even harsher.

CHAPTER SIX

We Meet

A year had gone by, and I marked off each passing day in my calendar. There were still more than three thousand agonizing days until my release, and I could only dream about freedom. Over that time there hadn't been a case of anyone being pardoned, although many had appealed to the Presidium of the Supreme Soviet of the USSR. There were some happy moments, though, and one of the days of the year that had gone by had been a red-letter one for the whole camp, I think.

As usual, I had come back from work in the evening, washed, and was getting ready to go to supper when suddenly I heard my name called: someone was looking for me. One of the prisoners who worked without an escort came up to me and handed me a note. As soon as I opened it I recognized the handwriting. My arms and legs began to tremble, and I couldn't imagine where the woman who wrote the note could possibly be. When I pulled myself together I read: "Sashok, I've come to you and I'm waiting at the guardhouse. Your Anya." Yes, it was a note from my wife. I simply couldn't believe that my wife had really come here, but it was so. She was close by, but we were still on opposite sides of the barbed wire.

My appeals to the camp administration to allow a meeting led nowhere. They wouldn't allow me to meet with my wife. On the third day I bribed a camp guard, and Anya and I met in the workers' compound. Our meeting lasted about an hour. They were already searching the settlement for my wife so that they could take her away from the cape under threat of arrest. And so, after an hour together we parted again, now for some long years.

News of my wife's visit spread through the whole camp. People came to me and asked if it was really true that my wife had come; and when they found out that she had been here they thrilled at her courage, the fact that she dared to enter these highly restricted areas. And it's true that she was the first woman who came to Cape Lazarev to visit her husband. The administration questioned me about how my wife could have found me. Of course, I didn't give up our secrets.

The administration began treating me with suspicion, and for a while they didn't even allow me to go out to work: I was kept under observation inside the camp. They were afraid that I might be able to escape. I was searched a few times, but eventually they convinced themselves that I had no intentions of escaping and sent me out to work again.

Then the gray days of camp life resumed. Some time after my wife left, people began saying that all political prisoners were going to be transferred to Sakhalin. This rumor soon turned out to be true.

As I end my recollections of Cape Lazarev, I want to confirm once more that situated here was one of the camps designated as P/Ya 241/15 that was part of Project 500. The project was secret. Project 500 was run by the

MVD from the town of Sofiisk. The head of construction was Lieutenant Colonel Arais. The head of camp P/Ya 241/15 was Major Zarubin, the security officer Senior Lieutenant Nadeikin. (My information might be useful to someone writing a history of the Sakhalin tunnel.) There were both criminals and politicals in the camp. My friends among the politicals in this camp were Anatoly Boev and Anatoly Yemshanov.

In the MVD's archives for Project 500 there are record books that were compiled quarterly; from them one can find out precisely how many criminals and how many politicals there were. Prisoners with good handwriting were also used to compile these records. I myself took part in the compilation several times. Even now I can remember just what they looked like. They measured thirty by forty centimeters and had about a hundred pages.

CHAPTER SEVEN

Sakhalin

And so we were on Sakhalin, not far from the settlement of Pogibi in the Rybnovsk Region. Here the work on building a causeway really had begun. The plan was to link the settlement of Pogibi to Cape Nevelskoy (a distance of some forty kilometers) by a causeway and link Pogibi by a land railway to the town of Aleksandrovsk; the railway was to come out of the tunnel somewhere in this area as well. The winter was a severe one; work went on in two shifts and in some sectors even three.

It was a new place with new worries, and to make matters worse I came down with jaundice. But I got a good deal of moral support, knowing that my wife had made her way safely back home: I was getting regular letters from her. She supported me materially as well. All this was the central factor in my life, and I was thinking about the future.

Many of the camp guards from Cape Lazarev turned up on Sakhalin. In our short breaks from work we would recall our old lives and dream about our future ones. Recollections of our past and our childhood didn't add any brightness to our current lot, because the nightmarish time spent in the camps overshadowed everything that was good and didn't allow any hope for the future.

One could write a great deal about how the camp administration treated the prisoners, and it would all be only bad, with the exception of a few separate instances.

The administration was afraid of the prisoners, not only the living but, even more, the dead. The regular burials on Sakhalin made me recall the whole procedure for burying prisoners.

As it happened, I had dealt with burials even as a child. I had not had to bury my relatives, but I did bury a good number of others, complete strangers. I well recall the year 1938. I was twelve and we lived in a settlement. My father worked in the local hospital and he had been given a horse. It was a large settlement: there were two mines in operation, a sawmill, a hydropathic center, a generating station, and a number of other enterprises. There were two schools. I went to the large, two-story school. Discipline in the school was excellent. We respected our teachers and feared the principal. There was only one cleaning lady for the whole school. She managed to do everything: she rang the bell, washed the floors, and supervised the cloakroom. I went to school in the winter. In the summer there was a lot of work at home, and in addition, my father would take me to his job when he had too much work to manage on his own. Such heavy work generally piled up at times when I was on school holiday.

As far as I recall, at the time, for some reason patients from other areas who were in serious condition would be brought to our hospital. These were people who had been badly beaten during NKVD interrogations and, as a rule, they didn't survive; their relatives were not informed of their death. So they were the ones my father and I had to bury. In the evening, my father would warn me that I had to come to the hospital the next day by breakfast time; by then the grave, which he had dug himself, was already prepared. In the second half of the day we would harness the horse, go to the morgue, and pick up the body awaiting burial (they would tie a bit of white cloth to the foot of the corpse), lay it in a coffin, fasten down the lid, load the coffin on the cart, and take it to the cemetery. There we would use planks to lower the coffin into the grave and cover it with earth. We set up no cross or other marker, and there was only a mound of earth that would, for a time, indicate that someone was buried beneath it.

In such a way we buried a lot of people—three or four a week, all through the summer. They made us use various places in the cemetery for the burials. Then my father quit his job at the hospital and went to work in the generating station; but I dreamed of corpses for a long time thereafter.

I mentioned this because those burials were linked with the repressions that took place in the distant prewar era. And now, when I myself was one of the repressed, I learned how people were buried in the camps.

I had witnessed burials of prisoners even on Cape Lazarev. We lived in harsh conditions, and prisoners began dying during the first year of the camp's existence. The deceased was brought to the guardhouse, where a doctor did an autopsy to determine the cause of death; then the body was brought back inside the zone and laid in a ready-made coffin. The coffin lid was placed alongside and everything was taken back to the guardhouse. Then the guard on duty would walk up to the corpse and with all his might hit it on the head with a heavy mallet; and then he would pierce the stomach of the corpse in two or three places with a metal rod. Only then, in the presence of the duty guard, would two other guards nail shut the coffin and take it away to the burial place. They buried people somewhere at the foot of a hill; I don't know precisely where, since this was an MVD secret. I know that a bit of plywood with the deceased's name, year of birth, the article under which he had been convicted, and his prison term was placed in the coffin. Relatives of those who died were not informed. And so people vanished from the face of the earth, and no one knew where they had gone. One prisoner, a trusty, told me that some bodies were burnt along with their coffins.

As soon as we—mainly politicals—had been shifted to Sakhalin we were put to work. Part of the brigade was sent to cut cribs—supports for the causeway; two brigades were sent to haul fill for the railway line. There were about two hundred kilometers to fill. Because of that, the work, both on the water and on the roadbed, was done in two shifts. We knew that somewhere nearby the construction of the underwater tunnel across the Tatar Strait was going on, and though the work was managed by the Ministry of Transport, there were prisoners working there as well. While we were still on Cape Lazarev we began leveling a hill to make a sort of large, flat field and had started to sink a shaft, but then free workers appeared on the site and we stopped working there. Our brigade also worked in two shifts filling the roadbed.

We had filled some twenty kilometers or more, and the road had reached a small river about twenty meters wide. A ramshackle bridge had been built across it. The riverbanks were already covered in ice, and the river was full of fish. We always ate our lunch by a bonfire. We made good use of what the river could provide, and it was a huge help to us. Now we began having some work stoppages, since the excavating machine that loaded the soil into trucks was already quite a distance away from the brigade. We were ordered to get the excavating machine to a sand pit on the opposite bank of the river. It weighed twenty tons, and the bridge could barely support empty trucks. They ordered us to get the excavator across the river no matter what. There was no ford across the river, and it was three meters deep.

The higher-ups in road construction told us to shore up the bridge with extra piles. And so we built a few bonfires in a circle with a clear space in the middle; and then we began plunging down into the frigid, seething water—in our underwear, of course. After spending five to seven minutes in the water we would jump out to the bank and warm ourselves among the bonfires; and then back into the water. In the course of a day we made as many as thirty such dives into the water. And so it went for two days. We reinforced the bridge, and to test it we sent across a fifteen-ton scraper: the bridge didn't seem to shake at all. Then the excavator started across. When it got about halfway it stalled, and the bridge began to crack. But it all came out well: they were able to tow the excavator across, find out why it had stalled, repair it, and in a couple of days it was working in the new sand pit. The river by now had completely frozen over. The bosses were pushing hard on the work in our sector. They kept telling us that we were lagging behind the Ministry of Transport's schedule. We knew that the tunnel was being built under the strait. And those prisoners who were left in the camp on the cape were shifted to tunnel construction; we learned that in February 1953.

I personally never saw the tunnel, but I know for certain that it exists; and besides, there is a ventilation shaft in the strait itself.

It was the beginning of March 1953. The work on these critical projects never ceased. The winter of 1953 on Sakhalin had turned out to be a mild one, and so we barely noticed the coming of spring. The snow began melting, and it was hard going to work in wet boots. There was an outbreak of jaundice, and I came down with it as well. I lost my sight. But my blindness didn't last long: I used all my savings for medicines and fish oil. I drank fish oil, got my strength back, and wanted to keep on living. The jaundice went away, but then the scurvy got me.

We didn't know what was going on in the wider world and not even in our own country. There weren't any newspapers, and no radio either. What news we had came from the free workers on the project. By now I had been in prison three years. On the morning of March 5, 1953, we went off to work as usual, but inside the compound they had set up a long post and attached a loudspeaker to it. The prisoners realized that something of national importance had happened. In the evening, the two thousand or so prisoners in our camp gathered around the loudspeaker. And it was here that we heard of the death of J. V. Stalin.

I have to say that we all stood without moving a muscle, and even though we had been deprived of our freedom, no one rejoiced in his death. Separate groups of nonpoliticals started to discuss what had happened. The politicals said nothing, and in fact what was there to say at the time? After all, it wasn't that long since the war had ended, and our troops had gone into battle with Stalin's name on their lips. It was under his name that they sealed off the gun ports of enemy pillboxes and perished in detachments of partisans. His name was the name of our Motherland—that was what we believed then. We knew about the repressions, and we ourselves were in prisons and camps, but we believed it was our whole system of state control that was responsible and put the blame for the repressions not on Stalin alone but on the whole leadership of the country—on Molotov, Voroshilov, Bulganin, Malenkov, and the others.

My attitude toward Stalin is another topic. After his death, the camp authorities were all in a commotion, and the guards were unsure of themselves. Soon there was a decree about amnesty for the criminals. They were rejoicing, but we politicals didn't know what to expect. There were rumors that all politicals were to be executed; we heard that even from the guards. In short, after the amnesty decree, the millstones of the major projects— Ministry of Transport Project 508 and Ministry of Internal Affairs Project 500—stopped grinding. The construction sites quickly began to be cut back; then, toward the end of March, all the projects on Sakhalin were closed, and we politicals were loaded into dump trucks and taken across to Cape Nevelskoy.

I think that we were taken to Cape Nevelskoy so as not to break the secrecy of Project 500, connected with building the tunnel under the strait.

CHAPTER EIGHT

Cape Nevelskoy

Cape Nevelskoy was some fifty to seventy kilometers south of Cape Lazarev. Here, just as on Cape Lazarev, work was going on connected with the building of the tunnel. The whole region from the town of Sofiisk to Cape Lazarev, Sakhalin, and Cape Nevelskoy was a restricted zone. Entry was forbidden. You could only get into these areas if you were alone and without any transport.

When we got to the camp we found out what else we would be working on here. There were a few hundred politicals in the camp and some repeat-offender criminals as well. They took us out to work on an eight-hundred-meter dock that had been started before we arrived. There was no stopping the rumor that this was the end of the line for us, that we were to die here building this dock. We got no letters, and all links with the world outside were cut off.

I remember how one day we were taken into a small ravine with cliffs on either side; they set up machine guns on the heights and aimed them at us. I don't know what they had in mind for us, but in any case they kept us here a very long time. Our guards fell back much farther than they normally did. We didn't do any work that day. They might even have been checking how they could bury us after an execution. In any case, something was being planned against the politicals.

Two days after that incident we learned about the arrest of the Minister of Internal Affairs, Beria. The camp administration was in some confusion, but it was prepared to carry out an order to eliminate the political prisoners. All work came to a halt; there was a general mood of uncertainty, yet somehow the fear that we would all be executed disappeared. We knew that they weren't going to let us out and we also knew that there was no escaping Kolyma. Thousands had already given up their lives there, thousands just like us.

It was the beginning of August 1953. They began getting us ready to be sent off, but we didn't know where we were going. A medical commission arrived. They picked out the young and healthy. I recognized one of the doctors in the medical commission: he was the brother of Vovka Pavlov, a schoolmate from before the war. He recognized me and said that the camp we were in was to be closed for good and that we were being sent somewhere even beyond Kolyma.

After the commission had spent three days with us, the freighter *Feliks Dzerzhinsky* appeared in the roads of Cape Nevelskoy. We knew that the ship already had a big load of prisoners, about two thousand men. They set about taking us on board. We were taken to the ship in small groups. There were eight hundred politicals—that's an exact figure.

We were loaded into a separate hold with no criminals. And so there we were, on board the ship, and there are no words to describe what happened during our voyage.

The tweendeck hold which under normal conditions would house 150 men now had 800. Even though summer was ending, the August days were very hot, and so the heat in the overcrowded hold was unbearable.

Two hours or so after the loading, people were already gasping for breath. There was no ventilation in this iron box. The bulkheads were dripping with moisture. The one and only hatch that could bring outside air into our hold was shut tight. People began collapsing from heat stroke, while those still standing were breathing heavily and covered with sweat. Even though we pleaded for help, the authorities gave no sign that they were going to do anything to solve the problem.

It was a critical situation, and even the most hardened among us were beginning to give out. The only thing to do was to move some of the people out of the hold, but the authorities weren't about to do that. There was only one thing we could do: refuse to accept food and declare a hunger strike. But who could organize it?

Suddenly the hatch opened and we heard the guard's command:

"Collect your meal!"

The group of prisoners, including me, who had gathered at the ladder to the hatch refused to accept the food. The hatch slammed shut. There was a murmur in the hold, and we could hear noises from on deck. No one could understand the whole situation: those in the hold didn't realize what was happening on deck, and vice versa.

I knew something about international maritime law and decided that it was up to me to represent the prisoners and then lead the struggle to have our demands met.

I turned to the whole group and said:

"This is how it works, boys: as long as there's a hunger strike on board, the ship won't go to sea; that's a law of the sea. We have to officially declare a hunger strike. If we don't do it now, the ship will put to sea and we'll suffocate in here."

There were shouts from all sides: "He's right! He's right! We trust you to lead the hunger strike, and we'll do whatever we have to!"

From that moment they began calling me "the diplomat" for some reason, and even gave me a new last name, Diplomatov. The lot of us discussed what to do next. I perched on the ladder, took a piece of paper, and began writing out the demands we were presenting to the administration.

That was more than thirty-five years ago, but I still remember word for word what I wrote then. Our legitimate demands were as follows:

To the commanders in charge of the transport of political prisoners
To the members of the ship's medical staff
To the captain of the vessel *Feliks Dzerzhinsky:*

800 men have been loaded into the tweendeck built to accommodate 150. There is no ventilation and no cold water. There is no ventilated toilet, no place for receiving hot food, no dishes. Cases of heat prostration have occurred during our three hours in the hold and they are receiving no medical attention. All this runs contrary to the medical norms for the transport of people. Because you have not observed these norms we, all 800, declare a hunger strike and DEMAND:

1. That medical attention be given to those in need of it.
2. That up to 500 men be removed from the hold and moved elsewhere, to the upper deck if necessary.
If our legitimate demands are not met within two hours, there may be grave consequences resulting in deaths.

Five of us signed on behalf of eight hundred men, and my signature was first.

We passed on our demands to the guards and began our wait. The hold hummed with human voices. By chance, we discovered that a few meters from our hold was another filled with criminal prisoners. Using the prison alphabet we began communicating with them. There were about two thousand of them. They realized that we had declared a hunger strike and were prepared to support our further actions.

We formed a committee to coordinate our actions. We knew that we had a hard struggle ahead, but our determination, strong spirit, solidarity, and sense of justice kept us united. We took as our slogan, "One for all, and all for one." They elected me to head of the committee.

There were many officers, from lieutenant to colonel, among the MVD guards. After we had passed on our demands, some of the ordinary guards wanted to conduct the negotiations with us. We insisted on seeing those in charge, and our committee decided to negotiate only with the people to whom we had addressed our demands. Therefore, I had to prepare for the negotiations and live up to the name my comrades had given me. Everyone in the hold supported me and told me, "Don't give in, diplomat," and we weren't prepared to give in. We worked out a plan of further action. We did what we could to help the sick, collected the moisture from the bulkheads, and shared the water with them. We posted sentries on our side of the hatch leading into the hold; their job was not to let in any low-ranking guards under any circumstances. Our sentries knew full well that I would negotiate only with the people at the very top, and so they didn't trouble me with minor questions. We could hear threats shouted to us through the closed hatch. Then the hatch opened again, and we heard them shouting at us to stop the hunger strike or they would set the guard dogs on us. This showed that our demands had not reached the ship's captain. We then had more discussions of what to do if the dogs were let loose in the hold. It turned out that there were some prisoners among us who had experience in dealing with guard dogs. All of them had been a prisoner of the Germans, and though they had been emaciated, hungry, and exhausted, they had managed to stand up to any dog. There were about thirty such people here, not all that many. We found out that the criminals really had declared a hunger strike, and that raised our spirits.

More than three hours had gone by since we had passed on our legitimate demands. Once more the hatch opened, and above us we saw a reinforced team of guards with dogs. A group of representatives came down the ladder into the hold: the deputy head of the whole guard detachment; the ship's doctor; the captain's deputy for political affairs; and with them a group of people a rank lower. Through the hatchway we could see the muzzles of machine guns and hear the snarling of dogs. The officers introduced themselves, after which a lieutenant colonel asked where Diplomatov could be found. The prisoners grinned, knowing that this was not my real name but one they had invented for me. I replied that I was Diplomatov.

The lieutenant colonel was surprised and asked:

"So why are you so short?"

Indeed, I was short, but at a critical moment I turned out to be needed by eight hundred men.

Negotiations began right there, in the hold, in the presence of everyone. I realized that our demands had reached their addressees, and from the way the commission behaved it was clear that we had won our battle.

After ten minutes of talks the lieutenant colonel said:

"Well then, Diplomatov, let's go up on deck and have a look at where we might put some of these people."

The thought occurred to me that perhaps they only wanted to isolate me from the others. Our committee suspected the same thing and wouldn't let me go alone. The officers agreed that someone else could come with me. Three of us went. Those left in the hold said that if anything happened to us or if we didn't come back, they would take measures to have us returned.

We went out on deck; a gentle breeze was blowing. The *Feliks Dzerzhinsky* stood at anchor; this was now the fourth day. I was well acquainted with the layout of merchant ships, and so I knew where we could put the people from the hold. The best place was the bow section of the deck. Once we had agreed on this, the three of us went back down to the hold and began getting people ready to go up on deck. A half-hour later the hatch opened and we were asked to go up the ladder. First went those who were most weakened, then those who volunteered; I went as well. We spread out our padded jackets and greedily swallowed the fresh air. Ventilation was set up for those left in the hold.

Toward evening we were given hot food and a dry ration for our day of hunger strike. We got ourselves back to normal, while the ship stayed at anchor. During the night we heard the command, "Weigh anchor," and realized that we were under way. At first I couldn't understand why we set off at night. In the morning I realized that in order to avoid any problems with the Japanese, the ship's commanders did not want to cross La Pérouse Strait in daylight. What would happen if the Japanese were to stop the ship and ask about the cargo in the hold and what sort of passengers there were? No one could tell how it might end if that were to happen.

In the morning we were sailing along the southern part of Sakhalin, places I knew since I had sailed in these waters several times. We crossed the La Pérouse Strait, as I said, by night.

That day we wrote a note stating who we were, where we were going, and on what sort of transport. We sealed it in a glass jar and threw it overboard in hopes that someone might find it. I still don't know what happened to the jar. The voyage was uneventful: there was no gale, the sun shone all the way, and five days later we were in the capital of Kolyma, Magadan.

CHAPTER NINE
Kolyma

The ship was not allowed to tie up at the dock. I noticed that the signal-man sent a message to the port that there was a valuable cargo on board. Permission was given for entry into a bay, and there we moored. Here, in the port, we heard the radio announce that the ship *Feliks Dzerzhinsky* with a valuable cargo was at mooring. We remained on board for a couple of hours more, and then they began taking us ashore for transfer to a camp located five kilometers from the port.

And so, in columns of five and under a reinforced escort with dogs, we marched from the port through the whole town. People looked at us with compassion, some wept and asked, "Why are they treating them so sav-agely?" MVD troops were stationed at all the crossroads, and the traffic police were also from the MVD. The windows on the first floor of every building were barred. Magadan was one huge prison.

We arrived at the camp. It was built to hold ten thousand people. This was the transit prison for the whole of Kolyma. It would have been good to stay a little longer even in this place, since my lot in life seemed to be getting a bit easier: the whole time I was in the camp I didn't have to work at heavy labor. They took me on temporarily as a clerk. It was here that they made up groups of prisoners to be sent to various points in Magadan Oblast. They were sent out in Douglas aircraft and also by vehicle. From the reports of these drafts of prisoners I found out that the whole of Magadan Oblast was dotted with camps, both active and inactive.

The camp administration feared political prisoners, and so they tried to ship them as far into the taiga as possible. And so a couple of weeks after our arrival, a large group of politicals was made up, of which I was a part. They loaded us onto trucks, and we set off on our journey to Ust-Nera. This was more than a thousand kilometers northwest of Magadan.

If I were to say nothing of our journey, the whole 1,050 kilometers that I traveled in the truck, then my recollections of my stay in Kolyma would be incomplete. Now, of course, it's difficult to establish the precise dates when all this happened, but I can recall it by the seasons of the year. I wanted to keep a diary, but how could I have written about it all at the time? They were always making full-scale inspections and would confiscate everything:

letters from our families, novels and poetry, blank paper and envelopes, scraps of old newspaper. And so keeping a diary was out of the question.

In 1950, while I was still on Cape Lazarev, I got a reference book on timber issued by the MVD Publishing House. I patched it up, rebound it, and made a little secret compartment in the binding in which I always kept a hundred rubles, just for a rainy day. When they searched me they would take a look at it, but seeing the MVD stamps everywhere they wouldn't confiscate it. And so it went with me through the camps and is with me to this day. True, in 1988 I put all the charts and tables in a new binding and gave them to my son-in-law, Kolya Romanov. But I hung on to the old one. They would also confiscate family photographs. And, in fact, it seems to me that keeping family photos had its risks. Despite the death of Stalin and the arrest of Beria, the MVD and MGB agents could still grab anyone they pleased, charge him, and leave him trying to figure out what had happened.

At the beginning of October they began loading us into vehicles, twenty of them. They put twenty-five men into each truck; we sat, squatting, in rows of five. There was a shield at the front of the truck box and behind it were stationed three guards, two with rifles and one with a submachine gun. Beside the driver in the cab sat one more guard who was in charge of the vehicle.

We left Magadan in the morning. People going to work would stop, their faces expressing compassion. Magadan's population is the whole flower of Russia's exile community; these were people who had been let out of the camps but who had no right of return to the "mainland." And so they knew very well what was awaiting us.

We drove through the town at a speed of fifteen kilometers per hour. When we left the town the trucks sped up. Now we were on the Kolyma highway. It bears little resemblance to a road; it really is a highway. It has a broad surface with a first-rate covering of sand and crushed rock that looks like asphalt. The road is well marked, and at every kilometer there is a pillar with an inscription showing how many kilometers from or to Magadan; every kilometer is divided up and marked by numbered pickets painted white.

The truck rolled along smoothly. After fifteen kilometers we passed the first empty camp by the roadside; two or three kilometers farther there was a huge cemetery; and then more and more camps, some empty, some half empty, some chock-full of prisoners. We passed camps very often, but there were no settlements at all. We were given our hard rations—three hundred grams of bread and one herring. It's very difficult to sit on your haunches. At one spot not far from the road was a camp full of prisoners; the trucks stopped here and we were allowed to relieve ourselves while standing in the back of the vehicle. That was our rest break.

And off we went again, squatting as before. The picture of the highway never changed. Every three or five hundred kilometers we would come upon prisoners making road repairs. The road was excellent, and the trucks could go fast enough to make the tires hum. I heard in the camp in Magadan that this highway had been built like a railway bed, "an iron road," and that it rested on the bones of prisoners. Most likely that's true: if they built a road like that through forests and swamps, in blizzards and extreme cold, then there had to be many victims. It was all built by hand, and the basic machinery was the pick and the wheelbarrow.

Toward evening we stopped near an abandoned camp where there was no one apart from some guards. We all spent the night in that camp. There were small barracks made of blackened logs with two-tiered bunks and no bedding. Our supper was again hard rations. We were glad to find a toilet in the camp. After this hard journey we quickly fell asleep.

Reveille was at seven, and we were given a breakfast of hot *balanda*—thin soup. We took our places in the trucks again, but the guards were changed in nearly every truck. And off we went once more. Soon we caught sight of a large village. Here we saw some huge locomotive sheds, railway materials, and carriage wheels, and I was convinced that this highway really had been built for a railway.

The village really was quite a large one. On one of the buildings I read that the village was called Yagodnoe. We had covered more than five hundred kilometers and just a bit more than that lay ahead of us. We met a great many cargo trucks of various makes. Yagodnoe is a key junction in Kolyma. From here there are roads to the north, south, east, and west of the oblast.

I got a place near the side of the truck. I spent some time counting how many trucks passed us and how many we met. If you average it out, then there were 800 to 850 trucks passing a given point in the course of twenty-four hours. We spent another night in a semi-abandoned camp. It was cloudy the whole time, and now the weather was changing for the worse. There was a cold wind blowing when we got into the trucks the next morning, and the farther we traveled north, the colder and colder it got. There was snow in one of the passes. We got fairly well frozen, but later, when we moved down into a valley, it was warmer.

And then the thousand-kilometer pillar flashed past, and we didn't have much longer to sit on our haunches. We drove into the village of Ust-Nera, and we were now in the Yakut Autonomous Republic. And so the journey of 1,050 kilometers from Magadan to the settlement of Ust-Nera was behind me, and I had traveled all this distance squatting on my haunches in the back of a truck.

CHAPTER TEN

My Wife

It would be unfair if my recollections of prisons and camps told only of my own hardships; all my torments and suffering were shared by one other person, though she had not been by my side. This person was my wife, Anna Petrovna Khabarova, born in 1925, a native of the village of Tolvuya in the former Karelo-Finnish Republic. Khabarova was her maiden name. When she became my wife in 1949 she became Butskovsky; after my arrest she again began using her maiden name. I don't need to write of how fate linked me to this woman. I will only say that before we met we were living far apart from one another: I was serving in Vladivostok, she was working in the town of Pavlovo in Gorky Oblast. When she decided to share her life with me, in the summer of 1949, she moved in with my parents, and in October of that year to Vladivostok.

We didn't manage to rent a room, just a "corner" of some 5.5 square meters and a ceiling only 1.8 meters high. There was no heating—our corner got heat only when the lady who owned the house opened the door to the kitchen. The washbasin was also in the kitchen. In our corner—later we called it a room—there was a bed, an army cabinet, and an old chair. That was all our furniture. Above our bed hung a flannelette blanket that we called our "Persian carpet." There was no daylight—the room was without a window. It had enough space to serve as a home for my wife, to begin with at least; I, on the other hand, would be a away a lot while on duty. I was able to come home more and more seldom, a maximum of twice a month.

207

Altogether this would amount to eight hours. We paid ten rubles for our corner, with extra for lighting plus more for heating the kitchen. Our room was like a closet or an entry hall. It was located on Dalzavodsky Street, number 2.

But my wife lived in that room. She didn't whine or grumble and never asked for any luxuries. She kept in mind that a sailor's wife mustn't whine, and so she didn't. When I was gone—and this was almost all the time— she would read the works of Balzac, Hugo, Turgenev, and Nadson in the evenings by the light of an electric lamp. And when we were together we would go the Ostrovsky Theater. I truly loved the theater and believed that only here one could find genuine culture and art. I also loved the circus.

But my family life didn't last long, and as I've already described, March 4, 1950, was the last day of our life together, the day of my tragedy and her sorrow. My wife didn't know that I had been arrested. When she came home that evening she didn't find me. She searched for me the next day, and the next two, but couldn't locate me. Then she managed to find out from the ship that I had been arrested, and a day or two later she already knew for certain that I was in prison. By that time they had already made a search of our room. What the agents of the MGB Military Detachment 25084 were looking for I'll never know. Yet they took a photo from our album of an American sailor with whom I had served in Alaska in 1945.

Later, the interrogator Guryanov called the American a spy and demanded that I confirm that this was really so and that he had given me an assignment. Guryanov had invented this assignment himself, but his plan didn't succeed. The American sailor was an honest fellow, a helmsman by training, and since I was also a helmsman this specialty had brought us together when the American fellows handed over their frigates to us.

After our apartment had been searched, my wife was called in a few times by night to report to the MGB. They frightened her and tried to force her to say that I had been meeting with some unknown persons in Vladivostok. Each time they would keep my wife there for hours. But she never wavered and always told them the truth about me. The MGB put our building under surveillance. When they had cobbled together my case, the surveillance was lifted. They suggested that my wife leave Vladivostok and get a divorce. She did get a divorce after my trial, but remained in the city for the time being, and once they had shipped me out of Vladivostok they forgot about her. The MGB had other things to worry about. When I was still in the city, my wife gave me moral and material support. *Her* thoughts and hopes were centered on me. *Her* moral support gave me strength and made it easier for me to bear the hardships of a harsh life.

When I was in my first camp, on Cape Lazarev, she not only managed to support me in every way but, without thinking about all the prohibitions, cordons, and security posts around the area, managed to make her way to see me on the cape. And I am so grateful to her for that and always remember it. Through all the years that followed, she continued to support me with all the strength and resources she had, and I felt her presence next to me. I often dreamed of her, but that was in Yakutia.

She always supported me, even though she had no assurance that we would ever be able to meet again. She knew that those convicted under a political article were not set free when their sentences had been served but were given new sentences, and so on endlessly.

CHAPTER ELEVEN

Yakutia

And so, over quite a brief time in the late summer and fall of 1953, I had made my way from Sakhalin to the settlement of Ust-Nera. "Made my way" isn't the right expression, though: they took me, along with thousands of others, by sea and by land under reinforced guards with dogs, never leaving any of the hardships behind.

They didn't keep us politicals long in this settlement, only for about ten days. I remember that they put us to work building barracks. This was a transit camp, which meant that we still had farther to go.

And in fact it was here that they made up parties of prisoners to be sent even farther north. There was snow on the ground in the settlement, and the temperature dipped below freezing, but we were in our summer clothes. The day arrived when I was included in one of the parties to be shipped away. We boarded a Douglas airplane. This was an American transport plane, and I had seen similar ones in Alaska. There were eighteen prisoners and two guards in our group. There was fear in the guards' faces while we were in the air: they were afraid that we might kill them, but we had no such idea.

After a two-hour flight, we arrived in a camp at the settlement of Batygai. It was a huge camp that could hold about three thousand people. There were both politicals and nonpoliticals here. The prisoners worked in mines, digging cassiterite and other ores. There was an ore enrichment plant here in the settlement. At designated times, the enriched ore would be sent off by air in small bags of various colors, under a strong guard, to be transported farther. I think that these shipments also included enriched uranium. Those who worked in the mines got extra credits toward their time served.

If the production quotas were met by 151 percent, the prisoners would be credited with two additional days for each one they had served, and so their terms were shortened. Aside from this, there was early release, after two-thirds of your term had been served; but this decree didn't cover everyone.

In my first days in camp I found out that many prisoners had credits of two, three, four, and even five years, and if you were to apply the two-thirds reduction then they should have already been released, yet they were still here in the camp as before.

The people in this camp generally had long sentences—from ten to twenty-five years. I met quite a few people here who had been with me in the hold of the ship *Feliks Dzerzhinsky*. I was really pleased to meet some men who shared my ideas. They were all organized into brigades. Our group was also assigned to brigades. I got into a construction brigade and worked for a few days. They were in need of people to make brick stoves. I decided that it would be easier being a stove maker and accepted the job.

I had learned how to make brick stoves back when I was in the navy, thanks to one sailor. This was in 1948 in Sovetskaya Gavan. There turned out to be two of us making stoves in the camp. Just one guard would escort us to work, and he carried a Nagan revolver, not a rifle. Somehow this eased our minds. The temperature was already thirty degrees below freezing. Our boots made of artificial leather would freeze on the way to work, but we could warm ourselves when we got to the work site. The buildings were well heated.

We built stoves in houses that were generally for the camp staff. We worked conscientiously, since it was a sensible job. We got a decent rate for building a stove and could earn some money, though we got only 30 percent of the rate and the rest went to the camp. Still, we got 150 rubles each for our first month of work, and this was real money. Life was a lot easier with money. Now we could buy ourselves some extra food. When we worked in someone's apartment we would ask the lady of the house to buy us a few groceries. And, using our money, she would. These were wives of camp employees, and some of them were sweet, kind people. They tried to lighten the lot of prisoners every way they could. And they did it all behind their husbands' backs, asking us not to tell anyone who was buying us groceries now and then. I'll say something about one such woman later, because she played a big role in my release, though that was almost two years later and in another camp.

We were issued some winter clothing and kept on building stoves. It was now 1954; our guards got tired of escorting us from one house to another to build stoves, and so they let us work unescorted. We didn't violate any camp rules. We'd go off to work precisely at 7:00 and come back at 6:00. Our food situation improved: people would give us a bite to eat when we worked in their apartments, and we managed to buy a few things ourselves. We'd only bring back to the zone the amount of food that was allowed. You could bring any food products into the camp except tea and alcohol, and the overall weight of the goods couldn't exceed two kilos. We were given temporary passes to leave the camp unescorted to go to work. There turned out to be a real demand for stove makers, and we had no end of work to do. Once we got our passes we were allowed to work until 8:00 P.M.

By now I'd slipped seven or eight hundred-ruble notes into my secret hiding place, just for a rainy day. I never let myself forget that a rainy day might come. One day, the oven in the settlement bakery collapsed, and both the settlement and the camp were left without any bread. They quickly sought us out and took us to the camp commander, where we were told to set up a baker's oven. My friend Lenka, who had been an "honest thief" but had given up his life of crime, had worked at various jobs in the camps for many years and he knew the stove builder's trade better than I. So we took on the job of laying the bricks for the baker's oven. We saw the collapsed oven when we arrived at the bakery. The old oven had operated twenty-four hours a day, producing ten to twelve batches of bread. We decided to set up two ovens on the old foundation.

They gave us some extra helpers and all the materials we needed. We worked sixteen-hour days—the settlement and the camp had no bread, after all. In fifteen or twenty days the ovens were ready; we heated them up and the bakers made their first batch of bread. We earned five hundred rubles each for those ovens.

After that job we were again put under escort. I was sent to a hard-labor brigade, for what reason I simply couldn't understand. Only six months later I found out that my record had the notation "Politically dangerous." This comment had appeared after I had headed the political prisoners during our hunger strike on the *Feliks Dzerzhinsky.*

There's no need to explain in detail what "very dangerous" or "politically dangerous" means. If this comment had appeared in my documents when Stalin was alive, my bones would have long been rotting. They would try to get rid of people like that under the pretext of an escape attempt. As a rule, the guards would do things like that in winter. This is how they did it.

They would bring the prisoners to the work site; the guards would take up stations on the site so that they could see all the prisoners and also see each other. The senior guard would go on the work site and take one or two "very dangerous" or "politically dangerous" prisoners and make them build a bonfire for the guards. But the firewood was beyond the limits of the site, and that was where they would send these "dangerous" prisoners. And as soon as the person crossed into the forbidden zone, the guards would open fire on him without warning. Then the camp authorities would arrive, pick up the dead man, and write up a document with the standard statement, "Killed during an escape attempt." Whether the man was shot in the chest or in the back, the guards were always in the right. If he was shot in the chest they would write, "Attempted attack on the guards"; if it was in the back, "Attempted escape."

So you always had to be on the alert and not fall victim to some trick or provocation by the guards. The guards shot at me once, on Cape Lazarev, but it seems that I was just fated to remain among the living.

Living in conditions like that was becoming unbearable; even sunny days became gray, and if a little patch of clear sky appeared, it would be covered by storm clouds.

Then they shifted me to another camp, in the forest about eighty kilometers from the base camp. It was a small camp of about four hundred prisoners, most of them with long sentences. The basic work was cutting firewood. By then my scurvy had come back. My legs ached, my gums bled, but I was still herded off to work. The work norm was very high: each man had to cut by hand fifteen cubic meters of firewood. No one could fulfill the norm, and so we were badly fed; and there was nowhere to buy food, just forest and swamp all around.

They gave us six hundred grams of bread, with watery soup three times a day. All the service personnel in the camp were criminal prisoners. They worked in the kitchen, in the bread-cutting room and the laundry, and a few of them didn't work at all. These were "thieves-in-the-law." There were about forty of them in all. They lived better than everyone else, and entirely at the expense of us workers. They would give short rations of bread and take the fats from the kitchen, along with all the other things that were due to the prisoners. But everyone kept quiet about it, afraid to raise their voices against the lawlessness that reigned in the camp.

The camp administration knew all about it but took no measures against the criminals. A conflict was brewing between the workers and the criminals. Preparations were under way for battle, a battle we had to win. I didn't know anything about the events that were about to unfold. But I did notice that there were birch sticks under many beds in our barracks. These had been brought in from the forest. They were the weapons of slaves against their oppressors. Later, two spades appeared in the barracks, and they were hidden under the floor. My bunk mate, a young lad named Genka, a well-muscled fellow, also worked in the forest but in another brigade. Once he asked me what I thought about the mob rule in the camp. I said that I was against it.

"Then help us."

I asked him what kind of help he needed.

"You'll see what we need, just don't stand at the sidelines."

I realized that the birch sticks and spades were going to be used to overthrow the power of the criminals.

From that time on I began watching the criminals very closely. When weighing the bread they really did give every ration short weight by forty or fifty grams. They took food from the mess hall and ate it within their own circle. If one of the prisoners even tried to protest, he was scared off by threats with a knife. All the criminals had knives that had been skillfully fashioned by some craftsman. As a rule, the criminals didn't throw their knives, they used them in fights. I realized that you had to keep your distance in a fight unless you wanted to be badly cut. And all the while the conflict was building up, and you could sense that something would flare up at any moment.

I can't remember which day this happened. Our brigade and another had come back from working at night. This was about seven in the morning. Some began washing up, others went to get their bread ration. For some reason, the criminals were even more brazen that day and were giving short weight by about a hundred grams. I had just finished washing. Two fellows came to our brigade, furious that they hadn't been given their full ration. I went to get bread and also got a short ration. When I came back to the barracks I saw a lot of prisoners holding their cudgels, and someone shouted, "Let's go!" Everyone ran off. I didn't have a cudgel, but I remembered the spades, lifted up the logs under which they lay, grabbed one, and followed all the others.

Inside the zone I noticed that all the criminals were in a cluster near the mess hall; a few others were running out of the barracks to join the group. Each one of them was flashing a knife, but we began closing in on them in a tight circle. Some of the criminals took refuge in the mess hall, the rest of the group moved toward us. It was knives against cudgels. They shouted at us, "Throw down your cudgels or we'll cut you all to pieces!" "Throw down your knives," we shouted back. A strapping criminal with a knife was coming at me. It was a matter of seconds before one of us would be giving it to the other. "Throw down your knife!" I yelled, but he was already two paces away, threatening me with his knife. He was certain that I wouldn't be able to do anything to him. I jumped aside and with all the strength that was in me I hit him with the spade on the shoulder close to his neck. He stopped, dropped his knife, and began slowly sinking to the ground. I could see that our side was winning at every point, and the criminals had begun retreating to the mess hall. We all advanced for the final battle. The criminals in the mess hall still hadn't surrendered. We began breaking the windows and tearing the ceiling apart. Earth poured down and everything was covered in dust. We demanded that the criminals come out and lay down their knives; they kept quiet for a long time. We decided to set fire to the mess hall. Then they began coming out and throwing down their knives. What happened to the criminals and their knives I don't know, but from that moment on the camp was peaceful.

As before, I was overcome by scurvy and my legs began to fail me. The camp administration was preparing for a meeting with some of their superiors, and so a medical commission was making the rounds of all the local camps. It came to our camp as well. Along with the civilian doctors were some prisoners. I recognized one of them as a doctor who had been with me on the ship back in 1953. At that time he was also serving out his sentence: he had been convicted as a political, but his sentence was fifteen years. He made a conclusive case to the commission that I had to be sent back to the main camp.

And so I got back to base camp again, among many who had been with me on the hunger strike on the ship.

CHAPTER TWELVE

Hope

The winter of 1954–55, the second Yakutia winter of my stay in the camp, was approaching. And it was only thanks to my knowledge of stove making that I had not yet had to work in the cassiterite and uranium mines. There were no stove makers to be found in the camp, and there was a lot of work to do. First we made repairs to the stoves in the camp, and then we began building them in the new settlement that was being constructed for the camp guards.

Once when we were laying firebricks for a boiler in a new boiler room, one of the officers of the camp guard stopped by, took a close look at our work, and then said that he needed a new stove for his apartment. It was already fall, and the temperature had dropped to thirty-five below. Three or four days later we were sent to see this officer.

When we came to his house—he lived in the new settlement—we were horrified. If the temperature outside was thirty-five below, then it was twenty below inside his apartment. Two little kids were walking about the room dressed in winter clothing, and his wife was wearing an army sheepskin coat. Then the head of the household arrived and asked for our assessment. We determined where best to place the stove so that it would heat the whole apartment. I won't describe how we managed to get the clay and warm water and make the mortar. We spent two days on the preparations, and on the third we set to work. We did a good job: these were people who needed help, after all. Though the owner was a prison guard, his children weren't to blame for anything and they needed some warmth.

The wife, a likable young lady, turned out to be a warm-hearted Russian woman. It's true, after all, that the world is not without good people. On the first day she cooked a meal for us over an open fire and we all ate together—she, the children, and us. We told each other about our lives. They had come here from another department of the MVD. She asked us about ourselves and about our parents. We worked in this apartment for as long as the camp administration allowed, believing that people in tough situations needed to be helped. When I told her about myself and why I had been imprisoned, she asked who made the decision on early release. I explained the system to her. We talked of many things during the meal, but when her husband arrived we tried to avoid conversations on such a topic. Just the same, every day this kind woman would ask her husband to find ways to make our life in the camp easier.

I think it was on the fourth day that we got the main job done and could get a fire going in the stove. In a little while the apartment got warm, the children were able to take off their heavy clothes and the wife her warm coat. We had our supper in what was now a cozy apartment. The next day we had to plaster the stove.

We arrived at the well-heated apartment, had a good meal, and set to work. The wife told us that at nights she would pass on what we had said to her husband. Her husband had said that arranging an early release was too complicated, the more so that my file had the notation "Politically danger-ous." Still, he promised that he would help as much as he could. I think his wife was the one who played the decisive role here.

After we had finished our work, we said our good-byes to the wife, hoping that she would not forget about us. After that we worked in many homes, and this woman and her children would visit us almost every day and bring us things to eat. My little cash reserve for a rainy day had scarcely increased, since I had been forced to use some of the money to treat the scurvy I had had in the forest camp.

I had saved about eight hundred rubles. I kept all the money in my secret hiding place. The year 1955 was approaching. It was December, and the temperature was sixty-nine below; at times it sank as low as seventy-three. We spent the whole winter working in the settlement; there was enough work building stoves to last for ten years. And for a long time we didn't see the person in whose hands, perhaps, our fate lay.

Winter had passed, and we had already lost all hope. Once, while return-ing to camp after work, I counted up how long I had already spent in the camps. It turned out to be 1,850 days, just a bit more than half my sentence.

A rumor started going round that some sort of commission would soon be coming to the camp to review our cases. No one knew just how and when this would happen, but all of us lived on this hope. Our work went on. As before, we were escorted to work by a single guard. At times he would go off to the store, leaving us without any surveillance, but we never repaid his kindness with evil.

In the middle of April 1955, a commission really did come to our base camp to prepare our "cases" for early release for submission to court. A few people were called in for interviews. I was not one of them. I had already adjusted to serving out my sentence, the more so that they had a great need for someone to make stoves. A few days passed. Lenka and I were coming back from work at six o'clock. Our evening meal still wasn't available; people said that the mess hall would be used as a courtroom to consider the cases for early release. No one was allowed into the mess hall; the judges and camp administration were in session there.

They began calling in people for review in alphabetical order. Within half an hour we knew that several cases had already been reexamined. They were calling in the "M" and "N." I realized that my case wasn't coming up and went off to my barracks to lie down and rest for a while. About a half hour later, one of the prisoners from my brigade came running in to tell me: "Get to the mess hall, on the run, they're waiting for you."

I don't remember running to the mess hall, but when I came in they were all sitting at a table. Among them was the officer—the husband of that good woman for whom we had made a stove in the winter.

They asked my name, article, and sentence. I told them, and then they asked what sort of work I would do after I was released. After a brief conference they announced that the court considered it possible to release me early.

Thirty cases had been dealt with that day, and mine was the last.

Now I had to wait for confirmation of the decision by a higher court. I felt my strength growing and I could sense freedom. A couple of days later, the lady we knew came to our work site and told us that we would be released on May 10 or 12; that conversation took place around the end of April.

The days dragged on like months. We began working even harder. I had to earn a bit of money to buy myself a few things. For eight hundred rubles I had some gray wool pants and a jacket made in the camp tailor shop, and I bought another sturdy pair of pants in the settlement store. Now I had some decent clothes to wear and still a bit of money left over. I also bought myself a "Star" watch as a souvenir of Yakutia.

And so the long-awaited day arrived, May 12, 1955. We were not sent out to work. We formed up inside the zone and they began issuing our documents: a certificate of release with a number beginning with two zeros. This indicated that we were forbidden to live in border towns, provincial capitals, and large cities. With that certificate in hand I set off for Siberia.

As I left the harsh land of Yakutia I thanked the Russian woman with a good soul who had been able to influence her husband; and he, too, had made his contribution to this good deed.

From Siberia I wrote a letter of thanks to these people who had saved me. What they did for me I remember to this day.

That was how I spent five years, two months, and eight days in prison and in the camps.

N. R. KOPYLOV

MY WANDERINGS

CHAPTER ONE

From Birth to Captivity

I, Nikolai Romanovich Kopylov, was born on May 5, 1918, in the city of Melitopol in Ukraine. My father was an electrician, my mother a housewife. We had a large orchard that filled the air with the scent of blossoming trees in springtime and that gave us fruit in the fall. My mother was always busy: aside from me there were three older children, my brother and two sisters. Ours was a musical family: my father played the balalaika, my brother made his own accordion and taught me how to read music. I had quite a good voice—everyone in Ukraine sings, some better than others, but almost everybody sings.

The Revolution passed through my childish mind as something that took place far away. Sometimes we would have White troops billeted with us, at other times, the Reds. During the NEP period everything was cheap, but my mother often wept. They were destroying the churches. Mama never threw out our icon and always said her prayers in front of it; she would lovingly decorate it with embroidered towels, and the icon lamp beneath it was always lit. In school they said that God did not exist; there were only the leaders, Lenin and Stalin. Mama said that they were the Antichrists. I still had to sort it all out for myself, but I was more inclined to believe Mama.

In 1934 I enrolled in the Sevastopol Technical College of Construction. They were arresting teachers in the college, and we were told that they were enemies of the people. This raised some doubts in me. While I was at the college I would sometimes earn a bit of extra money playing in the Simferopol Concert Hall on Sundays. I played the balalaika and tried to copy jazz tunes. My balalaika stood me in good stead here! The student grant in the college was thirty-nine rubles; one performance in the concert hall paid a hundred rubles, and so I was able to help out my family and my classmates.

I finished the college in 1938 and was called up for army service so quickly that I had no chance to send a telegram home and passed through

Melitopol without even seeing my parents. I went off to meet my fate not knowing what awaited me.

I was stationed in Tver, where I served in the 19th Reserve Artillery Regiment. There I completed an NCO course and was promoted to senior sergeant.

In May 1939 the regiment was transferred to Vyshny Volochek and was designated the 481st Reserve Rifle Regiment. In 1941 the regiment was redeployed to the village of Pukhovichi near Minsk, and we became part of the 7th Parachute Brigade, though we continued to function as a rifle regiment.

We first went into battle on the Berezina River. We fought for about three months, withdrawing, but with fierce resistance—and then we ran out of ammunition. At last, near the town of Klintsy, we were surrounded and I was taken prisoner. Our officers disappeared instantly, leaving us at the mercy of fate.

The Germans formed us up in the middle of a road, alongside a ditch. An officer stepped up to each person in our column and looked him over; anyone who looked like a Jew was pushed down into the gully. I was one of them. People shouted to me from up above:

"Mykola, you're a Ukrainian, tell them."

Several times I shouted, "I'm a Ukrainian, not a Jew!"

Finally the officer heard me and asked, "You're not a Jew?"

He called for an interpreter. He turned out to be a fellow from my town and spoke to me in pure Ukrainian. The interpreter said that I really was Ukrainian. I was let off. I quickly scrambled up the bank, but those left in the ravine were immediately shot. In shock and with heavy hearts, we dragged ourselves along the terrible path that fate had marked for us.

CHAPTER TWO

In Captivity

They marched us to the town of Starodub, giving us nothing to eat or drink along the way. It was good luck for us that it began raining, and we would fall on our knees and greedily drink the dirty water. We were marched to Surazh, and from there to the town of Unecha. We were so worn out we could barely drag our feet. The local people would toss whatever they could into our column. The German guards kept very strict watch to see that we didn't pick up any of the food, yet we still managed to get our hands on a few things. One prisoner jumped out of the ranks, and the guard killed him with his bayonet. From Unecha we were marched to the town of Mglin. There were about twenty-five thousand of us. During that whole time we had nothing to eat or drink and were soaked with rain. I ate my leather army belt.

When we reached our destination they took us to the market square. There was a well in the middle of the square, and deep pits had been dug on each side of it. The prisoners went down to the well and when they had drunk all the water they tried sucking it out of the sand. Many of them never left that spot. After a while, the Germans set up some cauldrons and boiled water. They put flour made from chicken bones into the boiling water and made a thin soup. Everyone got into line, holding out their field caps or whatever they had. We ate with our hands, just to get something into our bellies. Then we rushed to the latrines, in those same deep pits, but the flour had hardened in our bowels like cement, and those down in the pits never came out again. I hadn't had much of that soup and I stayed alive.

One day, as I was standing by the gate of the compound, some trucks drove up and we were loaded on them and taken to the town of Roslavl. There we were all put into an abandoned three-story building. The water taps in the building were working, so we were able to drink our fill. The local people would bring food up to the fence. I ran up and was hit on the head by a guard, though once I did manage to get a boiled potato.

We spent the night in that building, and then we were all herded out to the square. Trucks arrived, and we were again taken somewhere and put into a camp. They set us doing hard labor: we loaded coal and fished logs out of the cold water—some died in the water without ever getting the log back to shore. Everyone was vicious, hungry, and exhausted. At night they would lock us up in potato storehouses where there was still the odd potato to be found in the cellar. A few people ate corpses.

CHAPTER THREE

I Am a Performer

One day they dragged us out of the cellars and took us to a camp. It was a clear, sunny day. We weren't sent off to work. There was a barracks beside the compound, and the Ukrainian police there were playing balalaikas, and playing badly. I said:

"Give me a balalaika and I'll show you how to play."

One of them passed his balalaika under the barbed wire and, mustering strength from somewhere, I played so that the balalaika flew right around my body without the music ever stopping. The mouths of the *Polizei* dropped open in astonishment.

"You're a performer?" they asked.

"I am," I replied, and returned the balalaika.

A week passed and then the *Polizei* sent for me. There was an NCO there and he asked me to play. He was very pleased and had my name taken. The *Polizei* gave me something to eat and took me back to the compound.

After some time they called me out of the compound and took me to a room where there were a lot of officers. They offered me a drink, but I turned it down, telling them that I wanted to rehearse with the accordionist first. Then I played some jazz improvisations. They gave me something to eat and brought me back to the compound. They took my name.

One day they counted off ten of us, loaded us onto a truck, and took us away to parts unknown. When the truck stopped, we were in the courtyard of a military hospital. They put us into a barracks where there was only straw in place of beds and told us that this was where we would sleep. We were fed some disgusting, thin soup. We were doing heavy physical labor—carrying away slag from the furnaces, unloading coal from trucks, splitting wood. At nights they would lock us up.

Some time later they chose three people to work as orderlies in the hospital, and I was one of them. We would bring in chamber pots and bottles, take amputated arms and legs to the furnace, and spend our nights on duty. One time an officer's watch went missing and he, without a second thought, took a shot at me. I managed to jump away in time. He reported to the chief surgeon that a patient had told him I had stolen his watch. The surgeon began looking and found the watch in the pocket of the officer's overcoat. He put the officer to shame and confiscated his pistol.

They fed us poorly, and we went around hungry. Russian girls were serving food to the patients, and they would carry home buckets of leftovers. Finally we couldn't stand it any longer and told them: "Aren't you ashamed of yourselves? We're starving here, and you're giving leftovers to the pigs!"

They shed some tears and began slipping us things to eat. One day some officers arrived, and when they found out that I was a musician they took me into an ensemble of Russian performers. It was there that I got to know Baulin and his wife and became their friend.

We performed in prisoner-of-war camps and for the villagers in communities near Gomel and Borisov. The rumor was that they were sending us to Germany. People said there was famine there, but the main thing was that we could expect to be sent to a camp.

It was autumn. We talked things over and decided to run away and join the partisans. Our escape was successful. The partisans (this was the 13th Partisan Regiment, commanded by Grishin) fed us and told us that they had been to our concerts. We were welcomed, but the Security Section kept a very sharp eye on us. We had been with the partisans for about two and a half months when our group was surrounded and took a lot of casualties.

During the bombardment we took refuge in a bunker and camouflaged ourselves, but the Germans spotted us:

"We'll count to three and then we'll toss in a grenade!"

We came out.

"There's a woman here as well," the Germans said when they caught sight of Baulin's wife.

And so I was a prisoner again. They searched us and marched us off to some village. We were held in a tiny room. I was called out, held on a school desk, and beaten with a log since they thought that I was the one who had led the whole performers' group to the partisans. My lungs have been weak ever since. They beat me unconscious, then dragged me back and threw me into the little room. Early next morning they took us out and made us sit on a log; soldiers with automatic weapons took their places in front of us. We figured that they were going to execute us. They marched us outside the village and took us up to a ditch. The soldiers formed a row and aimed their weapons at us. Meanwhile, a car, its engine racing, was driving across a plowed field. The soldier in command ordered his men to lower their weapons and ran off to the car. A colonel, the chief field surgeon, got out of it and asked, "Are these the partisans?"

The soldier replied that we were.

"Are you going to execute them?"

"*Jawohl.*"

The colonel looked at our faces and then said:

"I recognize you. You're the performers I saw at the concert." And he turned to the soldiers: "These are Russian performers, take them back to headquarters."

They took us to the headquarters (thanks to His Majesty, Fate), where we spent the night in a little room. The next day they took us to Minsk. When they found out that we had worked in the Propaganda Section, they gave us a room where we lived under guard. But then the SD found out that the Russian performers had been in the partisans and were now living almost in freedom. They arrested us and put us in prison. We spent two months there, and were terribly fed and had our heads shaved bare.

After two months we were shipped off to Berlin on a transport. There turned out to be a lot of performers on this transport. They took us to a concert hall called "The Vignette." The head of the concert hall was very fond of birds, and after he had a look at what we could do he named our group "The Pink Peacock." He also added another female dancer to the group. An armed *Reisenleiter* traveled with us. I was designated the artistic manager. We performed for the *Ostarbeiter* and the Vlasovites.

One day they told us that they were sending us to perform for Cossack troops in Yugoslavia. We gave concerts for the Don, Kuban, and Terek Cossacks. We once saw General Shkuro. We spent time in the cities of Sisak, Nova Gradiška, Kostajnica, and Zagreb. Then they took us back to Berlin. The city was all in ruins. It was 1945.

They sent us off to Italy. We went on foot and sometimes managed to catch a lift on a truck; and that is how we made our way to the border town of Brenner. There we managed with some difficulty to persuade a driver to pick us up and went the rest of the way by truck. The landscape was enchantingly beautiful. We passed through Ravereto, Bolzano, Merano, Verona, and other towns.

From Verona we returned to Merano since the Red Cross was there, and they weren't shooting at us. We had to earn something on which to live. Since there were a lot of hospitals with wounded Germans in the town, our *Reisenleiter* managed to arrange for us to give concerts in them. The Germans paid us in cash: they would toss money in the caps that their girls would pass around. When the local people found out we were Russians they treated us very well. And that was how we lived.

CHAPTER FOUR

It's Decided: I Go Back to the Soviet Union

The month of May 1945 arrived and the Americans entered the city. We learned from them that the war had ended. Our *Reisenleiter* fled. We performed in the American club; they liked what we did and heaped us with food. Before long the Soviet representatives arrived and pasted up posters urging us to return to the Soviet Union. Homesickness overcame our fear, and we decided to go back.

We were sent to a collecting station. They took us in American trucks led by Soviet vehicles. The Americans urged us not to go back, saying that we would all be arrested, but we didn't believe them. There was a large "Welcome!" painted on the gates of the collecting station. They lined us all up in the courtyard; there turned out to be a lot of Russians there already. A few officers put their rank badges back on their shoulders, but they were immediately torn off. That was when we realized what was going on. But it was too late.

They assigned us to rooms and kept us under guard. The next morning they took us to the Austrian town of Melk, where there was a filtering camp. Everyone was interrogated separately. I, my partner, and Baulin's wife were reenlisted in the army and took our oath for the second time; then they sent us to the headquarters of the 4th Guards Army under Colonel General Gusev in the town of Eisenhüttenstadt.

The director of the club told us that we would be working as performers. We appeared in Vienna and in other cities. Then the army was redeployed to Hungary, to Balatonfüred where, by decree of the Supreme Soviet of the USSR, I was demobilized.

The Central Military Group knew of our garrison artistic troupe and invited us to perform at their officers' club in Vienna. Marshal Konev learned that we had been sent to Vienna and ordered us back to Baden, where his headquarters was located. He had often seen and enjoyed our performances. We were now free employees and lived in a hospital run by Colonel Zlatkin. I worked there for a time but then applied for voluntary termination and went back home to Melitopol. The Baulins came along as well, though they were headed for Moscow.

There was no end to the joy at home. Mama simply couldn't get enough of me and kept saying, "It was I who prayed to the Lord for your return." It was autumn, and I would walk around the orchard listening to the crickets chirping and thinking I had come to paradise.

I found a job teaching music and singing in the Melitopol Railway College.

Chapter Five

Sentenced to Twenty-Five Years

I worked for seven months. On April 1, 1947, a two-wheeled cart drove up. The man sitting in it asked my name and told me that the City Committee had sent for me—all the instructors in the arts were being called in. I accepted what he said, got into the cart, and we drove off. But I soon saw that we weren't going to the City Committee, and when I asked where we were bound he said that I'd find out soon enough. He told me that I was under arrest and took me to the Melitopol Prison.

In the prison they shaved my head, took away my belt, cut off all my buttons, and then took me to the railway station, on foot through the whole town. I was humiliated. They put me into a Stolypin car and took me to Moscow, to no. 7, Lubyanka. My parents didn't even know I had been arrested.

I spent a couple of days in a common cell. Then the interrogator, Captain Volodin, sent for me and presented my charges under Article 58, points 1b, 10, and 11. I denied all these accusations and refused to sign anything. Then he took me into an empty cell and began using illegal ways to make me give in. He wouldn't let me sleep at night: he would call me into his office and sit there without saying a word. He wouldn't let me eat, go to the toilet, or sit down during interrogations. I basically didn't eat or sleep. I'd come back to my cell and see a lot of bowls of food there; I'd find the warmest one and just when I got the spoon in my mouth I'd be called out for interrogation again. There were many times I lost consciousness and was revived by doctors and given something to eat; then the whole thing would begin again.

He also beat me. He told me, "If you don't sign, you'll croak in that cell."

My solitary cell was very small—two meters by a meter and a half; the *parasha* was under the bunk. It was dark. A dim bulb with a grill around it barely gave any light. There were many rats. The interrogator would call me in at night and keep me in his office by day as well. I couldn't drink or eat. Seven months passed this way. Once when they opened the cell door I was lying unconscious on the floor. They revived me, called the doctor, and began giving me a bit of food. They gave me fish oil and some kind of porridge. As soon as I could barely stand on my feet again they took me back for interrogation. It was in that condition that I signed it all—anything to put an end to this vicious treatment.

Three people in an office somewhere tried the three of us, Baulin, his wife, and me. The trial lasted ten minutes. They gave us twenty-five years each, plus five years deprivation of rights—Stalin's decree on the replacement of the death penalty by a twenty-five-year sentence had just come out.

Chapter Six

In the Zone on the Baikal–Amur Mainline

Two days after the trial I was sent to the Butyrka Prison. There were sixteen men crammed into a cell meant for six. A week or so later I was sent to the transfer prison in Krasnaya Presnya and then shipped off on a transport. They loaded us into cattle cars and took us to Siberia. We passed Lake Baikal; it was below freezing and everything inside the car was covered in hoarfrost.

I had a boil on my neck that had come to a head and was very painful. One of the prisoners offered to squeeze it for me. He did, and I immediately went blind. I tried standing, I tried squatting, and finally hid my face on the floor and wept bitterly. I wept for some twenty minutes, praying fervently to God, and then opened my eyes: I could see the light, and again burst into tears, but now tears of joy.

And so we came to Svetlaya Station (I'm not sure if that's the right name); then the train turned sharply northwards to Urgal Station. We were taken to a camp, but no camp would accept prisoners with sentences as long as ours. It was Stalin who thought up the twenty-five-year sentence in order to get a larger unpaid work force. People were no better than animals as far as he was concerned.

Our camp compound had a double fence, and there were huge dogs running between the two rows of barbed wire. They put me in a barracks and showed me my bunk. My neighbor turned out to be a decent fellow, a former criminal. He told me that he'd long ago called it quits on the thieves' life and told me, "Just stick with me, I'll help you out."

I told him what had happened to me. On the day they gave out our little ration of sugar the criminals would grab it at once, but my neighbor didn't let them get their hands on my sugar.

They took us out to work on the railway line that was later called the Baikal–Amur Mainline. We were cutting through a hill that was sheer rock, and the work norm was removing a square meter of rock five centimeters deep. For that we would get a crust of bread. It was impossible to meet the norm. The crowbar was frozen and your hands would get frostbitten. It was minus sixty-three degrees. One prisoner climbed out of the excavation to pee and the guard immediately shot him.

And so we lived and worked in these inhuman conditions. There happened to be an accordion in our barracks, and sometimes I would play it. One day a *suka* came by and said, "Bring your accordion and come with me."

Along the way he said threateningly: "You're going to play very loud; whatever else happens is our business."

We went into a barracks and I saw a man lying on a bunk; the criminals had woken him up and were talking to him about something; then they began pricking him with their knives. I turned away and fell silent, but they ordered me to "Play loud!"

They continued cutting him until he suddenly pushed them all aside, jumped across the table, and made straight for the window. He broke through the window frame and tried to run, but got tangled in the frame and fell. He did manage to make it to the guardhouse, and there he died.

There was no investigation. "Go now," they told me, and I left. There were more than a few incidents like this.

CHAPTER SEVEN

A Transport Farther East

We lived in this camp for about a month and then were sent away on transport. We traveled for a long time and crossed the Amur River on a ferry to the city of Komsomolsk-na-Amure. From there we were taken to the port of Vanino on the Tatar Strait. There were twenty-two camps here. The authorities put political prisoners in the same camp with criminals and nonpoliticals.

I found myself in a large barracks with three-tiered bunks. There were western Ukrainians there who were called Banderists. Once one of the criminals walked into the barracks:

"Now then, boys, get busy and collect some grub for me and my buddies, and get a move on!"

The barracks senior went up to him and said, "This isn't the mess hall, you'd better clear off."

"So, you think you can talk to me like that!" said the criminal, and stuck a knife in his stomach. "Now bring all your grub out here, to the middle of the room."

The Ukrainians stuck together, and they thrashed him until he was half dead and barely able to crawl out of the barracks. A little while later, about a hundred criminals burst into the barracks and a brawl began. The same thing happened in other barracks as well.

I couldn't stand on the sidelines and so I began helping the Ukrainians. I fought until I was hit, probably in the solar plexus. I gasped for breath and lost consciousness. When I came to there were about twenty men lying dead in the barracks, while in the camp compound something terrible was going on: the guards in all the towers opened up with bursts of machine gun fire on the people fighting in the zone. Then the shooting stopped and I looked out of the barracks. I saw some trucks drive in. A detachment of camp garrison troops began loading the dead and the dying onto the trucks. They loaded three trucks, covered them with tarpaulins, and took them away. I heard that there had been nine trucks, but I saw only three.

Somehow I found out that there was an orchestra and some performers at the commandant's camp sector and made a request that I be transferred there, adding that I was a professional performer. My request was approved. It turned out that there was a concert group with an orchestra there. I played my numbers for them, and they were happy to add me to their program. And so one day General Derevyanko and the head of the Kolyma Cultural Department, Tsudner, arrived. They had a look at what our brigade could do and selected four people for the Magadan theater: Mukhin, a singer; Evald Turgan, a violinist and professor from the Tallinn Conservatory; Artur Torni, an accordionist; and me. Then we got instructions to give a concert in Sovetskaya Gavan, but since I had a twenty-five-year term I wasn't allowed to go.

Then the bosses from Kolyma said:

"Here's what we'll do. The others can go, while we'll put together a transport for Magadan and you'll be on it. They'll put you ashore when you get to Nagaevo Bay; a woman will drive up in a car, and she'll be dressed in black (she's the wife of General Nikishov, the head of Maglag). When she gets out of the car, you stand up so she can see you."

With that they left. The next day they began loading the ship *Dzhurma*, remembered with horror by everyone who sailed in her. I recall that we went down into one hold, then into a second and finally into a third. This third hold was below the waterline and the bulkheads were bitterly cold. A lot of prisoners were crammed in. They were old men and teenagers. There was no way I could stay there. Food and water never reached us. Once I realized that I'd never survive there, I began trying to force my way up to the middle hold but they wouldn't let me in. There was no air to breathe, no toilet, and people were dying from the cold.

Yet somehow I managed to make my way up to the middle hold. It was stifling there and people were fighting over food. I saw a group sitting on the upper hatch, criminals apparently. I had heard that they loved listening to interesting stories, and the idea came to me that if I could tell them some fascinating tale they might let me get a breath of air; if not, I would die here. I began pushing my way toward them. They caught sight of me and cried out, "Where do you think you're going, old man?" (My hair had already gone gray.) "Tired of living, are you? We can help you with that."

"Not at all," I said, "I'm a performer and I can tell you a good story."

"If you're a performer, then come on up here and tell us something interesting."

I told them everything I could think of: novels, little theater pieces, scenes from plays. I wanted to live. They began feeding me. I can't say how many days we sailed from the port of Vanino through the Sea of Okhotsk to Nagaevo Bay and Magadan.

CHAPTER EIGHT

Kolyma: "A Performer in Various Genres"

After the ship had moored, they began taking us out to the pier. There were guards with dogs all around; they made us sit down. And in fact a car soon did drive up. A woman in black stepped out of it. As soon as I caught sight of her I stood up, as we'd arranged, but the guard made me sit down; the dogs began barking, the woman looked this way and that and then left. We remained sitting until everyone had disembarked. Then they took us to the transit camp.

I found out that there was a group of performers there that included an Honored Artist from Leningrad and an actress from the Minsk Operetta Theater. They were happy to take me into their group, and we began giving concerts. *Zeks* came and went, and we entertained them.

One day a few people from the Magadan Theater arrived—my old friends were concerned about me. They went to the camp authorities with some document and took me back to the Magadan Gorky Musical and Dramatic Theater. Thank God, I was now in the theater.

At the tryouts the woman who ran the theater asked me what I could do. (The famous singer Vadim Kozin was standing next to us.)

"I perform in various genres, all of them different," I replied.

"Then show us something in just one genre," the theater director said.

"What sort of genres do you work in?" asked Kozin.

I listed them: "I can mimic a jazz orchestra, I perform little skits with mimicry, and I'm a balalaika virtuoso."

"I'll tell you what," Kozin said, "just ignore her. I'll introduce you, and you can run through your whole repertoire."

My spot on the program came up, and Kozin made the introduction: "And now, Kopylov will perform in various genres."

I gave my performance and it was a colossal success. Kozin shook my hand. Everyone particularly liked the number "A Lady at Her Dressing Table Before Bed."

After the concert, the theater director came behind the scenes and told me: "I didn't know what you meant by a performer in various genres, but that was wonderful, really wonderful." (Kozin winked at me: "We've done it.") "We'll take you on in our theater."

We began giving concerts for the townspeople as well. There was also an operetta group within the theater.

"Can you perform in operetta?" they asked.

"I certainly can, that's what I like best."

"Wonderful, we'll make the arrangements."

Then something unexpected happened. Some Gulag higher-ups from Moscow came to one of our concerts. The concert was a great success. One of the Gulag officials came on stage and, turning to the theater director, asked, "Do you have any requests, and is there anything you need, any problems in your work?"

"Everything is going quite well, but I do have one very big request: we have a performer (she pointed at me) who can appear on stage and play in the operetta . . ."

"So what's the problem?"

"The problem," she replied, "is that he has a very long sentence—twenty-five years."

"What!" shouted the Gulag official. "Twenty-five years, and he's working for you? You have to look at his sentence, not his talent. I want him out of here by tomorrow! I'll check on it personally."

So it was good-bye to the theater! I found myself back in the same transit camp again, in the same group from which they had taken me. There I began to work on a new program. I made a bad choice of a partner for a skit with two masters of ceremonies. I myself performed little scenes from a few operettas and included some of my own numbers as well. The concert was to end with a scene from Aleksandrov's operetta *A Wedding in Malinovka*. My program was ready, but suddenly I had a third attack of appendicitis.

They put me into the camp hospital where the chief surgeon was a Hungarian doctor; he had hot water bottles applied to the area, and that made things worse. My temperature rose to forty, but the next evening I ran away from the hospital so as not to wreck the concert, since I was the one holding it all together. We began the concert, and you can imagine the condition I was in when I performed. It's true, indeed, that you have to sacrifice for your art! I was in mortal pain, but I finished my performance. In the last number, when I spun my partner around in a dance, she was to fall and I had to slip my shoulder under her to carry her offstage to the laughter and applause of the audience. But something crunched inside me and I fell down with my partner and lost consciousness. They brought down the curtain.

When I came to, I was in the back of a truck; they were taking me somewhere, evidently to the Magadan hospital some twenty-five kilometers outside the city. I was lying right on the plank floor with nothing to cover me. They carried me into the ward; it happened to be at the very time that Professor Nikolai Minin (one of the Kremlin doctors imprisoned by Stalin in the Gorky Affair) was making his rounds. Everyone in the ward had shaven heads like regular *zeks,* but I had long hair and was still in my makeup. Minin recognized me (he often attended our concerts) and asked, "So why are you here?"

"Appendicitis," I replied.

"Oh, we'll fix that in no time." He was about to continue his rounds but then turned back and asked how many attacks I'd had. I told him it was my third. He quickly pulled back the blanket. He pressed firmly on the left side of my stomach and immediately jerked back his hand. I had bellowed so loud that the whole ward could hear.

"Are you ready to go under the knife?" he asked.

"Of course, that's why I'm here."

And so without continuing his rounds he told one of his staff to prepare for surgery and left.

They prepared me for the operation and put me on the operating table. The professor came in, and I could see that he'd had a good bit to drink. I told the nurse, "Sister, I'm afraid that the doctor's drunk."

The professor heard me: "What's that he said?"

"Nikolai Sergeevich, he's worried that you've been drinking."

"You're a queer one, you are," the professor said. "Here you are at death's door. You should be grateful that I've managed to have a good stiff drink; otherwise you'd be pushing up daisies."

They gave me a local anesthetic and opened me up. When they cut through the peritoneum something happened that was extraordinary even in their practice: a huge fountain of pus squirted out, spattering the professor and all his assistants. "A pump!" the professor shouted.

"Nikolai Sergeevich," the nurse said, "this has never happened before, we don't have a pump ready."

Thereupon he cursed them all with some choice expressions, cut the incision larger, and began raking out the pus with his hands. I didn't cry out once, though it was incredibly painful. This, apparently, was due to the fact that when I got my twenty-five-year sentence I decided that my life was over and started using drugs (I would inject myself with opiates and other rubbish and smoke hashish); and so the anesthetic had no effect. I was in a terrible sweat. The sweat dripped off me, and in fact it not so much dripped as flowed off in streams. The nurses were amazed. The professor pulled out a part of an intestine from the incision and kept saying, "Where is it, where's it gone?"

At long last he found the appendix under my bladder, did something with it, and then stuffed the intestines back in.

"Professor," I said, "I hope you're putting them back in the right place."

"You're still alive, then?" he replied. "Never mind, they'll sort themselves out." And he told his assistants, "Sew him up."

He patted me on the cheek: "Don't worry, artist, you'll live," and he left.

His assistants did all that was necessary and brought me back to the ward.

Everyone knows that stitches are taken out on the seventh day. On the fifth day everyone in our ward, including me, was taken to the bathhouse, and it was about a kilometer away. Even though I was very careful in the bathhouse, the bandage got wet, fell off, and water got into the incision.

They took us back to the hospital, where one of the professor's assistants examined my incision: the upper seam had detached itself. He cursed everyone who deserved to be cursed, cleaned out the incision, and said, "We'll have to sew him up while he's conscious, without anesthetic."

I refused. The doctor said that the suture would be unsightly, and they took me back to the ward. The professor visited me several times and asked how I was feeling. I didn't complain and felt tolerably well. They discharged me a few days later. Professor Minin had already served his sentence and was a free worker.

After I was discharged from hospital I was sent to a camp, but to a different one, not the one where the performers were. In this new camp my name no longer existed: it had been replaced with a number, Z-1-290, which was painted on my undershirt, on the back of my padded jacket, on the knee of my trousers, on my sleeve, and on my cap. We were sent by airplane to the north of Kolyma, to the settlement of Seimchan. That was the location of the Seimchan Mining Complex, but we were taken by truck farther on, to the Kanyon mine.

When we arrived, they ordered us all to sit opposite the gate to the zone. The camp was fenced on three sides, and there was a cliff on the fourth side. The gates opened, and they began escorting the prisoners to work. We had the impression that they were all covered with flour, but it turned out to be dust from the ore. They went off to work, and we went into the zone and were assigned to barracks. I was sent to a tent barracks. Then they took us to the mess hall. The meal consisted of prison soup, then porridge and a bit of seal meat (seal meat is black as coal, and the seal's organs are like those of a human). Next to the serving hatch stood a barrel of water boiled with pine needles; we were supposed to drink this mixture to prevent scurvy. The next day we were assigned to brigades and taken to work in the mines. We had to climb high into the mountains on foot to get there.

They took us into the galleries, and there we found pick hammers, picks, and shovels. Our job was to mine the ore. I worked at that for two years.

One night in camp there was an avalanche, and a mass of snow crashed down on one of the barracks—the one where the fourth wall was the cliff side—right onto the sleeping prisoners. The barracks was smashed to its very foundation. We had to rescue the people, but they were so tightly packed in snow that we had to dig them out with crowbars and picks. Those who were still alive were rubbed with alcohol and sent to the sick bay. Many were dead.

Once when we were being marched off to work in the morning we saw the bodies of two *zeks*. They were lying near the gate so that everyone could see them. Escape attempts were rare in Kolyma: if the camp garrison didn't capture them, then they'd be killed and eaten by bears in the taiga. There were cases of three people making an escape—one of them would be taken along for the others to eat.

I got to know a man who worked in the ore enrichment plant, and he persuaded me to go and work with him (he was training a replacement since he was due for release). I brought this up with the camp bosses and they gave me permission to work in the plant. I quickly mastered all the processes apart from flotation—that was a job for a specialist. My friend was released and I became the brigadier.

About six months later the camp authorities sent for me and, for the first time, they called me by name: "Well, Kopylov, it seems as if you're going to be released. You're being called to Moscow. Get yourself ready, you're flying out tomorrow."

CHAPTER NINE

A Transport That Lasted a Year

I was overjoyed and wanted to believe it, yet I couldn't. They cut the numbers off my clothing, and the next day I and two others were taken by truck to Verkhny Seimchan. They sat us on the floor of the aircraft, put us in handcuffs, and made us spread our legs so they could make a place for another, then another, and so on. We couldn't stand up. My handcuffs were automatic—with every movement they squeezed tighter and tighter. I tried to hold out, but the pain became unbearable. I told the guard that I had automatic handcuffs and he loosened them and the pain became less.

And so we arrived in Khabarovsk, where they took us to prison. I spent ten days there, and then we went to Irkutsk by train. I spent a month in prison there. Then we were taken in freight cars to Chelyabinsk. The prisoners in the car lay on the floor and in bunks. At every stop the guards would pound the walls of the car with hammers, right under our heads, it seemed. They had special, red-handled hammers for that. We weren't fed while in the freight car. They would open the door, chase everyone off to one side, and then order us to move to the other side one by one; that was how they counted us to make sure that no one had escaped. Then the door would close and we'd move on. The same thing happened over the whole of our trip. I also spent a month in Chelyabinsk. From Chelyabinsk they took us to Kuibyshev, and I spent about the same amount of time there as well. From Kuibyshev we were sent to Kharkov Prison.

They would take us out for exercise. I managed to throw a note for my parents over the fence. Some kind and honest people passed this note on to them. Before long, my father arrived with a food parcel and requested a meeting with me. They didn't accept the parcel and refused the meeting. He went to the prison authorities several times but was refused. Over that period my father would spend the nights sleeping on a bench in the square.

I spent a month in Kharkov Prison, and then they sent me not to Moscow but to Kherson. Why to Kherson? I had never been in Kherson. I was put into Kherson Prison. Everyone there was delighted, telling me that they had been searching for Kopylov for a long time and at last he'd been brought in. I was called in to the prison authorities, who asked my name and the article under which I'd been convicted—it turned out that they had brought in the wrong Kopylov. The "right" Kopylov also had the initials N. R., but he was under a different article. It was amazing: "You're not the Kopylov we need!"

I remained in Kherson Prison waiting for a transport. They sent me to Vorkuta. I can't say how long the trip lasted since we stopped at every telegraph pole. Finally we arrived in Vorkuta. They put us into a transit prison. This was May 22, 1951. I had left Kolyma on May 22, 1950: I'd been on transport for a whole year.

CHAPTER TEN

Vorkuta: Working in the Mine and Organizing Amateur Talent Shows

They changed my number in Vorkuta: instead of 3-1-290 I became 1M678. Our camp in Kolyma was called Berlag (Riverbank Camp), in Vorkuta it was Rechlag (River Camp). They assigned us to all the various mines, and I went to No. 9/10 Mine. They immediately sent me down to Level 6, where I worked at the coal face. I had never been a miner, but now I had to become one. I stayed on Level 6 until 1953, i.e., until the death of Stalin. Strikes broke out in the mines, and Aleksandr Solzhenitsyn has written a lot about them. No one could do this better than Solzhenitsyn.

I forgot to mention that the barracks in all the camps were locked up at night. They did allow us to organize some talent shows. I began going round the barracks looking for performers. In one barracks I discovered an actor from the Moscow Ermolova Theater, Yury Volkov; in another a performer from the Lvov Zankovetskaya Theater, Boris Mirus; I also found the head director of the Riga Operetta Theater, Voldemar Putse, and many other talented people. Among them were the accordionist Aleksandr Selednevsky and the saxophonist Vasily Bender. Bender (he also worked in the mine) was in an accident: the cage car broke loose and he plunged down into the mine. The neurosurgeon Tulchinsky, another Kremlin doctor, literally had to pick him up in pieces.

And so I organized an amateur group of performers in which Gleb Zatvornitsky, a professor, also took part. Bender put together a variety orchestra; Boris Mirus, Zatvornitsky, Volkov, and I organized a dramatic group; and later a clown from the Moscow Circus, Yury Belinsky, joined us.

Even though the work in the mine was exhausting, we prepared our first variety concert and performed for the miners in the mess hall. It was a complete success, and some of the miners even wept: after all, we didn't even have movies in the camp. Later I staged an adaptation of Sukhovo-Kobylin's play *Krechinsky's Wedding* and Ostrovsky's *The Forest*. The female roles were played by men. I was the artistic director of this group. The mine officials were pleased and even decided to make my life easier: they sent me to work on the surface.

I got a job in the library, but before five days had passed the Security Section sent me back to work in the mine, down to level 6. The mine officials gave me a job in the pump room on level 2, pumping water from the mine to the surface. The Security Section was curious to know where Kopylov was working, and the head of the mine replied, "On level 6."

"That's just the place for him," replied the man from the Security Section.

During the time I was mining coal on Level 6 there was an accident: our friend, a musician, lost both his hands. We had great sympathy for him and felt his grief as keenly as if it were our own. I wrote a verse about this young lad as a way of expressing my participation in what he was going through:

> The sky hides the stars in black clouds
> A terrible blizzard is coming on,
> But someone is quietly weeping in the barracks,
> Bowed over the bed and weeping.
> Soothe this poor prisoner lad,
> Help him so he moans no more—
> He had been a fine musician,
> And played the accordion so well.
> The lad's had grief and sorrows aplenty,

And now he's lost his hands down the mine.
All night he's been weeping in his bed,
Thinking of home and his native town,
Next door someone's quietly playing
The waltz "In the Forest at the Front."
The sounds tear at his heart,
He knocks sharply on the wall
And asks that they give him the accordion
Even though he has no hands to play . . .
My hands, my hands, oh if you only knew
I'll never make these sounds without you.
He asks the young lad playing the song
To play the waltz "Autumn Dream,"
The prisoner's heart has grown so weary,
And he makes a quiet, pitiful moan.
Dearest Mama, my beloved, my own,
Twice I've now been punished by fate,
And so, my dearest, it means that you and I
Will never see each other again.
Gaze upon my portrait, dearest Mama,
And know your son now lives without his hands.

The camp regime got easier after Stalin's death. We tore off our numbers, and they stopped locking the barracks at night. And they allowed us to organize a cultural brigade of both men and women.

One day General Derevyanko appeared at No. 9/10 Mine and said that he was organizing a male cultural brigade. I was the first to approach him, and he recognized me: "Were you the one who played the balalaika? I remember you, we'll take you on."

Volkov was next, and he introduced himself as an actor from the Kamerny Theater, and so on.

Those of us who were chosen were sent to No. 6 Mine. When we entered the club we heard the overture to the operetta *Silva* being played by an orchestra under a remarkable conductor, the pianist Nokirev. We felt as if we had been set free, listening to the divine music we had been deprived of for many years.

They made a similar selection of performers in the women's camps. We were transferred to No. 3 Mine, where the general cultural brigade had made its home. It was headed by Viktor Lavrov. All of us were allowed to move about without escort. We gave concerts in all the camps. It was in this cultural brigade that I met my future wife, Viktoria Videman, with whom I was to spend the rest of my life.

Once we were giving a concert at No. 6 Mine with Yury Volkov, and on our way back we got off the truck at the wrong place. There was a terrible blizzard and we couldn't see more than two paces in front of us. We sat down to rest and began drifting off to sleep. I could feel that I was freezing. I remembered that we had a quarter-bottle of vodka, so we had a drink and with an enormous effort of will we forced ourselves to go on. We fell many times as we strayed off the path. By morning the storm began to die down. It was almost dawn when, covered with ice, we came up to the guardhouse. The guards were overjoyed to see us return (they had to answer for all of us, and we were supposed to be back in the zone at the appointed time). They almost kissed us. Once inside the zone, they took us to the barracks, rubbed us with snow and, in short, brought us back to life.

Everyday life in the cultural brigade went on. My wife was set free in 1954, and she found a place as an actress in the Vorkuta Dramatic Theater. She lived with friends. We rarely saw one another: she was touring with her company, I with mine. One day I was coming home to the camp at No. 3 Mine and I had to cross an open field in front of No. 4 Mine. At the time the prisoners in No. 4 Mine were being marched off to work. The guards were drawn up along both sides of the column, the miners walked between them. So as not to walk around the whole line of guards I cut through the ranks to get to my mine. The guards stopped me: "Halt! Where are you going? Who are you?"

"I'm a free man," I replied.

"Show me your passport."

"I only show my passport to the police, not to you," I said.

"That's our artist, don't lay a hand on him!" the miners shouted.

I went on, with the sentry right behind me. There's no point in going farther, I thought, I'd better turn back. The miners raised a terrific noise and demanded that I be let go; they threatened not to go to the mine. The guards evidently got frightened and let me go on to my passageway since it was very close. The guards at the guardhouse said not a word to me (it wasn't Stalin's day anymore), and I quietly went to my own barracks. Some of the miners from No. 4 Mine crawled through the fence and came to my barracks. When they found me they asked: "They didn't do anything to you? Didn't beat you or make threats? Didn't call for the security officer?"

"You can rest easy," I said, "everything's fine, boys."

And the miners went off to work.

Soon a decree came out from the Supreme Soviet of the USSR on amnesty, and my sentence was reduced by half. I kept on giving concerts at the mines with my cultural brigade.

My wife fell seriously ill and was put in hospital for an operation. She was very weak when she came out. At that time in Vorkuta there was a commission reexamining cases that might be eligible for release. There was a huge line of people waiting. I wrote an application, and my wife took it to the commission so that it could be heard without my waiting in line. They came to meet us. I was called in, questioned, and told to wait. My wife stood beneath the window, nervous and praying.

The duty officer whispered to me as he passed by: "Pack your suitcase, you're being let out."

Chapter Eleven

I Am Free!

Literally within a few days they issued me a passport at No. 5 Mine. Hurray! I was free and going home! They gave me money for a ticket to Melitopol. I got into the train alone, with no guard, for the first time in many long years.

My wife, meanwhile, was finishing her season in the theater. I had no idea of what lay ahead of us, but I was young and filled with optimism. I stayed in Melitopol, since my parents were seriously ill. I worked as an artistic director and as a director; I organized a vocal-instrumental trio that became famous all across the Soviet Union. I went to Poland, but they wouldn't let me go any farther: I was still a security risk for travel abroad.

They also watched me closely in Melitopol and would drag me off to the security officers: they couldn't act any other way, these security organs of ours.

Let me add a few words about my wife. She joined me, of course, after finishing her tour. My papa and I went to meet her at the station. The train pulled in and I could see her dear face through the window. We smiled at each other and I knew for certain: whatever might await us in the future, we would not be parted again; we would go to the end together and we would be happy!

I've finished my brief description of my wanderings, my humiliations, and my sufferings. I had been in ten prisons and twelve camps. I mourn for these wasted years of life.

May there be eternal memory for the prisoners of the Gulag, whose only memorial is the Stone of Solovki in Moscow and nothing more!

V. V. GORSHKOV

MY LIFE
AS A GIFT

The most terrible part was not when I stood, my knees trembling, and heard the chairman of the Military Tribunal of the City of Moscow pronounce the verdict.

"In consideration of the offender's status as a minor . . ."

I could hear what he was saying, but the words seemed to be coming from far away, almost muffled, and I simply could not comprehend that they referred to me. My mind was still focused on the fact that the three men on the tribunal and the prosecutor Doron on the left had only just demanded that I be executed, never imagining how terrified I was.

"Ten . . ."

This is not a fateful number, it is a magical one. The trembling in my knees stopped at once, as if a switch had been thrown. They had given me the gift of life. Later, on my journey through seven camps and camp sectors, death became something accepted more calmly, even as a matter of indifference.

That time has long passed. I was lucky, and I survived. On March 5, 1953 I realized it had all ended permanently. Yet something stayed with me the rest of my life, like a post-operative scar, like a broken bone that has not properly knit. There was always a sense of inferiority, the same awareness that causes a cripple to feel isolated among healthy people.

CHAPTER ONE

"The Government Building"

It all began with the ace of spades. It fell point downwards, like a needle into my heart.

"A shock!"

Then came the "government building," "official conversations," "a long journey." My mother would lay out the cards in her idle moments, but neither she nor I took her fortune-telling very seriously. Yet I was left with an uneasy feeling.

"They're going to draft you into the army," my mother concluded.

If only that had been it.

The knock at the door came at night, at 2:00 A.M. I was still awake and had just set aside my book. "I wonder if they've come to check our passports?" I thought, not alarmed. Almost a year had passed since I turned sixteen, the age when you received your official documents and an identity card.

My mother answered the door. Four men came in. The first was an officer in an overcoat and a light blue forage cap. He asked brusquely: "Last name? First name?" And then: "Get up and get dressed."

They already knew that I had no passport. How many times had I meant to get one . . .

The officer thrust a small yellowish paper at me. I read: "Warrant for Search and Arrest." There was a brief catch in my throat. I wasn't surprised.

They spent the whole night rummaging through the apartment. I guessed what they were looking for and was glad: only a little earlier Rodka Denisov had come and taken away the magazines to read, those very last four issues.

The search ended with a robbery. Apart from my manuscripts and letters they took away my stamp collection, some rare old books, cameras, binoculars—and not all of these things had been listed on the record of the search, as I discovered many years later.

The snow was melting. There were a few spatters of rain. It was damp and slippery underfoot. One of my escorts dropped a camera. I watched it slide across the ice, fearing that it might have been smashed. I still didn't comprehend that my whole life had been smashed into tiny bits.

I spent the rest of the night on a hard sofa in a building next to the police station. I couldn't sleep. It wasn't that I was afraid. I assumed that they would hold me for three days and then let me go. Then I was taken around to various offices where I was questioned by each of the men in turn: Nogtev, who was in charge of my arrest; the head of the city NKVD office, Major Lukyanov; and another man with an ugly, pockmarked face who had been the last to arrive at my arrest.

"Any idea why you've been arrested?"

"No."

They looked and spoke seriously, as if they had captured some hardened criminal. But from time to time they appeared a bit perplexed: I seemed to be a very small fish indeed. They gave me some cabbage soup and bread. I couldn't eat, just as I couldn't sleep.

The next morning they gave me a sheepskin coat and put me into an "Emka" jeep. We left early, and it was still quite dark. The road couldn't be seen for the blowing snow. On the back seat next to me sat a woman I knew, Sutormina, who, I think, ran the snack bar at the place where I had spent the night.

I whispered quietly to her so that Lukyanov, who was sitting next to the driver, couldn't hear: "Tell my mother that they've taken me to Gorky."

Of course she didn't do as I asked. Doing something like that, apparently, was akin to divulging a state secret and was strictly punished.

On a bend in the road somewhere near Gorky we skidded into a snow-filled ditch and the car turned on its side. Not far off, a tank was driving across a field, plowing up the snow. Another tank was parked on the road. There was a platoon of soldiers crowding around it; the tank troops were on exercises. Lukyanov had the soldiers come up and lift our jeep back on the road.

The little houses of Myza flashed by and then the barracks of Voroshilov Settlement. Everything looked sleepy and commonplace in the snow. We stopped at a large red building on Vorobyevka. I already knew about this building and its reputation. But now my prejudice toward those who worked in it was pushed aside by my curiosity: it would be interesting to have a look into the den of our guardians of public order, the more so that I wasn't reckoning on abusing their hospitality by a long stay.

They left me in an office in a passageway, and for the rest of the day, it seemed, no one paid me any attention and no one asked for me. People in uniform and in civilian clothes came and went. All of them were busy with their own affairs and no one showed any curiosity about me. Once, though, some civilian picked up a box camera from the pile of "booty" that had been sent with me and asked: "What's this, a radio transmitter?"

He gave me a long but empty look that expressed nothing. I made no reply, but thought to myself: "He's in state security, and he's an idiot."

One tenderhearted person did turn up, and he surmised in the second half of the day, evidently after wandering in after his own lunch, that it might not be a bad idea to give me something to eat as well. In the tiny office adjoining they served me a plate of meatballs and stewed cabbage. The only delicacies I had known since the war began had been black bread and hard flatcakes, and so I remarked to myself that with grub like that one could get by quite nicely here.

The short winter day was drawing to its end and I, seeing no sofa, was beginning to wonder where I might sleep. Then I heard someone say, apparently into a telephone, "Take the prisoner to the cells."

At first I didn't understand which prisoner he meant, but then I realized it was me and thought: "Why do that? I'm just fine here in the office . . ."

Nevertheless, they came for me. At the end of a long corridor was a completely respectable door upholstered in black oilcloth. Next to it was a bell push. Behind the black door was a second one made of thick steel bars. A steep staircase led downwards into some netherworld from whence came a breath of cold and melancholy. Deep below, as if in the hold of a ship, glimmered a faint light. Were they actually going to take me down there?

I had clearly formed my first impression of the prison, and it was not a good one. I realized that I would have to spend the night here and, evidently, more than just one night. My fears were borne out, and many times over.

I did not have to go down to the cellar. On the landing that joined the two flights of stairs was an ironclad door with various accessories on it (as later became clear, these were a little hatch for passing through the food; a "Judas hole"—a little round window with a cover for checking on the prisoners; and an enormous hasp lock more appropriate for the gateway of a fortress).

There was a tremendous clatter, unlike anything I had ever heard and much louder than seemed appropriate to the semi-darkness and narrow stairway. This was the warder who had come to meet us unlocking the door. The heavy door gaped wide like sinister jaws. The warder, silently and

249

with a slight nod of his head, gave me to understand that the maw of the prison had opened to swallow me whole.

The one-man cell was not large, barely more than a meter wide. Directly opposite the door was an iron cot covered in planks that had darkened with time. They were unplaned but polished to silky smoothness by many years of prisoners' squirming on them. Next to the cot stood a filthy bedside table of the same material. On the right was a rusty, covered canister that could hold about ten gallons; I understood its function when I raised the lid and the acrid stench of the toilet struck my nostrils. The free space among these furnishings was enough to take three paces in one direction and another three back. Above the cot was a large window with a grille as solid as a cage for a beast of prey. The exterior of the window was covered with an iron visor with the flared end upwards, thanks to which you could see a little patch of the open sky.

Despite the hospitality extended to me, I had scarcely slept at all over the past two days and so, after briefly acquainting myself with the facilities in my new lodgings, I felt that the time had come to catch up on my sleep. I collapsed on the bare boards just as I was, in my hat and overcoat, and thanks to my ascetic habits I found my resting place to be quite acceptable. Yet I couldn't manage to fall asleep at once, mostly because of the fierce cold in the cell. Twisting myself into every imaginable position and even trying to discover some unimaginable ones that might draw forth every little bit of heat from my body, I mentally cursed those who had provided this comfort as I writhed about like the princess on the pea.

Sleep had barely managed to gain victory over the cold when the lock clattered again and once more I was given evidence that I was being treated humanely: someone kindly threw a mattress and some objects resembling a pillow and a blanket through the cell door. All the bedding was threadbare, the dull color of an army greatcoat; but it bore no traces of any insect population. While making up my bed I realized that in prison anything that was not harmful must be considered a blessing. Through my sleep I heard a bell and guessed that this was lights-out; I had at last got warm, and for the first time in my life I fell asleep on a prison cot.

Several features of a night's residence in prison distinguish it from a night in a hotel. First, a light is kept on in the cell all night; it is not a bright light but it is bothersome when you are unused to it. Second, no matter what position you assume while sleeping, you must not cover your head or your hands—the warder must be able to see them at all times. This discomfort is felt very keenly at first, particularly when your shaven head is very sensitive to the beastly cold. It is true that you feel this only until the constant interrogations have reduced you to a state in which you can be dead to the world while facing theatrical spotlights and under volleys fired by 124 artillery pieces.

I made a closer acquaintance with the "government building" the following morning. I did not hear the bell. The door banged open and the warder greeted me: "Reveille!"

At this point I learned that I was to roll up the bedding so as not to spend the whole day languishing on a government-issue mattress.

I could sense the prison coming to life. Locks clicked open like shots on every floor of the building; I could make out the sound of footsteps; from time to time I could catch muffled words of the warders.

The lock clattered in my cell as well. The door opened: "To the toilet."

I took a pace out of the cell.

"Take this . . ."

I did not understand what I was supposed to take. It sounded as if he had said *furazhka,* a peaked cap, and I was surprised that he would call my warm fur hat a peaked cap.

"Over there," the warder said, pointing at the canister in the corner, "the *parasha.*"

I don't recall whether it is in Chekhov's tale *Sakhalin* or in Dostoevsky that I encountered this word, but I realized at last what he wanted me to do. Embracing with both arms this foul vessel that has, through some unknown associations, received a girl's name that has been celebrated in Pushkin's verse, I carried it gingerly before me like a *kulich* at Easter, trying to hold my breath.

After breakfast, which consisted of a day's ration of bread and a mug of unsweetened tea that I used only to warm my hands and my nose, I was left with some free time. Having the inclinations of an educated person, I decided to do some reading and unfolded a newspaper that I had picked up as I left home. My cultural pastime was interrupted, however. The Judas hole in the door winked and then with a clatter (in this prison everything was built around sound effects) the little hatchway in the door was thrown open and the warder announced in an even, unruffled voice: "Reading's not allowed." And he stretched out his arm for the newspaper.

I was not particularly perturbed since I had another newspaper in reserve, and I at once became absorbed in reading it. But again the Judas hole winked open; there was the clatter of the hatchway in the door, the same monotone announcement, "No reading"; and the second newspaper met the same fate as the first. Thereafter I had to find a new occupation. I began to whistle the melody of a Balakirev polka. The result was the same: "Whistling's not allowed."

For a time I was completely perplexed; it seemed that I had no weapons to fight against idleness. But my confusion was only temporary. I was attracted by the sounds of radio music that wafted through the window. Impelled by curiosity and a natural need for activity, I didn't stop to think and began to lift myself up along the wrought iron grille over the window—the celebrated holy of holies of all the Newgates and Bastilles through the ages—in the hope of catching a glimpse of the world outside and determining the source of the demonic temptation that had led me away from prison resignation and penitence. I had already been able to establish that the window of my cell faced Dynamo Stadium where a cheerful loudspeaker had been set up, when behind me I again heard the authoritative, didactic voice: "No climbing on the window."

With great reluctance I drew back from the prison bars behind which I had caught a brief glimpse of a bit of life that such a short time ago had been my everyday experience. Though wartime conditions had made that life less than pleasant, it was something that I now saw as a different world, magical and unattainable: yesterday's reality had become today's dream.

The next amusement in my individual program of entertainment was prompted by the severe microclimate within the space I was trying to make habitable. In order to warm up I began doing physical exercises at a quick tempo. Boxing moves turned out to be particularly effective. But here again I heard the repulsive grating of iron and that same tiresome voice: "No physical exercise allowed."

"So what am I allowed to do?" I said, unable to contain myself.

And then I had a sudden sense of dread, dread because nothing was allowed: I was not supposed to do anything. How could I live in conditions like that? In addition to all of the things mentioned, sleeping after reveille was not allowed, and you could not even lie down—that was permitted only in the specially designated quiet hour after the noon meal. The whole day long I was supposed to remain in a state of passive wakefulness.

The temperature in the cell dropped. The radiator, blocked by the bedside table and the back of the bed, had given off some heat in the morning but now it was cooling. The cold compelled me to act. I moved aside the table and squeezed into the narrow well formed between it, the wall, the bed, and the radiator; I pressed against the radiator so as to feel its warmth, as faint as the breath of a dying man. I heard the shield over the Judas hole clicking nervously, once, twice. Finally there came the familiar clattering of the bolts.

"Where are you?" I heard the uneasy voice of the warder.

"I'm here, keeping warm."

"Crawl out of there. You mustn't do that. You have to stay where I can see you."

I had to crawl out and put the bedside table back in place. And with that I had run out of ideas.

My perplexity at this endless and complete inactivity did not last long, however. I figured out that I had a large store of mental activities available and that they could not forbid me to think, even though they tried every possible way to do so. My first bit of mental gymnastics was the schoolchildren's game of naming cities, each of which began with the last letter of the previous one. When that became boring, I simply began recalling the cities of the world beginning with each letter of the alphabet. In addition to that, my guardians helped me while away the hours of my first day in prison. Apparently the senior warder, having learned that I had committed such a seditious act as reading a newspaper, realized that his underlings had slipped up. Through the door I could even hear him say, "Don't tell me you haven't searched him?"

And so they took me out of my cell to inflict a *shmon*—a body search—on me. This was a procedure every bit as essential as the little walk with the *parasha,* as soon became clear. They carefully ran their hands over my whole body and every scrap of my clothing; they turned out all my pockets, and at the same time took away my belt, pulled the laces out of my shoes, cut off all my metal buttons and clasps. My trousers suffered particularly. I returned to my cell disheartened as I pondered an insoluble problem: how was I to carry the *parasha* with both hands while simultaneously holding up my trousers?

The construction of a trouser harness filled the time remaining until the noon meal.

Again, to the accompaniment of that same clattering of bolts—a sound that, as it turned out, was a distinctive feature only of the prison on the Vorobyevka and one that subsequently would cause my heart muscles to contract and my breath to quicken—I was served my first real prison dinner. In a metal bowl they passed me a hot soup that smelled like badly processed offal and consisted of water and large chunks of unpeeled potato. The war years had weaned me away from delicacies, but this dish had no appeal at all. I drank some of the broth with whatever bread I had left and decided to wait and see what would be served at the main course. I had given up hope on meatballs. But it turned out that there was nothing at all to hope for. The main course—oatmeal porridge—came only toward evening, as supper.

I was more deliberate in the days that followed: I would pick out the chunks of potato, remove the skins, and eat them along with the stinking broth. Soon, when my supply of homemade bread ran out, I cast aside all my prejudices and would attack the sour, half-cooked prison bread ration, made partly from those same unpeeled potatoes, like a wolfhound with a honeycake and gulp it all down in the morning. Just as a hungry Tatar will eat the forbidden pork and a Russian, when there is no beef, will be amazed that he never regarded horseflesh as a proper meat, so I would champ with pleasure, swallowing the uncomplicated prison cuisine while recalling the wisdom I had absorbed in school—that it was specifically the skins of root vegetables that were especially rich in vitamins and trace minerals essential to the human organism.

CHAPTER TWO

Interrogation

The most difficult thing in recollecting my years in confinement is to give a faithful account of the initial period, the investigation and the interrogation.

First, after almost half a century it is impossible to recall in detail how it all happened. And second, I still feel guilty for behaving in an unworthy manner, faintheartedly, perhaps even basely.

What was it: fear, confusion, a weak will, a lack of character? I was not beaten or tortured, unless you consider sleep deprivation as torture. Was it my age, my inexperience? No, above all it was cowardice, a fear of something I did not even know. Before my arrest I had hardened myself physically, learning to tolerate cold and discomfort. I would pour cold water over myself and go on swimming until late in the autumn; I would sleep almost on bare boards and dress lightly in winter; and this helped me in the years to come. But I had not prepared myself morally, and this troubles my conscience even now.

Someone—I think it was the Gorky writer Kochin, who shared a cell with me for a time—told me: "There's no point resisting, they'll convict you just the same."

I understood that very early.

It was some time before I adapted myself to the interrogation procedure. As a rule, immediately after lights-out, when I had barely managed to close my eyes, the lock of my cell would clatter, making me shudder. The warder would enter, poke my shoulder, and say: "Time for interrogation!" And he would leave, allowing me time to get dressed.

Escorted now by a different guard, I would climb the stairs and walk along the corridor with my hands clasped behind my back as per prison ritual. The office of my interrogator, Captain Yevdokimov, was on the first floor, and the trip there was a short one, though it left many impressions. The lighting was dim and the silence was of a particular kind, a tense silence as if even the walls were watching and piercing you through with their gaze.

Yevdokimov was about thirty-five. He was tall and slender. Neither his appearance nor the expression of his face suggested anything bestial or pathological, qualities that would not have been surprising in a man of his profession. He was still wearing an old-style uniform, a service jacket with a broad lay-down collar and a rectangular rank badge in his buttonhole. His office was not large, and a white curtain covered its single window; he sat at a broad desk with a telephone, his back to the window. Some distance in front of the desk stood a single chair. That was for me.

He would gaze at me for a time, then shuffle the papers on his desk. Yevdokimov, evidently, was carefully studying his newest client and, as I could see, not without a certain amount of surprise: this enemy of the people sitting before him was a pretty puny specimen, one he could lay flat with a single blow.

The first interrogation began in the usual fashion: "Last name, first name, patronymic?"

Everything was recorded on paper. Then, suddenly, it came like a slap in the face: "So, tell me about your anti-Soviet activity."

I stared wide-eyed at the interrogator and, I suppose, answered as anyone in my situation would: "I've not been involved in any anti-Soviet activity."

Although probably, unlike most people who sat in this chair, I realized full well why I was here and what the interrogator meant.

Later, in the camps, I heard things like this many times: "Article 58? A chatterbox, eh. What was it, telling a joke that got you here?"

They gave seven, and sometimes even the full ten years for telling an "anti-Soviet" joke. And I came across cases that in themselves were like political jokes. For instance, in camp sector No. 3 of Chistyunlag, as my friend told me, there was a deaf and dumb old man who was imprisoned for having "links with Hitler." Hearing something like that made me seem a full-fledged state criminal.

This is how it all began. Back in 1941 my friend and neighbor Vovka Vinogradov brought me a handwritten magazine called *Druzhba* (*Friendship*), colorfully and skillfully designed, filled with poems and epigrams. It was put out by Vovka's classmates who were two years older than I. Knowing that they would soon be leaving school, they wanted to pass on the magazine to someone younger.

"So, shall we keep putting it out?" Vovka proposed.

I didn't agree. "We'd be better off creating one of our own."

And we began putting out our own magazine, *Nalim* (*The Eelpout*).

Later, during the interrogations, Yevdokimov would ask: "Why a magazine with a name like that? Something slippery that can't be caught?"

It was much simpler than that. We planned it as a humor journal: we were very keen on the stories of Zoshchenko. And the movie theaters just then were showing a screen version of some of Chekhov's stories, including "The Eelpout." Through some association it seemed to me that this title would suit our magazine.

The first three issues of *Nalim* appeared in accordance with the plan that we had worked out, but with the fourth—when Vinogradov was already serving in the army and when I had managed to increase the staff of the magazine to eight (all students in the upper grades)—the tone changed sharply. This was reflected even in the outward appearance of the magazine. In place of the pretty vignettes on the cover there appeared a black silhouette of Nekrasov and the epigraph: "The tears are few, but of grief there is a river, a bottomless river of grief." For later issues we proposed to add the silhouettes of Radishchev and Herzen. The contents of our publication changed accordingly.

In the seventh and final issue, which remained unfinished, I had included my poem with a very long title: "A Conversation on a Moscow Street on the Evening of August 23, 1943." Though the poem went on for eleven pages, I wrote it in a single day, beginning at seven in the morning on August 24 and finishing it by lamplight. Its point of departure was the fireworks display that had taken place in Moscow the night before to salute the liberation of the city of Kharkov from the German invaders; the point of the poem, however, was the inept leadership of our army, something that was obvious even at the very beginning of military operations and was the result of our country's lack of democracy, freedom of expression, and freedom of the press. Even the few excerpts from it that the military censor had found in my letters were enough to ruin my life and those of my two comrades.

I was aware of how dangerous our undertaking was, but I myself believed—and I convinced the other authors in the magazine of it—that as long as we were minors we had nothing to fear, and at worst we would get off with just a scare.

I was wrong.

"Well, then," Yevdokimov asked, "are you going to tell me about your activities against Soviet power?"

But how could I tell him about something that did not and does not exist? I was brought up under Soviet power and I believed—and even now I do not reject the idea—that Soviet power is a just power. But this does not mean that certain individuals who seized that power without being entrusted with it by the people were to be unconditionally supported, the more so that no discussion of their actions was allowed. Freedom of speech, freedom of the press—those are the guarantors of the preservation of justice.

"I am not against Soviet power," I replied to my interrogator with complete frankness, "but I don't support the actions of certain of its representatives."

"But don't you see that it's these representatives who are Soviet power?" Yevdokimov objected.

And so we were in a closed circle: the person who holds power is himself that same legal power, and criticism of that person means dissatisfaction with the existing political order, which is a state crime. The same is true of freedom of speech. No one is denied such freedom, but only so long as you do not use it to the detriment of Soviet power. If you express some criticism, if you disagree with something, it means that you are campaigning against Soviet, people's power, and that means you are a criminal, an enemy of the people.

That was more or less the spirit in which my conversations with Yevdokimov took place; the conclusion that followed was that I shouldn't have expressed opinions about anything, because even my very highest aspirations and desires already represented unlawful criticism of an ideal power—anti-Soviet agitation, in other words. In accordance with that axiom, all that was left was simply to admit that everything I had said, written, and even thought was a crime. But it turned out that it was not enough to admit that I was a criminal, I had to reveal my accomplices as well, and not only my school friends: the main thing was to list the adults who, supposedly, had been guiding us. And this was where things became particularly complicated. Even if they had been slowly killing me, I would not have been able to name a single adult: there were none.

The interrogations became harsher. After lights-out, when I had barely managed to slip into my icy bed and begun to warm it with my body, the lock would clatter. And again: "Time for interrogation!"

I would come back from interrogation in the morning and quickly slip into bed so as to get at least a few winks of sleep. But I couldn't manage it. No sooner would I close my eyes than the bell outside the door would announce reveille. After rolling up my bedding and eating the day's ration of damp, salty bread I would sit on the bare boards shivering from the cold, lacking the strength to keep my eyes open. Lying down for a moment was not allowed. I would sit, nodding, waiting for the midday meal—no, not the meal but the hour after it in which I had the right to sleep. But just before the meal I would hear: "Time for interrogation!"

And once more I would sit before Yevdokimov. As always, he would slowly and deliberately get out a sheet of yellowish lined paper, pick up a pen, and . . .

"And so who assisted you in your anti-Soviet activities?"

Dusk would be falling when I returned to my cell. On the bedside table would be a bowl of soup, cold as meat jelly from the cellar, made from unpeeled potatoes. I would eat it automatically and, befuddled from lack of sleep, wait for lights-out. I could not keep my head from falling; sensing, apparently, that I was about to collapse, I would manage to come to my senses at the last moment. Sleep, sleep . . . And at last the long-awaited bell for lights-out. I would quickly unroll the mattress, undress in the fierce cold, and dive under the blanket. Sleep!

But it was not to be. Through the sleep that instantly overcame me I would hear: "Time for interrogation!"

And once again I would be on the chair before my captain, looking at him in amazement and feeling sorry for him: how can he keep this up?

But he seems perfectly fine. He takes a smoked roach from a packet, picks out the bones, and chews it with relish, not looking at me, as if I were not there. It's warm. The lights are bright. The aroma of smoked fish makes my mouth water. I try to hide it when I swallow my saliva. With every swallow, I force myself to open my drooping eyelids. I'm so sleepy that my eyes smart.

Yevdokimov shoves a piece of paper toward me: "Check it and sign each page."

Check it? Can that be possible? And what will it matter, in any case? I sign the pages without reading them, anything to get back to my cell and get some sleep.

But everything, evidently, has been well calculated, and everything is repeated. The following night, though, Yevdokimov does not eat smoked roach; he makes a telephone call. By the tone of his voice and by the semblance of a smile on his face I surmise that he is speaking to a woman, a girlfriend as I imagine, who works somewhere nearby, in the building on the Vorobyevka. It's probably love. I listen in to the conversation and I am perplexed: "Are these people really capable of love?"

Now my interrogator is wearing one of the new uniforms. In place of a service jacket he has a coarse wool tunic of lizard green color with a stand-up collar and shoulder boards of poisonous yellow. He still feels awkward in his new regalia but he is pleased and admires himself.

Soon, a little diversity was added to my life: I was transferred to another cell at the very lowest level of the prison. The cell was a large one, with two cots. I walked around in it as if in a hall. And what amazed me was that along with the *parasha* there was a mop. For a cell with the temperature of a cold cellar this was a godsend. I soon figured out that though they might forbid exercise, they could not prevent me from mopping the floor. And so during most of the time I was not being interrogated I would prance about the cell with the mop in my hands, less concerned with the luster of the floor than with making all possible moves that would help raise my body temperature. Of course, I had to adjust the duration and the briskness of my dances with the mop to suit the caloric value of the prison ration.

Each day I was offered the chance for a twenty-minute walk in the fresh air. I never refused one of these promenades. The exercise yard was small and was surrounded by windowless brick walls, yet overhead was a genuine winter sky from which dropped genuine snowflakes, and underfoot there was a pleasant crunch that kept time with my deliberate pace. On occasion I could hear music from outside the walls (evidently from the skating rink at the Dynamo Stadium nearby), music that reminded me of a completely different life, as if on some other planet, a life from which I had been torn away so long ago that I had forgotten what it was like.

One day when I came back from interrogation I discovered that the population of the cell had doubled. It was a man a good deal older than I, with an emaciated appearance, taciturn, and with a rather wild or confused look in his eyes. All I could find out from him was that he was a soldier. And in fact the two of us spent only one evening together. At night they called me out for a meeting with Yevdokimov, and on the next day I found myself once more in a new cell.

This time I was lucky. The cell, on the third floor, turned out to be warm and, by comparison with my former ones, somehow cozy and even fit to live in. There was already a young lad in it, two years younger than I, whose name was Kolka; he came from the Vach District which was next to ours.

"What are you in for?" I asked him.

"I was pasting up German posters."

"You really are a fool," I blurted out to him.

It is true, though, that during the search of our apartment I myself had a German leaflet confiscated, one that the Germans had dropped over the area where work on the defenses was going on. I never showed it to anyone and kept it for the time when the war would end, as a historical artifact. Kolka, on the other hand, did something quite stupid, and I certainly did not approve of his action.

"Kochin is here in the prison," he told me, "the writer."

I knew scarcely anything about Kochin. It's true that I had his book, *Kulibin,* from the "Lives of Remarkable People" series, but I never managed to read it. I did not ask how Kolka came to know about Kochin. As happened with the soldier, we spent only a day or two together, and I have no idea of his fate thereafter.

This time they moved me to the cell next door, one that I might say was even more "comfortable." It was similar, with a barred window and a visor, the window being opposite the door. On either side was an iron cot with the bedding rolled up in a cylinder so that the dingy, grease-stained planks were visible. In front of the window was a small table with a mug on it. The open space from the table to the door was about four paces long and wide enough so that two people could just squeeze past each other. A man was standing in this "corridor." He was rather short and shaved bald, as a prisoner was supposed to be; he wore gray trousers and a greenish, unbuttoned checked jacket. His face, a regular oval with rather coarse features and a reddish bristle of beard, looked more like a villager's and not at all like that of an educated person.

"Kochin," he introduced himself.

There was a distinct pause before I realized that before me stood the well-known Gorky writer. Nikolai Ivanovich spoke very quietly and said scarcely anything about himself; his movements were careful and he often fell into deep thought; and from time to time he would press his eyelids together very tightly so that deep wrinkles would form on the bridge of his nose. As I came to understand, this was something involuntary—he had a nervous tic. I don't know if this was a hereditary trait, a consequence of the shock of his arrest, or the result of his worry over his court appearance, which was due to take place in the coming days. The trial of Kochin and his comrades—the writer Patreev, a few of the staff of a Gorky publishing house, and some other person—had ended; they had all confessed to being enemies of the people who were involved, as Article 58 of the Criminal Code read, in "anti-Soviet agitation, the manufacture and storage of anti-Soviet literature." The outcome of one of the sham trials of those times was impossible to predict.

Nikolai Ivanovich was forty-one, but despite the fact that he was more than twice my age we quickly got on friendly terms: prison, like travel, brings people together.

He was keenly interested in who I was, where I came from, and how I had come to Vorobyevka. When he learned that I was in the tenth grade in Pavlovo he recalled with obvious pleasure: "That's a lovely little town. I spent some time there as a teacher."

Then, after a brief pause in which, evidently, he was regretting what had happened, he added: "I thought about writing a book about Pavlovo and the teachers there." Then, as if shaking off this idea, he turned to me again with a question: "And what about you, young fellow, how did you get into this place? What kind of talk got you into trouble?"

"It wasn't talk," I replied, "I was also writing."

His face reflected genuine astonishment. He went on questioning me insistently, and I told him about the magazine *Nalim,* how it had come into being, how a circle of senior students had eventually formed around it, how we had moved from inventing harmless comic stories to the realization that tyranny and lawlessness reigned in our country and how we had made it our task to struggle for genuine freedom of speech and of the press.

Grasping his prickly chin with his five fingers, Nikolai Ivanovich fell into deep thought for some time, evidently assessing the weight of what I had said. At last he asked:

"So how was it they pinched you? Someone turned you in?"

That was far from what I believed: "No, it was my fault. I had hoped that, given our ages, nothing would come of it."

"And did they take all the copies of your *Nalim*?"

"No," I said happily, "Rodka Denisov, a school friend, has them. He's older than me and dropped in not long before the search and took them home to read. They're still at his place."

One evening after lights-out, as we were unrolling the dirty mattresses on our cots, Nikolai Ivanovich asked, "Recite something that you published in your magazine."

I felt very awkward reciting my verses, whose flaws I admitted, to a genuine writer, but I gave in to his request, plucked up my courage, and in a half-whisper so that the warder wouldn't hear through the door I began reciting my poem. Nikolai Ivanovich listened very intently and, contrary to my expectations, with complete seriousness; he would smile at some passages and even laughed from time to time, quite approvingly as it seemed to me.

Meanwhile, prison life ran its course. Sometimes the section head would come in during my interrogations. He would shake his fist in my face and shout: "You'll die before you ever get out of here."

And I believed him. Yevdokimov would start a heart-to-heart conversation with me from time to time.

"Just think," he would say, "your comrades are living in freedom, going to school, working, some already in the army defending the Motherland. But you made yourself out to be some sort of political activist and went against Soviet power. Now you've wrecked your life, yet you could be a decent person."

It was difficult for me to determine what was sincere in this and what was fakery, the more so that I had been accused of something I had never intended doing: they had profaned and distorted my patriotic feelings.

Befuddled from lack of sleep, I would return to my cell each day to the cold prison soup. It is impossible to describe the state a person is in after being continuously awake for many days: the vast riches of the Russian language have no appropriate word for it.

It was at this point that Nikolai Ivanovich saved me. In the daytime, he would sit on my cot closer to the door reading a book that he deliberately held high; I would place my hands on my knees so that the warder could see them, hide behind him, lean against the roll of bedding, and instantly fall asleep. And although the moments of sleep I could snatch were measured in minutes, they helped restore my strength.

One day I came back from interrogation deeply disheartened. Whether the interrogator had done it deliberately or accidentally, I noticed a corner of the cover of the last issue of our magazine *Nalim* protruding from under the papers of his desk. I told Kochin about this:

"Do you think that they've actually arrested Rodka?"

Instead of expressing sympathy Nikolai Ivanovich burst out laughing as he had never done before. I was puzzled.

"But this Rodya's the one who sold you out," he laughed, as he told me what he had supposed.

"Rodka? No, that's impossible. He's the kind of person who . . ."

I could not immediately find the lofty words to characterize my friend.

"He's a rat, your Rodka, a stool pigeon."

I could not believe this, but later on I had to admit that no matter how painful it was, it was true. I followed Nikolai Ivanovich's advice, and during the interrogations I began deliberately citing conversations with Rodka, noting the positive comments he made about our magazine (which he in fact made); but his name was never once entered into the record of the interrogation.

In prison, just as in cloudy weather, there are some rays of sunshine. One of these bright spots that has remained in my memory is meeting Nikolai Ivanovich, and especially the chess games we had. I don't recall how we got the chess set in our cell. After the inner prison in Gorky I spent time in four other prisons, but nowhere did I see any such board games. It's most likely that it was the property of Nikolai Ivanovich. He loved the game and was a top-grade chess player.

"Shall we have a game?" he suggested at some appropriate moment.

We set up the chessmen. And when we began playing he kept up the banter: "Ouch! Young Vsevolod, what a move you've made there!"

And what a face he made—amazed and, I think, even abashed when I triumphantly declared: "Mate!"

We played a second game and the outcome was the same. And at that my string of victories ended; I never won again, not even when Nikolai Ivanovich let me have an advantage by removing one of his bishops or even a rook before the game began. Even the prize he promised me didn't help.

Just before New Year's I turned seventeen. Nikolai Ivanovich had received a small food parcel, and on my birthday brought me a sizeable chunk of white bread. Ever since 1941 even rye bread had tasted like gingerbread to me, but here suddenly was some white bread. Ah, how good it tasted! No one in our family was religious, no one ever said prayers or went to church, even before the churches in our town had been destroyed by local barbarians. But we did keep up the traditions of pre-revolutionary days by coloring eggs at Easter and by baking *kulich* and pressing Easter cakes of curd cheese in wooden molds. We children and the adults as well, I think, loved all these special delicacies. No shortening was spared for the *kuliches;* they were generously larded with raisins, sauced with beaten egg whites, and even decorated with some sweet, multicolored confectionary beads. The bread to which Nikolai Ivanovich treated me seemed just like that *kulich.* And he suggested a game of chess and for my prize, another such piece of bread. I tried as hard as I could, but I never won another game. My partner truly was a strong chess player and I, probably, was thinking not so much about chess maneuvers as the fabulously tasty prize. And so I was left to content myself with only my ration of prison bread—damp and heavy, with salt crystals and pieces of unpeeled potato, like the soup. But I would gulp down this daily ration in the morning at one go, like a dog attacking a cutlet.

In the middle of January, Nikolai Ivanovich was summoned to review the evidence in the "case" against him and to sign Article 206 regarding the completion of his investigation. He returned silent and depressed, and in the days that followed he would pace wordlessly back and forth across the cell, his hands clasped behind his back in prisoner fashion, furrowing the bridge of his nose even more deeply than before when troubled by his tic. Then he began making ready to appear in court. His deliberate movements and the way he avoided looking in my direction were enough to tell me how nervous he was. And, indeed, it would be strange to see anyone indifferent about going off to his own execution. We said our farewells with some warmth but without excess emotion: he now had larger concerns than me.

But a strange thing happened: toward evening of the same day they brought Nikolai Ivanovich back to the cell. As a rule, those who had been sentenced were not sent back to the inner prison. I could see that he was preoccupied and depressed. To my unspoken question he replied in his usual weak voice, measuring his words: "Ten years, and five years deprivation of rights. With confiscation of property." He fell silent, and then added as if sighing, "It's a pity about my library. Six thousand volumes."

The sentence had hit him hard; evidently, until the trial he had been hoping for some miracle.

A day later we made our final farewells.

"I'm going to Burepolom or to Sukhobezvodny," he surmised gloomily.

"The names themselves sound frightening," I thought to myself. At the time I still did not know that there was a mass of camps far more terrible than these scattered all across our country.

Soon I too left the prison on Vorobyevka. But I had to undergo one more ordeal before that.

"You're going to see the general," said Yevdokimov with a grin, as if to say, "Imagine what an honor you've been given."

It made no difference to me: if it was to be the general, then so be it. It was evident that my interrogator was more excited than I.

And so after a brief stay in the waiting room, Yevdokimov accompanied me into the office of the commissar of state security for Gorky Oblast. It was an enormous, bright office. The paneled walls gleamed; there were carpets and a bronze clock under a glass dome. Somewhere in the depths of the room, behind an enormous desk the same color as the walls and which held a multitude of telephones, I at last made out some gleaming shoulder boards and then the bald head of the general, also gleaming.

Yevdokimov humbly took a seat on a chair by the wall and placed his hands on his knees, obviously trembling, like a schoolboy before an exam. Almost in the middle of the room, about four meters away from this high-ranking official, stood a single chair for me. I felt completely calm and examined with curiosity the room's furniture, the likes of which I had never seen before, and the elderly Jewish general with a stern, frowning face who sat at the desk before me.

The interrogation began. Unfortunately, I can't remember a single question the general asked me. I recall only that the questions were put in such a tricky way that any answer of mine might be interpreted not in my favor. At first I made an effort to wriggle out of the trap, but in so doing I only earned "His Excellency's" displeasure; I soon realized that it was best for me to make no reply, so I kept silent. The general would ask a question and I would say nothing but just look at him. Finally he fixed his intimidating stare at me, thinking, evidently, that he could break me psychologically. I was suddenly seized by a fit of stubbornness and I began looking the general in the eye without blinking. The pause continued. Neither of us spoke, but we went on intently looking at each other.

"My eyes may burst," I thought to myself, "but I'm not going to blink."

And I held out. My eyes had already begun to ache when the general could stand it no longer; he pounded his desk with his fist and shouted, "Take him away!"

I rejoiced in my victory.

CHAPTER THREE

My First Transport

The unknown weighs down on people because it gives rise to fear, just as darkness does to a child. This is not a weakness or a flaw, it is the normal response of self-preservation. A person also becomes accustomed to his circumstances, no matter how difficult they may be. Even a prison cell, with time, brings a sense of stability and peace to a prisoner. Therefore, a transport, as a change from the existing order to something unknown, always inspires alarm bordering on terror.

I marched through the city of Gorky experiencing contradictory feelings simultaneously. After six weeks of daily twenty-minute walks inside the bare walls of the prison courtyard I was suddenly walking along streets, looking with delight at the buildings, the snowbanks, the trams, the free people. At the same time, I was separated from all of that by an invisible wall, as if I were looking at the city spread out before me from a distance, from some other world. I can see everything before me, and at the same time I am no longer here; like the soul of one departed, I cannot take part in this life.

Behind me marches a soldier with a rifle slung across his shoulder, and so I'm not on my own; someone is taking me. No, it's not my mother, holding my hand; it's not in a group of schoolchildren marching in pairs; it's not even being marched like a soldier in the ranks, "Left, right, left!"

The faded sky is shedding snowflakes. They circle about, seeking the earth, turning in a merry circle dance before they die as they meet it. Everything seems to be moving to meet its end. By the time we had come down the hill to the bridge across the Oka the snow was falling heavily. It swiftly formed a curtain beyond the railings of the bridge, hiding the Strelka and Kanavino. Everything around was covered in a fresh coat of white, and only the tram rails stubbornly cut through the snow, gleaming like knife blades. We encountered few pedestrians on the streets, and there was no one at all on the bridge; this spared me from the oppressive feeling that people were looking at me like some captured thief. Little by little I began to calm down, and then a happy thought flashed through my mind: maybe they were going to take me to Moscow. I had never been to our capital, and the prospect of spending some time there, even as a prisoner, was somehow encouraging.

My supposition grew stronger when, having made our way through a series of backyards, we reached the tracks of the Moscow Station. Well away from the main station we found a dirty green Stolypin carriage. Its doleful look, the bars on its windows, and a certain unhealthy, ominous silence around it brought back my despondent prison mood.

The Stolypin carriage resembles a traveling menagerie. On the side where the windows are located is a narrow corridor. It is separated from the open-air cages of the compartments by a wire grill; looking through it you almost need to guess that the creatures inside are human beings.

I was pushed into one of these cages. In the semi-darkness I could not immediately make out distinct people as I entered a human mass so tightly packed that, it seemed, there was no room to place your foot let alone place yourself. Into a space intended for four people under cramped conditions of travel they had crammed more than twenty. I couldn't imagine the poses they had to assume so as to sit, lie, or hang. I felt guilty for taking up their last bit of living space and expected their displeasure to fall upon me at once in some savage way. I was amazed and relieved, however, when, without my asking and with the help of some well-wishers who took my arms, I managed to take a step without knowing where and on what and ended by sitting on the carriage seat among some male bodies that, by some miracle, had managed to move apart in this crush of people. I realized at once that the only people who could accept me this way were ones who had already endured more than it was possible to endure.

When my eyes became accustomed to the semi-darkness I could see that I was surrounded by soldiers, though they were wearing various uniforms.

There were green German tunics, yellowish Hungarian service jackets with roomy patch pockets, and even some Italian greatcoats with capes.

"Who are you?" I asked, utterly baffled.

"Prisoners of war."

Yet they all spoke perfect Russian. Whenever did they manage to learn the language?

It took me some time to comprehend their explanation that they were Soviet soldiers who had been captured by the Germans, then freed by our troops and now, our own people again, they had been imprisoned by us. They had no idea where they were being taken. They knew only that they had first been taken from west to east, and now they were going from east to west. Some hoped that they would be returned to active service, others were more pessimistically inclined, believing that they would go before a tribunal and be given longer sentences or something even worse.

I spent three days in the carriage with the prisoners of war. It was only on the second day that we were given bread and herring. I got nothing. Then I realized why, not long before I had been taken out of prison, they had given me a second ration. I was surprised at the time and happily ate it all, but, as it turned out, this had been my hard ration for the journey. One of the soldiers broke something off his crust of bread for me and I was given a piece of herring. This was all I had for three days. After the herring, the prisoners asked for water and to be let out to the toilet. The guards, who were Tatars or Kalmyks, paid no attention to these requests—evidently, their officers had issued no orders about letting people go to the toilet. Only after we began shouting, cursing, and rocking the whole carriage did the guards bring some water in a bucket and then begin to let people out in ones and twos.

The train still remained stopped. Some time toward the end of the second day our cage became even more crowded. This was because of the arrival of a man about forty, short, lean, black-browed, and dressed in a white, almost new officer's sheepskin coat and officer's ear-flapped fur cap.

"Vadim Kozin," he introduced himself, "Colonel."

Who knows if he really was a colonel, but one could sense in him a certain free-and-easy manner, the independence of a former front-line soldier. He was not dejected.

"I won't be with you for long. I'm off to Dzerzhinsk, to my trial. And then they'll shove me in some punishment battalion."

He didn't tell us what he had done to get here. But with his lively manner, his easy chatter, his detached view that what was happening did not concern him in the least, he managed to reassure us all. He seemed to inspire us with a faith that prison and the barred Stolypin carriage were things temporary and unsubstantial, belonging to another world. Man lives for a purpose, one unknown to him and determined by something higher.

During his short stay with us Kozin managed to divert this group of despairing people from their oppressive thoughts. He was able to instill in us the idea that not all was lost and that after the bad there would inevitably follow something good. In order to go on living we had to hold on to this faith in a better future. He became a friend to all of us in that cage, even someone we relied on. He was particularly friendly to me, despite our difference in age, and when they took him out of our carriage, late at night and unseen, he shouted a few words of farewell to me from the platform: "Vsevolod, pray to God and everything will be fine."

I never met him again, but I have remembered him all my life. Why? Probably because he simply loved people and had no other motive than that. Genuine feeling is easy to understand and it touches people.

CHAPTER FOUR

I Come to Know Butyrka Prison

When I jumped down from the Black Maria, my legs gave out and I fell. Evidently, the guards who were there to meet us were well accustomed to such problems. Two of them seized me by the arms as if carrying out a drill and led me away. I only managed to catch a glimpse of a courtyard, small but deep as a mine shaft, surrounded by greenish-yellow walls the color of a scorpion, walls seven or eight stories high with many windows. They brought me to a brightly lit, clean white basement and after taking me a little way along a corridor put me into a single cell. The ceiling was vaulted, the floor concrete; there were no windows, but the bright lights made it seem dazzlingly white. There was a small ventilation grille and it was very warm, even hot. I collapsed on the cot, looked around, and for some reason thought, "This place could serve well as an execution chamber."

Evidently this occurred to me because of the absolute silence all around. If no sounds could reach here from the outside, then cries and shots could not be heard from the outside either. In the silence and warmth I fell into a sound and untroubled sleep.

The next day they again took me somewhere in the Black Maria. When we arrived at our destination I saw an unusual building. It was surrounded by a rather high stone wall of bluish-gray color; immense and gloomy, with round towers on the corners, it resembled an ancient fortress. The entrance door stood out in sharp contrast. It was of enormous proportions, like a huge gate; its top was rounded and it was made from some costly wood that was carved and polished, and so it looked much more like a piece of fine handicraft than the gate to a prison hell.

The anteroom struck me even more: it was spacious; the walls had figured facings; the floor was tiled; and it was as clean as a pharmacy. I was even pleased that I had been brought here and had been able to see such a thing. I sometimes asked myself how I would have felt had I come in and seen an artistically engraved guillotine blade: would it have been terror or delight? Perhaps even the sling in David's hand is more attractive than terrifying.

"Into the box!"

These words brought me back to reality as I guessed that they were directed at me. And I was not mistaken. After a perfunctory body search—right there, in the anteroom—a narrow door opened in front of me and once more I found myself in a cage not more than a meter square, though with a very high ceiling; the floor was tiled and the walls faced in vitreous tile of bottle green color. The only furnishing was an electric light hanging from the ceiling. One pace this way, one pace that way is not walking but simply turning around, and it quickly tires you. I sat on the floor, trying to stretch out my legs, then tucking them under, listening to the shouted commands that filtered through the door. That meant that more people had been brought here, taken away and hidden in "boxes" like this one.

I completely lost track of time. There were no clues whatsoever that would allow me even to approximate if it was now daytime, evening, or night, or how many hours or days I had spent in this stone pencil case. Many times I would stand up, make some attempts to walk, and sit down again. At last I began to feel sleepy. I tried lying on the floor, tucking up my legs, but I could not manage to fit myself into this little den. After twisting this way and that I at last managed to find a position I could tolerate: I lay on my back with my legs propped up vertically against the wall. And in this way I fell asleep. I don't know how animals do it, but it turns out that a man can sleep with his legs in the air.

The next day began with my making closer acquaintance with the prison. I continued to be struck by its gigantic dimensions and by the finishing of the interiors that were more reminiscent of ancient palaces or tower rooms. They made me stay for a time in a corridor as huge as a stadium whose floors and walls were all just as carefully faced in two-colored ceramic tile with perfectly patterned ornament. Along both sides of the corridor were enormously high doors through whose transoms, covered in mesh-enforced glass, came some light. As I examined this unusual structure I once again forgot that I was in a prison and that, perhaps, the most terrible part still lay ahead. But in truth I was filled with admiration. What I saw was not a prison but a creation of the talented hands of men.

I was brought back to reality when they pushed me through the nearest door, smaller than the others and without a transom. I found myself in a strange room, rather spacious, with a linoleum floor that absorbed the sound of footsteps and with padded walls covered in tightly bulging, regular squares of yellow leather. The appearance of the room puzzled me. "What sort of cell is this?" I thought. "And why did they put me in it?"

But everything was explained. They threw some clean linen on the floor for me, along with a pair of hospital slippers.

"Put these on," came the command.

While getting undressed and still gazing around me, I realized that this must be a room for the violently insane or for one who was trying to kill himself by hitting his head against the wall. They had thought of everything in this prison.

Wearing only my underwear, my large slippers slapping on the floor, I was put into a cell or, more accurately, into a ward of the prison hospital with two cots; in one, to the left of the door, lay a man with his blanket pulled over his head. The ward was spacious (two more cots could easily fit into it) and quite bright; aside from the cots it was furnished with two bedside tables. It was rather cold and, assuming the rights of a patient, I quickly dived under the blanket.

I lay there for a long time, yearning for something to do, the more so that there was absolutely nothing to look at inside the ward. I was only drawn to my neighbor, lying there motionless, whom I still had not seen and who amazed me by his ability to sleep so soundly and for so long. But over the day we managed to make an acquaintance.

My bundled-up neighbor began showing signs of life. First he turned over, without uncovering himself, but very cautiously and slowly, without making any big movements. Then his head appeared from under the blanket. I was immediately struck by his face: it was thin, emaciated, and with skin of some deathly shade—not white, but without the least sign of color. As I examined him I could determine that he was a man of fifty or so, that he was tall, and by some signs that were barely perceptible, that he was a man of culture. It took him some time, evidently while gathering his strength, before he introduced himself in a weak, hollow voice: "Lvov."

He spoke with great difficulty, making long pauses. Yet I did manage to learn that he was a former professor at the Frunze Military Academy. When the Germans were moving on Moscow, the academy was evacuated to Tashkent. There he was arrested, along with many others, for anti-Soviet activity. A man who lived by strict rules, decent and honorable, a born intellectual of the type that has died out as a species among us in our day, he would not admit to the fictitious charges brought against him. When they could make no headway with him in Tashkent the authorities sent him to Moscow, to the Lubyanka. Over the course of two years they were unable to break him morally, but they did break him physically. Before me lay someone who was no longer a man but a corpse, one that had not yet given up its soul.

"I decided to die," he told me. "I declared a hunger strike."

And in fact he never touched the food that was put down for him on the bedside table. Over all the days that we were together he never once got up from the bed. But each time I returned from the prescribed twenty-minute walk, he would ask me something in a fading voice or tell me something using only a few words. It was from him I learned that we were in Butyrka Prison, built in the days of Catherine the Great. Once he asked about the courtyard in which I took my exercise.

"It's a small one," I replied, "with an irregular shape, by the round tower."

"That's a famous tower," he said, as if disclosing a secret. "It was there that Emelyan Pugachev was held, in chains, while awaiting execution."

Sometimes the silence of the hospital was broken by a powerful male voice. He would shout out panegyrics, first to the doctors and all the medical personnel, then to the workers in the glorious organs of state security, to the interrogators who worked so tirelessly, and to the valiant prosecutors. Gradually this exaltation would turn into abuse and cursing and would end with a long streak of the foulest language directed at those same persons.

I could make nothing of this but I managed to pick a moment when I could ask Lvov, "What's going on?"

"It's the lunatic in the cell opposite," he replied.

And the next day, when they brought in our meal, I could see this unfortunate across the corridor. His arms spread as if crucified, he managed by some miracle to hang from the transom and pronounce his regular panegyric.

I was not held in the hospital for long. For some reason they always and everywhere show heightened concern for the health of those whose lives they intended to take.

I left the ward without saying good-bye to Lvov. He lay there, stiff as a corpse, his head covered with the blanket as if he were in a shroud. His life was being measured out by hours.

CHAPTER FIVE

The Lubyanka Inner Prison

The corridors of the Lubyanka inner prison are covered with strip carpets. Unlike the Vorobyevka, the locks here made no noise, yet when they brought me to the cell at night all its inhabitants raised their heads. Prisoners under investigation, at least those who have not been worn out by interrogations, sleep lightly, and even in their dreams they are expecting to be summoned to the interrogator.

The cell was quite large: three cots were arranged along one wall, three along the other. A large painted table stood in the center. There was the same dark-green wainscoting, a parquet floor, a huge window covered by a shutter that cut off the light. A large red copper teapot and some enameled mugs stood on the table.

All the cots were occupied, so they brought me an additional one and placed it in the center in line with the table. They provided some bedding. But I could not get to sleep immediately: the bedbugs attacked me. There was a flurry of activity in the cell when the others learned why I was so restless. They called the warder. And only after they had brought me another cot, one with even some bits of snow clinging to it, did the cell settle down again.

From my first day there, life in the Lubyanka struck me as amusing. Something comic showed through even dramatic situations. It's true that everything in life can be looked at from two opposite points of view, the comic and the tragic.

One of the first procedures after reveille in the morning was the procession to the toilet. We went in pairs, and the first pair—the cell orderly and his deputy, who had served as orderly the day before—triumphantly bore the *parasha*. Why was it that this stinking vessel was carried in front with the rest of us following in its wake, as in a religious procession? Usually a procession is led by a flag or a religious banner. In prison they carry a rusty, eighteen-gallon vessel filled with our collective urine as if it were some holy relic. The procession is brought up by a prison screw, a *vertukhai*. A second guard meets us at the open door of the toilet and passes out pieces of toilet paper, though not always. In any case, given the prison grub there is no regular need for paper.

After this solemn rite, a watchful silence reigns in the cell. Someone is smoothing wrinkles from a handkerchief over his knee, another is reading a book, but everyone, even those who may be talking in low voices, has his ears pricked up: the "happy moment" is drawing near. Amidst all the sounds that are carried into the cell from outside the prisoner can infallibly discern that unique, metallic one made by the cover of a bowl or the lid of a teapot that announces the imminent arrival of the food.

"It's coming!" And the whole cell at once becomes animated as if regaining consciousness.

The bread rations are laid out on the table; they are chosen in a strict order of precedence. I was the last to arrive in the cell and therefore I can count only on the leftovers. Smirnov chooses first. He was a student from Moscow State University, very stout, round-shouldered, with puffy red cheeks covered in gypsy-like bristles and wearing frameless glasses without which he is almost blind. His crime against Soviet power was committed when the students in the History and Philology Faculty of Moscow University came to the conclusion that the country could only be ruled by people with special training. Specialized educational institutions were needed to train such personnel, and in their opinion it was their faculty—the nursery for members of the government, as one of our cellmates, Yagodkin, called it—that was best suited to do this.

Smirnov approaches the table. Bending down toward it he carefully examines every ration. It's a critical moment. He's been waiting a whole week to exercise his right to make the first choice and now he must be careful not to make a slip because the rations include both crusts and inside pieces.

The crust is drier and so its volume is greater. Another thing to consider is that additional pieces of various sizes have been fastened to each slice with wooden pins so as to make up the proper weight. Yes, indeed, you need experience, composure, and a sharp eye in order to pick out the biggest ration.

Blind Smirnov almost runs his nose across the bread laid out on the table. He's in agony, unable to make up his mind, but . . . the selection is finally made. He seizes a crust, brings it close to his eyes, and then looks back at the table: no, I think I've made a wrong choice; the one over there with two extra bits, near the edge, is bigger. Smirnov holds back a sigh. To-morrow he'll be last in line and will have to take whatever is left. The others choose their rations with the same care.

The ration includes the daily allotment of six hundred grams of bread. In the morning there is nothing else except tea. The noon meal is soup; sup-per is porridge. Each man divides up his ration in his own way. The microbi-ologist Kulinsky from Krasnodar, an elderly man, taller than average, with a pointed beard and a gold crown on one of his front teeth, carefully cuts off a third of the bread with a short piece of string and cuts the remainder in half—for lunch and supper—and wraps them up neatly in a handkerchief.

Yagodkin—in his words, a member of the Amnesty Board of the Su-preme Soviet of the USSR—is a tall man in an expensive but well-worn suit of mousy-gray color; he also uses a piece of string to cut up his ration into small cubes, but he keeps nothing in reserve. When the cutting pro-cedure is finished, he squeezes each cube in his fist to compress it and then pops it into his mouth, washing it down with hot, unsweetened tea.

The architect Arkhangelsky, who seems to be the oldest one in the cell, digs the soft portion out of the crust and saves that for his noon meal.

Smirnov finishes off his ration in animal fashion. He tears it into bits with his powerful hands and eats them greedily, hurriedly, as if taking re-venge on the bread for his poor choice. He eats without drinking, cast-ing quick glances at the others and bitterly comparing the way his large crust melts away faster than my smallest piece from the middle. Doing this he brings to mind Sobakevich: just as massive, just as coarse. He quickly gobbles up his ration and then seems to droop once it has disappeared. Just like Sobakevich, sitting before his empty plate after devouring a whole sturgeon, he looks around as if amazed at where it had all gone; he adjusts his glasses and picks up a few stray crumbs that have survived by chance, rejoicing that these barely visible bits are still left on the table and on his trousers. Aware at last of the hopelessness of his situation, he pours himself a mug of tea; he grasps it with both hands and bending down begins to drink leisurely, his now lusterless eyes glancing occasionally over the top of his glasses.

I can't wait and also eat up my whole ration at once, though I eat unhurriedly, savoring the bread and not drinking so that it lasts longer. First I tear off all the crusts "for smoothing down the meal," as we used to say at home about dessert; then with special delight I chew the soft part of the bread, while recalling the potato pancakes with caviar during Lenten meals in the refectories of trans-Volga monasteries that were described with inimitable art by Melnikov-Peshchersky.

Every day a floor cloth is brought to the cell: the duty prisoner has to polish the parquet floor. In this, as in the eating of bread crusts, everyone has his own approach. In the classical approach, that's to say the one most widely used, the prisoner clasps his hands behind his back and, putting one foot on the rag, scuffs it back and forth, making little curtseys in time to his movements. The result is a distinctive kind of dance that is by no means as easy to perform as might appear. When a prisoner, month after month, has had only a piece of bread and hot water in the morning and a half-bowl of Lenten soup at noon, the floor-polisher's dance, even at a slow tempo, leaves him dizzy and out of breath. Still, the floor is polished until it gleams. Once a month some paste wax and a brush are brought along with the polishing cloth. Each and every one of the prisoners takes part in polishing the floor.

After the noon meal, which consists of just one dish that most people have to eat without bread, there is an official quiet hour. In the Lubyanka, as a special indulgence, there are two hours. You do not have to sleep, but you must lie down, even if it is with a book in your hands. Books are brought twice a month, and they are in sufficient supply. You may request whatever you like, even forbidden literature published abroad. But all the prisoners regard this as an unjustified risk and content themselves with choosing among the books that are delivered.

Twenty minutes are set aside each day for a walk outside, but it is not compulsory. The whole time I was in the prison I never missed one, no matter what the weather. In cold weather, the walk is preceded by the outfitting. They toss in a heap of nondescript mackintoshes or loose smocks made of black material, boots of different sizes and caps; we get dressed without delay. We are taken to the seventh floor by an elevator. Boxlike exercise yards have been set up here, each walled off from the other by a high iron fence painted gray. There are several such fenced-off areas, and at the place where they join stands a sentry box. It's arranged very efficiently: one screw with his rifle can watch over several exercise yards.

We walk in a circle in pairs, our hands clasped behind our backs. Kulinsky whispers to me: "Breath deeply. Four paces in, four paces out."

From the street below come the soft tones of the horns of the "Emka" cars competing with each other; sometimes, as if right next to us, we hear the Kremlin chimes, whose slightly hoarse ringing I've known since childhood, measuring off the passing hours of our lives. Somewhere nearby, just beyond this iron wall, a normal life is being lived; people are working, going to school, relaxing, socializing. We see nothing of this. No one sees us; it never occurs to anyone that here, on the roof, there are people moving around who have been torn away from the world. And even if we did imagine someone suddenly catching sight of us, they would still only say, "Those are the enemies of the people over there, traitors and fascists."

We walk in measured paces, dragging our oversized boots across the concrete slabs that form the bottom of this iron box.

A little snow has fallen and it is growing dark. Here in Moscow lived a girl with whom I've lost touch. Is it forever? Could she know, I wonder, that I am nearby?

The twenty minutes are over. We return to the cell, bringing with us a breath of freshness.

Soon there were some changes in our cell. Turner, a correspondent, he claimed, for the English newspaper *Daily Mail* and the American paper *New York Herald Tribune* hopped about the cell, hammering on the door and filled with indignation at how he, a foreign citizen, could be imprisoned. He was taken from our cell literally the day after I arrived. A new man appeared, a poet, Ulin, from the Far East, who had something in common with Turner but different from the rest of us, since we already understood the situation we were in. Like Turner, he could not comprehend how he, a communist, front-line soldier and poet, could suddenly be put away in a prison. He would helplessly lift his hands in dismay and shrug his shoulders, repeating: "I can't understand it."

"You will," Yagodkin told him, "after you've sat here for a month or two."

Not everything was clear to me either. Back in the Vorobyevka, when the head of the Investigation Section had shaken his fist in my face and shouted, "You'll die before you ever get out of here!" I had realized there was no point in resisting: any explanation I tried to give would always be turned against me. But even during the interrogations, when we had reached the critical point at which they were unable to squeeze any more invented crimes out of me, the hardest thing to face in prison life was still the summons to the interrogator. This was done in a quite genteel manner in the Lubyanka. At night a warder would silently enter the cell and touch your shoulder: "Time for interrogation," and he would leave, allowing you some time to get ready.

The Lubyanka, i.e., the Main Administration of the People's Commissariat of State Security, is an immense building covering the whole perimeter of a city block, seven stories high on one side, eight on another; it is greenish in color, with a base of funereal black marble. The pediment of the front facade was crowned by two symmetrical, reclining naiads that have now been removed, leaving only two protruding spikes in their place, something that, perhaps, serves as a better symbol of the building which they crown. In the depths of this enormous well within is the five-story addition that is the inner prison, whose rooms have rather high ceilings, large windows, and durable parquet floors.

At first I was taken to interrogation along a short prison corridor. The guard escorting me walked along in his accustomed loose gait, tapping his key against the metal clasp of his belt, thereby signaling others that we were coming. Whenever we happened to meet another prisoner under escort coming our way, one prisoner would have to stand with his face to the wall or be taken around a corner so that two prisoners were never allowed to meet. Then I would be taken by elevator to the appropriate floor, and the procession would continue along the corridor of the main building. The corridor was not wide but was sufficient for three or four men to pass by each other. There were times when I had to walk around almost the whole perimeter of the building. Even at night the corridor was filled with people. There were flashes of gold from the new shoulder boards; officers, majors for the most part, were walking about here; they clearly liked their new uniforms and even seemed to be deliberately squaring their shoulders.

Sometimes I managed to catch a glimpse of the green naiads on the pediment or cast a glance at the broad stairway with its massive figured railings of ivory color that led downwards; that meant I was on the top story. But none of these observations lessened my inner tension. To the contrary, the closer we got to the interrogator's office, the more my chest seemed to tighten as if under pressure of the air being pumped into it; my throat would catch in a spasm and my breathing become difficult. I had no confidence that this night, with yet another interrogation, would end well. Total disregard for the law on the one hand and boundless tyranny on the other left not the slightest hope for fairness, justice, or common sense.

Captain Motavkin was in charge of my case.

"Well, that fellow will slap a case together for you," Yagodkin told me in my first days in the cell. "He's their specialist in literary matters."

Not all the interrogators are the same: there are some who deal in literary matters, others in industrial or agricultural cases. Their tactics during interrogations were grounded in rough, utterly unprincipled behavior and in inspiring fear, since what was demanded of them was not uncovering the truth but confirming some dogmatic idea that was invented, fantastic, and completely unfounded. All interrogations were built along the same scheme and boiled down to primitive sophistry.

"Do you admit you are guilty of anti-Soviet activity?" the interrogator would usually ask.

"No," was the first and natural response of the accused.

"Yet in your conversations you made unfounded criticisms of the leaders of the Communist Party."

"I made some remarks about specific people."

"But they have been chosen by the people and are the representatives of Soviet power," the interrogator would say, taking the bull by the horns, "and that means you are against Soviet power."

Given such a conclusion, along with a series of other accusations made in the same style, you yourself would conclude that, yes, in fact you were involved in anti-Soviet activity.

In the case of my friends and me, things were much more straightforward. As material evidence of our activity, which in their interpretation could be labeled as nothing other than anti-Soviet, they already had four issues of the manuscript magazine that our group had published; one of them contained my poem where I openly complained about the lack of freedom of speech in our country and about the situation on the front in the early months of the war. I had also made brief mention in the poem of Stalin's inability to manage the military operations of our army, comparing our leader to a calf trying to play chess. Such things were not forgiven.

But the interrogator had a different task ahead of him, and that was to learn the names of the adults who ran our group, since the authorities could not believe that a few schoolboys, independently and with no one's help, had been able to organize a magazine that sharply criticized political conditions in our country. It remained a mystery to me how agents of Beria's investigatory apparatus, capable of any bestial act and merciless in their zeal, could at last convince themselves that no one was leading us and do so without having to break our bones in the process.

The interrogation in the Lubyanka was a repetition of everything that I had already gone through in the inner prison in Gorky. Our "case" was later handled by the interrogator Perevozchikov, a man distinctly civilian in manner, who had barely achieved officer's rank and who, by all appearances, had not yet picked up much experience and was learning his trade on us. At the interrogations I soon realized that he was one of the new reinforcements who had come to fill out the ranks of the organs of state security.

Kulinsky, Smirnov, and I were moved to another cell. The fourth person in it turned out to be a professor from Moscow's Gorky Institute of Literature named Urbanovich-Nabatov. Like the rest of us, he had been under interrogation for several months. No longer young, single, accustomed to luxury, at least by comparison with our lives, his thoughts in prison ran less to what lay ahead of him and more to what he had been forced to give up. It was strange to hear him maintain that it was best to drink coffee with a piece of chocolate in your mouth since, in his opinion, that produced a particular gustatory bouquet. Or to hear him tell of how much he disliked the dark parquet flooring in his apartment and so he had workers come in to plane it down to bare wood, scrape it smooth, and polish it with wax. He regretted being without his deck of cards with gold edges and his little ivory letter knife. He had spent some time abroad. He took a certain satisfaction in exhibiting his Paris-made overcoat to us: "That's what I looked like before Lefortovo Prison."

And, in truth, all the prisoners in our cell could have easily fit inside Urbanovich's capacious overcoat and still left room for Urbanovich. More than once we tried to find out from him what the strict-regime Lefortovo Prison was like. He would begin telling us but his voice would start to quaver and then break, and each time he would begin to cry. There was only one thing that we heard clearly: "I tried to hang myself from the window bars but didn't succeed—they cut me down."

One day he announced that Easter was drawing near and walked about the cell quietly humming an Easter hymn. Then he began teaching me church music, and the two of us, our voices hushed so as not to attract the attention of the warder, would sing: "Christ is risen from the dead, conquering death by His death, bringing the gift of life to those in the tomb."

Odd as it may have been in those times, the feast of Christ's Glorious Resurrection was marked in prison. On Easter eve they issued us the necessary supplies to give our cell a holiday appearance. We washed the painted wainscoting, stained and polished the floor, and polished the teapot until it gleamed. On Sunday morning the warder came into the cell and graciously announced that anyone who had money could buy tobacco in the prison shop. Kulinsky was the only one among us who smoked. And the real miracle was that we had a ration of light-gray, properly baked bread on that festive day. That served as our prison *kulich*.

Despite the forty-year difference in our ages, I developed a very good relationship with Ivan Osipovich Kulinsky. Before the war he had been a research worker at the Krasnodar Institute of Microbiology and had also taught there. The war destroyed a great deal in his life, as it did in everyone's. When the Germans were approaching, he and his fellow workers buried their scientific files and their specimens and fled the city. They did not manage to go far because the German advance was so swift, so Kulinsky and his colleagues had little choice but to return and continue their work in the institute. When Krasnodar was liberated by our troops, the microbiologists were arrested as traitors to the Motherland and dispatched to the Lubyanka in Moscow.

Fate moved in a strange way when it brought these two antipodes, Urbanovich-Nabatov and Kulinsky, together in the same cell. Before his arrest, Urbanovich-Nabatov had been a gourmet, whereas Kulinsky had followed a very basic diet when he lived as a free man. He would add some porridge to a bowl of borsch, and this single dish served as his entire lunch. He did not allow himself any confections, took his tea usually with sugar, and instead of a pastry he would have a piece of white bread with butter and honey. He dressed just as simply and did not even own a suit; he wore a Russian *kosovorotka* blouse outside his trousers and a narrow, plaited belt. These were the clothes in which he had been arrested. And his temperament, by contrast with the nervous and overly talkative Urbanovich, was calm and balanced. He spoke slowly, rarely, and quietly; he never got involved in group discussions and particularly avoided the petty quarrels that broke out in the cell every day, though at the same time he listened attentively to everything.

One day Urbanovich, our literary man, corrected me: "You mustn't say 'I'm bored about something'; what's correct is simply to say 'I'm bored.'"

I did not agree with the professor, and we got into a major argument. Kulinsky did not intervene. But literally on the next day he found an expression in a book that proved I had been correct and he silently showed it to me.

Every day Ivan Osipovich Kulinsky would give us lectures on health, on venereal diseases in particular.

"Try to remember this," he would say in a pleading tone. "You might find it useful in the camps."

Using some bits of soft bread mixed with tobacco ash and some burnt matches, he would fashion models of microbes and medical instruments.

"There," he would show us a helix made of bread, "that's what the *spirochete pallidum* looks like." And he would follow up with a lesson devoted to syphilis.

Thanks to Kulinsky's lectures, the stories from biblical history of Urbanovich-Nabatov, and the books that we literally devoured, our time was well spent. On the other hand, we knew nothing of what was going on in the world, in our own country and on the front lines. One April evening we suddenly heard an artillery cannonade.

"They're firing a salute!" cried Smirnov, in a soft voice tone unlike his usual one.

I carefully pried open an edge of the grille "muzzle" that covered the window, and after the last in a series of volleys I could see a multicolored fan of fireworks in the dark sky. Only by some miracle did the news percolate down to us that Soviet forces had broken through to the border with Romania. It was difficult to describe our feelings. We had been deprived of the right to celebrate our successes along with everyone else, as if they were of no concern to us. This sense of inferiority, a feeling that we were social outcasts, remained with us for the rest of our lives.

The May 1 holiday passed without being noticed. And I cannot even recall whether it was before or after that date when they took me into a little closet next to our cell and placed two thick files on the table before me, saying: "Your investigation is over. You can familiarize yourself with your 'case' and sign Article 206 to acknowledge its completion."

As I paged through the papers I found transcripts of all the interrogations, both my own and those of others who were called in after my arrest. I found my own "Selected Works" bound in hardcover, clearly typewritten on coated paper, and specially chosen with the aim of documenting my anti-Soviet agitation and propaganda. There was not a single word about Rodka Denisov, who had taken my magazines and given them to the People's Commissariat of State Security, the NKGB, the person whose name I had deliberately mentioned many times during my interrogations. On the upper corners of the files were stamped two phrases: "Top Secret" and "To Be Preserved Forever."

CHAPTER SIX

My Second Encounter with Butyrka Prison

Very soon thereafter, I left Lubyanka and had my second encounter with Butyrka Prison.

This time the Butyrka struck me as less interesting. I passed through an unsightly, dreary corridor with high windows, beyond which stood a melancholy church building surrounded by greenery; then I reached a rather large cell, desolate, gray, and without the slightest sign of any comfort. The walls were gloomy, and the concrete floor more appropriate for a cellar or a storehouse. On both sides towered rows of *vagonki*—unpainted wooden two-tiered bunks. Between them was an enormous empty table with a bucket-sized teapot on it, a vessel with battered sides that in its time had served thousands of prisoners. In the corner stood the prescribed *parasha*, this one huge enough for mass employment. The windows were neatly divided into squares by the bars, and through them, at the top of the massive iron louvers outside, I could see a patch of clear blue sky and against it the fresh, spring green of the leaves that were just coming out on the poplars. When you looked through the window, you would feel your chest begin to ache and your eyes burn painfully with involuntary tears.

The population of the cell was sizeable—more than twenty people—and the group was as varied as any to be found in a bazaar. But we also had something in common, something that matched the outward look of the cell: an overall grayness, the absence of any bright spots in the clothing and the faces. Everyone's eyes even had the same expression—downcast, apathetic, as if no one was thinking about anything: everything had already been thought through, considered, decided. And once again there was absolutely nothing to do: no books, no newspapers, no sounds of any kind coming from outside. It was a stable. I would be in it until my trial, in complete ignorance of my subsequent fate and of the time when it would be decided.

They showed me a free place on the bunks. I sat down and began to feel nostalgic for the Lubyanka. There at least I was close to people of my own kind and could associate with members of the intelligentsia. Here, as I realized, I was among criminals. I had never had anything to do with them before. I had only heard that they were bandits, thieves, riffraff. And suddenly I not only found myself among them but a part of them.

When I had had a chance to look around I discovered, nevertheless, that by no means everyone was a criminal. I watched the tall man next to me, and neither his speech nor his appearance gave any grounds for including him in the ranks of the criminals. Three of his neighbors, who spoke with accents, turned out to be Lithuanians. I assumed that they were part of my own fraternity, the Article 58ers, and I felt reassured.

The prison routine had become habitual: reveille, toilet, giving out the crusts of bread, the twenty-minute walk in pairs in the stone courtyard. Two weeks passed in this monotonous fashion. Only once something happened that stirred up the whole cell and revealed some of the peculiarities of the criminal world.

The tall man received a food parcel: a loaf of bread, a tin of meat that the warder opened in front of him and placed in a prison bowl, and a few other small things. He invited the Lithuanians to share his food and gave me some as well, acting in a very friendly manner. This evoked a protest from the criminals, who made up the majority in the cell. According to their unwritten laws—and each one of these laws reflects above all the interests of the strong—it is only one's official ration that is untouchable. All food products received from outside are to be shared. How they were to be shared and among whom gave rise to a quarrel that almost ended in a bloody battle. Some of them maintained that the tall fellow had behaved properly by sharing his food with those he thought were in need. Others insisted that he had to give the greater part of it to the thieves. A third party took a compromise position: the parcel should be shared equally by all. That solution suited the majority, who would have received nothing under the first two proposals.

The noise grew louder, the passions more heated, and a brawl was about to break out. Particularly zealous was one unpretentious, thin criminal of rather weak build who bore the traces of a severe head wound. A triangular section of the bone of his skull was missing, either through an operation or as the result of a fracture. It was quite a large section, more than two fingers wide, and thin skin had grown over it. Looking at him I thought in horror: when the fight breaks out someone will shove a finger into that hole in his head and squeeze out his brains like toothpaste from a tube. He himself was afraid of this, and so he had armed himself with the heavy cover of the teapot which he could use to smash someone's head; but he used it like a cap to protect his own, holding it to one side to cover the hole in his skull.

The boundaries between the two contending sides were already clearly drawn. There was noise and cursing. People armed themselves with whatever they could lay hands on. The warders did not interfere—evidently they had seen things like this more than once, and no one had been killed yet. Unexpectedly, at the most critical moment, the tall fellow who had received the parcel decided to kiss it good-bye: "To hell with you, eat your fill!"

In fact, there was nothing to eat. When the remains of the parcel had been carefully divided and placed in piles on the table for those who had not been given anything, each person's share was so small that it barely allowed them to get a taste, let alone soothe their hunger. When they received this unexpected ration on the palm of their hands and had licked it up like a dog with a spoonful of cream, each one felt not so much the triumph of justice as the bitterness of loss: for some it was the loss of this treat that had gone by leaving scarcely a trace; for others it was also the irreplaceable loss of the link with their conscience.

CHAPTER SEVEN

The Trial

On Saturday, May 13, 1944, they took me out of the Butyrka in a compartment of a Black Maria as cramped as the cockpit of a fighter plane. Through a narrow gap and the little window in the back door of the vehicle I could see the concrete wall with the prison doors begin to recede. And then the broad streets of Moscow began flashing past. It was a sunny, warm day that seemed somehow joyous. I recognized the colonnade of the

Red Army Theater from the pictures on postage stamps and was happy because it made it seem as if they were taking me somewhere other than to court. Nearer the city center, the Black Maria stopped at an intersection, and against the bright facade of a building lit up by the sun I saw a soldier walking down the sidewalk holding a little girl by the hand. They looked very happy. I could not take my eyes off them; it seemed to me that their happiness was my own, and the only thing that troubled me was that the Maria would drive on and put an end to it. But at that moment a blue trolleybus blocked my view of the soldier and the little girl and when it had passed they were no longer there. Then I remembered that I was being taken to face the tribunal.

I sat between my friends. Yury was on my right and Aleksei on my left. A guard stood behind each of our chairs. Before us were the three members of the Military Tribunal of the City of Moscow, on the right, two defense lawyers, on the left, the prosecutor. Back in the Butyrka I had heard that a trial before a tribunal, just like one before a Special Commission, lasted no longer than fifteen minutes. They must have been making an exception for us. We listened to all the speeches without interruption, and then they began asking questions. The working day was ending, and the trial had to be carried over.

When I returned to my cell everyone was terribly surprised: "How did this happen? Why are you back?"

What could I tell them but that the trial was still not over and that I would have to wait until Monday for its continuance, since the members of the court are entitled to a day's rest on Sunday. We were not losing our rest day either, since one day in prison was the same as any other. But my nervous tension kept growing.

On Monday everything repeated itself, only this time I traveled to Ka-lanchevka, where the tribunal was held, as tense as a drawn bow, full of dark thoughts, though they continually circled around one thing: what would happen? No matter how I tried to direct my thoughts they would always circle around, like a person lost in the woods, to return to this same question, trying hopelessly to guess the answer to it. Only one thing was clear: everything would be decided today.

I conducted myself no better, and when the defense lawyer asked me a lead-ing question—"Which Russian writers do you find most interesting?"—

thinking that I would name Herzen, Ogarev, and Chernyshevsky and that their influence might in some way at least justify my urge to rebellion and seeking the truth—I didn't anticipate what he had in mind and could only blurt out: "Pushkin, Turgenev, Chekhov."

How could I not mention these names when in the Lubyanka I had read ten times in a row Turgenev's story "Forest and Steppe"?

When the summations on both sides had been heard, the prosecutor Doron (that name has stayed in my memory all my life) demanded that I, as the leader of the group, be given the supreme penalty. The members of the court did not leave to confer but merely whispered among themselves and then they all rose. The verdict was read out:

"In the name of the Russian Soviet Federated Socialist Republic ..."

And my knees began to tremble.

CHAPTER EIGHT

The Transfer Cell

All of us were taken back together. Aleksei, who had received a food parcel just before the trial began, slipped me a good-sized piece of salted pork fat. It tasted so good that I attacked it greedily and finished it all, without any bread, while we were on our way. Now everything was clear; now everything was over. I was still alive, and the corrective labor camp lay ahead, a place where, from what I had heard, living was easier than in prison. There is good reason for calling prison the hardest punishment of all.

My place of residence changed once more. It turned out that the prison church in the Butyrka, like all the churches in our country, was now offering quite different but no less necessary services to sinners. It had been remodeled and divided into three storys; each story was divided into six or eight cells where they held those convicted and awaiting dispatch to the transfer prison in Krasnaya Presnya. This church became my next refuge.

The large cell held some two hundred people who slept on continuous wooden shelves. It was very hot. People in undershirts yellowed from the disinfection ovens lay prostrate on the bedboards, worn out by the heat and lack of activity. The corner farthest from the door was the "thieves' corner." This was where the hardened criminals, the *urki,* naked to the waist and with tattoos of blue eagles and crosses on their fat bodies, sat noisily playing cards.

A handsome, slender, dark-haired fellow stood out from all the rest. He was wearing a steel-gray uniform which might have been that of an artilleryman or a tank soldier. He was cheerfully whistling some stylish foxtrot, keeping time by clacking some dominoes together to create a jazz effect. This was Volodya the Azerbaijani. He was neither an artilleryman nor a tank trooper. He was a thief. He had a happy-go-lucky nature. He loved walking about the cell, striking up conversations with people. Sometimes he would play practical jokes, and rather mean ones, on the Green Crocodile.

The Green Crocodile was an elderly man who looked even older than his years. He wore a threadbare woolen service jacket of dark-green color that had been the source of his nickname. He was meek, submissive, and helpless, yet that had not prevented him from having collected repeated convictions: devils hang out in quiet pools, as they say. Obviously, Crocodile's false teeth fit him badly and so he kept them in his jacket pocket. This fact was enough to provide Volodya the Azerbaijani with some amusement. He handed Crocodile a crust of bread: "Like something to eat?"

Crocodile's narrow, rheumy eyes looked blank: who would refuse a bite to eat? Not really believing his luck, he nevertheless stretched out his hand. No, everything was fine, there was no trick, he needed only to get his false teeth out of his pocket. But his teeth had disappeared. Crocodile looked despondently at the bread crust, squeezed it between his toothless gums and tried to suck it. It was an old crust, hard as a rusk. He was not able to get anywhere with it. Roaring with laughter, Volodya the Azerbaijani condescendingly passed Crocodile the false teeth he had stolen from his pocket.

There was no end to Azerbaijani's pranks.

"Had enough to eat?" he asked Crocodile in a concerned voice. "Well, then it's time for a smoke."

He knew that Crocodile never had tobacco or paper and he passed him a tiny hand-rolled cigarette made with a twist of newspaper. Crocodile, with the avidity of a starving man, took one puff and then another. Suddenly the cigarette exploded, showering his face with large sparks. Azerbaijani held his sides with laughter: he had rolled some sulfur from match heads into the tobacco. The others laughed as well, pleased to have some diversion. Crocodile, wiping his face, looked reproachfully but silently at his offenders: if you don't have your own tobacco you have to pay for someone else's.

Just as in all the cells, one of the more impatient prisoners would hang about the door well before the midday meal, listening intently.

"They're already giving it out down below!" he would announce joyfully.

Everyone would come to life: it's about time! Now they are all listening, avidly picking up every sound. A general joyous exclamation bursts forth when they hear the clanking of the food containers on our floor. A line quickly forms by the door. The door of the food hatch is flung open with a clatter that announces the arrival of the solemn moment like a fanfare. The man whose turn has come watches with suppressed hope as the server ladles out the soup: maybe he'll get a portion that's a bit thicker. The thieves' lackeys, who do not have to stand in line, carry the hot bowls around to the "thieves-in-the-law" sitting on the bunks. These members of the prison elite regarded themselves as human beings; everyone else was a mere insect.

I looked closely at the dimensions of the courtyard during our exercise period. Surrounded by red brick walls, the crowd of two hundred men was literally lost within it, seeming no more than a tiny handful. I began to consider how many various courtyards, large and small, there were in the Butyrka and how many warders were needed so that all the prisoners could be escorted out for walks each day.

Leon Iosifovich, an Armenian, walked alongside me. I noted that his name and patronymic were similar to Kulinsky's. He was a kind, even-tempered man who offered Aleksei and me a place beside him on the bed-boards, crowding himself and others to save us from having to live next to the criminals.

"I wonder," I asked him, not expecting to get an answer, "how many prisoners the Butyrka can hold?"

"Fifty thousand, I've heard," he replied. "A whole city."

All prisons have at least one thing in common, and that is the routine by which they handle the prisoners. What stands out most in that routine are the searches, or *shmony,* and the trips to the bathhouse. Prisoners resent the searches and sometimes make a mockery of them, but they look forward eagerly to bath days even though they can cause problems for those who have many belongings.

There are body searches after arriving in prison and again upon leaving it, though these are not always done in the same way. A prisoner leaving on transport is searched with special care. He is made to undress completely and then given a series of commands: "Raise your arms! Spread you fingers! Turn around! Bend over!"

The guards run their hands through all clothing. And only after the guard is convinced that there is nothing to be found comes the final command, now without shouting and in a calmer tone: "Get dressed."

There is also the search that is merely superficial, a pure formality. The screw hastily passes both his hands down your sides, from armpits to feet. I have no idea why they do this, because such a check could uncover nothing smaller than a machine gun or a pack of grenades. Sometimes the cell is searched while the prisoners are out for exercise. The beds are examined as well as the bundles of personal effects and the bedboards: perhaps they may discover some playing cards, metal objects, or homemade knives. Prisoners are very good at finding things they can cleverly fashion into knives.

The bath is a noisy affair, full of action and a veritable ceremony. It is a diversion from the stagnant prison routine. The most important part is the opportunity to get out of the unbearably boring cell and experience a little taste of freedom. There is palpable excitement, both in the preparations for the bath and in forming up to leave the cell.

In the anteroom to the bath all clothing—under, outer, and spare—is hung on large hooks and then placed on moveable metal racks to be sent off to the chambers for high-temperature disinfection. A tiny bar of soap of about twenty grams is thrust in your hand. What follows depends entirely on your own alertness and agility: you have to grab a bucket at once, get a place on the bench, and find something to use as a scrubbing cloth. Your body, wasted away by the stifling atmosphere of the cell, rejoices in the steam, the soap, and the hot water.

There is a special bustle when you get dressed again. Your clothes are hot, a bit reddish from the heat treatment, and smell as if freshly baked. The anteroom to the bath is full of this smell, and the prisoners bring it back with them to the cell, where they remain in a state of bliss for a time—clean, rosy, and elated.

There are many sorts of bathhouses—spacious and crowded, comfortable and uncomfortable—but in each one is performed the mystery of the ablution of the human body, cleansing it from filth and ailments and instilling it with the spirit of joy, conciliation, and universal forgiveness. A man cannot leave the bath irritable, embittered, and hating the whole world. Even the very rooms where the bath is located have a special significance. The baths in the Butyrka Prison were built, evidently, with that in mind. Low, arched ceilings, walls, and the benches of polished natural stone set into them, floor tiles arranged in a carpet pattern—all these features were rather heavy but restrained, in soft tones and a defined style. It was not a bathhouse, it was a veritable medieval chamber. As long as you do not fall into despair, you can find things to add charm to your life even in prison.

CHAPTER NINE

The Prison in Krasnaya Presnya

After the Butyrka, the size and the wretched architecture of the transfer prison in Krasnaya Presnya failed to impress me. But the cell they shoved me into was small and neat, with continuous sleeping platforms painted with red lead. I looked around and at once spotted a free space on the upper level to the left of the door. I had already picked up some prison skills and I nimbly clambered up on it. No sooner had I slipped off my hat and coat when an elderly man came up to the bunk. Leaning his hand on the stanchion, he gazed at me silently but in a friendly way. I noticed something familiar in his face but I did not recognize him. And only after he had smiled, exposing a glittering gold tooth, did I cry out happily: "Ivan Osipovich!"

It was Kulinsky, but without his pointed beard.

"I didn't recognize you at first either," he said. "I thought you were probably an *urka*."

We laughed, and then caught up on each other's news. He had been given seven years "for assistance to the Germans." We were happy to meet again and hoped that we would be put on the same transport. But that, unfortunately, did not happen.

Life in the transport prison was a constant whirl: people would be shifted to other cells, then there would be shouts about a transport; it was continual noise and bustle. A few days later I wound up on transport as well. And again there were the hated body searches, the bathhouse and disinfection, standing and waiting in the corridors, and endless roll calls:

"Last name? First name? Patronymic?" And then the hastily mumbled formula, "Article, sentence?"

We were loaded onto an open truck. There was room for us only if we remained standing, but they packed us all in. "This way no one can fall out while we're moving," I thought.

And suddenly there was the command, shouted out as always: "Sit down!"

"Sit? How?" I thought. "There's barely room to breathe when we're standing."

We all hesitated.

And again, like the barking of a dog: "Sit down!"

Strange as it was, we all in fact sat down. It turns out that a man can be made to do anything, even something that at first seems impossible. Thinking this, I recalled how in the summer of 1942 they took us, the senior students, off for some military training to Balakhno, near Gorky. For days on end they made us run, half-starved, carrying rifles, gas masks, and sappers' shovels, along a sandy beach. We were not given any water to drink. As for food, we used to say that we had water and semolina for our first course and semolina and water for our second. The two kilometers from our camp to the beach we also covered at the run. Our legs would give way, our mouths were dry. And at last we would march up to the kitchen in formation.

The platoon officer, Lieutenant Trofimenko, would give the command: "Sing!"

We could not open our lips.

"Mark time!"

We would shuffle our feet.

"Forward march . . . Sing!"

Our mouths were dried out, our tongues thick as if covered with fur. What we produced was not a song but some dissonant mumbling.

"Mark time . . ."

And so it went until we managed to sing as required: "When Comrade —— sends us into battle . . ."

But even then, if I did pronounce the name of the "Comrade" it was with concealed loathing.

CHAPTER TEN

The Transport to Vyazma

They took us to the Belorussky Station. They unloaded us somewhere behind the left wing of the building, inside a cordon of soldiers with rifles and dogs.

"On your knees!"

We got down, as if to pray.

It began raining, gently at first and then in buckets. We continued kneeling for perhaps an hour or more. Water ran in streams down our collars and a puddle formed beneath us. Wet and frozen, we could only shiver. Moscow held no more attraction for me. On the contrary, I began to hate this city. It was already growing dark when they herded us into the railway cars.

"Six months and three days," I calculated the time since my arrest.

A new period in my life as a slave was beginning: prison life had ended, camp life lay ahead.

The train journey lasted all night.

"They're taking us west," someone remarked.

"Maybe to the front!"

We poured out of the cars early on a gray and cloudy morning. Low overhead, shaggy shreds of storm clouds sailed quickly past. After many days of rain everything had become saturated with the damp. Even the air, it seemed, had grown heavy and swollen from an excess of moisture.

Alongside the railway tracks were huge concrete slabs grown black from the rain. This was all that remained of the station.

"Vyazma." The word passed along the column.

We had at last found out where we were.

The guards shouldered their rifles: "Forward march!"

The gloomy crowd, arranged in ranks of five, moved off. We splashed through puddles and mud, indifferent, vacant, depressed, not so much because of our own situation any longer as by the marks left by the war. From the top of a small hill we could see the city spread out before us, destroyed and empty. One lonely bell tower stood up among the ruins.

"There used to be twenty-two churches here," said the man next to me.

We came to a small meadow, or perhaps it was an uncultivated field that was beginning to turn green. The ground grew firmer, and we could hear cartridge cases jingling underfoot: rifle, pistol, and, more rarely, heavy caliber. We could hear the hurried chugging of locomotives from the railway line. Freight trains clattered by, linking the front with the rear many kilometers back.

We marched for a long time, getting farther and farther away from the city and sinking into torpor as we stared at the backs of those marching ahead, listened to the lazy champing underfoot, breathed in the fresh, washed air mixed with the stench from the dense crowd of human bodies. It was rough terrain without a single tree. Everything had been mowed down by the wave of war that washed back from this place. From time to time we would come upon a knocked-out German tank, black and absurd against the fresh greenery that was emerging into the light, or great chunks of twisted metal. Not having eaten since the day before, exhausted from our trip, we had climbed yet another deserted hill when someone cried out softly, "There it is, our own dear home!"

CHAPTER ELEVEN

The Zone

When I looked ahead I saw nothing but mud. It was only after we had gone on another hundred meters or so that I was able to make out a tower built of planks standing on four logs and a barbed wire fence running in two directions from it; then as we drew nearer I could see, blending into the dark background beyond, the low mounds of earth dugouts covered with tar. Beyond the fence was more mud, but it was pitted and trampled as if a large herd of cattle had been driven over it. There was not a blade of grass, not a single scrap of shrubbery. It was damp and blustery.

"So this is the camp," I thought, looking around fearfully. "How on earth can anyone live here?"

At last we came to a halt. Some guards and a jailer carrying a scrap of wood for making notations emerged from a log control post no bigger than a bathhouse in the country: "Form ranks!"

There was a bit of jostling and then we were still.

"How many have you got?" asked the jailer.

"A hundred and sixty," replied the head of the guard detachment.

"And we're all here for no reason," someone in the group cried.

They began the count: "First rank, second . . ."

One after the other each rank took two paces forward. The numbers tallied, it seemed, and no one had escaped.

"Unfasten your clothes!"

The *shmon* began. Soldiers hastily ran their hands over our sides, arms, and legs and looked through our meager belongings. The gates, made of rails and barbed wire, were flung open.

"Pass through! First rank, second . . ."

And so I'm in a camp, inside the zone. My impression was painful. I couldn't believe that people could live in such conditions. I recalled the many people I had met in prison—people who had experienced the system—who eagerly awaited being sent off to a camp again. This made no sense to me now. Prison seemed like a cozy home.

The dugouts looked like animal burrows, only they were as deep as a man's height. The walls, ceiling, and the two-tiered bunks were all made of spruce rails, rough and with some protruding branches. When it began raining at night, the liquid clay from the ceiling dripped onto the beds and plopped down in puddles on the floor. Squeaking rats would dart around our heads, gnawing on whatever they could find. They ate the lamb collar of my overcoat and slashed the cheek of my bunk mate.

The camp was not large, little more than a cattle pen made of barbed wire. Each corner had a guard tower that had been thrown together hastily, every which way. Three or four meters inside the fence around the zone was another row of barbed wire that marked the buffer: this was the forbidden zone, and anyone entering it would be fired upon from the guard towers. The main area was taken up by the gloomy sarcophagi of the dugouts. The most distant of these was the women's. A slightly smaller sarcophagus housed the mess hall and kitchen. Somewhat apart was the medical unit of similar construction and in the corner, near the women's dugout, was a small bathhouse with a chimneyless stove such as was found in the poorest type of peasant huts. When we went there for a bath, the smoke would sting your eyes and you would have to grope your way about to find anything. Once when I was fumbling around in the darkness I put my hand into a pot of hot water—thank God it wasn't boiling.

There was a little garden inside the zone. Two benches had been fastened in the earth in front of the mess hall, and alongside a few tiny spruce seedlings had been thrust into the ground. This had been done not long before, and they were still green.

Beside the control shack at the entry stood a post with a crossbeam from which hung a section of railway track. A large metal rod hung there as well. At the same time each morning and evening a warder or, if he felt lazy, the prisoner work assigner, hammered on the rail with this rod. When they heard the ringing, the orderlies in the dugouts would announce reveille or lights-out.

Every morning a muddy crowd of *zeks,* after eating their half ration of oversalted bread and half a bowl of thorny oat porridge, clusters near the camp gate. The work assigner runs about the camp shouting, "Form up for work! Form up for work!"

Meanwhile, the duty overseer with his scrap of wood with the work brigades listed on it stands near the camp gate and gives the order: "Fall in!"

The *zeks* jostle about, reluctantly forming ranks of five. There is a restrained commotion and murmur of conversations. Finally the gates are flung open. And again comes the command: "First rank, second..."

The *zeks* leave the boundaries of the camp. They are met by troops with rifles at the ready and sometimes with dogs.

Thanks be to God, the overseer's numbers do not tally with those of the guards and there has to be a recount. And again: "First rank, second..."

The *zeks* are happy enough: these are working hours being used up.

Then comes the final command: "A step to the right or a step to the left will be considered an escape. The guards will open fire without warning. Forward, march!"

The column moves off slowly, as if everyone's legs have been hobbled. Hands clasped behind their backs and looking like people seriously ill or bearing burdens beyond their strength, the *zeks* shift their feet no more than a foot's distance per pace. Walking slowly is also an art, and not everyone has mastered it. Because of that, the first rank is always made up of those who are better at it than the others. There's no reason to complain: the *zeks* are marching; and there's no one to complain to: the guards are also serving out their time.

Very slowly, like a ship without a sail, the column disappears from view. The camp falls silent. The only people who remain are the *pridurki* who look after camp maintenance and the invalids. The warder and the work assigner count those who stay behind. Neither one is fully literate and they spend a long time confused over how to balance the numbers. From time to time they discover a malingerer or a "goner" who is hiding from work. Such people may be sent to the punishment cells, but more often they are escorted to the work zone under special guard.

CHAPTER TWELVE

The First Summer at Hard Labor

Work on the Airfield

The work zone covers a vast territory, including the airfield runway and the adjoining taxi strips. The airfield was built by the Germans, and they made a solid job of it. The runway, as wide as a stadium and longer than the eye can see, is paved with concrete slabs three meters square. The slabs are set tightly together and designed with a precisely maintained slope toward the drainage collectors. The taxi strips are built in the same fashion. The areas between the concrete have been carefully sown with grass.

The Germans blew up the airfield when they retreated. The field was pitted by huge craters, and concrete slabs had been thrown along the drainage collectors. This whole area was high and open; the wind, finding no obstacles, blew freely, bringing relief when it was hot, chilling you to the bone when it was cold. No inhabited spot could be seen, and no clusters of trees remained: the war had swept them all away. It was utterly lonely and silent.

Spread out in a sparse cordon around the airfield, the soldiers of the escort would sit, rifles pressed between their knees, on anything they could find; their red shoulder straps could be seen in the distance. The middle of the meadow between the guards and the concrete was dotted with squatting *zeks*, both men and women: there were no toilets within the work zone. Scarcely anyone could be seen around the airfield itself. They were all working in various craters. Using blunt shovels, they were shifting up the damp, heavy clay from one man to another and then to a third. The clay would stick to the shovels and accumulate. The shovels would get as heavy as sledgehammers. The crater had to be cleaned out until it was dry, and then dry soil packed down in layers so firmly that it would not settle.

The entire population of the camp was involved in this project. The only exception was our brigade of twelve men. For some reason, from the first day we had not been thrown into the general work zone. They loaded us onto a three-ton truck with our own guards and tossed in some square-faced shovels and pickaxes.

"We're going to the quarry," the brigadier announced.

We passed the column of prisoners that had left the camp long before and bowled along the smooth taxi strip; then for about ten kilometers we bumped down a once-paved road pitted by shellfire.

The Germans had excavated the quarry when they were building the airfield. It had eaten into the side of a steep hill and looked like the crater of a volcano with one side open where the lava had burst through. The sloping sides were as high as a four-story building; they glistened with red pebbles of even size and were studded with cobblestones as round as melons. A pool of pure rainwater lay at the bottom. Some distance from it was the framework of an excavator without tracks. Through the gap in the quarry ran a well-worn road along which three-ton ZIS trucks hauled out the gravel. We were broken up into teams of three for loading the trucks. Our work quota was seven minutes per truck. Out of curiosity we noted the time by the driver's watch. It took us ten minutes to throw on a load of gravel. But we did not have to work precisely by schedule. The trucks did not come in too often, and between trips we had time to loosen the gravel, pick out and pile the cobblestones, and even take a little rest.

Summer was in full swing. The weather was clear and sunny. After having sweated over the stones, it was delightful to collapse, half-naked, atop them; they were cool and had only just been drawn out of the bowels of the earth. It was quiet in the enclosed quarry. The June sun baked it, creating its own microclimate. Occasionally a puff of wind would come from somewhere above, wafting fresh, cool air across our overheated bodies.

The guards dozed in the distance, propped up on their rifles. Looking at them, it occurred to me more than once that we could very easily slip away from here. I happened to mention this to the Chemist, a man a bit past his prime who had graduated, as he said, from the Institute of Red Professors and had taught chemistry somewhere, hence his nickname.

"Escape?" he asked. "It's not worth the risk. The war will end, and they'll let us all out anyway."

We were all hoping for that. And every day we counted the days we had been in prison. Those who had served half of their sentences counted the days remaining. Each one thought his term was endless.

Outside the gates in the morning, while we were waiting for the truck, we would be joyously greeted by a reddish-brown mongrel dog. She would snuggle up to us and dance around, briskly wagging her tail. Her eyes would sparkle, so glad was she to find people who, though they had no treats to give her, would play with her, pat her, and stroke her.

I knew that the dog belonged to Fedka the baker, a prisoner who was allowed to move about unguarded and whose bakery with its lean-to where he slept was just a little distance away. The *zeks* hated Fedka for his soggy, heavy bread laden with salt crystals. He, like a slave who has gained his freedom, no longer considered himself on a par with the prisoners. This well-fed fellow had broken solidarity with us, never suspecting that for the least infraction or by some caprice of fate he could find himself behind the barbed wire again where he would hardly be forgiven for his oversalted bread and temporary privileges. And so even the prisoners' relationship to his dog was ambiguous. Among the endearing words you would suddenly hear an angry voice, "She's fat, the bitch!"

And then someone else would chime in, referring to Fedka: "And he's fattened her up on our rations."

One day when they were taking us to work, I was surprised to see that the dog was in the back of the truck with us. She had been covered up with some rags and people were petting her, keeping her calm so that she would not give herself away by barking. The dog wasn't concerned: she knew she was among friends and had nothing to fear.

As soon as the truck had stopped at the quarry and the guards had gone off to their posts, the *zeks* spilled out of the truck. The rags covering the dog were taken away. She danced about with joy. But then the point of a pickaxe smashed in her skull and a shovel cut her throat. It was all done quickly and silently. One person gutted the dog, another cut up a shovel handle for firewood; a piece of cotton wadding was rolled until it broke into flames. The first truck had not left with its load before a bonfire had begun to blaze and soon the appetizing aroma of cooked meat spread through the quarry. The *zeks,* unable to tear their eyes away from the sooty black cooking pot, gulped back their flowing saliva.

Not everyone took part in the banquet, just the hardened criminals and those who in one way or another had helped organize it. I was also offered a bone with a little bit of meat. The Chemist, who was not offered anything, consoled himself: "When I'm let out of here I'm going to make myself a pressure cooker so I can cook bones till they're soft as potatoes."

The dog's head and paws were wrapped up in her skin and hidden under some stones.

"Tomorrow we'll make noodles out of that hide."

But they didn't manage to make any noodles. The next day our brigade was sent to work inside the general work area with the others. For a long time thereafter we remembered the quarry where the work was, as they say, a piece of cake.

At the airfield we were assigned to work at the stone-crusher. This small but very solid machine driven by an electric motor was a glutton. It would crunch up cobblestones like sugar and without any apparent effort. The crushed stone then poured out of its belly in a stream. We had to fill it continuously with wheelbarrows and then wheel them back for a new load. Unless you know how to manage a wheelbarrow this is sheer torment, not work. It was almost impossible to steer a fully loaded wheelbarrow along the wooden duckboards; it would slide off the boards or tip to one side; and then, being heavy, you couldn't bring it upright again. The load weighed more than a hundred kilos. To keep it balanced, you would have to keep your legs wide apart. Walking with both your hands and legs spread out is uncomfortable. But after a day or two passed you could already move confidently along the planks if you have loaded the wheelbarrow properly. You have to make sure that the center of gravity lies right above the wheel; then you can go confidently and use less energy.

The weather was hot. We worked stripped to the waist, bathed in salty sweat, casting glances at the hated stone-crusher in hopes that it might yet break down. It did not break down, though, and kept chewing up the stones while we waved our scoops and wheeled our barrows until our legs trembled.

Nevertheless, we found a way of getting a little rest, and it was the machine itself that suggested it. We would pick out a heavy stone, smooth and round, and raise it above the greedy maw of the stone-crusher whose iron jaws moved powerfully back and forth. Choosing the moment when the jaws were opened widest but had not yet begun to close, we would throw in the stone as hard as we could. The machine would jam. It would stop, the long drive belt would fly off, and silence would reign. We would all sit down, relaxing our strained muscles and gloating about our victory over the malicious beast. Then, in turns and taking our time, we would use a crowbar to smash up the stone we had used to jam the machine. One of us would work at this, the others would have a delightful rest. We would do this more than once each day, and no one could charge us with malicious intent because such stoppages could happen even without our help. Just the same, when we marched back to the zone our legs would be weak from exhaustion and poor nutrition.

Volodka Verbitsky from our brigade said to me once as we were going back to camp, "I heard they're giving out fish oil at the medical unit after supper."

The medical assistant, a former front-line soldier who had come to the camp after being wounded was, perhaps, the only one of the free-worker service staff who treated the prisoners without prejudice and with obvious sympathy. He wore his soldier's uniform but with no shoulder straps and, as we learned, did all he could to ease our lot. Later I found, even among the warders, some decent people who did not deliberately multiply the evils of the camps and who maintained their humanity in their inhuman jobs. But there were not many of them. They showed their sympathy toward the prisoners in various ways. Some would do so only when there was an opportunity, when the bosses couldn't see; but there were also others who went on honestly carrying out their duties and never considered themselves better than the *zeks*.

That evening I went to the medical unit with Verbitsky. A line of people stood in the narrow passage, revetted with planks, that led into the dugout. There were men here and also some other creatures that I did not immediately recognize as women. Shaved bald, thin, in worn and dirty prison knit skirts, the response they produced was not pity but repulsion, as if they were no longer humans but exhausted animals at bay, creatures no longer capable of work and so no longer needed. Stooped over, they looked without seeing, having completely lost interest in their surroundings and in themselves. I could not believe that representatives of the fair sex could look like this. And then I remembered the picture that had so struck me just after my arrival in camp: men and women sitting next to each other doing their business. The conditions of camp life had taken something away from the common stock of emotions.

The line slowly advanced to the unpainted plank door; those who wanted to treat themselves to some fish oil nimbly darted through it; they emerged just as briskly, licking a wooden spoon as they went and passing it on to the next person in line.

"You take that same spoon," Volodka prompted. "It's bigger than the others."

A few lucky fellows poured the contents of the spoon into a pot of boiled potatoes while expressing their pleasure aloud: "*Batsilla!*"—meaning "fat" or "oil."

A Few Words About the Criminal Community

Seven months of my imprisonment had gone by. Even before my arrest, the war had deprived me and other schoolchildren of summer holidays; it had introduced us to heavy physical labor. I spent one summer building defensive works, another building narrow-gauge railways to bring turf from the fields to the city. It was as hard as the work now. You were always hungry, and getting an extra portion of porridge meant having to work until your hands were covered in bloody blisters and your whole body ached. But even though this labor was forced, we did not feel it as such, whether that was due to our childish lack of understanding or to the absence of armed guards constantly drawing limits on the space in which we lived. Nevertheless, my first summer behind barbed wire did not seem something truly terrible. Obviously, my earlier experience carrying earth in an overloaded handbarrow and grubbing out deeply rooted stumps had been a rehearsal for the exhausting labor in the camp. I found that the worst torment was not physical fatigue but living alongside the genuine criminals among whom we politicals were placed. We were not a part of their society.

They are, first of all, a community, a cult, having their own language, ethnography, art, and culture, distinct from others. Nationalism is also a characteristic, if one recognizes the criminal world as a separate nation. The fact is that this community does not tolerate those who are different from it. To become a full-fledged member of the community one must first of all master its language: you must learn how to use the crudest language with artistry, to replace as many ordinary words as possible with words from the criminal jargon. You absolutely must smoke. It's a good thing if you know how to tap-dance (*batsat'*). And you must accept the hierarchy without question. On the highest level are the "thieves-in-the-law" who have won the recognition of the ordinary thieves or *urki* through their demonstrated banditry and knowledge of the thieves' laws. They have their own lackeys, the *shestyorka,* who carry out appointed tasks—cleaning, cooking food, fetching food parcels. In exchange, they enjoy the protection of their powerful bosses and, like all lackeys, regard it as their right to threaten, behind the backs of their bosses, anyone who does not belong to the criminal world.

Supreme power among the thieves-in-the-law, should a number of them gather in the same place, belongs to the one who holds seniority in his criminal career, having had the most and the lengthiest prison terms and so, usually, the one who is the eldest. He is called the *pakhan,* which, translated into normal language, means "father," "elder," and, in practice, "sovereign."

You would often see a group of still untested young fellows, gathered in a *kutok*—the thieves' corner—on the bunks, squatting around the *pakhan* and listening to him as intently as schoolchildren listen to their teacher. And he, in his underwear or sometimes with a jacket (*lepen'* in the thieves' language) thrown over his shoulders, is teaching them the thieves' law. These laws, though based on some primordial notions of justice, are usually observed only to the point where they begin to hinder the criminal.

One of their immutable laws, for example, is that the so-called "life ration" is inviolate. In accordance with this law, a criminal who can only acquire the necessities of life by stealing them from someone else must not take that person's prison ration, on pain of a most severe punishment, up to a sentence of death. However, I have seen criminals in punishment cells who had no other means of augmenting their rations and who were as hungry as wolves: they would violate this supposedly sacred commandment.

On the lowest rank of the criminal hierarchy are the *shkodniki,* who do not even have the right to proudly call themselves thieves, though in essence they are the very same racketeers as the others except that they are less discriminating in the value and size of what they steal. They dart about, looking for anything left carelessly lying around, observing no law and not fastidious in their choice of plunder. I encountered one other variety of criminal. Once in the cell of the Krasnaya Presnya transit prison I shared a bunk with a man no longer young. He was a stocky fellow, evidently physically powerful, calm and taciturn, who took no part in what was going on in the cell. The criminals gathered in a *kutok* opposite us. With their undershirts hanging out of their trousers as usual they were having a *tolkovishche,* a primitive meting out of justice, discussing some vital problems calmly and quietly, then excitedly, waving their arms and almost reaching the point of threats.

"I hate them," my neighbor suddenly blurted out.

I did not understand.

"Over there," he said, nodding toward the *kutok*. "The *shkodniki*."

Little by little we began talking. My neighbor was also a thief, though he did not squander his talents on little things. And when I asked him where he stole from he replied, confidentially and without the slightest emotion, "Banks, jewelry stores."

Among thieves of this category you can find people with higher education, often engineers who have raised their "second career" almost to the level of an art form.

Our brigade was enlarged. In it there were only five of us fascists, that's to say people sentenced under Article 58: Aleksei and I, the Chemist, Volodka Verbitsky, and Ivan Mikhailovich, an elderly man over sixty. The others were nonpoliticals and criminals, among whom there were even two thieves-in-the-law, Sasha the Cook and the Beard. These two never did any work but demanded the ration of a top worker.

They always went about together. The Beard, whose nickname came from his small, neatly trimmed reddish beard, was just past thirty, of average height or slightly more, lean and fit; he would wear a peaked cap and either a greatcoat of officer's cut with the buttons torn off or a loose smock whose shape and color made it look like an overcoat. He had rather relaxed, free-and-easy ways, though without the insolent, defiant manner in which the other thieves-in-the-law treated the "insects," i.e., everyone else, including guards and warders. Some even said that the Beard was not a criminal at all but was only posing as one; his father was supposedly an influential man in Moscow, and the Beard was nothing more than a pampered son.

Sasha the Cook was his complete opposite. He was short, fat, with narrow eyes like slits in his round, swollen face. As a proper "honest thief" he would not tuck his undershirt into his trousers. He went about barefoot, picking up his feet and carefully choosing where to step as if there were broken glass all around. He spoke in a thin nasal twang that was in keeping with his shifty nature. Whenever he caught sight of a bonfire or a group sitting around a cooking pot he would approach, squat down, and wordlessly dip his spoon into whatever was cooking. If anyone objected he would snarl, "Shut your mouth, scum, or I'll smash it for you."

Or he would explain, carefully measuring his words: "That's the way it is, I'm a thief-in-the-law."

And indeed, the criminals believed that by their law, people who had food in addition to their ration were obliged to give them a portion. The lackeys would usually approach anyone who had received a food parcel or a money order and state in a quiet, calm voice, confident that they would not be refused: "You have to share."

And share they did, for fear of losing even more.

The Accursed Crater

At that time, we, like the majority of the *zeks,* were working at filling in the craters. Using shovels that no one ever sharpened (and in fact there was nothing to sharpen them with), we began by digging out the sticky clay, swollen with water, until we reached dry ground. It's tedious, exhausting work. The dull spade resists; it's like trying to drive it into a piece of rubber. Then you have to fling up a heavy chunk of clay to a height of three meters or more. The clay sticks like glue. A sizeable lot stays stuck to the shovel, so you have to clean it off with a scrap of wood. The shovel gets heavier, and in the course of a day even the handle acquires a layer of dried clay paste.

And so, layer by layer, we dig down deeper. There seems to be no end to the mass of clay.

"Till you hit dry ground and a firm bottom," insists the work superintendent, a free worker in civilian clothes.

The sun and the shovel squeeze the sweat out of us. From the angle of the sun and the shadows it casts we can unerringly tell the time; we spend the morning longing for the noon meal and the afternoon longing for the return to the zone and our supper. But when are we going to hit this dry ground? We seem to have dug out all the damp clay, yet the ground beneath us feels like a springy mattress. At long last, our strength gone and our spirits sunk, we decide that it's enough, we're done; we'll tamp it down as it is. And we begin filling in the crater, ramming down dry clay with a tamping iron, as per orders, in ten- or twelve-centimeter layers. We make an honest job of it, checking the firmness of the soil by hitting it with a crowbar. Settling is allowed only around the edges. We beat it down layer by layer. It's hard work, but it's much better than shoving a spade into the earth. For some reason, though, the surface of the fill still remains uneven. We labor on for another day, two days, three days. We're now high enough to be out of the pit and can see the airfield; the sun beats down on us again. But the soil underfoot is still elastic, like a poorly inflated soccer ball. Never mind, we'll ram it down! Just so long as the superintendent doesn't see.

We've rammed down the soil in the whole crater, yet the uneven surface is still there. We're amazed: we'd gone down more than three meters.

The work superintendent comes to take a look. He doesn't curse us out and says only: "Clear it out again."

"It won't make any difference," we say, trying to justify ourselves.

"Shovel it out."

That means digging it out right to the bottom. All that work for nothing! And what sort of ration do we get in return? We collapse, some on the concrete, some on the clay, utterly crushed.

What can we do? The next day, angry and taciturn, we begin digging out the soil we had so conscientiously tamped down. And again, the sun, the shovel, the sweat, the waiting for the noon meal, some *magara* soup and oat porridge, prickly with chaff. Meter by meter we dig down once more. And again there's no dry soil. A tiny puddle of water, scarcely more than half a bucket full, forms at the bottom of the crater and won't disappear. But it's enough to torment us. After every layer we excavate it comes to the surface, like blood on the grave of some innocent victim. At last, enraged, we throw down our shovels.

"No more!"

The smokers managed to scrape from their pockets a pinch of tobacco mixed with bread crumbs and bits of rubbish and pass around the slobbery butt.

"Bah!" says Radzikovsky, suddenly slapping his forehead. "Idiots!"

He points to a flat slab of concrete from the wall of a drain that has been flung aside after an explosion. We don't know what he means.

"We just have to plop that slab over the puddle and that'll be it."

"But it must weigh over a ton."

"And what if it falls on its side?"

Still, the idea captivates us all. We find some tools. Using crowbars and heavy sticks we shift the slab to the edge of the pit, our exhaustion forgotten. And then comes the moment of triumph: the slab tumbles down and, as if by plan, covers the puddle. And now hastily, so the superintendent won't see, we shovel back the soil and tamp it down. But what if the surface is still uneven?

This time everything goes well, though. Layer after layer is tamped down tightly, burying the concrete slab and the puddle.

"That's how you should have done it the first time," says the superintendent approvingly when he comes by.

"So why didn't you tell us how?" we reply as he leaves. "And you're supposed to be an engineer."

The Two of Us

The muffled ringing of the piece of rail would find its way into the dugout every morning.

"Reveille!" the orderly would bawl.

I did not want to get up. My body ached as if I'd been badly beaten.

Another shout urged me on: "The chief's already at the bread cutter's!"

We could not delay it any longer and hurried off to the mess hall. The rations were carried out in large, flat boxes, as if on trays. Bits of bread to make up the weight, sometimes more than one, were attached to the basic bread ration with wooden skewers. The brigade assembled around the box. Everyone was frozen in silent tension, staring greedily at the rations: which one was the biggest? Everyone wanted a crust; they were lighter and so there was more in them, and they had make-up pieces as well! But it all depended on the will of the brigadier. Those who got crusts were pleased and stepped aside with relief; those who got the center pieces turned them over in their hands, distressed, while swallowing the insult and looking at the box where there were still some better rations. No luck today!

Then we would drag ourselves, in line, to the food hatch of the kitchen and get our bit of porridge made of oats or green foxtail. They would serve out the "premium," more of the same porridge with a spoonful of American tinned beans added. But this was not for everyone: our daily output wasn't high enough to cover us all.

On one such morning, clear and calm, heralding a fine day typical of the midsummer, Aleksei and I sat on a bench in our little garden by the spruce cuttings that were beginning to drop their needles. Between us stood a cooking pot made from a food tin that was full of boiled potatoes. The night before we had managed to flog Aleksei's sweater for them and now, after having breakfasted on two helpings of porridge and our bread ration, we were looking forward to continuing our pleasure, burning our fingers as we pulled the skin off the potatoes. We did not even notice Sasha the Cook appear in front of Aleksei.

"Was it you who packed off with my premium?" he intoned in his nasal voice, showing obvious aggression in his tone and his manner.

"But you didn't do any work," replied Aleksei with complete calm, even with a bit of a smile.

"You bitch's tit!" howled Sasha and gave him a powerful slap across the face.

I never expected this from Aleksei: suddenly, without thinking, he gave Sasha a jab to the nose. Sasha, of course, never anticipated such a thing; to make matters worse he had been standing in some unsteady theatrical pose, and so he tumbled down head over heels. Furious at this unheard-of outrage, he jumped up with surprising agility and threw himself at Aleksei. But the two of us knew how to stick up for ourselves, and I rushed into the fight as well. We both got on top of Sasha and began walloping him. But at this point the Beard showed up and the fight began taking a turn that was not in our favor. These criminals and bandits are well known for their merciless treatment of others. Things like caution, pity, or fear of inflicting too much injury don't hold them back. That's precisely what gives them the upper hand, the initiative that allows a minority to dominate the majority.

This time everything ended well for us. At this very moment, the other men of our brigade were coming back from the mess hall along with our brigadier, Fomin. He was young, powerful and, it seemed, had not lost his human decency. When he saw the fight he quickly put an end to it. That same day the news spread around the camp that the young "fascists" had beaten up the thieves-in-the-law; most important was that all the *shkodniki* realized that there were two of us, and that they had to keep that in mind in an attack on one of us. Most remarkable in this episode was something only I knew. When I got up from the ground after the fight I found an unpeeled potato in my hand, completely whole and undamaged. Such was its value to me that without thinking I had instinctively kept my hold on it even in this unlikely situation.

A day or so later we witnessed the second defeat of Sasha the Cook.

It happened well before the noon meal, the period of most intensive work when your body has warmed up sufficiently but you haven't yet exhausted your daily store of energy. We were busy tamping down our crater when suddenly we heard a truly odd combination of sounds coming from some distance away. Someone was shouting, someone was screeching, a dog was barking. We stopped work and tried to see what was going on. At last, as the noises came closer to us, someone realized what was happening.

"They've got Sasha under escort."

Sure enough, Sasha the Cook, in his underwear as always, barefoot, his arms extended, picking his way with every step, was slowly tottering past a group of working prisoners. He was accompanied by two guards, one of whom held a lunging shepherd dog on a leash. Sasha would stop every now and then to protest: "I'm a thief-in-the-law. I'm not going to work."

"You're going to sweat your guts out," the guard replied and set the dog on him. The dog, enraged and with fur bristling, seized him by the calf. Sasha howled wildly and had to continue his march. This same thing was repeated several times until Sasha was brought to our brigade and left in peace. Sasha squatted, casting wild glances around him, and said through clenched teeth: "Bloody screws! Fascists!"

Tears rolled down his cheeks.

We looked at him and rejoiced.

Fugitives

About the same time a small transport left for Moscow. Among those leaving were the movie director Slutsky and the Beard. The rumor about the Beard was that his high-ranking father had been able to use his influence on behalf of his son. Sasha the Cook was now an orphan. But there was one more notable thief-in-the-law in camp, Vitka Glukhov. He was thirty or more, tall, muscular, and always stripped to the waist. He would pace about the airfield, bothering no one and maintaining his dignity. He reminded me of Gorky's Chelkash. I never saw him laugh or even smile. His powerful, tanned body was decorated with tattoos. The largest of these, on his chest, was an entire picture, executed rather skillfully and not without dramatic effect. Against a background of the sea, cliffs, and a setting sun an eagle, its wings spread across the whole of Vitka's chest, bore a naked woman in its talons.

On one occasion when he stopped near our brigade and squatted among us as the criminals did, Vitka noticed that I was staring at his tattoo. Obviously flattered, he explained indulgently: "I got this in Japan when I was a sailor."

Then he warmed to his topic: "They really know how to do these things there. They apply a whole stamp made of needles and bang!—it's done. You pick out a drawing—anything you like. It doesn't have to be all in blue, they do colors as well. Real lifelike."

He was lying, of course.

Glukhov began to pal around with Korobko, who was different in every way from his protector. He was short, puny, and even in hot weather never took off his outfit, some sort of brown uniform with green piping and matching peaked cap. Korobko was clearly trying to ingratiate himself with Vitka and tried to imitate him in everything, though he never sank to the level of a lackey. It's possible that Vitka had him as an equal partner because he had a strong body and a strong will as well, and the frail Korobok, as we called him among ourselves, simply couldn't stand up to him. As became clear later, this friendship had other grounds which no one was aware of at the time.

Our brigadier Fomin took me on as his helper. He was working as a bricklayer, installing brick sections in the concrete sides of the drainage collectors that had been blown up.

"You'll learn how to do it," he told me.

But my learning proceeded more like the many afflictions of Vanka Zhukov. Part of my job was keeping two bricklayers supplied with all the materials they needed, which meant ensuring that they had both bricks and mortar at hand. I also had to mix the mortar myself, hauling the cement and sand for some hundred meters by wheelbarrow and using a German helmet with a hole in it to scoop up water from a puddle. Even though I was exhausted, I managed to learn something of how to lay bricks and plaster them. The three of us worked apart from the others at the very boundary of the work zone. One day after lunch, when we still had twenty minutes of free time, I was sitting by myself in the little meadow. It was a warm, sunny day. An unusual silence had fallen over the whole area. No one was working; a few slept, others were dozing. Even the guards, who had eaten much better than we had, were beginning to nod off. In the distance, a group of gravel trucks was parked on the concrete. The drivers would use one of them to go back to their homes for lunch each day. And above the whole scene flew a lark, serenely singing as if there were no war and no prisoners at forced labor.

I was also beginning to doze off when I suddenly heard the noise of an approaching truck. A ZIS with open sides was rushing down the middle of the runway at great speed. When it came abreast of me it looked as if the half-naked Vitka Glukhov was sitting at the wheel; next to him, in his invariable peaked cap, sat Korobok. But this was such a ridiculous notion that I at once put it out of my mind.

Normally, when a truck left the work zone, the guards would stop it for inspection, but since the back of the truck was open, it was obvious that it was empty and no one stopped it; the truck, never slowing, left the boundaries of the area under guard.

Without another thought of the truck, I lay down on the grass and fell asleep at once. I was awakened by someone's shout and immediately noticed unusual activity on the airfield. The brigades, in turmoil, were quickly forming up, and I could sense that the guards were nervous.

"It's an escape," I heard when I had found my brigade.

They formed us up and, as always when we were taken off work, they began counting: "First rank, second . . ."

They counted us a second time. No, the figures did not tally: two were missing. They began checking by their card files: "Last name? Article? Sentence?"

Glukhov and Korobko were missing. They quickly marched us back to the camp. Then I remembered the truck rushing past at lunch hour. So I hadn't been mistaken: it really had been them. I told Verbitsky, who was walking beside me.

"Keep it quiet," he told me sharply. "They'll round them up, and you'll be dragged in too, as an accomplice, because you didn't report it at the time."

He was right, and I bit my tongue.

That whole evening the only topic of conversation was whether the two would be caught. Nearly the whole of the guard platoon had been sent to chase after them. The *urki* were triumphant. There had been one other escape attempt earlier. One dark rainy night four boys managed to crawl unnoticed under the barbed wire of the forbidden zone and the fence and ran off to the airfield, where they made contact with some airmen. They fed the boys but held them and turned them over to the camp guards on condition that they would not be called to account. That was the end of the escape. The boys were pleased enough with getting a tasty, ample meal.

Glukhov's escape was a bolder one, obviously planned carefully, since he had used the only truck on the airfield that had no ignition key. To work the starter they simply connected two electrical wires. We all knew this truck since it had operated out of our quarry. Glukhov had figured out in advance that the sides of the truck box had to be taken down so it appeared empty and would thus arouse no suspicion from the guards. And the time chosen for the escape turned out to be a good one: it was toward the end of the lunch hour when the break had not yet ended; the guards were not so alert, but the trucks could already leave.

The whole camp was delighted with the escape, if only because of the difficulties it would cause the guards and the security officer; and we all hoped that it would end successfully. The next day a rumor went round that the truck had been found abandoned about twenty kilometers from the camp, that Korobko had been shot but Glukhov had escaped. It is quite possible that this is what really happened.

Summer Draws to a Close

Toward the end of the summer we could all see that the work on the airfield was nearing completion. No more did we have to pick at the tenacious clay. A huge heated vat stood smoking on the runway: they were heating asphalt. The *zeks* were already having discussions among themselves:

"So where do we go now?"

"Makes no difference. It can't be worse than here."

Those who had been around longer recalled some good camps with proper amenities, warm barracks, and even amateur entertainments. Listening to them, I also believed that I had fallen by chance into some temporary camp sector and began hoping for something better.

The weather changed, and now the mornings were cold. My overcoat, whose collar had been eaten by rats, had been stolen by some fellow who was being released; he had sold it to local people for home-brewed vodka. We never saw these locals, since their village had been burned to the ground and they were living in dugouts built into the slope of a hill. Although I reported the theft to the warder, and although my coat had even been found, they did not return it to me. I simply could not understand the legal grounds that made it impossible for them to return stolen property. Most likely it was because I had been charged under Article 58: a person under that article no longer enjoys equal rights; and if he wishes to live he may do so even without his coat.

There was often a cold, stinging drizzle. Such weather left us demoralized, and we counted the days we had served more frequently than usual. I was still in the first year of my imprisonment, and its end was as difficult to imagine as the end of the world. On one such raw day when we had formed up after work, they began the count and found that one person was missing. An escape! They counted once more. They quickly established that the missing man was Volodya Radzikovsky from our brigade. It seemed only moments before that I had seen him. When did he manage to run off, and from such an open area as well? Could he be hiding in one of the drainage basins? They began searching and found him asleep inside an iron pipe lying nearby. They dragged him out.

"I crawled into the pipe to get out of the rain," he explained, "and I fell asleep."

The head of the guards took out his anger on Volodya and gave him a good hiding. People laughed, but we all held to our idea that he had been trying to escape.

There were sunny days as well, and on one of them we saw a strange sight. Some distance away from us a crowd of prisoners, about fifty of them, were racing around on the airfield, rushing from one side to another like a flock of rooks getting ready to fly off.

It was Volodka Verbitsky who first guessed what they were up to: "They're trying to catch something," he said, and rushed to join them.

We watched from a distance as he rushed toward the constantly changing line of people, the tails of his buttonless overcoat flapping like wings. Then suddenly everything grew still. The pursuers collected in a group for a short time and then began to disperse. Verbitsky came back, happy and smiling.

"Look," he said, "I caught it."

On his palm lay the crushed body of a little animal, dark in color and scarcely bigger than a mouse.

"It's a *laska,*" Volodka explained, "a small weasel."

"What's it for?"

"What do you mean, what's it for?" he asked, equally astonished. "It's meat, isn't it?"

And in fact he found a piece of wire, skewered the body of the little animal on it, roasted it in the fire of the asphalt heater, and ate it.

"So how was it?" I asked.

"Not so terrible. A rat, now, would have been a kilo and a half."

CHAPTER THIRTEEN

A New Transport: Medvezhi Ozyora

The Guard Perepelochkin

On one of those days, when the weather was not very cold and the sun shone weakly, they made a careful search through our belongings and then loaded us onto the back of a truck, packing us in tightly as if we were not living beings. Guards with carbines sat on each corner of the truck box. Farewell, camp sector. We're off on another transport.

They took us to Vyazma, where the railway station lay in ruins. We assumed they would be loading us into railway cars. But we passed through the city and continued eastwards, in the direction of Moscow. We jolted over broken-up roads for what seemed an endless time. It was already night when we halted in a forest. We immediately recognized the familiar outlines of a camp zone: the barbed wire, the rickety guard towers, the little hut at the passage into the zone that for some reason was called the guardhouse. But everything here was much more substantial, sound, and carefully built. Even the light bulbs glowed more brightly here, where there was no fear of air raids, than they did in Vyazma. Beyond the passage was an area of barren ground that could have been a parade square. Beyond that was more barbed wire, and it was there, on the other side of the wire, that we could barely make out some wooden barracks in the darkness. We felt a measure of relief: here, it seemed, it really would be no worse.

They opened the back gate of the truck. I could barely straighten my numbed legs and was the last to jump down from the vehicle. My feet had only just touched the ground when I heard a shot behind me. We were all taken aback, unable to comprehend what had happened. And then, in the deathly silence came a voice as loud as the shot: "Perepelochkin has shot himself."

For some reason it is always the good people who depart this life before their time. After having been through seven corrective labor camps and a number of camp sectors I never came across a case in which the prisoners loved their guard as they did Perepelochkin, a private in the camp garrison of Camp Sector 6 near Vyazma. He was a simple country lad with very little education and a round, rosy, freckle-covered face that clearly expressed his artless nature. He had the gait and the manner of a country bumpkin. Despite his unenviable existence as a lonely soldier in a despised service, he was never downcast, never gave thought to a better lot in life and, most important, never lost those high moral qualities which at that time were still to be found among people from the remote countryside. These qualities had been spontaneously preserved and passed down in peasant families from one generation to the next; and their source was most likely to be found in the virtuous teachings of village priests whose way of life was little different from that of their parishioners. Perepelochkin did not recognize a difference between prisoners and free workers and, even more, had no idea that these prisoners he was to guard more carefully than the apple of his eye were supposedly enemies of the people. Everyone was the same as far as he was concerned; and not only that, he was as happy to see any of us as he was his closest friends. At the morning march to work I more than once saw him suddenly left off the contingent of guards. Downcast and apparently chastened, he would step aside, no doubt feeling he was a pariah. But how quickly he was transformed and how his face would light up with a broad, satisfied grin when, because of a shortage of troops, he would again be included in the guard detachment. He did not walk back, he ran, almost skipping along, as if he had been liberated; utterly pleased, he marched with the guards, smiling wordlessly at the column of prisoners. We understood him and returned the same silent greeting to him.

And suddenly Perepelochkin was no more. This awareness ran through all of us, guards and prisoners alike, like an electric current. What was it, an act of despair, a protest, or just a stupid accident? Someone replaced Perepelochkin, and we were again formed up in a column. And again came the endless repetition: "First rank, second . . ."

In Our New Camp

It's not easy to convey what a prisoner feels when he enters the zone of a camp that is still new to him. Above all, there is an animal-like deadening of the emotions, an almost total indifference. But against this background, like a few sparks in the darkness, come flashes of hope of a new and better beginning, that he'll be in a warm, snug spot and maybe even be fed. Then suddenly, the opposite: a stab of alarm that he'll find himself in a society run by criminals who will make his life so stressful and bleak that the loss of freedom is no longer the worst punishment.

It was night, the beginning of September, and rather cold. Rank by rank we marched through the gates and again were cut off from that freedom from which for a few hours we had been separated only by the muzzles of the carbines. Now there were a barbed-wire fence and frowning guard towers between us and the world outside. Shivering, we waited to be marched into the second zone, into actual warm barracks. After the dugouts of Vyazma, wooden barracks seemed the height of bliss. They marched us on, but away from the barracks. I can't convey the sense of bitter disappointment, the nagging ache bordering on despair that we felt as we approached our designated living space, a huge canvas tent the size of a house. I was wearing only summer clothing, and it seemed to me that spending even the remainder of this night here, with frost in the morning, was something truly dreadful, simply impossible when compared with the dugouts that we had left only today.

Disheartened and bewildered, we entered the tent. In the darkness, almost by feel, we could make out two rows of crudely built bunks. The meter-high windows had apron-like canvas covers that were tied down but flapped like loose sails in the wind, adding to the sense of cold. There was not a single sign of comfort anywhere. The entrance was covered by a curtain that surely could not conserve any heat, the only source of which was our own bodies.

It was a good job that I had been able to hang on to the old flannelette blanket passed on to me in the internal prison before my transport from Gorky. Aleksei and I climbed up to the upper level of bunks and covered ourselves with the blanket; exhausted from our trip, we managed to get some sleep on our first night in this new place.

We were in Medvezhi Ozyora, the northern part of the Moscow region. There were wonderful spots in this area, especially in the autumn, when the rich variety of plant life in the mixed forests displays a multicolored palette of leaves changing to gold against a dense background of motionless evergreens. Somewhere beyond the forest the sun was rising, its first rays lighting up the tops of the tallest spruces. Unseen in the tops of the trees, the birds would exchange calls in various voices, sending their greetings each morning to our sullen column that was so much out of harmony with the natural magnificence that surrounded us. Slowly, as if stretching a strong elastic with our feet, we shuffled along trying to cut a few more moments from our working day. Our hands were clasped behind our backs; our eyes were fixed on the backs of those in front. And all of us, probably, were consumed by one thought, one common wish: how to drag out our march, how to postpone the beginning of the loathsome labor as long as possible.

My outward appearance had changed noticeably. Nothing remained of the clothes I was in when I left home; they had all worn out. I was wearing an old, faded, padded jacket that had once been in camouflage colors. Its buttons were mismatched, it was already torn, and bits of padding were sticking out of it in places. I had soldier's riding breeches of the same color as the jacket. They were also torn and, for some reason, the tears went across the width of the trouser leg. Lacking needle and thread to mend them, I had sewn them up with some thin copper wire taken from a bit of electrical cable I had found. This had made them very prickly, and it struck me that I was beginning to resemble a hedgehog. Instead of boots I had some down-at-the-heel shoes taken from dead soldiers.

Aleksei had managed to keep his boots. He had replaced the laces with copper wire so that no one could take them off his feet while he slept. We slept in our clothes and footwear because it was warmer that way and our clothes were more secure. My footcloths, made from rags of unknown provenance, caused me many problems. Several people had shown me how to put them on, but each one in a different way. That's probably why I had to spend a huge amount of time wrapping them around my feet each morning. To make matters worse, they would unexpectedly come unwound during the day as well, and I again would have to choose among several possibilities for using them effectively. My head, shaved bare, was adorned with a black hood made of some sort of cotton or flannel material, thin, cold, and stretched tightly over my head like a stocking. This outfit was an absolutely proper match for my hands and face, which had grown dark from grime. We had not been able to wash for several days. The mornings were cold, and the frosts were growing more severe. To wash we had to get water from the well. The water was icy, and after a night in our drafty tent we could rarely summon up the courage to use it for our morning ablutions.

In Praise of the Shovel

We were building an airfield four kilometers from Shcholkovo. The work was quite intense. Many people were involved. Graders crawled about the site, leveling the crushed stone that would form a base for the asphalt runway. We worked as diggers, excavating deep trenches; thank God the soil was sandy. In the course of a day I could dig out eight or nine cubic meters. The ringing sound of someone hammering on a section of rail during the midst of work was the signal for a smoke break. Laying aside my shovel, I would sit down in a niche I had prepared in the wall of the trench and fall asleep immediately. The smoke break lasted five minutes. Roused by the ringing of the rail, I would again begin lifting my shovel mechanically, earning a large ration for myself and for the thieves-in-the-law.

Each person worked in his own way. Some worked fast, throwing up a complete shovelful at a time. Soaked in sweat they would quickly tire;

then, gasping for breath, they would have to rest for a long time. Some were simply lazy, others deliberately held back. Among the latter were the Lithuanians who rightly believed that an additional hundred grams of bread did not compensate for the added investment of labor needed to get it and that, generally, it was both useless and immoral to work for Stalin's regime. I realized that they were right, but for some reason I was unable to work listlessly and used my own method—unhurried, rhythmical, keeping my breathing regular. I thought that this saved my strength while giving me greater productivity, even by comparison with those who were physically stronger.

The tool you were using made all the difference. Somehow I had managed to get my hands on a spade with a broad blade and a handle that was thin, supple, long, and had a peculiar bend in it. This handle worked like a spring. Bending under the weight of a spadeful, it strove together with me to rid itself of the earth; as it straightened it would make an additional thrust that would make it easier for me to throw the soil up higher. At times this spade seemed to me to be a living thing that understood me and tried to ease my heavy labor. I cared for it and did all I could to keep it in good condition, wiping it clean after work, particularly in rainy weather. Every morning I would hurry to the tool shed, worried whether my unusual, silent friend was safe in its place. One morning, though, I did not find my spade. It stood out, the only one of its kind. On the other hand, I may simply have imagined that it did. But when I picked up another shovel with a stiff, unsupple handle, I realized at once that I would have a lot of trouble working with it, but there was nothing else to be done.

I recalled how, when I was a child, Aleksei Ivanovich Bokov would often stop by our house on his way home from work. He was a refined man who had been deprived of his civil rights because of "social origins," as they said at that time. Among those rights was the right to a job that was worthy of him—work in his area of specialization. Only unskilled, heavy, dirty labor was left for such "deprivees." Aleksei Ivanovich worked as a ditch digger, and he would stop by our house wearing canvas overalls and carrying a shovel that he would always place in the same spot in our entryway. His shovel gleamed, and its handle was always clean as well. Obviously he treated it as a friend, cared for it and treasured it.

I did not begin work that day and went off to look for my spade. The landing strip stretched on for three kilometers. There were hundreds of people working on it. Looking for my spade among all of them was like looking for a needle in a haystack. I went from one brigade to another until lunchtime and, O joy! I did find my beloved shovel. I was ready to fight for it in any way possible, the more so that I had become used to almost daily scuffles; and I did get my shovel back, by guarantee of a sizeable piece of the heel of the bread loaf.

Almost half a century has passed since the time of the events I have been describing. Many things have been forgotten altogether, many others are recalled only in general terms. The camp sector at Medvezhi Ozyora has remained a blank spot in my memory. I know only that Aleksei and I were constantly involved in fights as we stood up for our independent position among the *urki* or defended our rights to our food. Aleksei was from Moscow. Despite the great difficulties in this period of wartime hunger, his family visited him quite regularly and tried to help him by bringing food. I remain under obligation to Aleksei's parents and to him because he shared everything he received with me. And at that time, an extra piece of bread meant so much, even for those living in freedom! The honest people of our country who live only by their own labor understand this very well.

Getting Tougher

Getting a food parcel in camp, where you were hungry even after eating your main meal, was something to celebrate. Unfortunately, there was always a dark shadow cast over such a day. The criminals, like any power based on force, regarded it as a just principle that they should be supported by the labor and property of others. Therefore, anyone who received a food parcel was obliged to share it with the criminals under threat of a beating and the loss of not just a part of the contents but the whole of it. And every person who received a money order or a parcel shared it with them. But there were a lot of criminals, and after a few of them had made their demands, others would follow. Usually they would all claim that if you shared with them no one else could ask, such was their law. But the strong do not like going hungry, and hunger is everywhere and always more powerful than the law.

Personal items and parcels were kept in the storeroom. The job of storekeeper was a wonderful one, even given the soft jobs held by the camp *pridurki*. Everyone who came to collect something from his parcel had to treat the storekeeper. And he would also help himself, artfully making holes in the bags of sugar, grains, and other products.

"It's the rats," he would explain.

We realized that he was cheating us, but had to accept it since the rats, like the criminals, might well eat it all.

Two lanky, emaciated young fellows would usually approach us at the storeroom in the evening. They would watch Aleksei take some bread from the bag and sometimes even lard or other tasty food; then they would announce in an even, quiet tone: "You have to share."

"And who might you be?" we asked when we saw them for the first time.

Their reply astonished us: "Real people."

Sometimes, some of the criminals' lackeys would come and say the same thing: "You have to share."

But they would be more insistent, with no doubts about a refusal.

At first Aleksei and I did give them a little, but then we realized that there were countless hordes of "real people" and we stopped sharing. Each act of insubordination was accompanied by a fight. And we became so accustomed to fighting that it ceased to be a terrible thing and became a habit. We fought selflessly, desperately, sometimes against four or five people. We were no longer fighting for the food parcel, we were saving face. We were successful to some extent. Our persistence had an effect. They stopped pestering us with demands to share the parcels, but they never missed an opportunity to steal from us. Their thievery was sometimes masterful.

One time we had boiled some potatoes. Back in the tent we added some lard, mashed the potatoes and, literally for a moment, set the pot on the upper bunk above us while we took out some bread and spoons. But when we got up, the pot of potatoes was gone, although as far as we knew no one had been there, nothing was stirring, and there wasn't a single person nearby. We rushed this way and that, but our supper had vanished without a trace.

Life became more and more difficult. It was either frost or cold rain and wind. And we were still living in the tent with its flapping window covers. We went off to work when it was barely light and came back at dusk. The well-being of the slogger-*zeks* depends in great measure on their brigadier—the boss or *bugor,* as he was called—who knows how to get on with the camp authorities, the criminals, and with his own team. The first brigadier we had was Dagman, who not long before had been a colonel in the army General Staff, where he dealt with supply matters. Wearing a greatcoat of good sturdy cloth and a pair of dandified boots, he looked imposing and made an impression. That was probably why they made him a brigadier. But a corrective labor camp is not the General Staff, and ensuring a daily ration for an ill-assorted pack of men who have been brutalized by hunger and hardship is not the same as accepting indents and compiling summaries for an army of several million located somewhere far away.

We soon realized that he was not cut out to be a *bugor*. All day long he would sit somewhere with a piece of paper on his knee, wetting his pencil like some hopeless schoolboy, making calculations and trying to apportion the rations to be received for the output of two dozen men, as if he were trying to feed thousands with five loaves. Nothing came of his schemes, of course, and all the members of the brigade were angry with him. The criminals punched and beat him, the work assigner and the norm setter snarled at him for the delays in submitting his apportionments and for his general sluggishness. When he realized the hopelessness of his situation, this man began to go to pieces and die away right before our eyes. His greatcoat, peaked cap, and calfskin boots had long disappeared. When the cold weather set in, he went about in a white padded jacket and matching quilted trousers and a cap with earflaps that was as battered as my own. His light-colored padded suit became spattered with black asphalt and quickly lost its luster from grime; the colonel himself began to drool; his nose ran and he had a pathetic, even repulsive look.

Once, toward the end of the working day, the thieves gave the colonel a terrible beating—for what, I don't know, but probably it was the perennial lack of a big ration for everyone. I found out about it when we were getting ready to go back to the zone. Dagman, all disheveled, lay flat on the ground in his black-spotted white suit. At the same time, there was another young lad who had grown so weak that he was unable to walk and no one was willing to help him. He was not from our brigade, but what could we do? Aleksei and I, using the well-known method of holding one another's wrists to make a chair for him, picked up the invalid. Dagman, laid face down, was carried off on two poles. We formed a strange and terrible procession as we approached the camp. It was a Sunday, and in front of the camp entrance stood a large crowd of Muscovites who had come with parcels for relatives. And then we arrived. At the head of the column, the lifeless body of Dagman, arms dangling loosely, was carried on two poles. His quilted trousers had slipped down, exposing a backside whiter than his jacket and so skinny it looked like it had been slit with a knife. Following him came Aleksei and I carrying the second unfortunate. And behind us, this time much more slowly than was usual when returning from work, the column moved painfully along. The visitors stood paralyzed. Funereal silence reigned. The invalids were taken from the camp entrance straight to the infirmary. I never saw Dagman again.

Dreams of the Infirmary

Getting to the infirmary for some treatment is the dream of every *zek*. To fall ill so as to get out of work; to sleep as much as you liked, to rest; to eat, if not your fill, then at least a little better. And the *zeks* tried all sorts of tricks and resorted to all kinds of *mastyrki*—ways of feigning or inducing an illness—in order to realize this dream. I was told how one *mastyrka* was done. You take a needle and thread, rub the thread on your unbrushed teeth so that it becomes fully saturated, and then make a few stitches beneath the skin on your arm or your leg. Infection begins within a day or two; your arm swells, your temperature rises, and you are assured of a hospital cot. There was one unfortunate case of a young lad to whom the camp infirmary could not offer appropriate help. They sent him to Moscow, and soon the rumor went round that his arm had been amputated.

There are other methods as well. Volodka Verbitsky once suggested that we drink some salt water. But we had to drink several liters of it in the course of a day. This causes a person to swell up as if from dropsy and, naturally, he is sent off to be treated. Aleksei and I rejected this sort of self-abuse.

"Well, I'm going to try it," said Volodka.

"You'll croak for sure," we warned him.

Soon Volodka really did begin to swell up. His face got round and puffy, and he became so flabby he could barely move in his long overcoat. He looked quite dreadful, with inflamed eyelids and swollen hands. And, of course, he got into the infirmary. We thought he would never get out alive. Fortunately, our fears weren't realized. About a month later we met Verbitsky, healthy and rosy, and we could even tell that his eyes really were as blue as cornflowers.

"How did you manage to recover?"

"My sister came to visit."

It turned out that in fact his sister had come from Ukraine and brought some lard and shortbread and this saved Volodka.

I, too, had to use the services of the infirmary. One morning I was caught short, as they say. Hugging myself and bent over with pain, I managed to drag myself to the infirmary. There I found a Jewish doctor and a junior nurse. I explained what was happening to the doctor.

"Take his temperature," he said to the nurse.

"I don't have a temperature," I told the doctor.

But, evidently, that was how they did things.

I sat holding the thermometer. It was warm. Through the open door opposite I could see the ward, the clean sheets on the bed, and I could already anticipate how I would lounge blissfully for a day or two in such a paradise. The nurse took the thermometer, examined it very carefully, and handed it to the doctor. After barely glancing at it he fixed his gaze on me.

"Give him two thermometers, one under each arm."

"What for?" I asked, perplexed.

She gave me two thermometers. Holding on to them in good faith, I still failed to understand what sort of procedure this was and what point it had.

"He's faking!" the doctor suddenly bellowed furiously after they had removed the thermometers.

"But listen," I tried to explain, "it's my stomach that hurts, not my head."

"Clear out of here!" the doctor shouted, more angrily than before. "I can fix it so you get another Article 58 for this."

It was then I realized what had happened. Evidently they had first given me a thermometer that had not been shaken down, one that showed a high temperature that had possibly been set artificially by tapping it with a finger. I realized that it was useless to try to prove this and quickly fled the infirmary.

In the distance I could see that the morning march to work was in progress and, overcoming my pain, I ran to the gates so as not to be caught in the zone and find myself, as an absentee, spending several days in a punishment cell rather than in the infirmary. On the way my footcloth came unwound. I pulled it out of my shoe and, footcloth in hand, went out the gates and managed to join the ranks of my brigade. As we marched to the airfield the pain in my stomach subsided. There remained only the regret that I had not been able to spend some time lying in the warmth on a clean sheet and the deep mortification that they had taken me for a trickster.

Love Camp Style

In the evenings we would sometimes visit the wooden barracks. It was warm there, and the *zeks* sat undressed on their bunks, using their free hours late at night to attend to "household" matters: peeling potatoes, patching clothes, using scraps of paper to write letters that always asked for rye rusks or salted pork fat. There was no electric lighting in the barracks, and everyone used homemade oil lamps fashioned from food tins and having as many as five wicks. They hung by nearly every bunk like icon lamps and did little to dispel the general darkness of the barracks, but when the large building was filled with these lamps it looked rather like a church with many glowing candles. We were always reluctant to leave this barracks and did so with great regret and even with pain in our hearts as we returned to our cold tent.

Winter was drawing near. It would be deathly to go on living in the tent. Its roof was already white with snow. But at this point our prayers reached God's ear, as they say: they finally found it possible to move us into a barracks. Our lives improved tangibly. We were able to keep warm, our spirits rose, and we even began washing every day so that we looked like actual human beings again. The only thing that spoiled our mood was the thievery in the barracks. When I came back from work on the first day, I found that my blanket had disappeared from my bunk. Wine-red in color, it stood out from all the others. I went around the barracks and soon discovered it and brought it back it as was my right. But the same thing kept happening. Each day when I returned from work I would find my bunk bare. I was tired of this and stopped looking for my conspicuous blanket. One day I happened to see it hanging up and simply kissed it good-bye and never claimed my right to my own property. Instead, I would make a tour of the barracks each night before going to bed and pinch a government-issue blanket or two from some fellow who wasn't looking. These were woven blankets, heavy as doormats. They were all alike, so that no one was able to prove that I had stolen one. I would spread out one as a mattress and cover myself with another. And when I went off to work I was resigned to the fact that in the evening I would find nothing but bare planks in the place where I slept.

I began to get used to camp life. The cold, the hunger, the frequent fights—these things I accepted as ordinary and necessary facts. I even began to perceive all the adversities with a certain amount of humor, and when other men, older than I, showed a lack of fortitude and gave in to a despondency at times bordering on despair, I would sometimes catch myself smiling involuntarily when I looked at them. Was this cruel or heartless? Evidently, I simply did not understand them, not being weighed down myself with worries over my family. Once I even found a girlfriend. Her name was Lida. She was older than I and it was she who approached me during a pause between jobs. The snow that had fallen the night before had covered the earth like a fluffy fur coat; the many black clods of earth that seemed to have punctured holes in the white blanket created a sharp contrast against the monotonous gray background of the sky. A gusty wind penetrated the many holes in my padded jacket and made me shiver. I imagine I must have been a rather sorry sight in my worn prison outfit. But she struck up a conversation with me. She asked me who I was, where I was from, and the article under which I was in prison. She was sympathetic, even called me good-looking, and asked me to give her my fluffy blue wool scarf—the only thing I had left from home—which I wrapped around my neck for lack of a collar. Evidently Lida realized from the sour expression on my face that I treasured the scarf; with a look that made me want to disappear into the earth, she went her way, though she did turn and give me a smile.

I spent the rest of the day and the evening feeling as if I had been dragged through the mud. At last I decided to find Lida and present her with the scarf which had now become an indicator of my complete selfishness and made me look like a mama's boy unable to appreciate the attention and kindness of a woman.

The most terrible crime in camp, one that was punished without any mercy at all, was the visit of a man to the women's barracks and, likewise, the visit of a woman to the men's barracks. Although these things appeared in the camp regulations simply as prohibitions against visiting other barracks, the supervisors in all camps without exception interpreted them much more broadly and treated them as a general prohibition against meetings between people of the opposite sex, wherever they might occur. Love was unconditionally punished by ten days in the punishment cells without being taken out to work and with a daily ration of three hundred grams of bread, water, and a bowl of thin camp soup for lunch.

Still, despite the threat of such harsh punishment, I decided to find Lida. Aleksei and I went to the women's barracks. There was still an hour before lights-out. It was completely dark. Like thieves in the night we stole up to the women's barracks. And then suddenly before us appeared the huge figure of the head of the Culture and Education Section. We recognized him by the leather overcoat and fur cap he always wore.

"And where are you two going? So you want to pay a visit to the girls, do you?" he roared, adding some unflattering terms to describe us.

We stammered some words by way of explanation, trying to convince this boss that he was wrong about our intentions. He poured out curses by way of a reply, and to make his case more convincing he gave Aleksei a kick. The two of us were well pleased that the matter ended with only that and, with nothing to show for our efforts, we returned to our barracks.

Our place in the barracks was in the farthest, darkest corner. I was already dozing off when I suddenly heard a muffled woman's voice and then a man's voice on the bunk above me. I nudged Aleksei: "Who's that?"

"It's her, Lida, the brigadier of the women's brigade."

The bunk kept creaking and I could not sleep. Then a man climbed down and another climbed up in his place. Again, there were muffled voices. The barracks slept, the many sleepers snored, the homemade lamps flickered. In our corner the bunk rocked and groaned.

One of My Countrymen

It was December. The first year of my confinement was behind me. Snow covered the asphalt runway of the airfield we had built. The forest, now gray, gazed gloomily at the landscape we had defaced. We felt no sorrow at all, unless it was the sorrow each of us felt for himself. We saw our future only as a void and counted off each day as another day served. Each day was like another drop that had fallen.

On one of those evenings Aleksei brought some news: a countryman of ours was living in our barracks. This was Pavel Fedorovich Bakharev, the brigadier of the woodworking shop attached to the camp. As a lieutenant in the service corps he had been called back from the front and arrested under Article 58. Before the war he had lived in Pavlovo, then in Gorky. He had worked in insurance inspection. After he had chatted with us for a bit, he promised to ask the administration to transfer us to his brigade. This was just what we needed: winter lay ahead, and we could work indoors. When we parted to go to bed we were very pleased. But things happened in a way we could not foresee. Literally on the next day Aleksei and I were pulled out to go on a long transport.

As folk wisdom tells us, men may meet but mountains never greet. In 1955, the third year after my return from prison, I was working as the head of the repair and construction shop in the Kirov Metalworking Cooperative in Pavlovo. Our shop was located across the ravine behind the main site of the enterprise. The stables were located here as well: at that time horses were the main means of transport within the factory. It was here that I came to know the man who ran this operation. Although there was a

large difference in age between us, we were drawn together by my need of
transport and, generally, by something common in our outlooks and opinions on what was happening around us. We treated one another with polite
respect. Once he came to me and asked, unexpectedly: "Tell me, were you
in Monino in forty-two?"

"No," I replied, not understanding what he was getting at. "I was in
Medvezhi Ozyora."

"That's right!" he agreed. "But they sent you off a little earlier to parts
unknown, while they sent us to Monino."

I allowed that, indeed, this was what had happened, still not understanding what he was driving at.

"Do you recall talking in the barracks one night about a transfer to the
woodworking shop? Well, that brigadier Bakharev is me."

And so we met for a second time, though I was surprised at how he
was able to recognize me, while I had completely forgotten him. It turned
out that when he was in Metartelsoyuz, our parent organization, he had
heard that I was a former *zek* and a chance bit of our conversation—that
my mother was a teacher—had jogged his memory.

After that, the two of us stuck together. When I was posted to the Pavlovo Repair and Construction Department as chief engineer I asked him
to be head of transport. Seven years later, when I was head of rural construction for the district, he was my foreman. We were very close friends.
It turned out that we lived quite close to each other, and our friendship
expanded to include our families. He was sixty-two when I had to accom-
pany him on his last journey to the Pavlovo cemetery.

CHAPTER FOURTEEN

A Long Transport

And everything started from the beginning again: Krasnaya Presnya and
its transit prison; the bathhouse; disinfection of clothing; searches, the last
of which was a very thorough one. In a cold room I was ordered to strip
naked. I watched as two of the screws carefully, inch by inch, felt their way
through all my belongings. Yet I was able to outwit them. I had a fur cap

that had been handed down to me by an army doctor who had lived in our house for a time; he had visited me while en route to a new posting. I had hidden the blade from a safety razor in the earflap of the cap. It was an old cap that my father had made from the skins of polecats that had begun paying visits to our henhouse. The skin had dried with time and become tough but flexible, like parchment. They couldn't feel the razor blade inside.

After they had examined my things they turned to me: "Show me your hands; lift your arms; turn around; bend over."

The outcome of these gymnastics was that they found nothing, and indeed I would never have hit upon the idea of hiding something in the place where they looked so carefully.

Then the final commotion in the corridor, the issue of raggedy winter clothes to those who seemed inappropriately dressed. My padded jacket and old but sturdy padded trousers were sufficient, it seemed.

As was always the case for people on transport, we no idea where we were being relocated. Only when they had loaded us into heated freight cars did we assume that it was going to be far away.

The cold weather of late December had set in, with temperatures in the minus thirties. The heated car—which in no way lived up to its name since it was no more than a two-axle freight car or cattle car—was as cold as a barn. It's true that there was a factory-made *burzhuika* stove in the middle of the car, but there was no fuel, and the stove was as cold as a cobblestone. It gave off cold instead of heat. There were fifty men in the car. We danced about, stamping our feet and slapping ourselves, trying not to freeze. Our breath formed hoarfrost on the walls and ceiling. The door opposite the entry was partly drawn back, and through the opening jutted a tin sheet bent to form a trough. This was our toilet, the transport *parasha*. Some rags had been carelessly stuffed into the gap above the trough. A frigid draft blew through the *parasha*. A few planks on one end of the car were evidently meant to serve as bunks, but there were not enough of them for us all. The pessimists could not contain themselves: "We'll croak here for sure."

There was a restrained racket from our moving about in the car. Some people tried to joke about it: "How long are we going to keep dancing like this?"

Others guessed where they were taking us: "To the Crimea, of course. It needs settlers now that it's been liberated."

Those less optimistically inclined did not agree: "Vorkuta is smiling at us."

This latter prediction turned out to be closer to the truth.

Our first concern about ourselves was eased when in the gathering darkness a light suddenly came on in the freight car. It seemed that even this single light bulb somehow made it warmer. Then we heard a noise in the car next to us and soon our door rumbled wide open as well: "Here you go!"

They threw us some logs and passed over some buckets of coal; then the door slammed shut again. Fuel meant life.

Zeks are a very meticulous and resourceful lot. Only they could manage to cut kindling from a log without using a knife and light a fire without matches or a piece of flint. One leg of the stove which, it turned out, could be pulled off if the stove were tipped to one side, served as an axe. And making fire presented no problem for us, dressed as we were in jackets and pants padded with cotton. A wad of padding, rapidly rolled back and forth on the floor with the sole of your boot, quickly gives off the unmistakable odor of smoldering cotton. You carefully pick apart the wad of cotton; some smoke appears and, after blowing on it a few times, it begins to glow—and you've got fire.

The fire in the stove hummed like music. A damp spot appeared around the chimney pipe in the ceiling: the hoarfrost was melting just as our souls were melting, as if we really were in the Crimea.

At first we all crowded about the stove, stretching out our red hands, frozen to the point of pain. Little by little the heat spread through the length of the car and, exhausted from our jumping about for several hours, we were ready to sleep. Trying to find a spot as close as possible to the stove, we lay down on the frozen floor.

I woke up during the night. It was quiet and everyone was sleeping. There was the rustle of heavy breathing; the stove, glowing red, wheezed. The car quivered, its wheels slowly clicking against the rails. We had set off.

Then came the long days of the transport. We could tell by the sun that they were taking us eastwards. That meant Siberia. That word, branded by the stamp of many centuries of exiles, hard labor, nostrils torn out and the clank of leg irons, struck us with a shiver of horror. But as we left Shcholkovo, we again began hoping for a good camp and comforted ourselves by the thought that "It can't be any worse."

We slept in a row, one lot of us atop another: there was not enough space for fifty men. Although one of your sides freezes to the floor when you sleep on the bottom, it's very warm, but the weight of the bodies above you is heavy. At last you can't stand the weight any longer; your crushed arms and legs grow numb, and you can't help but try to force your way out of the tight mass of bodies. Being on top is easier, but the cold pierces you through, particularly if you haven't managed to find a spot close to the stove.

There was no reveille or lights-out in the cars. It's difficult to say why we got up in the morning, whether it was because we had slept enough or whether it was the cold that kept us from sleeping any longer. Even our little stove, red-hot as it was, was losing the battle with the cold outside. We would stand all through the daytime, stamping our feet until we were ready to drop. The sun would peep through the tiny barred windows near the ceiling. The freight car would rock and shudder, sometimes loosening the rags stuffed around the gap made for the *parasha* until they flew outside; then the frigid wind from the movement of the train would come bursting in on us as if through a ventilation shaft.

The train would sometimes come to a halt for a brief time to let a train from the other direction pass by. This was also a notable event. When, day after day, you are in a closed cage—a cell or a transport train—and the unchanging surroundings no longer provide anything new to think about, when your reasoning mind grows dull for lack of material to absorb, then your hearing grows more acute, like that of a blind man, and it picks up anything from the world outside, weak though it may be but enough to interrupt the usual monotony. Whenever our train stopped we could hear the throbbing of the coming train from a long distance away. The noise would grow clearer and louder with every second. From the sound I could tell which type of locomotive was coming, an FD or an IS. And somehow it was a joyful thing to pick up the sounds as they drew closer. Probably this was because they were a reminder of another life rushing past, right here next to us, one unseen but to which I had an agonizing longing to return; but that would happen only after another eight years, ten months, and twenty-six days.

Outside the walls of our freight car the train rattled past. Then the rattling broke off and died away. Awaking from my dream, I again found myself immersed in the cold, filthy, embittered, isolated little world of a prison freight car with a fresh ache in my heart. It was as if my eyes had been opened by the awareness of the full weight, helplessness, and endlessness of my terrible present and unpredictable future.

Without any whistle or other signal and without the least participation of any of us, as if we did not even exist, our own train began to move off, its couplers clanking. And once again the walls of our car began to rock, the wheels to clatter, the cold to descend on us.

Sometimes once a day, sometimes twice, our train would stop for a long time. A prolonged, alert silence would set in. And then, just as in prison, we would hear from a distance the clapping sound of thermos lids; then from a car nearby would come the clatter of bowls; and then, right next to us, the crunching of footsteps and the sound of voices. The door, broad as a gate, would fly open. The cold would instantly burst in, filling the car and piercing us through as if we had been splashed with water. The head of the guard detachment, wearing a new white sheepskin jacket and carrying a wooden mallet with a long handle, would jump into the car. Accustomed to this operation we, like a flock of sheep, would press ourselves into one corner. He would hammer at the walls and floor of the empty section of the car with his mallet and then give the command: "Like a shot! Like a shot!"

He would count us by striking each man on the back with his mallet, and so as to make the blow as painless as possible we really would dart across to the opposite side of the car like a shot.

They would give us some fuel for the stove and pass out aluminum bowls of thick, hot porridge and a ration of bread. The car would be locked again.

Some would find a place to sit, others would squat, and we would greedily gulp down the hot food, after which they would bring us some warm water. Dealing with the bread was more difficult. It was frozen and impossible to eat. We would put our crusts on the hot stove and eat it layer by layer as it thawed. The stove was small, and we would all reach out to place our ration on it, everyone wanting to eat as soon as possible. Sometimes this procedure was drawn out and would continue even after they had collected our bowls and the car was again rocking as it traveled on. On the other hand, if you were not in such a rush you could even toast the bread and eat it quite hot. After a feeding like that we would feel more cheerful, but we would have to heat up the car again.

One day the head of the guard detachment was in a bad mood. He stormed into the car like an enraged animal, kicked our remaining supply of kindling and coal outside, then kicked over our little stove, making the car frigid and leaving us to wonder what the problem was. We had to begin all over again—set up the stove and put together the chimney pipe. In time with the knocking of the wheels so as not to alert the guards, we broke up the last remaining plank that had been meant for the bunks. Once more, we used the leg of the stove in place of an axe.

But the plank burned up quickly and gave off little heat. So as not to freeze to death, an unconditional confiscation of anything that would burn and anything warm was declared. I was wearing a pair of so-called ChTZ—canvas boots with rubber soles and heels. Despite my desperate resistance, the heels of my ChTZ were torn off and used for fuel. The pack-sacks or bags of those who had them were checked, and any extra shirts or trousers were taken to heat the car or to stuff up the holes around the *parasha* through which the cold air blew.

It seemed that there would be no end to the transport. We went on for a day, a second day, a week. In the wooden boarding of the car I found a nail hole. If you pressed your eye close to it you could see the moving panorama outside. I would stand there for hours, watching as hundreds of kilometers of my native Russian land passed by. In some places a thick spruce forest came close to the tracks, but most often I could see only space, as flat as a table, a broad territory bordered in the distance by a white birch forest and the sky covered by winter haze. But there were sunny days as well. Then the snow sparkled, the blue sky stood high above, the shadow of our car raced alongside and the sun would peep in on us through the little windows; in-side the car it became bright and even cheerful like the New Year's school holiday. The cold weather hung on, and we could sense it since our clothes would be even more firmly frozen to the floor in the mornings. We were thirsty. Without any water we would suck the frost from the rivets on the walls.

Once we had stopped at some station or other. We could hear the loud voices of the passengers, the hurried steps on the crisp snow; somewhere nearby a puffing locomotive gave a whistle. As a rule, the doors on the cars of our train were not opened in populated areas and near large stations. But evidently, because of the next lengthy stage of our trip, it had become necessary to toss in a supply of fuel for our stove. And when they opened the door of our freight car, I saw directly opposite the illuminated windows of a passenger car of a long-distance train. For a few moments I caught a glimpse of another, happier life. Some adults and children, a family by all appearances, were sitting at a little table eating something and chattering without a care in the world when their attention was immediately drawn to the sudden exposure of the unattractive interior of our car. Our accidental neighbors, their meal interrupted, were amazed at this revelation of an area of life they had not known before. Their faces froze instantly in an expres-sion of bewilderment, as if through some complete accident they had made a great discovery confirming the existence of another world beyond their own. In our abode, we simply did not conform to the normal conception of a human way of life.

The door in front of us slammed shut as if a movie film—interesting, beautiful, magical, distant, and unique—had unexpectedly broken. It was as if something familiar and dear to us had suddenly disappeared, carried off by death. I went on staring at the blank, cold wall of the door and kept seeing the train window, the faces of free people, the life that had been taken away from me.

That evening it took me a long time to fall asleep. The station remained somewhere far behind us. Our freight car was rocking once more; its wheels seemed now to be knocking against the rails in a nighttime fashion, their hammering, clattering, and squeaking now muffled. The sleeping *zeks* lay packed in a gray, warmish mass, their bodies contorted and huddled together. At the opposite end of the car, four criminals were fiddling with something. Kneeling, they had pulled up a square of the flooring and were poking at it with that same universal tool, the iron leg of the stove. When I looked more closely I could make out a small, tightly fitted trap door in the floor, and it was this that the criminals were trying to open. I watched their vain efforts for a long time and little by little drifted off to sleep. Suddenly, through my sleep I heard a shot, after which the train began braking sharply. Everyone awoke. A great bustle began: there were shouts and the knocking of the wooden mallet on the cars. Our car's turn came. The door abruptly flew open and the guards burst in: "Like a shot! Like a shot!"

Then it all became clear: there were four people missing from our car; they had crawled through the trap door they had opened in the floor.

"Who saw them?" the head of the guards asked in a fury.

No one replied.

"Who was sleeping next to them?"

Again, silence. And suddenly someone said, as if joyfully: "The Fox was sleeping there. The Fox saw them."

The Fox was me. They had given me that nickname on account of my yellow cap of polecat fur.

"I wasn't anywhere near them," I replied reasonably.

But everyone in the car joined in, in concert: "The Fox, the Fox saw it all."

They had made me the scapegoat.

"Get out!" they ordered.

I jumped out of the car and the door slammed shut behind me.

It was night and it was very cold. Our train stood frozen like some monstrous black insect. The silence was broken only by the loud crunching of snow underfoot. It was cold, but I felt I was filling my lungs with air in some new way, intensely, greedily, as if drinking the purest fresh water after a long thirst. The whole of the long train seemed to be picking up its ears as we marched beside it. I relaxed somewhat, as if freed from fetters that had bound me; I was only half aware of the sharp yet pleasant bite of the frost.

They brought me to the car that served as the office. It was just another freight car but was well heated and well lit, its stove blazing fiercely. Preoccupied with thoughts of my own situation, one that promised nothing good, I paid little attention to my surroundings; I did not see so much as sense that a good deal was going on in the car and that there was little free space in it. The guard commander sat on a stool near the stove, and I sat on a crate in front of him.

"So, tell me what you know," he began, as all the interrogators normally did.

Following the same pattern, I replied with a question: "About what?"

In fact, what could I tell him? That just before going to sleep I had seen four of the criminals poking at the floor? What had happened was clear enough already.

"Who are they, the ones that escaped?" the commander asked. "What are their names?"

I sat there in torment. In the first place, I didn't know their names, and in the second place I felt that I was being cast in the role of a traitor, an informer.

"I don't know them," I replied.

My conversation with the guard commander became less and less pleasant. He began to get angry and picked up a piece of firewood with a handle hewn on it.

"Is he going to start beating me?" I wondered.

They had caught the fugitives and their names were known. So what did the guard commander want from me? Why would he need to beat me with that log? And how the whole car had turned against me! How glad they had been when they decided to dump it all on me. Why should I suffer a beating for them because of their cowardice? What was the right thing to do?

"Don't be afraid," said the commander. "Speak out. They won't do anything to you; I'll protect you."

Being so close to the hot stove began to make me tired, and I was ready to fall asleep. The talk with the guard commander and a general lack of sleep had worn me out. The train had long since carried on its journey, and its rocking was making me even sleepier. I could barely hear what the commander was saying and could think only of how nice it was to be traveling in such a warm car and how good it would be to sleep.

"You'll be had up as an accessory to an escape," I heard.

I had no idea what that threat might lead to. And in any case, why should I protect those who had sold me out?

"One of them was called Lekha," I said at last. "The others I don't know."

There was no beating. When the train stopped, they put me into a different car as an informer who had done his job.

The end of the journey turned out to be more auspicious for me. The car in which I now found myself was far better heated than the first one; there were bunks on both sides which were already taken by the most influential criminals. And so even though it meant sleeping on the floor, it was not as one part of two layers of human bodies. As soon as I appeared I was hauled off to the bunks: "Tell us a now-vel."

The thieves, who never read books themselves, very much like to listen to "now-vels," as they call them, especially ones about passionate love and adventures like *The Count of Monte Cristo, Queen Margot,* and similar things. Unfortunately, I have absolutely no talent as a storyteller and, indeed, scarcely ever read novels. After thinking a bit, I asked the *urki:* "Do you know Gogol's 'Vii'?"

It turned out that they didn't know it. I began telling the story but quickly realized that Gogol's "Vii" wasn't at all what they were expecting, and I had no talent whatsoever at spinning out an absorbing tale.

No one belittled my efforts or insulted me, but clearly I had disappointed them all. I was removed from the bunks and put on the floor as a complete failure who was of no further interest.

CHAPTER FIFTEEN

The Camp at Biysk

I Stay Alive

After a thirteen-day journey our train stopped. We had arrived. We were unloaded at night in terrible cold. A huge moon stared at us in wide-eyed astonishment. Curious stars spilled out into the heavens, winking at each other and gazing down at us as well. It was only here that we were able to see the full length of our train: it was dark, gloomy, and had fallen silent, abandoned without us. Along its side stretched an even darker, crooked column of some 2,500 *zeks,* surrounded by the figures of soldiers with rifles and dogs. The cold began to seize us in its grip. We did our best not to give in to it by stamping our feet as usual, while shivering and tucking our hands in our armpits. We tried to figure out where we were. I have to give credit to the guards: they were quick to get us formed up.

There was the usual formula: "A step to the right, a step to the left will be considered an escape . . . Forward, march!"

We marched quickly, trying not to get separated. We were driven on by cold, curiosity, alarm, and the wish to get to our destination, for better or for worse . . . We all had the same hope: "It can't be any worse."

We arrived at a patch of sparse pine forest. The trees were old and tall. Beneath them were some structures that might have been dugouts and might have been root cellars. They were long and wide with tiny windows right at ground level. There were no fences, no barbed wire. Everything was dusted with snow. The snow, crisscrossed by the blue stripes of shadows of the pine trunks, glistened with iridescence and reflected the moonlight so strongly that, unaccustomed as we were, we found it painful to look at. But the beauties of nature were of little concern to us. Even while in the freight car the tips of all my fingers and toes had become frostbitten, and now they were painfully sensitive to the cold.

We were all assigned to three dugouts, the men in two, the women in the third. The interior of the dugouts was a model of order. They were heated and the walls were faced in planks. The whole central area was taken up by huge, continuous sleeping shelves three levels high and twice as wide as the height of a man; there were a number of cross-passages through them. The bunks were painted green, and there were red stars along the middle overhead. Each corner had a stove surrounded by a log partition. Between the bunks were ovens made of brick, like the stoves, for drying footwear. Everything was whitewashed or painted. The floors were wooden and they were clean. It turned out that a military unit had been housed here before we arrived, and these had served as barracks. The men took their places on the bunks in order, carload by carload. Fifty men could fit in one row, tightly squeezed together, each on their sides with their knees tucked up. Warmed by our body heat we fell asleep, having disconnected ourselves from what we had just endured, as if we had turned a page of our lives after finishing one of its chapters.

The first evening, revived from the jolting of a two-week journey, the *zeks* swarmed about, getting acquainted with the new place, taking pleasure in being able to move in a space less confined than that of the freight car, jostling as if in a noisy crowd at a market, seeking human contact, new acquaintances and new ways in which to apply their talents, above all in the appropriation of other people's property. Suddenly I heard, "Hey, Fox!"

I turned and froze. The four fugitives advanced on me in a solid wall. I could read their intentions on their faces. I wouldn't say that their faces were angry or openly expressed a craving for revenge. They showed, rather, a touch of malice, the pleasure that was to come from the settling of scores, something akin to the magnanimity of a cat when that household predator toys with a doomed mouse. In the hand of one of the *urki* flashed what might have been a sharpened bit of metal or a shard of glass.

I sized up the situation in an instant. There could be no question of resistance to these four. There was no place to run either, and not only because I was trapped in a corner with only a blank wall behind me.

And then I recalled the words of the guard commander on our train—quite possibly, he was the security officer. He guaranteed my safety only while I was on the train, when he was there close at hand. What would happen to me later was of absolutely no interest to him, though he must have been aware that for me it was a question of life and death. Our lives were simply not taken into account; they were of little value, since so many of them were lost in camps, prisons, and in the front lines. Masses of people had perished from epidemics and from hunger in years of poor harvests.

My enemies kept advancing toward me. Blood pulsed in my temples like a hammer, helping quicken the work of my mind to find a way out, a way to save myself. My life was being counted out in seconds.

What happened next I cannot recall. But I was left not only alive but even unharmed. It may have been that something diverted my enemies or frightened them. Possibly it was an act of magnanimity on their part; possibly they realized that in fact I had done nothing that could have changed their situation for the worse. Yet the latter possibility does not stand, since it could apply only to explain the behavior of more rational, more developed creatures than these hardened criminals. What matters more to me is why this gap remained in my memory. Perhaps I had reached the limit of perception of my surroundings, after which, as if having been shifted to a different wavelength, my consciousness and psyche no longer responded to external stimuli and so they were not registered in my memory. I stayed alive. A miracle of some sort had occurred.

Hunger, Lice, and Illnesses

We slept uninterrupted for three months, entirely losing our sense of time. There was no radio, no newspaper, no clock, no cock's crow in the mornings. It was winter; the days were short and we scarcely noticed them. Day or night, it was all the same for us. It seemed that we wanted nothing more than to sleep all the time; and we would sleep without stirring, to the point of numbness, to pain in our sides and doubled-up legs. Then someone would give the command: "We're turning over."

And all fifty men would simultaneously turn on their other side, and this was the only way it could be done: if one person had tried to lay bent the opposite way he would never have been able to squeeze into his allotted space.

There was one other command. It is difficult to say how often it was repeated, whether once a day or oftener.

"Car twelve, to the mess hall!"

Who gave this command was unknown, but when we heard the number of our car we, though sleeping, reacted as if to a shot. In an obedient crowd we hurried out of the dugout like sheep. It was dark, and there was no way of telling whether it was evening, night, or morning. The mess hall was opposite. To get in we again had to step down a few plank stairs, squeeze ourselves tightly onto benches at long wooden tables, and receive our earthenware bowls of soup made from frozen, unwashed potatoes with a tiny strip of stinking entrails. We ate, indiscriminately, something dirty, scarcely cooked, disgusting to the taste; its only virtue was that it was hot. And, indeed, we would have eaten something cold with the same wolfish appetite.

Bread made largely out of corn was given out irregularly. We would get this every other day or every third day. There were times when we had no bread for three days. This made people angry and even led to outright insubordination. There were cases when the warders would come into the barracks and command: "Head count!"

But instead of the usual bustle and forming up into two ranks no one moved.

"Give us bread!" someone shouted in reply.

And everyone took up the chorus: "Bread! Bread!"

The warders tried various tactics. When they saw that their little sheep were becoming ungovernable and that this could lead to quite undesirable results in days to come, the warders resorted to persuasion and ingratiation: "Come on, what will it cost you? Just form up and we'll count you quickly..."

But the reply was the same shout, only with even more vigor: "Bread! Bread!"

At this stage, the warders would lose their composure and begin shouting, swearing, and making threats. And then something unheard-of would unfold. The thousand-man crowd would explode. The choice oaths, whistling, and hammering on the bunks became a continuous uproar. An earthenware bowl came flying toward the warders, and as it shattered on a post it showered them with fragments. The warders retreated toward the exit. The *zeks,* inspired by their victory, shouted in a friendly tone: "Bread! Bread!"

Then bowls came flying one after the other, shattering and spraying fragments about.

"Bread!" roared the hungry crowd.

Shielding themselves, the warders hastily withdrew from the barracks, abandoning their mission of carrying out a regular head count. The *zeks* had triumphed.

But hunger was not the only hostile element. We were not marched off to work, possibly because the camp had not yet been fully built. It was only after our arrival that construction began on a wooden fence around the rather large compound. Carpenters hammered at it day and night. There were no toilets either. Instead, under the watchful eye of a guard standing on the roof of the dugout with a rifle, we used the nearby adjoining area; this meant that as spring approached our dwelling was surrounded by a solid ring of frozen sewage.

The problem of heating the dugouts was also solved in a rather original fashion. As soon as we arrived and began complaining about the cold, we were offered the chance to take a saw and an axe and, supervised by guards, cut down the nearest pine trees. Not a single pine was sawn, however, and this was certainly not because the *zeks* felt particularly protective about nature. It was just because we had found a simpler method to get firewood. First we began to strip off the painted and quite artfully made trimmings on the bunks, leaving bare the posts, pediments, and corbels. Then we dismantled the partitions in the corners. And since these did not last for long we set about dismantling the floors and wall facings. What not long before had been a well-appointed barracks took on the appearance of an abandoned stable or a cattle yard that had suffered war damage.

But the worst misery of all was the lice. We had not been to the bathhouse for more than two months, had not washed, had not taken off our padded jackets and quilted trousers, had not cut our hair or trimmed our nails, and we had begun to look like cave dwellers. All this, along with the overcrowding, created a most favorable environment in which insects could multiply. With our legs bent at the knee we lay tightly together as if nested into each other; we would sleep until the hungry insects that had bred on our bodies would allow us to sleep no longer. Four times a day, awakened by unbearable itching, I would tear my body out of the solid mass of sleeping men. When I stood up I could hear a flood of lice pouring off my body, unhindered by my underclothes which had grown stiff and shiny. I needed only to pass my hand through my hair just once for all my fingernails to be filled with these little beasts. I would undress and begin killing them, first counting them by hundreds and then simply killing them without counting. The nails of my middle fingers that I used to kill them became sticky. I noticed that these little beasties came in a variety of shapes and colors: some were black, others blue, red, or yellow. After carrying out this operation I could manage to sleep peacefully again for a few hours, after which it all had to be done again in the same fashion. Some people would rid themselves of insects in a simpler way: they would go out into the cold, take off their shirts, and shake them. The lice would stand out against the snow like scattered beads.

At the very beginning, after our arrival, I had changed places with someone so as to get into the group from the car Aleksei had been in. Ivan Mikhailovich was with him as well. All three of us lay together on the bunks. Ivan Mikhailovich's beard had grown out. He asked us once to kill the little beasties that had multiplied in it. Unfortunately, there was nothing we could do. The lice and nits were so thickly entangled in his beard that they had formed a continuous mass that could not be torn apart; it was one resilient bundle, like a felt mat. His beard would have to be completely cut off, but we had no scissors, knife, or axe and were quite helpless. Aleksei and I were lucky that our beards had not yet grown.

It was not until March that they took us to the bathhouse for the first time. We were taken in groups—in the order of the railway cars in which we had traveled—to the town on whose edge our camp was located, a town that turned out to be Biysk in the Altai Region. In the bathhouse, our faces and heads were shaved; we were each given a sliver of black soap the size of a piece of toffee; and our clothes were put through the roaster. But our first wash did nothing to help. The relief was only temporary. The lice attacked our clean bodies with renewed fury, and once more we set about killing them, crushing them and shaking them off. Someone made a proper decision: car after car, day and night, we were continuously sent off to the bathhouse and our clothing put through the roaster. Only then did we begin to get some relief and, at last, complete liberation from these pernicious insects.

But along with the lice came illnesses as well. Over the winter a rather large territory around our dugouts had been fenced in. A little distance away from the mess hall they organized a hospital infirmary that was desperately needed. A wide range of illnesses broke out. I got to know a man from Belorussia. He was tall, a little older than I was, a quiet fellow who never hurt anyone. It was odd to imagine how people like him could be sent to prison. The law is the same for all. But how can there be justice when each person is different, when losing an index finger is enough for one, while the noose cries out for another, as they say?

Once this Belorussian and I were sitting on the bunks. It was daytime, but because the windows were high and covered with ice the barracks was cast in semi-darkness. He was telling me about his homeland, Belorussia. And like all hungry people, our thoughts were taken up with memories of food—simple, everyday food, the mere taste of which was now only a wishful dream. He told me that they didn't use the entire *bulba,* the potato, for food: they would eat only the outer layer and leave the core to feed the livestock. This was entirely reasonable. And he told me that his mother would fry potatoes for him.

"Ah, how rosy red they were," he recalled with pleasure.

Then he fell silent, bowed his head, and suddenly I noticed that a thin, straight red trickle was coming from his mouth. At first I didn't realize what this was, since the red color had showed only in a chance flash of reflected light. It was blood. I felt unbearably sorry for this Belorussian; I realized that he would never see his homeland again, nor his mother and the rosy-red *bulba.* The next day he was taken to hospital and I never saw him again.

Death began visiting us more and more often. One morning we got up, responding as if to an alarm, to go to the mess hall; we were surprised that Ivan Mikhailovich didn't move and didn't even seem to hear our cries. We tried shaking him awake, but he was dead. So I had slept that night embracing a corpse. What was even more terrible, perhaps, was the fact of my indifference. I felt neither fear nor pity. This dulling of the feelings is a product of captivity, a derivative of slavery. Somewhat later I was to learn that I was capable of regarding my own death apathetically. But that was only after mass deaths of others. Dysentery had broken out in the camp.

This disease was inevitable. People had no normal food. Starving, they would gulp down any rubbish. There was no question of any food hygiene. The same was true of sanitation in our day-to-day lives. We ate anything that seemed edible.

On one of those winter days that were not too cold, as our carload of men was hobbling off for our routine ration of food, a truckload of potatoes arrived at the mess hall. At the same time, another crowd of men who had just eaten was coming toward us. And suddenly, as if on some mysterious signal, people rushed to the truck and opened its back gate while still on the run; frozen potatoes tumbled out of it, thumping as they hit the ground. In a rush, the *zeks* grabbed at them, stuffed them into their jackets and pockets, if they had pockets, or simply scooped them up by the handful. The work assignment clerk, Boyko, a healthy, strapping fellow, appeared out of nowhere with some helpers. They struck out at these emaciated people with their sticks, keeping their own daily rations from them.

Another time, as we were going down into the mess hall, we passed a truck full of fresh cabbage that was parked right at the entry. The mess hall *pridurki,* whom everyone hated for the extra bowls of soup that always came their way, were unloading them. The *zeks* going down the steps stared greedily at the cabbage and contrived ways of stealing some while moving past. We had already sat down at the table when Aleksei, trying to avoid being spotted, drew back the skirt of the short overcoat he had still kept from home.

"Look at that," he whispered to me.

And I saw that he had a head of cabbage hidden away.

"How did you do it?" I asked, amazed.

Aleksei only gave a sly smile, clearly pleased with his lucky acquisition.

We left the mess hall, looking all around us. It was risky to go back to the barracks with a head of cabbage, since the starving petty thieves could simply take it away from us. It was already dark, and Aleksei and I went off some distance from the barracks dugouts. A young lad, aware of what was going on, had attached himself to us in the hope of picking up something, and we simply weren't able to get rid of him.

The cabbage was green and frozen hard as steel, so we couldn't tear off any leaves. We found a stump and began throwing the cabbage at it as hard as we could to try to break it. We managed to do so, though it was difficult. We gathered up every leaf that had been thrown off. We gave a few leaves to the lad who had come with us, to placate him so he would not tell anyone about our treasure. We tried chewing the frozen cabbage right there, but then we hit upon a better method. We returned to the dugout, found an earthenware bowl, put the fragments of cabbage into it and shoved it into the stove. The cabbage quickly thawed and warmed and now became a fully edible dish.

There was more and more room on the sleeping shelves now, as people were dying. Every other day, two carts loaded with corpses would regularly creep about the camp. The corpses—naked, white as ivory, frozen into every possible position, their twisted arms and legs as thin as sticks—looked more like roots than the remains of human beings. They hauled them around uncovered, with no formalities, no coffins, no clothes, and without observing rituals of any sort, as if they were rubbish or carrion. And it never entered anyone's head that these people had families, mothers, or children somewhere. Everyone was absolutely indifferent, though everyone was, as it were, standing in line behind them. Not only the infirmary but the barracks dugouts were filled with the stench of diarrhea from which masses of people suffered.

Once I also experienced all the symptoms of fatal dysentery. Aleksei wasn't around at the time. He had managed to find a job in the office through some of his Moscow acquaintances, and I rarely saw him. Obviously, being left on my own made me sense the danger hanging over me especially keenly. I ate nothing for three days and hid my daily ration beneath my jacket inside a bag made from a German handkerchief. Then, when I had accumulated almost two kilos of dry bread, I made myself eat it. I finished the first ration without any difficulty, and it seemed as if my appetite had come back. I had to force myself to eat the second ration. The third I was unable to finish without any liquid, so I poured some water into a bowl and finished the bread mixed with water. Nothing remained of my illness. I sighed with relief: this time, at least, they wouldn't carry me out as a stiffened corpse.

New Outfits

Sometimes I wondered where they were putting these corpses. With their extremities stretched out wide they would never fit into a coffin, never mind a grave. One day I happened to hear that they were asking for people to work in a grave-digging brigade. I decided immediately that I had to go to work, realizing that it was only through work, no matter what kind, that I could keep up my strength and good spirits and keep my system in some semblance of normality. Gravediggers were issued with new winter clothing. Through an irony of fate, as they say, the man assigned as brigadier to manage this work was named Mogilny. I signed up for his brigade. We had to sign for our outfits, which were quilted trousers—thick, warm, and of a light-blue color—and felt boots or, as the Siberians call them, *pimy*. I didn't manage to get a new jacket. The next day, before I had even left the zone to go to work, I met Aleksei near the dugout.

"Run off and hide somewhere, they're taking away the new outfits."

It turned out that the camp "operators," headed by the work assignment clerk, Boyko, had decided to make some quick money on a profitable business deal. They herded the *zeks* from one dugout to another and took away the new outfits from those who had them, giving them in return some rags from those who had died. The new clothing, for which people had signed, went to the city to be traded for provisions and home-brewed vodka.

Aleksei's warning had come in time. Since the zone by this time had been fenced in and we could move about freely within it, I ran off to the most distant dugout, one that was not being used to hold prisoners. When I went down into it I saw at once that it held stacks of corpses. They were white as ivory and just as grotesque as those on the carts; they lay atop one another like firewood or dry twigs, rough and gnarled as if they were not human at all. Concerned more for the safety of my new trousers, I was not frightened by the heap of the dead lying there and found a place for myself among them, even pleased to have them nearby. I hoped that Boyko's team would never think of searching for new clothing in the morgue, among corpses they had already stripped bare.

The next day, passing out of the gates of the camp for the first time, I went to work as part of Mogilny's brigade. It was a cold day and there were snowdrifts all around. The sun shone and the snow sparkled; I felt a half-forgotten sense of pleasure from marching along, from freely breathing the pure air, from simply being active again, from being able to tear myself away from the stench and filth. My new padded trousers and *pimy* kept out the cold, and a sense of invulnerability raised my spirits and separated and liberated me, at least for a short time, from the sordid dreariness of camp life and feelings of depression.

They marched us to the outskirts of Biysk. It was an empty, uninhabited area. Off in the distance we could make out the squat buildings of the boiler factory that was under construction. We cleared a patch of snow and began chiseling out the frozen earth with crowbars. We tackled the job eagerly at first, since we craved for activity. We warmed up and our faces became flushed; but soon the heavy crowbars drove away our longing for work, weakened as we were by prolonged hunger. Fifty degrees of frost had made the soil as hard as glass, and it was only with great effort that we could make it shatter into tiny fragments. Changing by turns from crowbar to shovel, we nevertheless managed to chisel out a pit about four meters by four and as deep as a man's arm. This was a fresh grave for those from our train who now lay stacked as dried-out corpses, frozen as solid as this ground.

Our strength began to fail. Nearby we found some straw beneath the snow and sat down; and, as is normal, we lit a bonfire and stretched our red hands, numb from the cold, toward it.

Suddenly someone behind me shouted: "Potatoes!"

Without even managing to size up the situation and find out where they were, I instantly turned around and, without standing up, shoved my hands into the snow-covered straw. I gave no thought to what I was do-ing, but my hands were working feverishly, tossing aside the icy, moldering straw. Here was one, a potato! My fingers felt out the round, frozen lumps. As mechanically as a parachute jumper pulls the ring of his ripcord, I drew my cherished little ration bag out of my jacket. Thoughts flew feverishly through my head, urging me on: "Turn around quickly before they've all been grabbed up!"

I rummaged through this burning straw hurriedly, greedily, trying to gather in my bag my share of these little edible balls that knocked together as if made of ivory.

"You're on fire!" someone suddenly screamed, tugging hard at my sleeve.

I got up, aware that something was wrong, and saw that the left leg of my new padded trousers was on fire above the knee. I managed to put out the burning fabric quickly, but the padding went on smoldering for a long time, giving off acrid smoke. I had to tear out pieces of it, and most of the trouser leg had turned into rags. Carried away by the potatoes, I had, it seems, put my leg into the fire and so ruined what even before had been an incomplete new outfit.

I came back from work in a dark mood. Hanging from my hand was my bread bag, one-third filled with potatoes no bigger than walnuts; tatters of the scorched, stinking padding of my trousers flapped on my leg. I was happy about the potatoes and worried about my trousers. Had I not taken any potatoes, my trousers would have been safe and sound. Had my new trousers remained safe and sound, there would have been no potatoes. But why on earth was I the one who had to get his trousers in the fire? Others with both new jackets and new trousers had even more potatoes than I did.

Depressing thoughts like these gnawed at me all the way back to camp. I tried to distract myself, wondering how they could dump several cartloads of corpses into such a tiny grave as the one we had dug and then somehow cover them over with chips of frozen earth. What would happen in spring and in summer? And this was not the only such grave, since there were hundreds of corpses.

It was with such gloomy reflections that I came into the dugout and found myself a bit of wire. I threaded the partially thawed, wrinkled little potatoes on it like the beads on an abacus and shoved them into the stove, thus cooking myself a peculiar sort of shish-kebab. Then I went to the women's barracks where a girl sewed a huge green patch on my new trousers.

Criminals' Justice

For some reason they never sent us out to dig graves again, though cartloads of corpses were regularly leaving the zone. The number of people in the dugouts continued to drop. And the dugouts themselves had been transformed over the winter. Almost everything that would burn had gone into the fire. Nothing remained of the sleeping platforms but a few posts that had been stripped of their casings; here and there a few planks had been fastened together at the tops of the posts like crows' nests. The *urki* still huddled together there. The *zeks* slept side by side on the bare earth: not a trace remained of the wooden floor or of the plank wall facings. Piles of sawdust that had been used as insulation now lay along the bare walls. There were heaps of broken brick where the stoves and drying ovens had once stood. The inside of the dugout, stripped bare, looked like a patch of woodland where all the trees had been cut. Hungry, feral people with nothing to do wandered about in silence as if they had lost their reason. From the latrines they had collected bones from the skulls of horses that had been used to make our soup and then discarded. These bones were completely bare, without the slightest sign of meat. But if you smashed the horse jawbone you could dig soft, edible veins out of it, thin as threads.

Using a piece of brick, I broke up some of these jawbones with their huge yellow teeth and pulled out these threads that had some resemblance to meat. The bones themselves served as food. To eat them you first had to roast them in the fire until they took on a chocolate color and then gnaw them before they had completely cooled. Once cold, they hardened again and lost their properties as edible food.

I soon realized that there was more harm than good to be had from such food, that it could lead to infection, and I summoned up the strength to reject it.

Late one evening I couldn't find any free space on the floor of our dug-out to nestle down for the night and went off to the one next door. To my amazement, it was almost empty. I walked among the bare posts as if in a burnt-over forest until I noticed a few planks that had been put together close to the ceiling; these seemed to be a suitable place to spend the night. Without thinking for long, I climbed up the post by grasping a few of the notches, nails, and bits of facing that remained from the sleeping platform that had once been here. I had almost reached my goal when suddenly I heard a shout from below: "There he is, that's the little bugger who's been stealing our stuff!"

The man who had shouted was one of the lackeys from the criminal gangs. I recognized him since I had seen him before, fussing about in a servile way while preparing food for the highest-ranking of the criminals. I didn't wait to see what would happen next but slid down the pole and hurried toward the door. I couldn't manage to escape scot-free, though; a gang of about ten criminals caught up to me and I was surrounded.

"Was it you that stole the *bobochka* (shirt)?" one of them shouted.

"And you pinched my *prokhorya* (boots)?" said another.

I thought that all these accusations had been invented, simply as an excuse to beat me up. And the beating was not long in coming. One of them struck me across the back with a stick as thick as a wagon shaft, another hit me over the head with an iron rod. When I looked up I could see this rod waving over me once more but I did not feel its blow.

When I came to, I was aware of lying in complete darkness. Everything was quiet. I remembered what had just happened and I was terrified, terrified from the realization that I had gone blind from the blow that I had not felt. I moved and felt stabbing pains all through my body; I had been beaten all over. I wanted to get up but couldn't; I didn't have enough strength. Then I spotted somewhere off in the distance, apparently at the end of the dugout, the faint glow of a cigarette. I felt better immediately: so I wasn't blind after all. I guessed that during the fight the lights had gone out and thanks to that they didn't finish me off.

I couldn't count on any assistance. Overcoming the pain, I managed to get on my feet and stumble out of the dugout into the open air. It was night, dark, starry, and cold. I thought for a moment and then limped to the infirmary, a small dugout in which *zeks* were dying every day but where, I hoped, I could get some help. The infirmary door was locked. I knocked. The reply came rather quickly: "Who's there?"

"Help me," I explained through the closed door. "I've been badly beaten up."

"There's no room," came the blunt refusal.

I tried to explain my situation and arouse the man's pity, but once again I heard: "There's no room."

I heard his footsteps moving away from the door and then all grew silent.

"And what if I was dying," I thought, "or dripping blood?" I felt so hurt that my eyes welled with tears. So where could I go? In one dugout it was packed to bursting, in the other they would finish me off. The choice was simple: I went back to the first one.

The dugout presented a depressing picture. It was enormous and cold, with bare poles thrusting up along the center and heaps of rotting sawdust along the walls, open toilets in the corners where once the stoves had stood within little enclosures; and all over the floor *zeks* were sleeping in every imaginable position. Their breathing merged into one general snore that rang out expressively in the silence. Barely able to find a spot among the bodies to place my foot, I made my way into the dugout in hopes of finding some room for myself on the floor. I got as far as the center, but there was not a place to be found. I stood alone over these human bodies that lay about like corpses on a field of battle. They were happy because they were asleep. Some distance away I spotted a heap of broken bricks from the destroyed drying oven; once more, with difficulty, I managed to make my way to it and collapsed on the bricks, beaten, exhausted, and swallowing the bitter insults. I fell asleep at once.

I Am a Carpenter

One result of all the things that had been going on in the camp was an outbreak of typhus. The complete lack of any organized medical service, the absence of hospital beds, and the endless despotism of both the free workers and the internal camp personnel threatened to wipe out the entire population of prisoners. It was terrifying: every one of us was facing death. At the same time, we could sense that the war was coming to an end, and the hope of an inevitable amnesty was growing among the *zeks*.

"We'll all be going home," was constantly repeated in conversations.

And even we 58ers could not entirely reject such a possibility. But then on April 13 or 14 we heard that Roosevelt, the president of the United States, had died. It seemed that everything inside me had been torn loose, that it had collapsed and grown dark. One quiet, sunny spring day, in a tiny puddle of melting snow far away from everyone else, I sat down on a stump and cried. Who could have known then that somewhere in the Altai, in a neglected corrective labor camp forgotten by everyone, ruined and defiled, an emaciated young prisoner lad was weeping over the death of the president of the United States of America! I had never ever, perhaps, felt as sorry for anyone as for Franklin Delano Roosevelt. I realized that with his death we political prisoners had no hope for any amnesty, not now or at any time over the course of our long prison terms. Unconsciously I understood that as long as Stalin was alive we would never see life in freedom. With Roosevelt's death that had become completely clear.

It may have been that the time had simply arrived—since nothing is ever without an end—or, more likely, the raging typhus epidemic had frightened some influential people in the city, but at last they began paying some attention to us. I learned from the talk among prisoners that the people running the camp had been arrested one after the other and that even some of the prisoners in administrative positions had been picked up. And soon we heard that Boyko, the work assignment clerk, had been given ten years. That was quite possible, because they quickly began getting the camp back in order again.

Once when I was in the barracks I heard someone say: "We've got work for carpenters and electricians."

Though I was neither one nor the other I immediately offered my services.

"Go and see brigadier Nosov."

They directed me to the farthest dugout where, not that long ago, I had spent some time in the company of piles of corpses. Nosov turned out to be a man still quite young; he was short, with a face that was artless yet conveyed a strength of will.

"What are you," he asked me, "carpenter or electrician?"

"Carpenter," I said, without giving it a moment's thought.

On the spot they presented me with a small saw, an axe, and even assigned me an assistant, a Belorussian lad named Kolka.

In the dugout, now completely abandoned, they had again laid down plank floors. Nosov gave us our first assignment.

"Over here," he pointed to a section of new flooring, "I want you to cut an opening for the foundation of the stove."

I can't say that I knew nothing at all about carpentry and woodworking. My father could turn his hand to anything, and even when I was a child, before the war, the two of us would work in the shed building a boat. I knew how to saw, plane, and square a plank. But I was utterly baffled at how I was to cut a hole through a flat, tightly laid plank floor. I hadn't the slightest idea of how to do it and where to begin. Still, I kept my composure.

"Kolka," I ordered my helper, "you begin here and I'll be right back."

I fled and hid, and when I returned I saw that Kolka was confidently working with the saw and had already cut through one plank; sawing the others didn't require much wit, and I set about it with the independent air of an experienced craftsman.

Then we got a new assignment.

"Trim up these posts," Nosov said to one of the carpenters, giving him the dimensions.

"You too," he told another, "but make them twenty by fifteen. And you do the same," he waved at me.

I had no idea what these dimensions were and how I was to measure them. I didn't hurry, though, and began keeping an eye on what my neighbor was doing. He set the log on a block of wood, took a length of string, and blackened it with charcoal. Then it all became clear, since I had mastered the skill of using an axe to square up a log.

And so, day by day, I became a carpenter. No one noticed that I was a complete novice at the trade.

Someone, evidently, was very worried: we were getting materials by the cartload. After decent lighting had been installed in the dugout we began working from dawn till dusk: the typhus epidemic urged us on. We built a hospital-infirmary: we laid floors, set up partitions, hung doors. I was already becoming a regular virtuoso at the job: I could drive in a hundred-millimeter nail with one blow when nailing down a floor. We slept right there, on the job site, after we had set up a *burzhuika* stove. And this was probably what saved us workers. We were isolated from the mass of people and even went to the mess hall separately, after everyone else.

Spring was already going full tilt; meltwater sparkled in the sun's rays; it became warm, and we would splash through the puddles in our gray *pimy*. They would get soaked through, and we had to dry them at nights on the stove and often scorch them. Then we devised some blocks to fit on our boots; these were like little benches that we tied to the soles with cords. Wearing these we had no fear of any puddle. Our feet would not bend, but we boldly splashed our way to the camp refectory without fear of soaking our felt boots.

Victory Day did not bring out any special enthusiasm in the camp. There was some excitement and bustle, enhanced perhaps by the lovely sunny weather—it was a truly warm day. No one shouted "Hurrah!" The *zeks* simply were happy that an amnesty would soon be declared and everyone would go home. It was a matter of complete indifference to me whether there was war or peace: war could not take anything more away from me, and peace promised nothing better. I had no doubt at all that the amnesty would not apply to us. It's true that in the depths of my soul there was an occasional flash of hope for a miracle, but common sense dampened that hope; life again became burdensome and dreary, and I was overwhelmed by a sense of doom.

In the Infirmary

Food in the camp improved somewhat, and all the *zeks* were examined by a medical commission. Those who were most frail were sent to recover in the infirmary, now set up in half of the hospital we had built. The carpenters and electricians in our brigade were also examined, and to my astonishment and to my delight that I could get some rest, I was admitted to the new sanatorium.

I hadn't experienced anything like this since my arrest. After our repairs, the dugout looked like new: the freshly planed boards on the walls made it brighter and filled it with the scent of pine. The bunks were now *vagonki*—double-tiered, in groups of four—and had new sheets, blankets, and pillows. Everything was white and clean. The patients were also issued new underclothes, and mine gave me an unaccustomed feeling of ease and freedom. We were on an enhanced diet. Our noon meal was a full bowl of *magara* soup with salt flatfish and porridge as well. We were allowed a portion of sugar daily, something we had not seen in a long time. Doctor Lysak would examine us every day in his dispensary behind a partition in the corner. He was a prisoner, about forty, a strapping fellow with a kind face and kind nature. A nurse attached to the infirmary would pass out thermometers regularly and record our temperatures three times a day. On the whole, I felt as if I had come to a resort.

The inhabitants of the infirmary were young people, scarcely more than boys. They fell upon the thick soup greedily and ate one dish after another. Emaciated and downtrodden when they were admitted, they put on weight and came to life right before my eyes. Soon they weren't able to remain lying in bed or sitting down. They ran and jumped about like goats, filling the infirmary with chatter from morning to evening. And to top it all, the long-awaited amnesty was then announced. With the exception of particularly dangerous repeat offenders, all the petty crooks, thieves, and hooligans, not to mention those who had a year's sentence for being late for work, were set free. And only those of us who were here under Article 58 or the law of August 7, 1932, who, as persons in responsible positions, had been sentenced for major theft and given ten years or a death sentence, were completely excluded from the amnesty. This no longer caused me any grief because I had seen it all coming; and though it is a painful thing to admit, I had steeled myself to the idea of erasing ten years of my life—the best years of my youth, as well—from my biography.

Unfortunately, I began to find the smell of the salt flatfish cooked with our *magara* porridge repulsive. Gradually, I became less and less able to finish my portion, and then I stopped eating that dish altogether. Then the oatmeal porridge began to make me feel sick as well. I stopped going to lunch and ate only my bread ration and drank sweetened hot water. It was obvious that I was losing weight; I felt weak and had to spend more time lying down.

The weather was wonderful and sunny. It was summer. They began sending the young, recovering patients to work at the Biysk meatpacking plant. They would come back in the evenings satisfied and full of enthusiasm, even though the sausage, lard, and other meat products they brought back had been confiscated when they were searched at the camp entrance. I didn't go anywhere and spent more and more time lying down. When I got up from my bunk, everything would go dark and I couldn't see. Before walking anywhere, I would have to stand for a time until my vision was restored. When I left the dugout, I would again go blind from the sunlight. I couldn't see the sun but only could sense the strong light. Again I would have to stand until things grew clear. Then I would be able to walk, but it was as if I didn't feel the ground beneath my feet, as if I were floating on air but somehow did not fall.

One day I asked the nurse who was collecting my thermometer, "What's my temperature?"

"Forty," she replied.

I didn't believe her and assumed she was joking. But no, she showed me her chart. Opposite my name was "40."

"And what was it yesterday?" I asked.

She showed me what she had recorded over many days. Everywhere, both morning and evening, my temperature was the same. Dr. Lysak had written on my card: "Dystrophy, second degree." I noticed that I could make out not only every bone on my body but even segments of bones. The little creases along the edge of the hip bone were particularly noticeable. And my arms and legs were nothing but bones, thin and protruding. I realized that my days were numbered. I would lie for days on end without getting up, eating nothing and even trading my bread ration for a portion of sugar that I would dissolve in water and drink. This became my only nourishment. When the boys came back from the meatpacking plant and saw me they would say, laughing, "Fox, you're going to croak for sure."

I already knew that. Yet I was indifferent: perhaps I had just reconciled myself to dying. It was the second half of July. I don't know why, but I had no doubts that I would not live until September; this was going to be the last month of my life. I wanted only to die on some date with a nice round number. I assessed the strength I had left and set the date as August 15. That date seemed appropriate, and I decided that no matter what, I would manage to live until then, firmly convinced that it was precisely on that day that I would die. I had no fear and did not think about anything, I simply lay and waited out the allotted span of my life, feeling neither pain nor hunger nor longing of any kind.

Life around me went on at its measured, sometimes even busy pace. Everyone else was in an elevated mood: any day they expected that they would begin being set free. They ate their fill at the meatpacking plant. There was even one major event: when he left for work at the meatpacker's, Muzover, a little Jewish kid, escaped. He was sentenced under the "seven-eight" (the law of August 7, 1932), and the amnesty would not include him. The rumor was that he had planned to escape along with the work assignment clerk, Balykov, who that day was also going to the meatpacker's. But Balykov stayed in camp. That day they brought the workers home early. The guards were furious, and there was a terrible fuss. The next day no one was taken out of the zone. All the guards rushed off on the search for Muzover. A week passed—Muzover had vanished. They stopped searching for him after requesting a countrywide manhunt.

At that time they began releasing group after group of amnestied prisoners. The camp was due to be closed. The remaining group of 150 people was prepared for transport.

On one of the last days in July I had a talk with Lysak.

"The transport's almost ready," he said. "Can you make it to the dock?"

"I'll make it," I replied mechanically.

CHAPTER SIXTEEN

The Transport to Chistyunlag

And then there was a miracle. The day the transport was to leave, I, like the others, got dressed and left Biysk Camp in a crowd of my fellow prisoners who still had to serve out their sentences. It was about three kilometers to the dock. First we had to pass through the city. Biysk, as I'd heard, had a population of one hundred thousand, but it was more like a village than a city. There were tiny houses, wattle fences through which hung the yellow heads of sunflowers, and small, unpaved side streets. Only one major street, Lenin Street, with a monument to the leader and a red-brick vocational school, had its traffic lanes paved with cobblestones.

I found it interesting to have a look at Biysk; it distracted me and because of that, probably, I was able to go on mechanically putting one foot in front of the other. These new impressions gave me added strength. We came down the river. The Biya is a small river, shallow but navigable. We crossed to the other side on a wooden bridge that led to a small dock resembling a barge. We settled ourselves along the riverbank to wait for the boat to arrive, and it was not long in coming.

To me, who grew up along the full-flowing Oka and knew the Volga with its many large ships, this little single-decker didn't seem like a passenger vessel at all. We were loaded into a compartment below that had portholes and hard couches. I found a place at the side of the boat and spent the whole trip watching the riverbanks slip past, low and with bits of greenery beyond the sun-dappled water.

I thought the Biya was a pretty river, a cheerful one. Every once in a while our little boat would make a stop right beside the riverbank and exchange a few passengers. Before one of these stops, as the boat was carefully tucking itself against a low but steep riverbank, I suddenly heard a shot and a loud shout from the deck above: "Hands up!"

I looked out of the porthole. On the edge of the bank stood Muzover, his ChTZ shoes slung over his shoulder, his face frozen in an expression of amazed surprise. More than a week had passed since his escape, and evidently, counting on the fact that they had stopped searching for him, he had decided to travel farther away by boat. How could he know that this was the boat carrying our transport escorted by guards who knew him and were furious at him?

Muzover was taken on board under guard and held in a separate cabin. "He's in for it now!" said one of our boys.

The boat sailed on all night, running aground a few times, and in the morning we disembarked at the mouth of the Biya. At this point, where the Biya flows into the Ob, there was a large village and a dock.

They had to help me off the boat, since I was unable to walk any farther unaided. We spent almost the whole day lying about on the riverbank, waiting for the next stage of the transport. Timidly at first, and one at a time, the villagers began coming up to us, one bringing some bread, another some boiled potatoes. But then, obviously growing bolder and seeing that the guards were not interfering, whole crowds of them, whole families, came up, all of them wanting to feed us. They brought all sorts of things: flatcakes, pans full of fried potatoes, dill pickles, meat, fermented milk. Never in my life had I seen such compassion from one group of people for another, the well-fed for the hungry, those who lived well for the unfortunate. We were literally surrounded by consideration and concern. I wasn't able to get up and was lying off to one side, but they noticed me and I could hear them saying, "Give something to that fellow over there, he's sick."

And they brought me all sorts of food. But I didn't need anything: I drank only some of the tasty *ryazhenka,* made of rich fermented and baked milk. I gave the rest to others, though they had been very well fed and had managed to stock up on supplies for the rest of the journey.

Then we set off by boat again along the Ob. The Ob is a broad, severe river. From midstream you can see both banks, covered in evergreen forest, far in the distance. On the horizon you can see the blue foothills of the

Altai. This is a gloomy landscape, one that leads you to deep thoughts, yet it is beautiful.

The next morning we disembarked at Uch-Pristan. It was a thirty-kilometer trip to our destination. I, the Estonian Loite, and three other weakened prisoners were unable to walk. They left us, and a little later we were taken on to a passing train of oxcarts. Teams of oxen were used to haul timber—huge trunks thicker than a man could reach his arms around—from Uch-Pristan to the camp. It was my luck that there was some sort of a door or fence gate on one of the carts. They laid me down on this.

This was the first time I had seen a team of oxen. They walked slowly, occasionally waving their tails, blinking from time to time to rid themselves of the flies that troubled them. By the end of the day we had arrived at the commandant's camp sector of Chistyunlag. Everything indicated that this camp had not been built yesterday and that it had been built in a proper fashion. The barracks were made of adobe brick that had been plastered and whitewashed. Not far from the camp entry there was a little grove of poplars; beyond it was the recreation room, and a little farther the two blocks of the hospital, the surgical and the therapeutic sections.

Kondakov, an old doctor and former prisoner who had served a ten-year sentence in this camp, examined me. He listened carefully to my heart, tapped my chest, shook his head and said scarcely a word. A day or two later he sent me to the second half of the therapeutic building where there was a section for tuberculosis patients. There I was met by none other than Dr. Lysak, who had arrived from Biysk after us. He was surprised when he saw me.

"When I sent you off on transport," he said, "I assumed that along the way . . ."

He stopped himself from saying more, but I knew very well what he meant.

There were two wards in the TB section, Ward 8 and Ward 9. Those from Ward 8 went on to the infirmary for further recovery, or to Ward 9. There was only one way to get out of Ward 9—on a cart inside a covered box painted in red lead. The cart would move past the zone and through the entrance, where the guard would open up the cover and strike the deceased's head with a hammer to ensure that there was no mistake—that no living person was being hauled out of the camp.

They put me in Ward 8.

I had spent twenty months in confinement. A hundred more lay ahead.

A. E. KROPOCHKIN

MEMOIRS OF
FORMER PRISONER
SL-208

On February 22, 1947, the iron door to one of
the cellars in the inner prison of the Tomsk MGB
slammed shut behind me.

Now, many years later, when I call to mind the
events of that terrible time, I can scarcely believe the
dread that gripped my very soul during the interrogations, the torture of sleep deprivation, hunger,
and isolation cells. The whole prison routine and the
system of "processing" a person through interrogation
almost always produced the result the torturers desired: a person in a state of semi-delirium would sign
whatever the investigator wanted. I signed as well.

Then, during the almost nine years that followed
my trial, came a succession of transit prisons, regular
prisons, camps, and transports.

The sixth and last transport on my journey was
to the copper mines of Dzhezkazgan. As the "leader"
of a counterrevolutionary group I was given the
"honor" of working at the ore face. Those who were
dying in the copper mines asked their comrades who
were destined to remain among the living and to
return to freedom to tell the whole terrible truth
about these camps.

As one of the survivors, I am carrying out the
request of my comrade, Aleksandr Aleksandrovsky,
with whom I shared four years of imprisonment and
who was not destined to see freedom. I was on five
transports before Dzhezkazgan, and the first of them
was to Asino.

CHAPTER ONE

The Transport to Asino

There were five of us in the cell: three students from Tomsk University; Vaska, a tractor driver from the Kozhevnikov Region; and a priest, Father Pitirim. We were all short-termers, the five of us having a total of thirty-three years under Article 58, paragraphs 10 and 11. Someone had slipped up with Father Pitirim, who had somewhere offered prayers to the glory of the Russian people who had taken up arms to overcome the enemy: he had ten years.

Vaska's story was rather different from anything I came to see and hear in the years that followed. When he was a little boy in the village, his grandmother Yermachikha had asked him to take some moistened bread and paste a piece of notebook paper on the door of the kolkhoz office. As he learned later, during his interrogation, the paper said that Soviet power came from the Antichrist because it had destroyed the church and that the kolkhoz likewise was not one of God's institutions.

He received a handful of candies for carrying out this little chore and thought no more about it. At the time he was only eight years old. In 1947, he was seventeen and was the best tractor driver on the kolkhoz. He had finished four grades in the village school, and Granny Yermachikha had long been dead. Then the organs of state security charged him under Article 58, paragraph 10, the distribution of leaflets with propagandistic intent directed at undermining the system of collective farms and socialism. Vaska's deed cost him ten years.

And so we were in the transport cell waiting to be sent to a camp. We had told and retold each other all the details of our arrests and interrogations and had described the behavior of our interrogators. When the head of the prison made his rounds we asked: "Could we please have something to read, Citizen Chief?"

To our amazement, the next morning, along with our soup, we were given a thick volume, its frayed pages so well thumbed that holes had worn into them. It was Victor Hugo's *The Hunchback of Notre Dame.* Three of

359

us took turns reading it aloud: the priest and Vaska were barely literate. Father Pitirim's eyes even welled up with tears when the reading was finished, and he said, "May the Kingdom of Heaven be theirs"—meaning Esmeralda and Quasimodo—though at first he had not wanted to listen to the reading of this heretical book.

These were the last days of August 1947. About a month had passed since my trial. On one of those days, right after breakfast, the cell door was thrown open. The head of the prison entered and with him was a man in civilian clothes. "Collect your belongings," came the order. We three students were taken out of the block. Father Pitirim made the sign of the cross over us, and Vaska's eyes were full of tears.

"Last name, first name, patronymic, year of birth, article, term?"

Now we would hear these six questions repeated many, many times on transports, in transit prisons, and in cells as we left or entered them.

"Hands behind your backs, no talking, no looking to left or right, no looking back. March!"

These five commands were to be a part of our lives until our terms ended.

Before us rose the blank prison wall of the old transit prison in Tomsk. A "Black Maria" stood at the gate. We stepped uncertainly over the cobblestone courtyard, our legs like cotton wool. The summer sun shone down, and our heads swam from the fresh air; there were smiles on our faces. How radiant the day seemed after the semi-darkness and stifling air of the cell! Just twenty or thirty paces and the barred door of the Black Maria slammed shut behind us.

We drove for ten or fifteen minutes and came to the station. We arrived just before the train was to leave. They pushed us into the prison car, where we found fifteen or twenty men. We spoke quietly among ourselves. And we had but one question: where are they taking us? Someone proposed, correctly as it turned out, that we were going to Asino (a settlement on the bank of the Chulyma River, a large center for transshipping timber, with a woodworking plant and a mill that made railway ties).

The camp guardhouse, and again: "Last name, first name, patronymic, article, term?"

And so here we were, inside the camp. We looked about us. The first things that struck us were the people bustling about, the rows of squat barracks, the windows without bars. Someone shouted, "Work assigner to the guardhouse!" Before us, as if he has sprung out of the ground, appeared a tall man with a piece of board under his arm and a pencil behind his ear.

"Put them into brigades," commanded a man in a lieutenant's uniform who then turned and went into the guardhouse; we followed the work assigner to the barracks. Two women were coming toward us along the plank sidewalk, and one of them seemed familiar to me. I couldn't believe my eyes . . . Yes, indeed, it was her, a professor of history at Tomsk University named Faina Heyfitz. The year before she had said good-bye to us as she left for Moscow (her new history textbook, coauthored by a professor from Moscow University, was being published there, and she was going to make the final editorial changes before it went to press). But she ended in Asino, not Moscow, with ten years under Article 58, paragraph 10. We didn't ask what she had done. It was all for the same thing—anti-Soviet agitation, and of course a professor has many more opportunities for that than does a student.

The next morning we went out to work for the first time. It was in the railway tie mill. When the sawn tie came out of the machine we had to roll it off the gantry and down a couple of planks laid aslant where two men would pick it up and add it to the stack.

From a distance, this seemed like easy work, but after about two hours my arms were aching; I saw spots before my eyes, and my legs began to give way. But the saws kept spinning, whining madly, and tie after tie came flying down. If I miss even one, I thought, I'll be hit by the next beam coming at me, but . . . there was the whistle for lunch. The whine of the saw and the crash of timber died away and everything came to a halt. People from every corner of the work zone were making their way to the overhang where they had brought two kettles of food. The soup was served into little pots, tin cans, cracked crockery. I had no dish and stood to one side, not knowing what to do.

They had nearly finished giving out the food when a young lad, covered with sawdust and no more than a boy, came up to me and wordlessly handed me a tin pot.

"Leave some," he said brusquely and went off.

The cook ladled some soup into this rusty pot and tossed in a scoop of porridge as well. For some reason, everyone ate their bread separately. I drank my portion from the pot and fished out the porridge from the bottom using a crust of bread. At this point, the boy came back, took the pot, and looked into it. It was only then that I realized what he had meant when he said "Leave some." I was supposed to pay for his favor.

"Cheap bugger," he said, as he grabbed the pot.

Thus I had my first lesson in camp law: you have to pay for everything—the butt-end of a cigarette, a ration, a portion of soup. Someone showed me where I could get a tin of the right size for lunch at the work site. You weren't allowed to bring these back to the camp, so each person hid his here, on the spot: one would bury his in a pile of sawdust; another would shove his under a log or a pile of chips.

I can't clearly recall how I managed to keep working until the shift ended, but I could see that all the joints in my shoulders and elbows had swollen to such a size that I was afraid to look at them. The next day I went to the camp infirmary and managed to get off work.

CHAPTER TWO

The Transport to Gorevka

About two weeks later some hundred men were not taken out to work. A rumor went round that a transport was being formed up. It was only later, when I myself had been on more than one transport, that I realized how worked-up the whole camp would be before a transport. The many unknowns are a worry: where are they taking us? Will it be better or worse? What if it's cutting trees or working in a mine? People would run through all the possible and impossible variants when they talked, but their speculations never proved to be right.

First of all, we realized that it was those with shorter terms—ten years or less—who were being kept back from work. Some even speculated that we would no longer have to work under guard. And with my five-year term I was sure to be one of them.

In any case, by evening we had all been photographed, both in profile and full face; our fingerprints had been taken and checked against our record cards; boots and pea jackets were issued to those whose clothing was in very bad shape (meaning that the soles of their boots were tied on with a bit of cord or wire and the pea jacket or padded coat was nothing more than rags).

We were formed up in fives and counted, first inside the camp and once more outside the gate; then, with our escort of guards and dogs, we moved off to the railway station. There we were handed over to the guards escorting the transport. Another check, another count, and into the railway cars. We had to stand packed tightly together.

"Do you think they're going to haul us away standing, like this?" asked some who had not been on transport before.

"No, they're going to assign us to two-berth compartments," others joked gloomily.

By evening we had arrived at Anzherskaya Station. It was early November. Again a check and a recount. There were ninety of us (eighteen groups of five) and, herded along by the guards and their dogs, our column stretched out along the road. Breaking ranks, barely able to drag our feet out of the mud mixed with snow, we moved slowly southwards along a road through the taiga.

A cold, gusty wind was blowing, blinding us with wet snow. Our jackets became soaked through.

"Close up! Close up!" shouted the guards.

The dogs bark hoarsely, choking as they pull at their leashes. As in a dream, we drag ourselves along through the driving snow, the barking dogs, the shouted commands. The dogs, now tired, are calmer; the guards, also tired, no longer urge on the tired prisoners. Around us on all sides stands the forest, like a solid, dark wall. We go on . . .

It had become quite dark when, in the midst of this dense, godforsaken taiga, we suddenly came upon some lights in the windows of houses. It was a forest settlement, most likely a logging enterprise. The guards do not escort prisoners through the taiga at night, so we'll get some rest. Let's get ourselves into the warmth, quick now; we'll get dry at least and maybe even get a ration. The deathly fatigue had dulled our hunger, but they halted the column. We stand and wait.

Fifteen or twenty minutes later, a sleigh drove up. A pair of emaciated nags was barely able to pull it. There were people lying on the sleigh. These were the laggers, the exhausted (the "goners"). The guard escorting the sleigh began pulling the people off to get them back in the ranks. Two of them, barely able to drag their legs along, got back in the ranks; two more stayed lying on the sleigh. The guard, in a rage, ran around the sleigh trying to rouse them with shouts and threats. And when he had convinced himself that he could not rouse them by shouting, he began beating them with the butt of his submachine gun. Suddenly, as if he had grasped something, he jumped away from the sleigh and shouted to the crowd of prisoners: "Any doctors here? Well, best have a look at them. They faked it so they could have an easy ride—right, you contras?"

A stocky man with a black beard—a doctor from a Kiev hospital, as we later found out—stepped out of the crowd. He later was to become the doctor at the camp first-aid post.

The black-bearded fellow went up to the men lying on the cart and checked their pulses.

"They're dead," he said, addressing not the guard but us. This had been obvious enough, though, when the guard was beating these motionless bodies with the butt of his weapon.

"So they got here," someone said quietly, but in the deathly silence everyone heard it. Even the dogs had stopped their howling and snarling.

It grew colder, the sky cleared and bright stars appeared. We stood, not knowing what was to happen next. The guards had a whispered consultation about something and then came the command: "Form up in fives!"

In the darkness it took us a long time to sort ourselves out and line up properly. Again there were shouts, cursing, and dogs barking, while we tried to squeeze into the middle of the row of five so as not be on the outside or in the last row, closest to the guard and the fangs of the dogs. Soon it was obvious that it was impossible to get us formed up. Two guards passed their weapons to their comrades and began pulling people out of the crowd. Punching them on the back of the neck, they led them off in groups of five to some sort of cabin without a roof, windows, or doors. In such fashion, after a half hour of turmoil and confusion, we had been counted and installed in this cattle pen. How they were able to fit ninety men into this partially built little cabin is beyond me. Now the only thing that was clear was that we would have to spend the night in the cold, standing. We were ordered not to make noise. People spoke in hushed voices, making speculations and guesses.

"They've herded us in here so we'll all freeze."

"Not all of us. There'll be a selection. Natural selection."

"They don't need any goners in the camp."

"Croaking's better than this . . ."

"They just have to pour water over us and we'll all be heroes, like General Karbyshev."

"That was the Germans . . ."

"Our own people here are worse."

"They should give us our rations. Let's demand that."

And so, first in uncertain voices, then louder and louder: "Rations! Rations!"

Then everyone, in a surge of despair, began yelling: "Rations!"

We would listen for a minute or two and then, again: "Rations!"

Bursts of machine-gun fire crackled from two sides, striking the top of the cabin; chips rained down on our heads and everything grew silent. And suddenly amidst this stillness rose up a high voice, almost in a screech: "Go ahead and shoot, you bastards, we'll all be dead by morning anyway!"

And again, ninety voices bawled out: "Rations!"

Once again we listened.

During one of those moments when we had all grown quiet we heard someone approach the cabin.

"Listen, now, you contras! There's one loaf for five men. Divide it up yourselves, and no noise!"

And after this warning loaves of bread began raining down on us inside the cabin. Immediately a silent scuffle began. We rummaged about at our feet; someone managed to grab a loaf from the shoulders of his neighbor. Then suddenly a deep bass voice rang out from the moving mass:

"All the bread goes to the center. If any one of you bastards even takes a bite from a loaf I'll rip out his throat. Now form a circle!"

And we did the impossible: we squeezed even more closely together and cleared a circle a meter wide in the center. From all sides we carefully passed the loaves from one to another and laid them out on the damp chips that covered the ground. That was all. Everyone began counting. There should have been eighteen loaves; we counted seventeen. The same voice said:

"We'll have a *shmon* right now. If we find somebody's stashed away a loaf, he can say good-bye to his life."

Someone suggested that we search around our feet, and a minute later from the darkness in one of the corners came the cry: "I've got it!"

They passed the eighteenth loaf to the pile.

A few dry wood chips were found among the damp ones on the ground, and by their dim, smoky light the loaves were broken up into individual rations of two hundred grams apiece. There was no need to check. There could not have been more than five or six grams difference among them, even if they had been weighed on the most precise scales.

Those who have been on more than one transport know how a loaf can be measured by eye and divided with absolute accuracy without a knife. A strong piece of string or cord was found, and the loaf was cut exactly into five equal rations. When they issued rations in the mess hall or outside, people would stand close behind each other—your turn comes, you get your ration. And woe to the one who gets into line a second time to pinch a second ration. They would take away what he already had and then beat him until the warder or the guard stepped in; and in such cases even they weren't in any hurry to rescue him.

But how were we to distribute bread here, in the dark, with people so tightly packed together that a bread loaf had no room to fall to the ground? There were many suggestions, but at last one was accepted: we would form rows of ten, everyone facing the center where the bread was and where a burning splinter of wood gave some light. It took us no less than an hour to get ninety men formed up in this way. Finally the bread began to be handed out. The first man in the row would get a piece, and he would pass it to the man behind him, and so on, until it reached the man at the end. This last man would say, "Got it," meaning that the ration had arrived. This would go on until the first man got his share, and then the same thing would happen with the next row, until the shout came: "Ten men fed!"

Thanks to the efforts of a man who obviously knew what he was doing, every one of us got his 200-gram ration of half-baked bread. We had to respect this fellow. He was tall, broad as an ox, and wore a canvas raincoat with a hood pulled over a uniform cap of a captain in the river transport. But that voice! I never heard a deep bass voice like that before or after the camps. He eventually became brigadier of a carpenters' brigade in the camp, but more about that later. We made short work of our ration.

The black-bearded man who had said he was a doctor when he examined our dying comrades stepped out to the light and said: "Listen, all of you who want to stay alive. Don't fall asleep! Falling asleep here in the cold means death. Move around a bit, press close to each other, but don't fall asleep!"

CHAPTER THREE

Sleep

How quickly the days pass! It is a quiet summer morning. I'm walking through a pine forest. Above me is a bottomless blue sky. The air is full of the fragrant freshness of birch and pine.

In the dark green grass covered with morning dew are patches of large, juicy wild strawberries. I don't want to step on the berries and go around the edge of the clearing.

I am very sleepy. I lie down under a pine tree. The leaves and pine needles aren't covered with dew, though, but with cold hoarfrost, and a voice keeps whispering to me, "Don't fall asleep! Don't fall asleep!" I struggle against it but . . . fall asleep from the cold that grips my whole body.

And then the terrible reality returns . . . A living mass of people, all in a state of semi-delirium, semi-sleep, were trying to get through this terrible, nightmarish night. The cold gripped our bodies more and more tightly. We didn't want to keep moving; we had no strength left even to stand on our feet, and we began squatting; and then sleep simply struck us down, one by one, and we managed to doze for twenty or thirty minutes.

At the first gleam of daylight we heard the command: "Come out and form up!"

Kneading our numbed arms and legs, we began to drag ourselves out of the cabin. And again: "Form fives! First five, four step forward! Second five! Third . . . Eighteenth!"

There was no eighteenth. Last night there had been three men in it, today not a single one. The guards rushed into the cabin. There were crude oaths and blows.

They dragged out three men, one after the other. Their unnaturally twisted bodies showed that they had fallen asleep forever. The dogs were about to attack them but drew back at once, growling, their tails between their legs. Now there were five bodies on the sleigh. Again the shouts: "Close up!"

The dogs barked. Soon the forest seemed to grow sparser; stacks of logs had been piled along the road. Now we realized that they were taking us to cut timber.

In the evening we reached the camp. The zone was fenced in by a stockade of tightly fitted logs with sharpened tops; there was a heavy gate made of slabs and a guardhouse—a little hut with two tiny windows. They marched us some distance away from the guardhouse, since we had to make room for a brigade coming back from work. They came in, emaciated, faces blackened with soot, heads bent. Later we understood why they all had black faces. At the logging site everyone tried to warm themselves by getting as close as possible to the fire. They were reluctant to wash in snow, and there was no water in the washstands in the camp.

And so we were in the zone. We hadn't managed to have a good look around before the warder commanded: "To the barracks, march!"

The order made no sense because we had not seen any barracks. We stood, gazing around us.

"What are you waiting for, a special invitation?" roared the warder.

Only then did we make out in front of us a dark hole with steps leading downwards. We felt our way down the five steps and opened the door. The first one who entered the barracks shouted, "Boys, this is an air raid shelter!"

Then, as if on command, we threw ourselves at the door, crushing one another. There were curses, a regular jam . . . If it was a dugout shelter, then it would have bunks, and each of us wanted a place as far as possible from the entrance, from the *parasha,* and, if fortune smiled on us, on the upper bunks where it was warmer.

The dugout into which they had herded us was quite roomy, dark, and damp. It had two-tiered bunks made of rough slabs and tiny windows at ground level that let in scarcely any light. Where the bunks ended, closer to the exit, was a stove made from an old oil barrel. The stove was red-hot, but the air in the dugout was damp and filled with the smell of fresh earth and pine. Flashes of light from the burning logs darted across the walls, lighting up a few faces in the darkness.

After the noise and the squabble for places on the bunks came a silence. Someone was rummaging in his bag; another had taken off his boots and was rubbing his feet. There was quiet talk about the dugout: some said it looked like a mass grave, others complained that the bastards had beaten us out of our supper. We had no strength left to beg for our legal ration, let alone demand it. Soon the talk died out completely; deathly tired, hungry people sank into a heavy sleep filled with snores, coughs, and unintelligible mutterings. The burned-out embers smoldered in the stove and then died altogether.

When the deep sleep of exhausted people was broken by the shout of "Reveille!" none of us could comprehend that the night had already passed.

The men got up reluctantly and drew on their clothes.

The next command came: "Outside and form up!"

No one was in a hurry to be the first out, since he had to stand in the cold and wait for all the others.

"Out you get, and nobody better be last!" shouted the work assigner.

This meant that the last man out of the barracks would feel the blow of a stick. We were formed up by the barracks. A man dressed in a short white sheepskin coat with the shoulder straps of a lieutenant came up; he was stocky, with a Mongolian-type face.

"So, did you contras have a good rest?"

There was only gloomy silence in reply. "You'll be working inside the zone. Keep at least twenty paces from the forbidden zone; the sentry will open fire without warning. Axes will be issued at the guardhouse and you'll sign for them. Losing or hiding an axe is considered preparation for an attack on the camp guards. You'll get fifteen years for that. Is that clear? Any questions?"

"Why weren't we given our rations yesterday?"

"Ask the guards who brought you here about that," said the camp commandant, with a barely perceptible smirk. "Don't leave the barracks at night, submit any complaints to me personally, through your brigadier. As for the rest, the law here is the law of the taiga and the prosecutor is the bear," he said, repeating an old camp saying that every *zek* had known for a long time.

From the way our young camp chief spoke, it was obvious that he enjoyed his unlimited power over hungry people who had no rights.

Our brigade of Article 58ers was building a barracks.

One day, as spring was approaching, we had a visit from some officials from Siblag.

"The camp authorities are complaining about your poor work," began one of the officials who had come to check on us. "We're going to find the saboteurs and send them to a punishment camp."

"It can't be any worse than this," someone said quietly.

"Who said that? Two paces forward!"

To our great surprise, out of the ranks stepped our brigadier—that same riverboat captain who had divided up the bread on our transport. He would rouse the exhausted sloggers from their bunks by force and by curses: if a man ever stopped getting up from his bunk he would never be able to stand on his feet again. We knew this as well as our brigadier did, but not every man was able to overcome the overwhelming heaviness he felt in every part of his body, particularly in his legs. The legs were the first to go. Every morning, we had to make the daunting climb up the five steps from the dugout; and we, pushing one another on, would overcome them, though the effort was greater with each passing day.

"I said it, Citizen Chief. And I'll say as well that they don't give us any bread for three days running, that we're being eaten up by lice, that we don't have any strength left to climb the walls we're building and have to push one another up to do the work. We don't fulfill the norm because we're on our last legs; the criminals are stealing our rations . . ."

We stood, our heads bowed, and a silence set in that was so oppressive we could hear the breathing of this whole group of filthy, ragged people with emaciated faces who pressed close to each other. The pause continued.

"We'll look into it," said the official, curtly yet in a tone somehow less than official, as he looked intently at the camp commandant standing stiffly at attention before him and who now seemed to us so insignificant and pathetic.

We waited in vain for any sudden changes for the better after the visit of the officials. Everything remained the same.

Spring in the taiga comes late, but April did bring warmth and bright, sunny days. We seemed to recognize each other anew. They allowed us to build a bonfire inside the zone to heat our clothing for disinfection. We would undress by the fire, trying to bring what were once called underclothes as close as possible to the heat. From a distance, this looked like some dance of skeletons covered with gray gooseflesh. The experiment with roasting our clothing ended with the underclothes getting even blacker from the soot and accumulating more holes from burns. The insects in the seams of the clothes went on living there.

Then some of the more inventive people tried heating two bricks and using them like an iron to run over the seams of their underclothes. This was also useless, and in a frenzy they would use the hot brick to beat the underclothes; bloody spots from the crushed insects would show where the men had struck.

By the beginning of summer, the size of the brigade had been reduced by half, and the barracks we were building was less than half done. Even before the winter, a pit had been dug just outside the zone so that there had been no need to dig separate graves in the frozen earth for every man who died. The corpses were thrown into the pit, earth was leveled over them and some grass and moss tossed on top.

No news from the outside came to this godforsaken taiga wilderness, just as there was no way for us to cry out from here to our families and dear ones.

The endless monotony of reveille, work, and lights-out that consumed the soul and the body and transformed a man into little more than an animal was broken one day when I was summoned to the guardhouse. For a *zek* in camp, a summons to the guardhouse means either trouble or joy. The joy might be a visit from relatives or an order for release; anything else that happens there may not be trouble, but it's no joy either.

When I stepped across the threshold of the guardhouse, I immediately spotted my sister Anya. She was sitting on a bench in the corner, and only a low partition separated us. It was her dear, kind face. But why did she glance past my face with a distracted look and then gaze at the warder who had brought me in? Of course—she didn't recognize me, though it hadn't been a year since we parted.

One spring day after it had rained I was bending over a puddle near the barracks to have a wash and I saw the reflection of my face as if in a mirror. Some stranger was gazing back at me, a man with sunken eyes and rough bristles grown over the dirty skin that covered his skull. It occurred to me at the time that even my own mother wouldn't have recognized me.

And now, what I had thought had come true. We stood opposite one another for a moment until I said: "Hi, Anya."

Fear and amazement flashed in her eyes simultaneously. She gazed at me wide-eyed, still unable to believe that her own brother was standing before her. The only thing I can remember from our brief, disjointed conversation was her question: "Why have they done this to you?"

Indeed, many years after they had taken away my freedom and after I had regained a relative freedom, I asked myself the same question again: "Why? What for?" And I answered it myself using the words of one seedy fellow who had told me when we were discussing the repressions, "They didn't arrest people for nothing."

And in fact they didn't. You only have to start digging back in your memory, recalling the things you've done. And if you've forgotten, the interrogator will remind you when he questions you: where, when, in whose presence was this sentence or this word uttered? And only a single word might be enough for them to suspect you of disloyalty, of disrespect for the existing order, for the "leader" or for your own boss. That was enough for them to roll out a whole case of anti-Soviet activity. "If we've got a man, then we'll make the 'case'"—that was the joke the interrogators made in those days.

They hammered into our stupid Pioneer-Komsomol brains, into our consciousness from early childhood, that freedom of speech and freedom of the press were guaranteed by the Stalin Constitution; and we believed in this, just as we believed that we were living in the happiest and freest country, "... Where people breathe so freely." We believed it, without realizing that by freedom of speech and the press they meant the glorification of tyranny, hypocrisy, universal lying, denunciations, and the other features of the movement toward the "radiant future."

And if you did not engage in the glorification, if you voluntarily did not give yourself up to the power of this enormous, many-eyed monster with its long tentacles, then it would seize you and devour you and those close to you.

This monster was the Gulag.

And now, many years later, I cannot help but recall the words of the head of the Tomsk MGB, Lieutenant Colonel Volkov, who favored me with a summons for a chat. He began spreading his net from a distance:

"So, young fellow, judging by your diaries and stories that I read with real interest, you are plucky and far from stupid. And your university friends will say that there was no reason for us to pick you up. But now, as the investigation of your case is coming to an end, you probably realize what you have to be if you want to be called one of our own, a Soviet person. Your arrest should serve as a warning to other students that it is not only the Komsomol and the party organizations that stand on guard for ideology but we Chekists as well. Your arrest might give rise to a few more people who are unhappy with the existing order and Soviet power. Still, we had no choice but to arrest you. It's people like you who, tomorrow, might move from idle talk to action. As we know, every illness can be cured at an early stage of the infection."

This whole sermon was delivered in a calm, even voice, and an unsophisticated person might think that, in fact, this was really so and give thanks to these diagnosticians who had caught the illness at an early stage of its development.

They didn't allow me to speak to my sister. They made a complete mess of the bag of food she had brought. The warder, in a near frenzy, crushed every flatcake; he twice sifted through the homegrown tobacco; and then, at last, he handed me the bag of food. I was the first to have received a parcel here, in this godforsaken wilderness.

The brigadier brought back the parcel from the guardhouse. The camp riffraff did not dare attack him and take it away.

Some time earlier in the camp there had been an attempt at this. Three *urki* came into our barracks to get hold of some tobacco. We weren't about to give them anything, but when they demanded a share of our tobacco, the brigadier seized an axe and chased them right to the guardhouse. Since then, none of them had ever paid a visit to our barracks.

The summer was drawing to an end. Early autumn is beautiful in the taiga. The forest was adorned in colors from deep green to orangey-red. A warm, gentle sun heated the earth; the mosquitoes and other insects that had caused us as much suffering as the hunger had now disappeared. It was terrible to think that ahead of us lay bad weather, rain, snow, cold. Once again, there would be the darkness of the underground barracks and the hunger. Less than half the men were left in the brigade, and those who were still among the living could just barely manage to climb up on the walls of the barracks we were building and pick at them with their axes, trying to conserve enough energy to make it back to the barracks after "stand-down."

On one of those fine days I was called out to the guardhouse. The camp commandant was sitting at a small table; in front of him lay a thick file, my prison record. He checked the facts: last name, first name, patronymic, date of birth, article, term, date of arrest, court in which I was tried. All these questions had to be answered quickly and clearly.

"In ten minutes I want you at the guardhouse with your things," the camp chief said as he closed the file. "Turn in your axe to the warder," he added.

Since I was wearing all the things I owned I needed only to turn in my axe.

I was overcome by joy and hope. When I had discussed my case with people who knew about these things, they had told me that I, a former front-line soldier who had never been in German captivity, ought to be released after my complaints to Stalin.

I had written in my complaint: "Our dear commander, we, your soldiers, who have served you and our Motherland truly and faithfully, who have traveled the road of war . . ." and so on. I thought that my strongest argument in the complaint was that I had a letter of commendation and gratitude signed by him stating that we had saved him and his ministers "from Hitler's noose" (literally). And now I was suffering under the violence and tyranny of the organs of the MGB. ". . . Dear Leader, help us, your soldiers, and restore justice."

It was a warm September day. The road from the camp went through mown fields with birch pegs marking the boundaries; there were stacks of hay and straw that had not yet been gathered from the fields. So here was freedom, right at hand, though I still had been warned by the guard: "A step to the left or a step to the right will be considered an escape; I will open fire without warning."

But he, our guard escort, was a kind, decent lad, and he was taking me to freedom.

A girl was marching along beside me. She looked to be eighteen or nineteen. Talking in the ranks was not allowed. We looked at each other and smiled. Where did she come from, and why was she coming along with me? There were no women's camps in the district. Had she been arrested in Gorevka, perhaps? But then why was she wearing camp boots and a camp dress? Her little turned-up nose, her cheerfulness and the mischievous look of her dark eyes reached right into my soul. When I looked at her I couldn't help but feel happy and free. I glanced at her and thought, would the guard really shoot at her if she took a step to one side?

I thought to try asking her a question—how did she end up in Gorevka—and if the guard didn't cut our conversation short at once, then we could go on talking while we walked.

And so I asked her that. The guard kept silent. So, we were allowed to chat.

Galya—that was the girl's name—came from western Ukraine. She had a five-year sentence. Her father and mother had been arrested earlier, and she had been living with an aunt in the same village. Her "case" stemmed from the fact that one evening she had brought some water to three young lads. She gave them a drink and then forgot about it. Two years passed. When she reached the age of eighteen—on her birthday—they came to arrest her. During the interrogations, they tried to link her with the Banderists and promised that if she would point out the three lads and identify them they would let her go.

After two years she wasn't able to identify any of the people they brought before her. Finally, they convinced themselves that she really did not know anything and charged her simply with offering assistance to the Banderists. And after that, as usual, came the transports, the transit prisons . . .

She had come to Gorevka from the women's camp in Asino, Tomsk Oblast, without an escort. She had been a fetch-and-carry girl for the camp commandant, she had washed the floors in the security chief's office, and here she was on a transport to God-knows-where.

"They might even let you out," she said, "but they'll never let us Banderists go."

I tried to reassure her by saying that prisoners who were allowed to move around without escort would only be taken away to be set free, yet the worm of doubt kept gnawing away at my insides: what would happen tomorrow? Now I wanted this trip through the fields and patches of woodland to go on as long as possible. I felt so free and joyous now: after all, I had torn myself away from that hell where slowly but surely my life was ebbing away.

Toward evening we came to Yashkino Station. We stopped to spend the night in some rundown little house attached to the station. Judging by the way the guard spoke to the lady of the house, this was not the first time he had been here. I used my jacket as a pillow and don't remember falling asleep. I awoke suddenly, whether from the clatter or the screams, and a second later Galya came running into the little room where I slept.

"Help me," she whispered.

The guard, evidently, had not been expecting any resistance from the girl. He risked being charged, not for rape but for having a relationship with a prisoner, and he backed off. And so we sat there, pressed close together, and decided that if he should order her to leave this room we would go together. The rest of the night passed peacefully, although we didn't close our eyes. This guard didn't know the western Ukrainians, who believe that dishonor is the same as death. She could only have relations with a man out of love and according to law. We exchanged addresses. She asked me to write to her aunt, if I had the opportunity, and tell her when and where I had last seen her.

The two of us were taken to the transit camp at Yaya Station. There Galya and I parted.

"Good-bye," she said, in a voice that was barely audible.

Never again did I see such sad eyes, filled with tears . . . The gates of the women's prison closed behind her, while I, for some reason, was sent on to Novosibirsk.

What happened later upset my life in the camps completely and never allowed me to fulfill her request; and then even the address was lost from my memory.

They unloaded us from the railway car into a blind alley between the old pumping station and the icehouse. This was the beginning of 1905 Street, on which the transit prison was located. As fate had it, I had lived in the corner house at the junction of 1905 and Saltykov-Shchedrin streets in the 1930s.

During those terrible years of the 1930s, the residents of this street had already become accustomed to the almost daily movement of prison transports down the middle of the street. People or vehicles who encountered such groups would draw back to the sidewalks. The group of prisoners, closely surrounded by guards with dogs, would walk past, followed by glances filled with compassion, curiosity, and terror. Who were these people? Why had they been arrested? What crime had they committed? That was what I thought in those days as well when, as a boy, I watched those columns pass by.

Everyone stared at me when I stepped across the threshold of the transit prison. The first question was, "How long since you've been on the outside?"

And when they learned that it had been almost a year, their interest in me ended at once.

I surveyed the group of people in the barracks, and the words of the poet came to mind unbidden: "a motley crowd of faces, clothes . . ." Nothing better than that can be said about the transit prison. Here people were sorted out, sent on to some designated place, to a face-to-face encounter with witnesses, for supplementary interrogation or to give evidence in court in a trial of some acquaintances who had been arrested after they had. Others here would go off to their permanent residence—a labor camp. There was a continuous change of faces . . .

And in the meantime, there was only waiting and uncertainty, uncertainty and waiting. People were continuously making the circuit in the corridors that ran along the whole length of the barracks between the row of bunks and the wall opposite. They held their hands clasped behind their backs, arguing or discussing something. My barracks mates tried to convince me that I had left the camp not to be released but to get a "bonus," since the General Public Prosecutor's Office had supposedly protested all the five-year sentences given by provincial courts as insufficiently severe, and so those who had a "fiver" would get an eight- or ten-year sentence.

"That's ridiculous," I thought. "How can they increase everyone's sentence with no regard for the seriousness of the offense?"

Saintly naivete. They can! Ten days later I became convinced of it. It was in the same Tomsk Provincial Court, with its full-length portrait of Stalin behind the judge and the two assessors. There was a prosecutor, a defense lawyer, and a secretary—the complete image of the "most humane and fair" system of Soviet justice. There were questions from the court, answers from the prisoners . . . The court withdrew for deliberations. Then the sentence:

"In the name of the Russian Soviet Federated Socialist Republic, the Tomsk Provincial Court, in accordance with Article 58, points 10 and 11 of the Criminal Code, sentences Kropochkin, Aleksandr Evdokimovich, to ten years deprivation of freedom in a corrective labor camp."

In response I smiled at the prosecutor.

"Why are you so pleased, prisoner?"

"There's little to be pleased about, but it is amusing that from beginning to end both you and the defense lawyer have been giving speeches of indictment, not speeches for the defense."

At this point, it seemed to me that the prosecutor gave a self-satisfied smile.

But we were even more afraid that the case would be transferred from the court to the MGB for further investigation. That was more terrible than any sentence. And when they made me out to be someone who had organized and led a nonexistent criminal counterrevolutionary organization whose ultimate goal was to bring down the existing order, I made no objection and did not try to prove the absurdity of such a finding.

How could I ever try to prove to an investigator that three students, former front-line soldiers, could not bring down the existing order? Only yesterday, they had been defending that existing order with weapons in hand, an existing order that a German army, well equipped and armed to the teeth, had been unable to bring down. I thought this was a case strong enough to refute the accusation presented in court. But the hellish machinery of investigation that had been set in motion pulverized all my arguments and did not stop until it had delivered another bit of its production to the Gulag. And none of our reasoning, arguments, or evidence concerned it in the least.

CHAPTER FOUR

Transport to Baikonur

It was the end of February 1949. Two years had passed in remand prisons, camps, and on transfers. And now a train of freight cars with tiny barred windows was rushing along, taking us somewhere. If we could just catch a glimpse of the name of some station we would know where we were bound.

The first station we saw was Barabinsk. So it's westward. Then the guessing began ... Where are we going? If it's the northern Urals it's not good ...

No one in the car could predict our destination until we arrived at Petropavlovsk Station. Here we turned south, off the Trans-Siberian Railway.

Someone speculated that we were off to the coal mines of Karaganda. But they didn't take us off the train at Karaganda, and then everyone was at a loss. None of us knew that a workers' settlement called Baikonur existed on this earth, or that there were places like Dzhezkazgan, Kengir, Karsapkai, or Balkhash, where Steplag held complete dominion from its headquarters in Karaganda ...

We detrained at Novorudny Station. It was the end of February. It was noticeably warmer than it had been in Novosibirsk. The sun shone. The sky was a clear blue, and there was boundless steppe as far as the eye could see in all four directions. Our heads were spinning after a week in the freight car.

We saw a building.

"First five, five steps forward; second, third ... No looking around, no talking!"

We marched for two or three hundred meters and were loaded in cars on a narrow-gauge railway. These had been adapted for transporting *zeks*. I had never seen narrow-gauge railway cars before, and they all struck me as toylike, tiny, and unreal. They counted off ten groups of five.

"Where are we going?" This brief question was almost whispered to the railway man who supervised the train.

He replied just as briefly and quietly: "Baikonur."

It turned out that this workers' settlement lay ninety kilometers west of Dzhezkazgan.

The formalities of sending off our transport delayed us almost until evening. The clear, comparatively warm day was transformed by a gusty wind; flakes of snow flew about. The locomotive gave a short whistle and the cars, rocking from side to side and clattering across the junction points in the rails, carried us off to parts unknown. I don't know how far we had traveled when the train slowed until it was barely moving and finally stopped completely. A blizzard was raging outside. The howling and whistling of the wind merged into a hellish roar. It seemed that these little toy cars would be carried off into the steppe with us inside them.

We sat, pressing tightly against each other. A freezing draft blew through the car. Night fell. But even before night came, the car had become totally dark because the windows had been covered by snowdrifts. Now the car became a bit warmer. We lost all track of time in the pitch blackness and the roar of the storm. We heard the stamping of feet on the roof of the car and a barely audible voice: "Open the vents!"

But who knew where to find these vents and how to open them? It became unbearably stifling. People felt their way along the walls and ceiling of the car but found nothing that could be opened. We were buried alive in these boxes under banks of snow. The stench of urine and excrement filled the air. No toilet or *parasha* had been provided in these cars. This made our critical situation even worse. People began fainting. We managed to break through one of the little barred widows. But this did no good. The tightly packed snow outside would let no fresh air into the car, which now had become our gas chamber.

There were heartrending cries; people beat on the walls of the car with their fists and feet; we strained to listen, but there was only the silence of the grave; and then we could hear only the broken, hoarse breathing of doomed people.

"They'll write us off, boys, on account of a natural disaster," someone said.

"Shut up! We might as well sit quietly; they'll write us off anyway."

"Let's break out of the car."

"With what?"

"With our hands!"

I could feel my head beginning to spin and my thoughts becoming confused; then suddenly it dawned on me. I remembered how in 1938 three of us, all on a Komsomol draft, were traveling on a train people used to call a "Maksimka." It was a mixed freight and passenger train that took eight or ten days to drag itself along from Novosibirsk to Vladivostok. Half the train was freight cars, the other half passenger cars. We were in a passenger car with common sleeping platforms and no bedding. It got quite hot, and I found a little metal handle on a disk in the ceiling above me. The disk had openings in it, and you could turn it so these openings lined up with similar ones in the ceiling of the car. As the train moved, air drawn into the car would whistle through these vents. We had to look for this little handle in the middle of the car.

I spent a long time feeling my way along the ceiling of the car, found the wretched handle, and tried turning it this way and that. The disk wouldn't move: probably it had rusted tight. I took off one of my boots and began hammering the disk with my heel. I tried turning it again, but the disk wouldn't break free.

"You have to kick it," someone advised.

"Let's try it."

Four of us held up a fifth man. He lay on his back on our hands and kicked at the place where we guided his foot. After the third or fourth kick some rusty bits of metal sifted down from the ceiling and his foot caught in the vent opening. A faint bit of cold air wafted from this opening. The guards, evidently, had cleared the snow from around the vent caps on the roof of the car. They were also responsible for getting us to our destination alive. And they could be punished—not for our destroyed lives—no, not for that! We all knew that very well. They could be punished only for failing to deliver a labor force on time.

By turns we would bring those who had fainted up to this opening in the roof of the car for a breath of fresh air. And as soon as that man opened his eyes we would bring up another one.

We had lost track of time. We guessed, though, that it must be morning. People had been overcome by a kind of stupor, and it wasn't clear if they had fallen asleep while sitting on their haunches or if they had died. But no. If you listened intently you could hear barely audible breathing, weak groans, mutterings. We might have been buried, but we were still alive. Then suddenly from outside we thought we heard voices we could barely make out; yet our heightened sense of hearing could catch the sound, and we could not have been mistaken. Then there was a scraping along the wall of the car on the side where the windows were. We could make out the dim square of a barred window, and then some blows, the crash of the window grille being torn away, and bits of glass from the window, broken with the butt of a machine gun, rained down on us with a jangle. A guard's face drew near the window.

"All of you sit on the floor. Don't stick your heads out of the window. We'll shoot without warning."

"Water! Water!" came the shouts from the car.

"Quiet!" barked the guard. "Or I'll give you a drink you won't forget."

"Water! . . ."

Fifteen or twenty minutes later, someone thrust a piece of caked snow through the window, and then another one. People rushed at the snow, elbowing one another and trampling on as much as they picked up.

"So, fascist, you decided to go on living, did you?" This was said by a Kazakh in a fox fur cap whose smiling face blocked the whole window. So it was the local population, the Kazakhs, who had dug out the train.

Once they had slaked their thirst, the men in the car began talking again. Speculations began: How long would it take to dig out the whole train? How long would it take to clear the track? Where would they take us—farther on, or back? Meanwhile, time passed, and outside the car we could hear shouts, curses, and the braying of camels.

The blizzard, evidently, had passed, since the trench dug through to the window during the day had not filled with snow.

In the second half of the day they tossed us, through the same window, some salt fish and a piece of bread apiece.

Again came the cries: "Water!..."

Again a few chunks of snow came through the window, and again there was silence.

After some time came a command: "Come out by fives for the toilet!"

Under the muzzles of machine guns we stepped down to the ground from the open platform and then back again.

"Next five, come out..."

The whole length of the train had been dug out. Evening was coming on. Did we really have another nightmarish night ahead of us? Around midnight the car gave a barely perceptible jolt, and then came the grinding and squeal of wheels on the snowy rails. We had started off, it seemed. Did it make any difference which way we were going? Through the night our train would stop, back up, and then crawl forward again.

Yes, now there were no doubts, we were returning to Novorudny, that same station from which we had left for Baikonur over two days ago.[1]

Later, in Dzhezkazgan, we met people who had been in Baikonur. A small detached camp of Steplag was located there, Camp P/Ya 392/7. A deposit of coal, a seam of 60 to 100 centimeters at a depth of a hundred meters, had once been discovered on the site. It was impossible to use machinery to mine a seam of that thickness, and so picks and wooden trough-like sledges with straps to haul them were used to do the job.

The forced labor of sledge haulers in the mines in tsarist Russia has been treated at some length in the literature; but in the twentieth century coal was not mined, either in the Donbass, in Vorkuta, or anywhere else using such a technique. But in Baikonur the coal-face worker would use a pick

---

1. The settlement of Baikonur that gave its name to the cosmodrome is in fact located four hundred kilometers from that cosmodrome, near the Tiura-Tam Station. *Author's note.*

to hew out the coal; he would load it into the trough, and then the sledge hauler, on his hands and knees, would drag it to the mine shaft. It was only there that he could straighten up to his full height, dump the coal into the bucket, and again crawl back to the mine face on his hands and knees.

After five or six shifts, knee pads and gloves would be reduced to rags, but they were issued for a full month's use. Then the miners would have to tie scraps of old, half-rotten jackets around their knees—a pile of them lay near the mine for that purpose. It was a rare day when they didn't haul a corpse up to the surface. People died, or went out of their minds, because a man working in the semi-darkness of the coal face is constantly terrified of being crushed or buried alive, and cave-ins happened regularly. These daily trips down into the grave-like mine reduced people to stupefaction, to indifference to everything around them and to their own fate. After that, the man would reach the "goner" state; after that, the infirmary; and after that . . . the "wooden overcoat."

In the barracks at night they would hear the groans and the inhuman cries of "Save me!" These were the newcomers who were getting accustomed to their new working conditions; this was the underground nightmare that came to people in terrifying dreams in their first days of work.

These underground moles had to produce their norm each day. And they produced it—at the cost of their own lives.

The elements had interrupted our journey to Baikonur, and it was all the same to us where they might fling us tomorrow. But today we wanted to eat and sleep after our two-day captivity in the snow.

CHAPTER FIVE

Transport to Dzhezkazgan

The Hard-Labor Camp of Dzhezkazgan (The Copper Kettle)

After the failed transport to Baikonur, they took us back to Novorudny Station, and it was there we faced what all the *zeks* brought to Steplag feared: the copper mines of Dzhezkazgan.

In the third volume of *The Gulag Archipelago* Aleksandr Solzhenitsyn describes how the *zeks*—and he was one of them—prayed to God that they would not be sent to Dzhezkazgan when they were brought to Steplag. "This was the famous Dzhezkazgan copper," writes Solzhenitsyn, "and the lungs of those who mined it never held out for more than four months."

It was three or four kilometers from the station to the camp. We marched in a column of fives, our arms linked, across slush mixed with sand. We could hear the larks singing in the high blue sky overhead. Today, even the dogs weren't straining at their leashes as they usually did when escorting us on a transport.

On my right was a tall, bony, wrinkled man of about sixty. What had once been a fine-quality blue suit hung on his frame. He clung to my arm more and more tightly. Without looking my way he whispered, "Don't leave me here . . ."

I realized that next to me was an exhausted and emaciated man who could barely keep his legs moving. My right arm grew numb, and I myself was beginning to stumble. My neighbor on the left looked at me, and I indicated the fellow on my right with my eyes; my neighbor understood and held my arm more firmly to give me some support. And so the three of us, clinging to each other, came up to the camp. The column had to sit down on the ground to one side of the gate, still keeping our rows of five.

No sooner had we sat down than the fellow I'd been looking out for fell face first on my knees.

"Stand up!" came the command.

We stood up. I tried to drag him to his feet but I couldn't manage it.

The guard noticed the disturbance in the column.

"What's going on over there, you want a special invitation?" he shouted.

He handed his machine gun to another guard and came up to us.

"He can't get up," I told him.

"Never mind, they'll soon cure him of that in here."

Meanwhile, some people came from the guardhouse with a stretcher and carried the poor devil into the camp. That was how I came to meet the former Soviet ambassador to England, Maisky. After he was released from the camp infirmary he ran the camp bakery. My friend Volodya Khomenko and I then were able to go to the bakery after our shift in the mine. We would unload and carry bags of flour and fill our bellies with bread and kvass. Through our early days in camp, this extra bread helped us get our strength back after the ravages of the transit camps, transports, and prisons and after the backbreaking labor in the mine. But before a year had passed, someone had attempted to kill Maisky, and he was transferred out of the camp sector. A Chechen began running the bakery, and he took on his own people as helpers.

As we approached the camp we couldn't help but compare its strong, high stone walls with those we had seen in other places—which were either plank fences or simply barbed-wire enclosures with guard towers at the corners and wooden barracks inside.

"A solid piece of work, that is," said someone.

The iron gates opened with grinding and screeching, and five by five they let us inside the camp.

The next morning we got ourselves rigged out in miners' overalls. We tied on our work boots with bits of cord or wire.

Then the mess hall. For breakfast, three hundred grams of bread, a bowl of soup, and a few spoonfuls of oatmeal. We were terrified. Were we really going down in the mine with empty bellies? I had never in my life seen a mine at close hand, and the dread of something unknown was terrifying as well. We marched across the bare steppe, surrounded by guards with machine guns and dogs. Some of us thought hard about taking a step to the left or a step to the right so as to be shot without warning.

We reached the small courtyard around the mine.

"Sit down!"

We sat down, right in the puddles of melting snow. Talking was forbidden. We were desperate to ask what would happen next. All we knew was what the brigadier had told us before we marched off to work: "Your ration is buried 150 meters down in the mine, and to get it you have to fulfill the plan."

These words, "fulfill" or "not fulfill" the plan, had already become a fixed idea, one that meant either 600 or 300 grams of bread in the evening.

The sound of muffled explosions came from somewhere. The ground beneath us shuddered. What was that? Twenty or thirty minutes later, three men with burning carbide lamps and wearing the same miners' overalls as we were, came out of the pithead and disappeared behind the engine house.

"Get ready to go down! First five, march! Second . . . third . . ."

The first five went under the pithead cover and within a minute they seemed to vanish into the earth. A dim light hanging somewhere overhead barely lit up a square opening leading downwards, into darkness. Damp warmth and smoke from the explosives wafted from this pit.

My feet found a support beneath; this was a ladder that stood almost vertically. One rung, a second, a third . . . It was slippery, damp. I reached the end of the ladder. There was a small platform, a "bridge," and then another hole and another ladder. By the fifth or sixth one I had lost count. Somewhere down in the black depths was a square hole with a light in it. I could hear the labored breathing of the people below and above me. There was no way to stop. We went down with an interval of thirty seconds. If you stopped, the person coming after you would crush your fingers. You couldn't pause to catch your breath on the platform either. That would hold up the descent of the whole brigade, since there was no room for two people to pass. And so we reached the spot where we had seen the light from above, but the smoke from the explosions was so thick and dense that the bulb gave off little more than a faint yellowish glow.

It was as if we were descending into a 150-meter smokestack. The Petro-2 mine shaft and the footway had only natural ventilation. We had managed to climb down twenty-one ladders, each one seven meters long, and now we were standing on solid rock. The lights here were more powerful, but even so, they could do nothing to dispel the smoky gloom.

Then the last man came down.

"That's everybody?" asked the brigadier.

We waited another minute or two, but no one else came down. So we were all here.

"Load your carbide lamps."

These were thick-walled cylinders with little spouts, like a teapot, and an opening in the lid to add the carbide. You had to moisten the carbide with some water to generate the acetylene. Then you touched a lighted match to the spout and a bluish-red flame would blaze up.

And so, in a long line along the mine gallery, lighting our way through the smoky gloom with the carbide lamps, we followed the brigadier to the mine face.

This procession reminded me of one of the ten circles of Dante's hell with its sinners shuffling along, but I'm not sure which circle. It even occurred to me that this was a test especially arranged for those coming down the mine for the first time. At that point I still had no idea that it had been like this before I came, and it would be like this after I left. It had been like this as long as this mine had existed.

"The Nazis would call this a *Gaswagen*," someone said.

"A gas chamber!"

People choked with coughing. We walked on and on, and it seemed that there would be no end to this journey. Yet as we learned later, the distance from the shaft to the mine face was only three hundred meters.

We thought that when this gallery ended we would come out some-where with light and fresh air. And we did come out. The walls of the gallery seemed to draw apart, but the smoke was even denser and more choking.

"Sit down!" commanded the brigadier.

There was no way we could work. You couldn't see your hand in front of your face.

This smoky gloom reminded me of the Kalinin sector of the front in No-vember 1942. A group of night bombers was flying off on a mission, and though the forecast had been for good weather, a fog suddenly rolled in, and such a dense mass of it that nothing could be seen. We lit bonfires and fired off flares, but in vain—the planes coming back from their mission couldn't see the airfield and kept circling above us in hope that they might find a gap in the fog and orient themselves for a landing. The fog didn't lift, and the planes were running out of fuel. Then the pilots began landing their planes wherever they could. The group lost eight aircraft, almost a whole squadron.

Then the security officers wanted to have the two poor girls from the meteorological station (at least if you can call a place with a field telephone and a wind direction indicator a met station) shot before our whole forma-tion. The girls would get the weather summary from our division, higher up, and our group headquarters would get the information from them. I don't know what stopped the security officers, but these "weathervane girls," as they were jokingly called at the airfield, were not shot, though we never saw them again.

I don't know how long it took before we could begin to make out the silhouettes of the people sitting tightly packed on boulders and piles of ore that had been mined out of the rock.

Then the light bulb seemed to glow more clearly, casting light on the mine face, which looked like a grotto five or six meters high. It was hard to believe that these burrows under the ground and these high faces in solid granite had been made by people like us, who looked like little cave dwell-ers in fiber helmets and torn miners' overalls.

The brigadier, Leshka Lavrikov, "a nonpolitical contra," as he introduced himself, said solemnly: "In this place I'm your prosecutor, your interroga-tor, and your judge. If you don't want to croak here, you'll sweat your guts out and you'll get your ration. And don't think of disobeying my helper: you'll find you're missing a few ribs—he's taught us how."

His helper, Pashka, was a man of indeterminate years and almost a midget, and he was truly terrifying and dangerous. No one knew when and why he might attack you and beat you mercilessly with a collaring bit. Complaining to the bosses about his methods was the same as writing your own death sentence. Pashka was a Banderist, and like the brigadier he had a twenty-five-year sentence.

The brigadier assigned jobs to us new people: some were haulage men, others railway men, a safety man, a boulder man, a drill operator, an assistant drill operator, a scraper operator, a timber man.

Many things have been erased from my memory and forgotten, but that first day in the mine I have remembered all my life.

"You'll be a boulder man," the brigadier told me, handing me a heavy sledgehammer with a long handle. "I'll take all of you around the work sites and show you what you have to do."

I thought that I could even hear a note of concern in his quiet voice. About fifteen minutes later he came up to me again.

"Look over there. A boulder like that won't pass through the gratings on the ore chute, so you have to break it up. You have to know what you're doing if you want to smash it. Don't use the sledgehammer on the edge of the rock, hit it on the flat side. So if the rock is sitting slantways or on edge, you'll have to turn it flat side up and hit it like this."

As the eighteen-pound hammer described an arc over his head, it seemed to me it didn't come down all that heavily on the rock. The boulder appeared to be still sitting there in one piece, but when he touched it with his foot I could see that it had all been smashed into sharp-cornered bits.

"Now you have a go."

I chose a smaller boulder, took aim while holding the sledge at chest height, and hit it. Tiny fragments scattered to one side, while the boulder remained in one piece. I hit it again: the result was the same. I turned over the boulder and began beating on it. Sweat and tears clouded my eyes and soon, exhausted and damp with sweat, I sank down beside the damned boulder, which by now was round.

"If you've got the muscle, you don't need the brains! You still haven't got the hang of it. You're tired out and hungry, but your ration is buried right here, under the boulder, and you have to get it before the shift is over," the brigadier said as he stood over me. "Grab that hammer!" he shouted sharply. "You're a damned fool. Now let your arms and body drop along with the hammer, don't keep it hanging in the air."

I think I put everything I had into the next blow and—a miracle! I still couldn't see it, but I could sense that the boulder had been smashed. And so, once I had mastered this simple art, I went on smashing boulder after boulder. I kept it up until everything went dark before my eyes. The last thing that flashed through my mind before I fell down among the boulders was . . . I had to rest. When I came to I was all wet. Someone had brought water in a helmet and thrown it over me. Through the haze of fog in my eyes there gradually emerged the walls of the mine face, the light of the lamps, the people scrambling about, each busy at his own work.

"So, you've figured it out? Then take a rest. We'll soon be going up."

I tried to get up, but terrible pain in the small of my back, in my joints, and in my arms forced me to sit down again. The long ringing of a bell told me that the shift was over. I can barely remember how I made it to the mine shaft. Everything told me that I wouldn't be able to climb up through the passage. I'd never be able to get up twenty-one ladders that were almost vertical. The brigadier sent his helper to get permission from the guards to take a sick man up in the cage. And so this was the one time—my first and last—that I came out of the mine in the cage.

Whenever we finished a shift every one of us was in dread, wondering if we would have the strength to make it up the 140 meters on the wet, slippery ladders. Twenty-one ladders, seven meters each.

Finally, everyone was on top. Those who came out first lay down on the ground—a chance for a bit of rest before the march back to camp.

"Form up in fives! Forward, march!"

I was in the middle of the rank of five. People took my arms, and I walked along, barely conscious. The gate, dogs barking, a body search . . .

From the guardhouse I went to the medical unit.

"Get undressed."

I tried to take off my overalls, but I couldn't straighten my fingers. I couldn't unbutton my jacket.

"Come on! Take your clothes off."

The Georgian doctor was getting furious. He tore off my top and my jacket, kneaded my muscles, forced my fingers to bend open and closed. I cried out with the pain, and once more everything before me grew dark. He put a cotton wad with liquid ammonia under my nose. He massaged my temples. I watched his hands, and it all seemed as if in a dream. My elbow joints had swollen to an incredible size. This was the second time since Asino.

"Now get out!"

He tossed my top and jacket over my shoulders. A doctor. So ended my first day's work in the Petro-2 Mine. This was a day when I trembled with fear. I was afraid that I would fall sick and be unable to work. An illness in camp means saying good-bye to life. You're a goner, a "candlewick," and the next inevitable step is the "wooden overcoat." That was not for me. Then there was only one way out: a couple of steps to one side while marching to work and that would be the end of it. A step to the left, a step to the right—that was no idle threat from the guards.

This was February 1949.

Ahead of me were still six long years in this hard-labor camp named P/Ya 392/1.

Hard Labor

In the autumn of 1950 an event took place that seemed trivial at first glance, yet had consequences we could not have even guessed at.

One day when we had come back from work and had eaten, the brigadier brought in some scraps of white calico with numbers written on them, along with a list of people in the brigade. There was a number after the last name of every person on the list. We stepped out of our ranks and each of us signed for four of these scraps; then we stepped back and, puzzled, examined these numbers.

"Everyone's got them?" asked the brigadier.

"Everyone."

"Now watch where and how you have to sew them on."

He showed us a quilted jacket and pants with numbers sewn on. One had to be on the back, another on the left breast, a third on the jacket sleeve. On the trouser leg above the knee we were to cut a hole the size of the number and sew it in. We finished this job before lights-out, borrowing needles and thread from each other. The brigadier hurried us on. Everyone had to come to morning roll call with numbers sewn on.

And so, from that day on, I became person number SL-208. People tried to puzzle out what the letters "SL" meant: did it stand for *spetslager* (special camp)? But others had all the letters of the alphabet, from beginning to end. The number might indicate the number of one's criminal "case." Well, to hell with it, what did it matter in any case?

In the morning we formed up to go to work. Aside from the guards and the warders there was the camp commandant, the disciplinary officer, the head of the Culture and Education Unit, the security officer, and another person as well. They were very finicky in checking each person. They tested to make sure that the numbers had been well sewn on. Two people from our brigade had a bit of luck—they were sent back to the zone. The disciplinary officer had managed to tear off the numbers they had sewn on badly. The guards and warders smirked with satisfaction. In the presence of the camp bosses, it seemed that even the dogs surrounding the column were more vicious than usual.

Along with all our other worries was now the added one of keeping our numbers in good condition, meaning that they always had to be clearly visible and legible. Every two weeks, the brigadier would bring a tin of black paint, and an artist from the Cultural and Educational Unit would touch up the numbers.

We could easily distinguish the *pridurki* and the camp aristocracy generally, because the numbers on their clothes were clean and stood out clearly on their jackets; but within a month you could barely find the bit of sewn-on rag with a number on any of the sloggers. It wasn't too long before they stopped putting the miners into the disciplinary barracks for violating the dress regulations—there was simply no way to keep your number clean, even after only one shift.

After we had sewn on our numbers we expected there would be more tightening of the prison regime, and it was not long before our expectations were fulfilled. Sudden searches of the barracks and body frisks at night became the norm, and they happened more and more often. If you forgot to respond to a warder when he called out your number, he had the right to take you to the guardhouse in handcuffs to explain why you didn't respond. After that you would remember your number for the rest of your life.

Now the warders would walk around the zone toying with shiny bracelets linked by a chain. Some said that it was the Americans who had sent over these ratcheting handcuffs; others who had been prisoners of the Germans said that they were of German manufacture.

Smoking was forbidden in the barracks, but after the barracks had been locked for the night you could see, here and there, the glow of smoldering hand-rolled cigarettes. The barracks filled with tobacco smoke.

That evening, as usual, the warder shut the door with a rattle of the bolt and the lock. As usual, people lit up their hand-rolled cigarettes. No one noticed how the warder managed to get back into the barracks again. The lights came on.

"Who's smoking?" he roared.

In cases like this, you not only had to keep your head down, you couldn't even stir; you just lay rigid . . . sleeping.

I was apparently just dozing off, and when I heard the warder shouting I mechanically raised my head; I was sleeping on the upper bunk. At that same moment my blanket was torn off and I was dragged down to the floor.

"Let's go . . ."

"I wasn't smoking; I don't even have any tobacco," I tried to explain to the Kazakh warder.

"We'll soon find out if you were smoking or not."

In the entry to the barracks, between the outside door and the one leading to the barracks itself, was a little room for the warders. It had two stools, a table, and a tiny barred window.

"Hands on the table!"

I was standing in my underwear, my hands behind my back, as was the drill when a warder took you somewhere.

"Are you deaf?"

"I wasn't smoking . . ."

The next second I felt a deafening blow to my left temple. When I came to, I was sitting on a stool wearing handcuffs. The warder pulled the second stool in front of me, put my hands on it, and pressed down on the bracelets with his knee—first on one wrist, then on the other. I soon stopped feeling the pain; little drops of blood welled up from under the bracelets, which now could barely be seen because of the bluish-red swellings around them.

How long this torture lasted I can't recall, only that I cried out from the unbearable pain when he took off the handcuffs: it was as if they were tearing the skin off my wrists at the same time.

The warders pushed me back into the barracks and locked the door.

"So, does it hurt?" the barracks orderly asked. He was a kindly Czech, Vasily Kirichek. Tall and thin as a rail, he had by some miracle survived three months working in the mine. He ended in the infirmary and from there as our barracks orderly.

"Here, just piss on this rag and wrap it around your wrists. The pain will stop."

It was morning before I had managed to put at least some of the shock and pain out of my mind, and then came the command: "Reveille!"

I could not bend my wrists. My friend, Volodya Khomenko, helped me put on my overalls, and I went out to march to work. Our brigadier, Leshka Lavrikov, was a merciless sadist and bandit who thought that the mine's daily plan was more important than the death of any one of us; still, when he looked at my hands he said:

"Go off to work. You can sit out your shift at the mine face. If you stay here you'll be taking your rest in the disciplinary barracks."

And so, for the only time during my whole sentence, I went off to work but didn't do any work. My mates took off their jackets and passed them to me. I spread them out beneath me, covered myself up, and went to sleep. The constant temperature at the mine face, both winter and summer, was four degrees above. This and the high humidity meant that it was not the best place for sleeping but, to the rumble of loaded mine cars, I fell asleep, warm under the pile of jackets.

The shift ended. One more terrible ordeal lay ahead—getting back to the surface. I had those damned ladders to overcome. The ladders in the shaft were mounted almost vertically; each one was fastened to a ledge about a meter square with an opening to reach the ladder above. Each ledge, then, was the base for the next ladder. The signal for work to end was a long ring that came from the engine house. I knew that with my swollen hands and fingers that wouldn't bend I wouldn't be able to climb even two ladders.

The brigadier asked me if I'd be able to get to the surface.

"I'll need at least an hour to make it up all the ladders," I replied.

We didn't have any clocks, so we had learned to measure the time left until the shift's end to within five to eight minutes. And so, about an hour before the end of the shift, I began climbing up. My mates gave me a bit of parting advice:

"Wrap your arms around the ladder. When you come to a manhole, prop yourself up on either side with your elbows. And sit down for a rest on each platform."

I can't clearly remember how, with the help of my mates and covered with sweat, I managed to climb the last few ladders. I was barely conscious on the way back to camp. Later they told me that when they were coming up to the surface they found me at ladder twenty, lying on the platform where I had been unconscious for some time.

So one year passed after another, without any events of note, unless you count yet another transport coming into or leaving the camp or the transports of goners to Spassk, near Karaganda. We called that camp the "All-Union Home for Invalids." Those who wound up there would face no more transports or transfers . . .

These were the years from 1949 to 1951. Over that time, the population of the camp changed twice, almost completely. A few names remain in my memory: Ivan Tsilyarchuk, Vladimir Khomenko, Vladimir Grigolavichius, Brigadier Leshka Lavrikov; there were two or three others whose names I no longer recall. They, like I, survived through some sort of miracle. The others went down the conveyor: from the infirmary to a transport to Spassk—and there they found their final resting place. Silicosis is a serious matter: "from Lat. *Silex* . . . 'flint': an occupational disease caused by prolonged inhalation of dust containing silicon dioxide . . . which causes a profound disruption to the vital functions of the organism . . ." (*Great Soviet Encyclopedia,* vol. 39, p. 30).

On one of those days when we had come to work our shift, the brigadier told me to stay on the surface.

"You'll be doing haulage on the surface. The work's simple enough, but you need some muscle power, and you need it to last from the beginning of the shift to the end."

The work was as follows: when a mine car full of ore came up in the cage we had to roll it out on a concrete slab, then shove in an empty one and send it back down. While the empty car was going down, we swung the full ore car around and rolled it along the rails to the dump. While I was pushing the empty car back to the pithead, a loaded one would be coming up in the cage. We would roll away the loaded car and bring back the empty one—and so it went for the whole shift. If a car full of barren rock came up, we had to shift it to the rails leading to the rock shaft, fasten the winch cable to the hook on the car, and turn on the winch. The car would crawl up to the top of the dump, where its box would tip and the empty car would come back down to the ground.

Sometimes a car would hit a restrainer and break loose. Then we'd be lucky if it managed to tip: the empty car would come flying down with a crash and a clatter and fly off somewhere in the dump. But if it broke loose and came flying down loaded, even the sentry would run out of his box, take his machine gun from his shoulder, and shout at us; we would hide behind the pithead. The car would always turn over at the bottom of the dump, and bits of rock would come whistling through the air in all directions. They would have to stop sending up the cars. Bells would ring in the mine, bells would ring in the engine house. We would send the cage down empty. Then it would start all over again: a car would come up, we'd send a car down . . . up and down. And finally, the long-awaited end of the shift.

Deathly fatigue would overcome us; we'd see spots before our eyes, and there would be no feeling left in our arms and legs . . .

Tomorrow, and the next day, and a month from now it would be the same thing. In the summer the sun would roast us without mercy; in the winter, on a cold day in a blizzard, there wasn't a scrap of shelter on the gantry and nowhere to take refuge. And if we had to stop the cars coming up for some reason, there would be big trouble. My predecessor on surface haulage got badly frostbitten, was put in the infirmary, and left on a transport as a goner. Only people who had served half their terms were taken on for surface haulage.

That was how the years 1951 and 1952 passed. In 1953 two events took place at the same time. The first was that I was transferred to work in the mine's machine shops; the second, joyous one—no less joyous than the end of the war—was the end of the tyrant Joseph the Bloody (that's what we called the "Father of All Peoples" among ourselves).

It is difficult to describe what happened in the camp. There wasn't a single person, even those who were serving twenty-five-year terms, who did not have his hope reborn that our lives would soon be changing.

This was in March 1953.

CHAPTER SIX

The Kengir Uprising. The Strike in Dzhezkazgan

But before any changes could take place, we had to face more than a few bitter, sometimes even tragic days and months at the end of May and beginning of June 1954.

Now they began showing movies to the camp. For an hour or more, we could lose ourselves while gazing on the freedom and life that were so far away.

On one of those Sunday evenings, just after the screen had gone dark, a man stepped out of the projectionist's booth onto the little balcony in the mess hall. He loudly announced that we were not going to work tomorrow and that anyone who took one step toward the guardhouse would be killed. Kengir had not been working for the past month, and we had to support our comrades.

Everyone understood the general sense of what he said, though the language of the speaker was some gibberish blend of Ukrainian, Belorussian, and Moldavian. It was clear that it was the "Westerners," the Banderists, as we Russians called them, who had planned the strike. They called us "Moskals" or Reds. Someone could write a whole study of this event that seemed so odd at first glance: all of us, bound by the same terrible tribulations and forced to live in inhuman conditions, found each day filled not only with exhausting labor and the struggle for a scrap of bread but also with implacable malice and enmity between the Moskals and the Westerners. And now, after this call for a strike, we were gripped by a kind of numbness; and our first thought was "How is all this going to end?"

They, with their twenty-five-year sentences, had nothing to lose, while many of us Moskals had served out half our terms, and some were almost due for release. And now we were supposed to be, if not participants in a strike, then at least hostages. Later, this is just what happened.

It was morning. The camp seemed desolate, and not a person was stirring, neither the warders nor the camp bosses. One of the warders had been at the movie the day before and had reported the strike to the bosses.

We trudged off to the mess hall as per schedule. Those who went to work first were the first to eat. I recall that on that morning, for the first time in many years, I had no appetite; I managed to drink up my portion of soup and eat some bread. Everyone was quiet. There was none of the usual bustle as the food was handed out, and none of the cursing. Our barracks was closest to the guardhouse and the corner watchtower. When I glanced at the tower, I noticed that along with the usual sentry and his machine gun there was a second man standing on the tower ledge and armed with a Degtyaryov machine pistol. Sentries had been posted in the towers between the corners—normally they were here only at night. So, measures had already been taken . . .

Nothing special happened the next day, except that they cut off the water into the cistern that supplied the camp. Luckily, the cistern had been filled to the top the day before, and if we used it carefully there was enough to last four or five days. Suddenly, an order came that water was to be used only by the mess hall. That same day, the gate by the guardhouse opened a little, and onto the path they pushed a handcart filled with boxes of salt fish: Lake Balkash was feeding all the camps of Steplag with its carp. They usually made something resembling fish soup out of it, cooking it up bones and all.

No one came near these boxes of salt fish. They remained sitting there on the path until the strike ended. On the third day, some time after the noon meal, they began transmitting a concert from powerful speakers set up on the towers. This amazed us more than anything. After many years of silence and without any news from the outside, suddenly we had radio.

> My native land is broad and fair,
> With forests, fields and streams;
> No other country do I know
> Where men can live their dreams . . .

Then Ruslanova sang the folk song "Felt Boots," then there was a silence, and a loud, strong voice said: "Prisoners!"

The gist of the speech was as follows: the mines are our common heritage, the wealth of our Motherland, and this wealth is now being wasted. The mines will flood, the machinery will break down. Go back to work tomorrow. Beginning next week a commission from Moscow will begin reviewing your cases, looking at rehabilitation and reduction of sentences. You will only worsen your situation by striking.

And then some completely unconventional words that had never before been used to address us:

"Comrades, friends . . . A little more patience and then you, many of you, will be working here as free citizens for the good of your Motherland, in this same mining complex . . ."

As we learned later, it was the director of the complex, Lomako, who was speaking.

There were replies to the speech from the prisoners: "The wolf in the forest may be your comrade, but not us." "First set us free, then we'll go to work," and so on.

The next event in the strike was the appearance of two men the warders shoved through the camp gate.

They were people from Kengir. They had been sent in to tell us how their strike had ended. The upshot was this: had they not created mayhem inside the camp and murdered some of the Moskals, and had they not torn down the walls between the zones, particularly the one around the women's zone, then perhaps the camp would not have been flattened by tanks and guns. The leader of our strike warned the two men that if there were any lies at all in their stories he would hang them.

Many years later, when I read the chapters on the Kengir uprising in *The Gulag Archipelago,* I realized that the two men's stories were very near to the truth. After we found out about Kengir, every day and, particularly, every coming night was spent in dread that we "Reds" would be dealt with mercilessly. And so, after surviving the torments of prison hell, the interrogations and hunger, and at a time when we could already see the dawn of our freedom glowing in the morning sky, were we now to die by someone's knife or be strangled while sleeping just because we were Russians and short-termers? This constant dread was more than we could bear. Still, if they wanted to get rid of us, would they have helped us keep watch in the barracks behind a barricaded door? They could have burned down the barracks with us inside. The camp, hushed and watchful, was like a powder keg. It needed only some chance spark for a blind, mindless wave of murders and violence to be unleashed on thousands of people who were already condemned. The anxiety became unbearable.

The day after the "envoys" from Kengir arrived, three people came to our barracks. One of them, a short, quite ordinary-looking fellow, was in fact the leader of our strike. His two bodyguards, hefty young lads wearing astrakhan caps and shirts decorated with Ukrainian embroidery, asked which of us Russians knew Ukrainian. My brigade mates pointed at me. I loved and still love the Ukrainian language. In university I picked up quite a good knowledge of Ukrainian and Belorussian, all in the course of one semester and mainly from textbooks. And later I used to listen to Ukrainian songs.

When I worked in the mine with Ivan Tsilyarchuk, we spoke only Ukrainian. At first he found my accent amusing, but after about three months we were chattering away like equals.

I still don't know why this barely literate young tough needed a Moskal who could speak Ukrainian. My closest friend was the Ukrainian, Volodka Khomenko; they called him in as well.

The ringleader began by saying: "It wouldn't be such a bad idea to hang someone, but there's not enough time," and he added that now we were to write down what he was going to say.

His "adjutants" set a plywood scrap on my knees, one that the work assigners used when the brigades were marched off to work; on it were a couple of squared sheets of notebook paper. I truly regret now that I don't have a copy of this remarkable document that was translated from Ukrainian to Russian. But I remember the gist of it very clearly. It was an appeal to the camp population that said we must forget all our personal conflicts and enmity, maintain order and discipline in the camp, and that if we repeated what happened in Kengir, we would all perish. Volodka Khomenko read the Ukrainian text to the ringleader, and it was clear that he was pleased with it. Khomenko wrote out the text in Ukrainian on a similar piece of paper. Copies were made of the text and hung up around the camp. This turn of events encouraged us, and there was hope that the affair would come to an end. And the end was not slow in coming.

At dawn we heard the roar of vehicles coming from all directions outside the zone, and I was overjoyed to catch the scent of diesel. They were tanks. Those of us who had served at the front recognized the noise and the smell. There could be no mistake. Now even a terrible end would be better than terror without end. We could hear dogs barking; the machine guns in the guard towers were aimed at the barracks . . . The iron gates rattled open. A tank surrounded by a group of people appeared in the gate's opening; they advanced along the path by the guardhouse; the tank halted at the gate. A command came by megaphone: "Brigadiers, report here; the rest of you, stay in your places!"

The brigadiers, gazing around, came out.

"I'll give you ten minutes. In that time, the brigades must be formed up on the pathway!"

They turned around and walked out of the camp as calmly as they had entered it; the T-34 tank stayed in the gate opening.

Our brigade of mine craftsmen was the first to form up. Our brigadier hadn't managed to finish giving his orders before we were jostling one another to rush out to the pathway. The tank drew back, giving us room to go out. Outside the zone we immediately found ourselves in a ring of guards with machine guns and dogs. Where did they ever find so many of them?

Baring their teeth, the dogs strained at the leashes; commands were shouted; tank engines roared: that was how we formed up to march to work that day. We marched to our hard labor in the mine that morning freed from terror, the unknown, and dread.

CHAPTER SEVEN

Liberation

Within three days, mine Petro-2 was fulfilling its plan, and everything had fallen back into the regular routine of camp life. Only now no one demanded that something be done over again; the warders were more tolerant; mail began flowing from camp to camp.

The most important and amazing thing was that this time they did not deceive us. A commission to review sentences did come to the camp. Vavilov, one of the assistants of the General Prosecutor Rudenko, did accept complaints in the camp commandant's office. On July 28 they did accept my complaint describing my "case" and the tactics the Tomsk MGB used in their investigation. This man's benevolent, forthright face and calm gaze inspired a certain hope and trust. I remember his words even now:

"We will review your case in the Supreme Court of the RSFSR, and if everything you have written in your complaint is corroborated, you will be rehabilitated within three or four months. After reducing your sentence to seven years, the commission will allow you to work without being under guard; you will work at the mine and report regularly to the commandant's office. An escape attempt means a term of twenty-five years."

In November 1955, in the commandant's office, the Kazakh commandant read out the document of my rehabilitation. A week later I was in Kengir, in the settlement's Council Office, where I received all my documents: in the geological prospecting party, where I had worked for the past year, they issued me a work service record stating that I had been working in the Mine Construction Department and in a geological prospecting party for all these eight years and ten months. A month later I was back home, in Novosibirsk.

I had to begin a new life. I was thirty-six years old. The army, the war, and prison had erased almost fifteen years from my life. Such was my university, one that extended over time and space for many long years.

Translator's Notes

V. M. Lazarev

6   **Ordzhonikidze:** Grigory (Sergo) Konstantinovich Ordzhonikidze (1886–1937), close associate of Stalin, in charge of heavy industry. He committed suicide after Stalin began to question his loyalty.

7   ***Ten Days That Shook the World:*** a sympathetic account of the Bolshevik coup of 1917 by the American journalist John Reed (1887–1920); ***I Love:*** autobiographical novel by the popular Soviet writer A. O. Avdeenko (1908–1996).

7   **Shakhty Trial:** a widely publicized trial of fifty-three engineers and technicians accused of sabotage in the coal mines that took place from May through July 1928. The affair was used by the communist leadership to cover up a sharp drop in coal production caused by poor management. All the accused confessed.

8   *faraony,* cops; *shkery,* trousers; *kozha,* a prostitute or promiscuous woman; *smetana,* narcotics in tablet form; *frayer,* a "pigeon," an easy mark.

10   **Troika:** a three-member board—usually the head of the local NKVD, the party secretary of the area, and a member of the Prosecutor's Office—set up to enable rapid disposal of "counterrevolutionary" cases. The board could impose sentences in absentia and without legal representation. In 1937 the boards were empowered to impose the death penalty.

11   **"kulaks' henchmen":** *podkulachniki,* poor peasants who resisted joining collective farms or who would not take part in the looting of the farms of the wealthier peasants (kulaks) during the forced collectivization of agriculture.

17   **Stolypin carriage:** a type of railroad carriage named after Pyotr Arkadievich Stolypin (1862–1911), prime minister of Russia from 1906 to his assassination in 1911. Among other things, Stolypin was known for his success in repressing the growing revolutionary movement.

18   **Sobakevich:** a clumsy, bearlike character in Nikolai Gogol's novel *Dead Souls.*

23   **the new Stalin Constitution:** adopted on December 5, 1936, the constitution remodeled the government of the USSR, instituted universal and direct suffrage, and guaranteed a range of social and economic rights. These rights were, however, granted "in conformity with the interests of the working people, and in order to strengthen the socialist system." The exclusive right of the Communist Party to define "the interests of the working people" remained unchanged.

23   **Bukharin:** Nikolai Ivanovich Bukharin (1888–1938), Bolshevik revolutionary, economic theorist, and political figure. He was the principal framer of the 1936 constitution. Stalin opposed his relatively moderate views. He was arrested in 1937 and was executed after a show trial in March 1938.

23   *The Golden Calf:* satirical novel (*Zolotoi telënok,* 1931) by Ilia Ilf (1897–1937) and Evgeny Petrov (1903–1942). In the novel, a group of elderly men wearing white piqué vests periodically appear, carrying on very serious but uninformed discussions of world events.

23   **Prince Sviatopolk-Mirsky:** Dmitry Pavlovich Sviatopolk-Mirsky (1890–1939), literary critic and historian. Mirsky came from an old aristocratic family and fought against the Bolsheviks in the Civil War. He eventually found refuge in England, where he moved in literary circles, lectured on Russian literature, and published (in English) a number of studies of Russian literature and history that remain influential. In 1931 he joined the British Communist Party, and the following year he returned to the Soviet Union, voluntarily and not by invitation, as Lazarev states. He was arrested in June 1937 and died in a camp hospital in Kolyma in 1939. Mirsky did not teach at Oxford but at the School of Slavonic Studies of London University, from 1922 to 1932. (See also note to p. 118.)

23   **Pulkovo:** astronomical observatory of Russia's Academy of Sciences, founded in 1839 and located near St. Petersburg.

26   **English interventionists:** American, Canadian, and British troops landed in Arkhangelsk in 1918 (and other Allied forces landed elsewhere) to prevent stockpiles of military equipment from falling into the hands of the Bolsheviks and to support the Russian anti-Bolshevik forces.

27   **Transpolar Railway:** the Salekhard–Igarka Railway (also known as the 501 Railway and the Railway of Death) was built between 1949 and 1953 to link a new Arctic port, to be constructed near the mouth of the Ob River, with the mineral-rich Vorkuta region. Building a railway over the Arctic permafrost proved all but impossible, and the project, costing billions of rubles and taking tens of thousands of lives, was abandoned soon after Stalin's death.

36   **Radek:** Karl Radek (1885–1939), an international communist leader who helped organize the German communist movement from 1918 to 1920. An ardent supporter of the Bolsheviks, he moved to Russia but eventually

fell out of favor with Stalin. In 1937 he was put on trial for treason and sentenced to ten years in prison, where he was executed in 1939.

36 **Sokolnikov:** Grigory Sokolnikov (1888–1939), Bolshevik revolutionary, people's commissar of finance, and Soviet ambassador to Britain. Arrested in 1936, he was tried, together with Radek and others, in 1937. Sentenced to ten years, he was killed while in prison.

36 **Tukhachevsky:** Mikhail Tukhachevsky (1893–1937), marshal of the Soviet Union, head of the Red Army from 1925 to 1928. Arrested on May 22, 1937, and accused of treason and spying for Germany, he and eight other senior military commanders were tried and executed in June of the same year.

36 *Krokodil:* Soviet satirical magazine, it often produced crude attacks on those designated as hostile to the regime.

36 **Yezhov's Iron Fist:** Nikolai Ivanovich Yezhov (1885–1939) headed the NKVD from 1936 to 1938, the peak of the "Great Terror." His last name is echoed in the Russian saying, *derzhat' v yezhovykh rukavitsakh,* "to rule with an iron hand, treat despotically."

38 **a bit of incense for Comrade Stalin:** Gide's book, *Retour de L'U.R.S.S.* (1936), appeared only a few months after his visit to the Soviet Union in the summer of 1936. The early pages of the book express his admiration for many of the regime's achievements, but the later portions are very critical and reflect his overall disillusionment with Soviet Russia. Although Gide did visit the Caucasus, he makes no mention of Rabinovich but notes that his translator was a woman, "Comrade Bola."

39 **Leshaft Institute:** an institute (now a university) for physical training founded in St. Petersburg in 1896 by P. F. Leshaft.

41 *tufta:* padding, forgery, work done only for show; a widespread practice in the camps (and in the world outside them).

42 *shmony (shmon, singular):* a frisk or search.

45 **Red Front:** Der Rote Frontkämpferbund, a paramilitary organization of the Communist Party of Germany that existed from 1924 to 1932. Members greeted one another with clenched fists raised and the words "Red Front!"

45 *bezprizorniki:* "street children." From World War I through the 1930s, millions of homeless children roamed the streets of cities and towns, living by begging, stealing, and prostitution. Some had been orphaned, some simply abandoned, others separated from their parents by the Revolution and Civil War, and still others left homeless after their parents had been arrested.

46 **"thieves-in-the-law":** criminals who observed the "thieves' code," an unwritten law that set standards of behavior and punishment for infractions. The code proscribes collaboration with the authorities, for example.

46 **"goat":** a card game with some resemblance to pinochle.

54 **Shukov boiler:** Vladimir Shukov (1853–1939) was a Russian engineer and inventor; among his many inventions was an efficient tubular boiler.

54 **Maliuta Skuratov:** Grigory Maliuta-Lukyanovich Skuratov-Belsky (?–1573), a much-feared henchman of Ivan the Terrible, whose orders for executions and bloody reprisals he faithfully carried out.

56 **Dostoevsky's words:** In part 1, chapter 10 of Dostoevsky's own prison memoirs, *Notes from the Dead House* (*Zapiski iz mertvogo doma,* 1860–62), he describes the prisoners' excitement and softened temperaments as they prepare for the Christmas holiday, a celebration that gives them a connection with the world outside. No mention is made of them polishing their shackles, however.

60 **pedology:** An approach to childhood behavior and development popular in the USSR in the 1920s to 1930s. It relied heavily on psychological testing to predict a child's mental development and so determine the level of education a child would receive. The principles of pedology were often applied mechanically, much to the detriment of Soviet education, and the approach was officially abandoned in 1936.

61 **Makarenko:** Anton Semenovich Makarenko (1888–1939), Soviet pedagogue and writer. He established self-supporting orphanages to house and educate street children (*bezprizorniki*).

63 **NEP:** New Economic Policy (1921–28), a period of limited private enterprise instituted by the regime to help the Soviet Union to recover from the ravages of war, revolution, and civil war. During the NEP small businesses were allowed to reopen and make private profits, agricultural production was restored, and by 1928 most economic indicators had returned to or exceeded their 1914 levels.

64 **Tumanian:** Hovhannes Tumanian (1869–1923), major Armenian poet.

N. N. Boldyrev

73 **Suvorov's crossing of the Swiss Alps:** Field Marshal Aleksandr Suvorov (1729–1800), a renowned Russian military leader, commanded Russian troops in the campaign against French forces in Italy. After driving all but a few of the French out of Italy in 1799, he was forced to lead his army on a strategic retreat through the Swiss passes.

74 **zemstvo:** a form of local government set up by Alexander II in the 1860s.

74 **Smolny Institute:** until 1917, an exclusive finishing school for young girls of the nobility.

75 **"Velvet Book":** a genealogy, compiled in 1687, listing Russia's most notable aristocratic families, many of whom traced their ancestry to Riurik (c. 830–c. 879), founder of the dynasty that ruled Kievan Rus and Muscovy until the sixteenth century.

75 **Mikhail Lermontov:** (1814–1841), major Russian Romantic poet and novelist. In 1840 he was exiled, for a second time, and sent to serve in a line regiment in the Caucasus.

75 **Petrashevsky Affair:** in April 1849 thirty-three members of a group of young intellectuals who met in the apartment of M. V. Butashevich-Petrashevsky (1821–1866) to read and discuss books prohibited in Russia were arrested and imprisoned. Several writers, including Fyodor Dostoevsky, were among them. Many others, loosely linked to the group, were questioned.

75 **Nikolai Chernyshevsky:** (1828–1889), literary critic, novelist, and revolutionary, nineteenth-century Russia's most prominent radical journalist. He was arrested in 1862 and spent almost all the rest of his life in exile.

75 **Russian-Turkish War:** Russia became involved in a war with Turkey in 1877–78 in order to help liberate the Balkan Slavs who had risen up against Ottoman rule. The siege of Plevna (now Pleven), which lasted from July to December 1877, resulted in a costly victory for Russia.

76 **Admiral Kolchak:** Aleksandr Vasilyevich Kolchak (1874–1920), Russian naval officer who headed the anti-Bolshevik White forces during the Civil War. Kolchak was named "Supreme Ruler" of the White forces after a military coup overthrew the existing and unpopular Siberian regional government.

80 **Sergei Mironovich Kirov:** (1886–1934), prominent Bolshevik leader assassinated in Leningrad on December 1, 1934. His death, which some suspect may have been ordered by Stalin, led to wide-scale arrests of those labeled Trotskyite conspirators against Soviet power.

80 **NEP:** see note to p. 63.

82 **Aleksei Nikolaevich Tolstoy:** (1883–1945), novelist and dramatist. A nobleman, he left Russia after the Revolution but returned in 1923, eventually becoming one of the Soviet Union's most popular writers. He wrote a number of stories paying tribute to Stalin, and his historical novel *Peter the First* (1929–45) implicitly identifies Stalin's policies with those of Peter the Great.

84 **Comrade Voroshilov:** Kliment Yefremovich Voroshilov (1881–1969), Soviet military commander and politician, close associate of Stalin.

85 **Otto Schmidt:** (1891–1956), Soviet mathematician and astronomer, famed for his explorations of the Arctic in the 1930s.

85 **Hetman Skoropadsky:** Pavlo Skoropadsky (1873–1945), leader (hetman) of Ukraine's struggle for independence following the 1917 Revolution.

86 **Special Board:** an extralegal body that existed from 1934 to 1953. An arm of the NKVD, the board was initially authorized to give sentences of up to five years, but this limit was gradually expanded to twenty-five years after 1948. It tried prisoners in absentia.

86 **Demyan Bedny:** pseudonym of Efim Alekseevich Pridvorov (1883–1945), poet, satirist, and propagandist for the Communist Party.

87 **Savinkov:** Boris Viktorovich Savinkov (1879–1925), Russian writer, politician, and terrorist responsible for the assassinations of two highly

placed Russian officials in 1904 and 1905. His novel *Pale Horse* is a semi-autobiographical tale of a terrorist.

87   **Plekhanov:** Georgi Valentinovich Plekhanov (1856–1918), Russian revolutionary and first Marxist theoretician. He broke with Lenin in 1903 and sided with the Mensheviks.

89   *bura:* a card game for three or four players whose aim is to take thirty-one tricks by trumping the opposing players' cards; *stos* (more commonly, *shtos*), gambling game in which the players bet the cards they have selected will be turned up by the "banker" into one of two rows.

90   **Princess Tarakanova:** an eighteenth-century adventuress of mysterious origins. She traveled through Europe, claiming to be a wealthy Russian princess, even insisting she was the pretender to the Russian throne. She died in prison in St. Petersburg in 1775. Boldyrev probably has in mind Pavel Melnikov's (alias Andrei Pechersky's) book *Princess Tarakanova and Princess Vladimirskaya* (*Kniazhna Tarakanova i printsessa Vladimirskaia*) (1868) or Grigory Danilevsky's *Princess Tarakanova* (*Kniazhna Tarakanova*) (1883). Gleb Uspensky did not write about her.

96   **full of people:** What Boldyrev goes on to describe is one of the consequences of "the great terror" of the Stalin years, which reached its peak in 1937. Mass arrests of people of all social levels and professions (mid- to upper-level bureaucrats and military personnel) filled prisons and labor camps to the bursting point.

97   **Karl Radek:** See note to p. 36.

97   **Uglanov:** Nikolai Aleksandrovich Uglanov (1886–1937) helped organize the defense of Petrograd against the attack of the White Army during the Civil War. Uglanov was arrested in 1936 and executed in 1937.

97   **Yudenich:** Nikolai Nikolaevich Yudenich (1862–1933), Russian general, commander of the Northwestern White Army in the Civil War. In October 1919 his troops came close to taking Petrograd (St. Petersburg).

98   **Kaganovich:** Lazar Moiseevich Kaganovich (1893–1991), Soviet political figure and Communist Party official; a close associate of Joseph Stalin. From 1935 to 1937 he was minister of railways.

100   **Special Judicial Collegium:** bodies formed in July 1934 to review cases involving state crimes.

100   **NKVD Troika:** see note to p. 10.

102   **M. I. Kalinin:** Mikhail Ivanovich Kalinin (1875–1946), Bolshevik revolutionary and titular head of state of Russia/Soviet Union from 1919 to his death.

102   **Yezhov:** see note to p. 36.

105   **Stakhanovite rations:** "shock workers" (Stakhanovites), credited for fulfilling 200 percent of the norm, received a higher calorie ration with 1,200 grams of bread.

106   **Berman:** Matvei Berman (1898–1939), head of the Gulag from 1932 to 1937. He was executed in 1939.

112 **Pletnev:** in 1938, Dmitry Pletnev (1872–1941) and a number of other Kremlin doctors appeared among the accused at Stalin's last and largest show trial, that of Bukharin, Rykov, and Yagoda. Pletnev, a renowned heart specialist and one of Russia's most admired doctors, testified that he had poisoned Maxim Gorky. Pletnev died in prison.

112 **Galina Serebriakova:** (1905–1980), author of a number of historical novels and memoirs.

113 **Count Mirbach:** in an attempt to undermine the Brest-Litovsk Treaty between Germany and Soviet Russia, two Left Socialist Revolutionaries, Bliumkin and Andreev, assassinated Count Wilhelm von Mirbach, the German ambassador in Moscow, on July 6, 1918.

113 **General Todorsky:** Lieutenant General A. I. Todorsky (1894–1965) was among those senior officers purged by Stalin in 1938. He spent eighteen years in the Gulag.

118 **Rokossovsky's army:** Konstantin Rokossovsky (1896–1968) was commanding a cavalry corps in the Red Army when he was caught up in Stalin's purges in 1937. After being arrested, tortured, and sent to the camps of Vorkuta, he was suddenly released in 1940 and restored to his former command. Rokossovsky commanded the Don Front during the Battle of Stalingrad. He eventually was promoted to marshal of the Soviet Union and served as Poland's minister of defense.

118 **Colonel Berling:** in early 1943 Stalin authorized the formation of a Soviet-sponsored Polish force, led by Colonel (later General) Zygmunt Berling. Berling's force, which eventually grew to more than 300,000 troops, fought alongside the Red Army.

118 **Prince Sviatopolk-Mirsky:** Boldyrev is mistaken here. Mirsky died June 6, 1939, in a camp hospital near Magadan. (See also note to p. 23.)

122 **Levitan:** Yury Borisovich Levitan (1914–1983), well-known announcer on Soviet radio during the war years. It was Levitan who read all the important communiqués, including the announcement of the beginning of the war in June 1941 and of Germany's surrender on May 9, 1945.

123 **Vlasovites:** General Andrei Vlasov was captured by the Germans in July 1942 after the 2nd Shock Army he commanded was surrounded. With German encouragement he formed the Russian Liberation Army of several hundred thousand Soviet prisoners of war to fight against Stalin. In accordance with the provisions of the Yalta Conference in February 1945, Soviet citizens who found themselves in the hands of the Allies were returned to the Soviet Union, sometimes forcibly. Vlasov himself was kidnapped by Soviet troops and taken to Moscow, where he was executed in 1946.

124 **Azhaev:** Vasily Nikolaevich Azhaev (1915–1968), Soviet writer. His best-known novel, *Far from Moscow* (*Daleko ot Moskvy,* 1948), is in the tradition of Socialist Realism and deals with workers (Azhaev does not mention that they were prisoners) building an oil pipeline in eastern Siberia during World War II. The novel received the Stalin Prize of 1949.

125 **SMERSH:** the Russian acronym for "Death to Spies" (*Smert' shpionam*), the wartime counterintelligence directorate of the Soviet Army. SMERSH was particularly active in interrogating former Soviet prisoners of war and those who had lived in areas under German occupation.

125 **Project 501:** see note to p. 27.

126 **Kwantung Army:** (also known as the Guandong Army), a Japanese army that in August 1945 was stationed in Japanese-occupied Manchuria. Overwhelmed by the advancing Red Army, it was ordered to surrender by Emperor Hirohito. Several hundred thousand of its troops were sent to work in Soviet labor camps in eastern Siberia.

127 **Law of August 7, 1932:** this law covered the theft of state property. Industrial managers and collective farm chairmen convicted of stealing could be shot, though with mitigating circumstances the sentence could be reduced to no less than ten years. It was often called the "ear of wheat" law, since collective farmers who cut a few ears of wheat from the fields to help feed their families could be sentenced to five to ten years in the camps.

127 **Article 39:** Article 39 of the Instructions on Internal Passports contained a secret attachment listing the areas in which the bearer of the passport was forbidden to live and the types of employment closed to him. The released prisoner's passport would contain a notation indicating that it was issued pursuant to this article.

127 **Industrial Party:** a group of prominent engineers and industrial planners accused of "wrecking" and counterrevolutionary activity. Their trial, in November–December 1930, was one of the early show trials of the 1930s.

128 **Actual State Councilor:** a civil service rank, equivalent to that of a major general in the army and fourth from the top in the Table of Ranks that existed in Russia until 1917.

129 **Ostap Bender:** the protagonist, an ingenious swindler, of the novel *The Twelve Chairs* (*Dvenadtsat' stul'ev,* 1928) by Ilia Ilf (1897–1937) and Evgeny Petrov (1903–1942).

131 **Golda Meir's arrival:** Golda Meir served as Israel's first ambassador to the Soviet Union from 1948 to 1949. She was welcomed with great enthusiasm by Soviet Jews. This, coupled with the increasing anti-Semitism and anti-Zionism of the later years of Stalin's regime, provoked a wave of arrests of Jewish citizens of the Soviet Union.

131 **Zinoviev:** Grigory Yevseevich Zinoviev (1883–1936), Bolshevik revolutionary and Soviet politician. He was a powerful figure in the early 1920s but broke with Stalin in 1925. He was arrested in 1934 and tried in 1935 and again in 1936 at the first of the major show trials of the Stalin years. Zinoviev confessed to a series of monstrous and improbable crimes and was executed in August 1936. Radomyslsky was his actual last name. Most of his relatives were arrested, as were those of other purged political figures of the 1930s.

132 **My native land is broad and fair:** popular Soviet patriotic song composed in 1935 by Vasily Lebedev-Kumach and Isaak Dunaevsky.

133 **Kolkhoz:** a collective farm, nominally a peasant cooperative. The kolkhoz became one of the main components of the socialized agriculture instituted in the years that followed the 1917 Revolution. The many peasants who resisted the forced collectivization of 1928 were sent to prison camps or exiled.

134 **workday units:** workers on collective farms were credited with workday units for the quantity and quality of their labor. When the farm had fulfilled its obligations to the state, anything remaining was divided among its members on the basis of the workdays they had accumulated.

N. M. Ignatov

141 *Jolly Fellows: Veselye rebiata,* a very popular film musical from 1934.

141 **Utesov:** Leonid Utesov (Utyosov) (1895–1982), Soviet orchestra leader, jazz singer, and comic actor, extremely popular from the 1920s to the 1940s.

142 **bare-knuckle fights:** organized fistfights had been a popular entertainment over the Christmas period for centuries. Two lines of young men from neighboring villages or city neighborhoods would face one another, fighting until a victor was declared. Babiy Gorodok was an area south of central Moscow, part of the Zamoskvorechye district.

143 **Mikhail Kalinin:** see note to p. 102.

144 *anasha:* marijuana.

147 *bura:* see note to p. 89.

151 **Bliukher:** Vasily Konstantinovich Bliukher (1889–1938), Soviet military commander. An outstanding leader on the Bolshevik side during the Civil War, Bliukher spent much of his subsequent career in Russia's Far East. He was promoted to marshal of the Soviet Union in 1935 but was arrested in 1938 during Stalin's purge of Red Army commanders. He died in Lefortovo Prison.

154 **our transport walked from Murashi Station to Chibiu:** the distance from Murashi to Chibiu, as the crow flies, is about 550 kilometers.

154 *Lev Gurych Sinichkin: Lev Gurych Sinichkin, or a Provincial Debutante* (1839), comedy (vaudeville) by Dmitry Lensky (1805–1860).

155 **Mikhail Nazvanov:** (1914–1964), director and actor in stage and film productions.

155 **Zinoviev:** see note to p. 131.

159 **Peltzer:** probably Ivan Romanovich Peltzer (1871–1959), actor and director.

163 **Pat and Patachon:** Carl Schenstrom (1881–1942) and Harald Madsen (1890–1949), Danish film comedians who were very popular in the 1920s and 1930s. They were known in Britain as Long and Short.

A. P. Butskovsky

176   **"Leningrad Affair":** in 1949–50 a series of cases were concocted against prominent party members in Leningrad. They were accused of treason or embezzlement, and a number of them were executed; about two thousand other prominent figures were imprisoned or exiled.

187   **Tatar Strait:** the strait that separates the mainland from Sakhalin Island, 7.3 kilometers away at its narrowest point.

199   **Beria:** After Stalin's death Beria was appointed as first deputy prime minister and reappointed to head the MVD (successor to the NKVD). He was arrested on June 26, 1953, by Khrushchev and others within the leadership and executed on December 23.

201   **the prison alphabet:** prisoners had a well-established system of communicating by tapping on cell walls. Letters of the alphabet were arranged, on paper or in one's mind, in a grid so that words could be spelled out by tapping first the number of the row in which the letter appeared and then the number indicating its position within that row.

203   **La Pérouse Strait:** the strait that divides the southern part of the island of Sakhalin from the Japanese island of Hokkaido.

204   **Ust-Nera:** a town near the village of Oymyakon, which holds the record as the coldest inhabited spot in the Northern Hemisphere. The temperature there has fallen as low as minus ninety-four degrees Fahrenheit.

210   **earn some money:** news of the vast complex of labor camps in the Soviet Union had reached the outside world, and in 1949 the United Nations was asked to investigate the practice of slave labor, which was defined as forced, unpaid work. In response, the Soviet Union began paying prisoners for their work, though with substantial deductions for food and housing in the camps.

N. R. Kopylov

226   *Ostarbeiter:* "workers from the East," civilians from the Soviet Union and Eastern Europe who were taken to Nazi Germany to work on farms and in factories.

226   **Vlasovites:** see note to p. 123.

226   **General Shkuro:** Andrei Grigorievich Shkuro (1887–1947), a decorated veteran of World War I, commanded Cossack forces against the Bolsheviks in the Civil War. He emigrated to Paris, but at the beginning of World War II he decided to join the Germans in fighting the Soviets and helped organize Cossack forces for the German Army. After the war ended, more than two thousand Cossack troops were returned to the Soviet Union by the British, under terms negotiated in the Yalta agreement. The troops were tried for treason, and Shkuro was executed by the Soviets in 1947.

227 **Marshal Konev:** Ivan Stepanovich Konev (1897–1973) led Red Army troops on the Eastern Front in World War II and liberated much of Eastern Europe from the Germans. After the war he served for a time as Allied high commissioner for Austria.

228 **Article 58, points 1b, 10, and 11:** point 1b is "subversion or weakening the national security of the USSR"; point 10 is counterrevolutionary agitation; point 11 is organized anti-Soviet activity.

230 **Baikal–Amur Mainline:** construction of this 4,234-kilometer railway line, known as BAM, began in 1933 and was completed only in 1984. It connects Taishet on the Trans-Siberian Railway with the Pacific port of Sovetskaya Gavan.

230 *suka:* literally, a bitch. A former criminal who has broken the "thieves' law" and cooperates with the camp authorities.

231 **Banderists:** members of a Ukrainian nationalist movement led by Stepan Bandera (1909–1959). Partisans belonging to the movement fought against the Soviet Union in the last year of World War II and for some years thereafter.

232 **General Derevyanko:** Major General A. A. Derevyanko headed USVITL (the northeastern labor camps, i.e., Kolyma) from 1948 to 1951.

232 **General Nikishov:** Lieutenant General I. F. Nikishov (1894–1958) was head of Dalstroy, the organization that managed the immense complex of camps in Kolyma, from 1939 to 1948. He and his wife, Aleksandra Gridasova, exploited prisoners, particularly those with artistic talent, to support their extravagant lifestyle.

232 *Dzhurma:* one of the fleet of ships used by Dalstroy to transport prisoners from Vladivostok and other Pacific ports to Kolyma. The horrors of a voyage in this ship are described in a number of prison memoirs, most notably in Eugenia Ginzburg's book *Into the Whirlwind* (*Krutoi marshrut*).

233 **Vadim Kozin:** (1903–1994), singer, songwriter, and poet. Kozin became well known in the 1920s as a versatile soloist. He gave many performances for Soviet troops during World War II and, with Marlene Dietrich and Maurice Chevalier, gave a concert for the delegates to the Teheran Conference in 1943. He was arrested in 1945 and sentenced to eight years in the camps; he was released early, in 1950.

234 *A Wedding in Malinovka:* 1937 operetta by Boris Aleksandrov (1905–1994).

235 **Gorky Affair:** see note to p. 112.

240 *Krechinsky's Wedding:* comedy (*Svad'ba Krechinskogo,* 1854) by Aleksandr Sukhovo-Kobylin (1817–1903).

240 *The Forest:* drama (*Les,* 1871) by Aleksandr Ostrovsky (1823–1886).

241 *Silva:* operetta (*Die Csárdásfürstin,* 1915) by the Hungarian composer Emmerich (Imre) Kalman (1882–1953).

244 **Stone of Solovki:** in 1990 a boulder from the earliest Gulag prison camp, on the Solovetsky Islands, was placed in Lubyanka Square in Moscow. The inscription reads, "As a memorial to the victims of a totalitarian regime." Similar memorials have since been erected in other cities.

V. V. Gorshkov

246 **March 5, 1953:** the date of Stalin's death.

248 **Gorky:** city (now Nizhny Novgorod) on the Volga River, some 400 kilometers east of Moscow.

251 *Sakhalin:* between 1893 and 1895 Chekhov published a study, *The Island of Sakhalin* (*Ostrov Sakhalin*), based on his own field research done in the summer of 1890 on social and economic conditions among the population of Sakhalin Island, where there was a large prison colony.

251 **Pushkin's verse:** the attractive heroine of Pushkin's poem "The Little House in Kolomna" ("Domik v Kolomne," 1830) is called Parasha.

251 *kulich:* a rich cake traditionally served on Easter Sunday.

252 **Balakirev:** Miliy Alekseevich Balakirev (1836–1910), noted Russian composer.

255 **Kochin:** Nikolai Ivanovich Kochin (1902–1983), author of a several novels of peasant life in Gorky (now Nizhegorod) Oblast.

256 **Zoshchenko:** Mikhail Mikhailovich Zoshchenko (1895–1958), Russian writer whose short comic stories have remained enormously popular since the 1920s.

256 **"The Eelpout":** early comic story ("Nalim," 1885) by Anton Chekhov.

256 **"a bottomless river of grief":** from the poem by Nikolai Nekrasov (1821–1878), "V polnom razgare strada derevenskaia . . ."

256 **Radishchev and Herzen:** Aleksandr Nikolaevich Radishchev (1749–1802), Russian poet and essayist whose *Journey from Petersburg to Moscow* (*Puteshestvie iz Peterburga v Moskvu,* 1790) criticized Russian reality from a humanitarian viewpoint and was regarded by the government as subversive. Aleksandr Ivanovich Herzen (1812–1870), writer, thinker, and strong critic of Russian autocracy; he spent the last twenty-three years of his life as an émigré in Europe.

259 **new uniforms:** in January 1943 Stalin introduced new military uniforms that had many similarities to those worn before the Revolution. Most notably, officers again wore shoulder boards with indications of their rank.

260 **Kulibin:** the second edition of N. I. Kochin's biography of the engineer and inventor Ivan Kulibin (1735–1818) appeared in 1940.

265 **Burepolom, Sukhobezvodny:** large prison camps in Gorky Oblast.

272 **Emelyan Pugachev:** (1740?–1775), leader of a major peasant rebellion from 1773 to 1775. After his capture he was brought to Moscow and held in the Butyrka Prison until his execution.

275   **Sobakevich:** see note to p. 18.

276   **Melnikov-Peshchersky:** Pavel Ivanovich Melnikov (1818–1883), Russian writer best known for his treatment of popular life, particularly among the Old Believer sectarians living between the Volga and the Ural Mountains.

287   **Herzen, Ogarev, and Chernyshevsky:** for Herzen, see note to p. 256. Nikolai Platonovich Ogarev (1813–1877), poet and essayist, close friend and collaborator of Herzen. For Chernyshevsky, see note to p. 75. As nineteenth-century revolutionaries, all would be considered "safe" reading by Soviet authorities.

293   **Vyazma:** small city some 200 kilometers west of Moscow. It was occupied by the Germans in October 1941 and liberated, after fierce battles in which the city was mostly destroyed, in March 1943, a few months before Gorshkov's prison transport arrived.

298   **Institute of Red Professors:** founded in 1921, the institute's aim was to train a new generation of Marxist scholars that would reflect the new values of the post-revolutionary regime.

302   *"Batsilla":* literally, bacillus. Camp slang for fats or rich food generally. Camp legend holds that in the 1930s camp authorities told prisoners complaining about the lack of fats in their diet that fats contain harmful bacilli.

306   *magara:* a millet-like grain with low nutritional value, much detested by the prisoners.

309   **Chelkash:** eponomyous hero of a story by Maxim Gorky (1868–1936). Chelkash, depicted in romantic terms, is a freedom-loving thief on the Odessa waterfront.

310   **Vanka Zhukov:** hero of Anton Chekhov's story "Vanka" (1886). Vanka is an orphaned nine-year-old peasant boy who has been sent to the city as an apprentice shoemaker.

318   **social origins:** the 1918 "Declaration of the Rights of the Toiling Masses and Exploited Peoples of the USSR" stated that "alien class elements" could be deprived of the rights "which they have used to the detriment of the socialist revolution."

332   **ChTZ:** the abbreviation for Chelyabinsk Tractor Factory. Crude footwear was made from tires produced by this factory.

335   **Gogol's "Vii":** horror story by Nikolai Gogol (1809–1852).

344   **Mogilny:** Russian for "grave" (adjective).

352   **the law of August 7, 1932:** see note to p. 127.

A. E. Kropochkin

364   **General Karbyshev:** General Dmitry Karbyshev was captured by the Germans in August 1941. Although there are a number of versions of how he died, the one circulated after the war was as follows: in February 1945,

Karbyshev and about a thousand prisoners were taken to the Mauthausen
concentration camp. In very cold weather the group was subjected to ice-
cold showers and sprayed with fire hoses until at least half of them, including the general, perished.

369 **Siblag:** a complex of camps in Kemerovo and Novosibirsk oblasts. In 1947
Siblag had 37,595 prisoners engaged in forestry, coal mining, and road
building, as well as various agricultural and industrial activities.

372 **". . . Where people breathe so freely":** see note to p. 132.

374 **Banderists:** see note to p. 231.

376 **"a motley crowd . . .":** from Alexander Pushkin's poem "The Robber
Brothers" ("Brat'ia razboiniki," 1821–22).

378 **Steplag:** a complex of camps in the Kazakh Republic engaged primarily in
mining and construction projects. The camps held a total of 18,572 prisoners in 1949.

383 **Maisky:** Ivan Mikhailovich Maisky (1884–1975) served as Soviet ambassador to Great Britain from 1932 to 1943. He was arrested in February
1953 and interrogated personally by Beria. Under torture, he confessed to
being a British spy. He was released and rehabilitated in 1956. Kropochkin
is mistaken here, however: Maisky was held in prison and was never sent
to the camps; his arrest, in any case, came several years after the time Kropochkin depicts here.

383 **kvass:** a slightly alcoholic beverage made from rye bread fermented in water.

396 **My native land is broad and fair:** see note to p. 132. The last line quoted
is, literally, "Where a man can breathe so free."

396 **Ruslanova:** Lidia Ruslanova (1900–1973), popular singer of Russian folk
songs. She was famous for the concerts she performed for Soviet troops
during World War II.

396 *The Gulag Archipelago:* Solzhenitsyn's account of the Kengir uprising is
found in volume 3 of his study. The uprising lasted for some forty days
in May and June 1954. Over this time criminals and political prisoners
joined forces to hold the camp compound and defend it against incursions
from the authorities outside. The uprising was suppressed on June 25 by
Soviet troops supported by tanks.